Organizational Communication

Principles and Practices in Canadian Organizations

Stan Klimowicz

McMaster University

THOMSON

NELSON

Australia   Canada   Mexico   Singapore   Spain   United Kingdom   United States

Organizational Communication
by Stan P. Klimowicz

**Associate Vice President,
Editorial Director:**
Evelyn Veitch

**Editor-in-Chief,
Higher Education:**
Anne Williams

Acquisitions Editor:
Bram Sepers

Marketing Manager:
Sandra Green

Marketing Manager:
Sandra Green

Publisher's Representative:
Chris Cirella

Developmental Editor:
Katherine Goodes

Permissions Coordinator:
Sheila Hall

Content Production Manager:
Jaime Smith

Production Service:
International Typesetting
and Composition

Copy Editor:
Elizabeth Phinney

Proofreader:
Carol Anderson

Indexer:
Edwin Dubrin

Senior Production Coordinator:
Ferial Suleman

Design Director:
Ken Phipps

Cover Design:
Johanna Liburd

Cover Image:
©Steve P./Alamy

Printer:
Thomson/West

**Library and Archives Canada
Cataloguing in Publication Data**

Klimowicz, Stan
   Organizational communication :
principles and practices in Canadian
businesses/Stan Klimowicz.—1st ed.

Includes index.

ISBN-13: 978-0-17-625191-8
ISBN-10: 0-17-625191-X

   1. Communication in organizations—
Textbooks.
2. Business communication—Canada—
Textbooks. I. Title.

HD30.3.K55 2007 658.4'5 C2006-
906006-1

Brief Contents

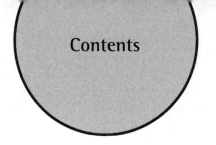

Contents

Part 3   *Traditional Approaches 59*

Part 4   *Contemporary Approaches 95*

Part 5   *Individuals and Groups in Organizations   149*

Preface

I know you've deceived me, now here's a surprise
I know that you have 'cause there's magic in my eyes
I can see for miles and miles and miles and miles and miles
Oh yeah.

—"I Can See For Miles," The Who

Communication has been making our worlds expand since people first made eye contact, and the speed of change seems to be growing faster. The forces of technology, globalization, and knowledge have given us new horizons. And today, as always, our reach exceeds our grasp. To respond to these challenges, organizations are taking an increasing interest in communication in order to understand what part they play in the big picture.

The workplace in particular has been compelled to adapt to radical and exciting new ways of working, new perspectives on relationships along the entire value chain, and new ways of thinking. Employees today are given greater opportunities for engagement in organizational life, not only with coworkers but with customers and suppliers. We are trained to show self-direction, not just to follow orders, and to display both technical and emotional intelligence. We are expected to use collaboration skills to deal with problems such as interpersonal and cultural differences. Our workplaces have become spread across distributed networks and virtual environments. And we are required to learn while in college or university, and then to become part of a learning organization so that we can continually bring new knowledge into our lives. The horizons are constantly changing. And as the pressure to perform becomes greater, we are expected to be able to deal with the stress of these ever-growing demands.

Organizational communication looks at how companies and their employees use communication to accomplish their day-to-day operations. The field has become a popular professional and academic area over the years as organizations try to deal with the new challenges of the business world. This text allows students to discover and experience the importance of communication in the workplace, and to understand its techniques and its potential for not only improving individual and organizational performance but for becoming better people and maybe even helping to make a better world.

This textbook provides a comprehensive introduction to the field of organizational communication for college or university seniors. It is suitable for students in communication studies programs with a humanities or social science orientation or in business administration programs.

Organization

The book begins with a look at the forces transforming today's organizations—information technology, a changing business environment, workplace diversity, and young generations with new values entering the work force. Next, communication theory is examined in the context of an organization so that the concept of organizational communication can ultimately be defined.

The next section looks at theoretical perspectives of organizations. Communication in the workplace is explored in terms of

- classical theories of management, where communication is one-way, the workplace is organized like a machine, and managers are responsible for thinking and workers for working
- human relations theories, which humanize the workplace by considering emotional and psychological factors behind employee performance and stress the importance of social interaction
- systems theories, which view a workplace as an organic learning network where relationships matter above all, concepts widely applied in today's companies
- organizational culture theories, which focus on collective meaning systems and shared workplace values
- critical theories, which see organizations as systems of power and domination, a revealing perspective for a global economy

The trend in workplaces is toward greater integration, so in our next part applied communication is examined in the following areas:

- communication networks in organizations
- communication in teams and project groups
- communication strategies for decision making and conflict resolution
- leadership and communication
- corporate communication, both internal and external, with an emphasis on strategic alignment

The final section looks at contemporary issues in organizational communication:

- workplace diversity, in particular how organizations make diversity efforts work for employees and for investors
- knowledge management, which focuses on using communication to collect and manage an organization's knowledge
- ethics and corporate social responsibility, in particular how organizations are dealing with unethical behaviour and becoming better corporate citizens

Chapters contain a mini-case in the middle, and a case study and classroom activities at the end. There are chapter notes, and a website is available for further readings and exploration.

A Canadian Perspective

This is a Canadian book on organizational communication—the first of its kind. So it includes discussion of Canadian communication scholarship, in particular Harold Innis and Marshall McLuhan, and others as well. Some attempts have been made to connect these traditions to the field of organizational communication, but these are only beginning efforts and are not the aims of a textbook such as this.

The book is steeped in examples, stories, and cases from Canadian businesses from all corners of the country, which was one of the main goals of the book. And there's even a few references to hockey. Nothing against our American neighbours (I have some roots there from my graduate school days); I just wanted, as a teacher of Canadian students, to discover what's in our own backyards before automatically jumping to a larger view of things.

Another goal was to promote the field. I have studied and worked in communication, mainly organizational, most of my life and consider it an extremely intriguing subject. Its interdisciplinary nature provides many new ways of understanding organizational life by putting it in the context of bigger issues from the arts, the sciences, the social sciences, and business. This book examines some of these exciting areas. The workplace has the potential to both increase performance and offer a far more rewarding experience for workers.

My final goal was practical. I am a communication professor who often works at two or three schools at the same time, and I have kids ready for college and university. So, it's a combination of my own job security and their educational opportunities. To my four sons, Joe, Mike, Eric, and Morgan, I hope this helps us all get to where we want to be in life. I dedicate this book to you as one way of giving back everything you've given to me. I also dedicate it to the thousands of students whose eyes I brought a smile to by opening them up to the world of communication. And, let's be inclusive, to those also, as Dylan Thomas said, "Who pay no praise or wages / Nor heed my craft or art." The field of communication is not only about vision, but also connection.

Stan Klimowicz

Acknowledgments

I'd like to thank Katherine Goodes and everyone else at Thomson Nelson Learning for the many e-mails, meetings, and phone calls that helped me to complete this project. And also the many great professors and students I shared learning with at the University of Western Ontario and The State University of New York at Buffalo. And many thanks to the reviewers for their kind, detailed, and astute comments:

Steffie Hawrylak-Young, Nova Scotia Community College

David Patient, Simon Fraser University

R.V. Rasmussen, University of Alberta

Danielle van Jaarsveld, University of British Columbia

Stephen Lynch, University of Guelph

Rosemary McGowen, Wilfrid Laurier University

Overview of Today's Workplace

Chapter One

The Changing Workplace

Organizational communication explains how organizations work by looking at how its members communicate with each other. It examines how we interact with the environment that we work in and the things, places, and people that are meaningful to us in our workplaces. Studying organizational communication is especially important today because our ways of working have changed so much.

Information technology has greatly increased efficiency and allowed us to conduct business in distant parts of the world without even being at the office. The business environment has changed. The key process today is integration through the breaking down of traditional barriers. People work more interactively, and more concurrently, to enable creativity and innovation to emerge. The forces of integration have connected internal and external operations, making networks of activity that are virtually limitless, whether it's multinational systems or university–industry collaborations. To harmonize with changes in markets and economics, organizations have restructured. Many workplaces have abandoned vertical hierarchies for lateral networks based on teamwork. Managers have adopted leadership skills. And people's perspectives of the workplace have changed. New generations of workers are tremendously more technology-friendly, yet more disconnected from established workplace values and practices than previous generations.

This book is written with two purposes: to explore how communication works in today's organizations, and to promote communication skills that will make our jobs more effective and more satisfying. The book will emphasize the Canadian experience in the workplace. Let's begin by looking at how today's workplace has changed, specifically in the areas of information technology, the changing business environment, and organizational restructuring.

Information Technology—Virtual Connection

The capabilities of modern business have been greatly expanded with information technology. For example, the Internet has been described as having as much impact on the auto industry as Henry Ford's mass-production methods did in the 1920s.[1] It has changed the face of industry. In fact, today's global business model, built on decentralized operational structures, virtual workers, and rapidly changing environments, couldn't exist without it.

According to the Canadian Telework Association, over 1.5 million people in Canada are working as virtual assistants, charging from $25 to $40 an hour for their labour.[2] With personal computers and the Internet, working at home has been the next logical step in the evolution of information management—a succession of communication technologies that started with clay tokens and parchment and has become ever more portable and powerful through the centuries. One of the advantages Canada has (along with the U.S., Britain, and Australia) when it comes to virtual work is that English is the dominant language of business. In fact, as a virtual worker, you would be eligible to join the International Association of Virtual Assistants. Among the types of work that are commonly now done at home are accounting, advertising, copy writing, data entry, marketing, real estate, answer and customer services, research, and event planning. Of course, the advantage of home-based employees for companies is the savings in benefit expenses and office costs. "You don't have to worry about medical, dental and other benefits for an employee. With a virtual assistant, which is a contractor, they provide all their own resources."[3]

There are negative impacts for workers, though. The trend points to greater numbers of people doing part-time and contract work. Isolation from colleagues and clients and the limited nature of virtual communication prevents employees from establishing good relations and experiencing the social rewards of the workplace. Author Jeremy Rifkin pointed out back in 1997 that, contrary to common belief, information technology hits the service sector harder that it does the manufacturing sector.[4] Bank tellers, hotel clerks, and office workers are seeing their jobs disappear rapidly. And today, the new jobs that are created as a result of new technology are likely to be in distant countries that offer the attraction of low wages. Since virtual workers are not limited by geography, they could be located in Manila just as easily as Moncton.

With the new work structures that technology enables, our notions of space, distance, and time become drastically rearranged. As television brought the sights and sounds of distant events into our homes, computers now allow us to shop, work, or go to school without taking off our housecoats. In fact, organizations have become places that exist in an electronic space. How often are we told, "Visit us at www.ourplace.com"? Technology has allowed the workplace to expand to wherever technology reaches—to our homes, our cars, even our campsites.

Information technology has changed our conception of what an organization is in today's business world. It is no longer defined by walls, rooms, and fences, but by mental and human geography. In other words, an organization is people and knowledge connected through technology. Canadian communication scholar Marshall McLuhan referred to technology as being *extensions* of people. A phone is an extension of our voices and ears; a car, an extension of our legs; a computer, an extension of the way we use a pencil. Whatever becomes part of our experience also becomes part of us. As we learn how to use our workplace technologies, we learn new ways of working. Think of the impact the punch clock, one of IBM's first innovations, had on the organization of the workplace. Workers in many companies are still being told by a machine when to start work.

As electronic communication eliminated the barriers of space and time, McLuhan's vision of the *global village* was realized, in particular in the business world. The traditional concept of "village" as a small community of people connected by regular communication activity now extends to global proportions with the help of technology such as television, cellular phones, and, especially, the Internet. The convenience of electronic communication has allowed many businesses to operate globally. This development obviously presents problems with intercultural communication, but it can also give immigrants in business a competitive advantage. Consider the case of Ashok Kalle, owner of Pathways Communications in Markham, Ontario, a provider of computer software and hardware that employs 70 people. The company operates a call centre in Pune, India, where a staff of 50 troubleshoots Internet problems for clients in Canada. Says owner Ashok Kalle, "We're a Canadian company with roots in India. We see India as a great opportunity." In fact, Kalle sees himself as neither Canadian nor Indian, but rather as a citizen of the world. According to Joseph D'Cruz of the Rotman School of Management at the University of Toronto, in the coming years, more immigrants will develop businesses in Canada connecting "the Indian production base for software and Internet-mediated services and customers in the U.S. and Canada."[5] Communication technology allows immigrants to retain business and personal contacts in one land while living in another.

The Business Environment—From "Machine" to "White Water"

As a result of technological developments, the evolution of industry over the past centuries has been characterized by periods of rapid change. The first decades of the twentieth century in Canada saw great social displacement as people flooded from rural farms to find new types of work in unfamiliar urban settings, thus forming Canada's industrial centres. An era of optimism was born. The faith in science and technology inherent in the Industrial Revolution led to industry being described as a "machine."

The current business environment is once again undergoing rapid change, and conditions are more complex than they were for our great-grandparents. To reflect the turbulence, researchers have changed the metaphor for organizations from "machine" to "white water"—a term that connotes the quickness of change, the unpredictability of direction, and the hazards caused by unknowns. A much greater awareness of the environment is required to provide information about changes in markets, the competition, technology, economics, and government policy. How have organizations dealt with this change?

Over the last few decades, many traditional organizational structures have been abandoned. As a prescription for the 1990s, William Blundell, then director of General Electric Canada, made three suggestions:[6]

1. maintain an external focus, emphasizing quality and customer service

2. establish people empowerment, focusing on employee training, greater employee involvement in decision making, and less reliance on policies and committees

3. eliminate boundaries, integrating the energy of employees to focus on the organizational goal and breaking down traditional barriers of status and departments

In the 2000s so far we have seen a continued emphasis on teamwork and communication, continued learning, diversity skills to help manage the growing differences among workers, a renewed focus on ethics and social responsibility, and an increased emphasis on employing the entire person—not just the professional part, but the emotional, personal, and even spiritual part in an effort to re-personalize the workplace.

Traditional corporate structure is based on principles of efficiency and control. Scientific methods were applied to the design of the work process. This resulted in division of labour. Jobs were broken down into small, repetitive tasks and put in sequence, so that an organization ran like a machine. The chain of command had many layers of authority, and communication usually travelled down the ranks, not up. Business organizations generally followed this design until the last quarter of the twentieth century. As routines became increasingly automated, greater efficiencies were achieved. Networks of organizations that did business together also created routines structures and then squeezed them for more output. The era's example of industrial excellence was General Motors, but nothing lasts forever. In the 1970s, two events changed business drastically: the oil crisis and the success of the Japanese car industry. Industries built on stable structures scrambled to deal with developments that were ushering in new ways of doing business. So, how do we build a corporate structure that embodies the efficiencies of routine activity, but can also handle change and diversity? This is a big question for organizational communication. Let's look at some techniques and examples of ways organizations have dealt with this issue.

Workplace Trends

Distributed structures involve any work arrangement where the employee is not physically present in the workplace. Employees can work away from the organization's physical location in a number of ways. We've mentioned virtual offices, where employees are connected electronically to the workplace though physically they are working from home. Traditionally the domain of sales people, distributed workers now do a wide range of jobs.

Outsourcing, another rapidly growing work system, is a method for using contract or casual workers to do the work that used to be done by regular staff. Organizations save money by outsourcing, for instance, their janitorial staff or their human resources responsibilities. Over the past few decades, outsourcing has grown steadily. In 2003, industry leader Labor Ready, a publicly traded, day-labour agency, had 790 offices in Canada, the United States, and Britain. Wal-Mart has a contract with Labor Ready for store cleaners and shelf stockers. Agencies like Labor Ready sprung up and grew so quickly that they are loosely regulated in terms of wage and safety laws.[7] This provides cost savings for companies that use them, but decreases employee pay and protections normally covered by workplace agreements. As the numbers of outsourced and contracted employees grow, ethical considerations are being raised: at what point does outsourcing become abusive to workers? In many college and university systems across the country, the percentage of contract faculty has approached 50 percent—creating essentially a two-tier system of teachers. In fact, faculty unions are organizing the contract teachers to help bring their pay, benefits, and working conditions in line with their full-time colleagues. In many industries, outsourcing is used on a global scale. The workforce in China and Southeast Asia contributes cheap labour in the production of clothing, shoes, and electronics as North American companies move their workplaces to these countries. The ethical issues raised by global outsourcing are similar. Nike, Gap, and Ikea, major global outsourcers, are gradually adopting a more socially responsible role by re-establishing benefits for workers and improving working conditions. They are doing so, however, only after realizing the business advantages of marketing themselves as companies with a social conscience.

Decentralized Management

Organizational structures based on a hierarchical, top-down chain of command have been decreasing in number since the 1980s. Their deficiencies first became particularly obvious during the big splash made by Japanese cars in the North American market in the late 1970s. Several years later, the huge growth of the personal computer industry again brought these deficiencies to the fore. To keep up with the competition, organizations adopted decentralized management structures that allowed for faster responses to changes in industry by passing authority and decision making down the ranks. In terms of product development, a top-down style was slow and status-oriented, whereas a decentralized structure focused on outcomes, eliminating the log jams caused by numerous committees and levels of authority.

The *decentralized structure* became known as the "flat" organization. Hi-tech companies found a flatter structure especially efficient, since faster product development often means getting a jump on the market. Many of their operations, such as the former head office of Nortel in Brampton, Ontario, are literally flat, rising a mere two floors—one for operations, one for top management. The flatness not only brings efficiencies, but eliminates many status barriers among coworkers. But "flat" structures are not suitable for all organizations. Big corporations are far more traditional in their organizational structures, since their priorities are security, stability, and power, as can be seen in the head offices of the major banks in Toronto or the oil towers of Calgary. Many organizations have several structures in one. The financial arms are hierarchical and top-down, while the production and research areas are flatter and more team-based—and often far away from the rigidity of head office.

Changes in the political and economic climate in the last few decades have created more interprovincial and international economic integration. In Canada, for example, free trade agreements and the removal of interprovincial trade barriers caused organizations to respond by restructuring their operations. Deregulation as a political and economic direction has been taking place since the mid-twentieth century, in an effort to remove controls on industry and dismantle costly social programs. Recently it has been called privatization. Numerous examples exist. Transportation companies, such as CN and Air Canada, that used to be publicly owned are now run privately, as are some hospitals, schools, and even highways.

Workforce Diversity

The increasing diversity in today's workplaces brings with it new attitudes, lifestyles, values, and motivations. Diversity emerges from numerous differences, with the major ones being gender, culture, and age.

Workplace diversity has always been a major factor in the Canadian economy and no doubt played a big role in developing cultural tolerance, one of this country's strengths. In 1910, 400 000 immigrants entered the country. The next big wave came in the years after World War II, with about 200 000 arriving each year, mainly from Europe. In the 1990s, the number of immigrants topped 200,000 per year, mainly from Asia. According to Statistics Canada, by 2017 one in five Canadians will be a visible minority.[8] Greater cultural diversity challenges our senses of tolerance, understanding, and cooperation. Other than Aboriginal groups, North American society is built on imported cultures, which have gradually formed an independent and individual identity. The importance today is the quickness with which the cultural mix is changing. In the United States, huge numbers of Spanish-speaking immigrants from Mexico and Latin America have profoundly changed the cultural mix in states such as California, almost overnight.

A possible bright light in terms of immigration and the global competition for talent was described by Richard Florida, author of *The Rise of the Creative Class*.[9] He explains that diversity is the key to economic growth because it attracts the "creative class" in society. In terms of talent, British, Australian, and Canadian universities are drawing their best talent pools ever. In fact, on a global ranking of creative workers, Ireland is first; Canada, eighth; the U.S., eleventh. Overall, the attraction of the U.S. for international students has dropped because of accessibility issues, while cities such as London, Amsterdam, Toronto, and Vancouver have become extremely attractive.

A more equal representation of both genders in the workplace has been taking place for decades and is still growing as more and more females raise their educational levels and enter the workforce. Today females represent almost half of the workforce, up from 30 percent in 1965. There are many more working mothers. In 1965, only one-quarter of mothers with children under the age of six were in the labour force; now that proportion has almost tripled.[10] The number of women entrepreneurs in Canada between 1981 and 2001 increased by 208 percent compared to a 38 percent increase for men. The total number of female entrepreneurs in 2005 was 821 000.[11]

The growing number of women in universities and colleges is making executives see the importance of females in the human capital of an organization. In addition to academic skills, "women have a particular ability," according to health care consultant Lisa Newman, "to define a task as collaborative, to share in the doing, to both value their connections with others for the sake of being connected, as well as to use these in the instrumental realm for power and profit."[12] There is also a good business case for hiring women. In Ontario and Alberta, both provinces that are experiencing shortages in skilled occupations, women have been filling the positions. In Alberta, women are starting to see construction as a satisfying career choice. An industrial employer in natural resources gained significant benefits by putting women into the driver's seats of heavy equipment. Maintenance costs decreased because women were more likely than men to bring in the equipment for servicing at the first sign of trouble, which led to earlier repairs and preventative maintenance. And, after Local 269 of the International Longshoremen's Association on the Halifax waterfront accepted Rosanne Weagle as its first female member, the local has successfully attracted and retained a significant number of women workers. To facilitate the arrival of women, union representatives reviewed workplace practices and developed training programs.[13]

Even traditionally male-dominated jobs in science, technology, and engineering show increases in female hiring, though the numbers are far from matching those of their male counterparts. Elizabeth Croft, assistant professor of mechanical engineering at the University of British Columbia, says, "Sometimes I feel isolated. I'm one of two women faculty in a large department." Only one in five professionals employed in the natural sciences, math, and engineering are female, according to the Manitoba Women's Directorate.[14] And in the energy sector in Calgary, fewer than 5 percent of executives are female. But Pamela Jeffrey, founder of the Top 100 of Canada's Most Powerful Women awards, sees definite progress being made: "More women are entering the accounting and engineering professions and as these women start to enter the workforce we will see them climb the ranks of the operating and financial groups."[15]

Hedy Fry, former federal minister of Multiculturalism and the Status of Women, admits that one of the biggest challenges facing women in demanding professions is time. "Women do unpaid work more than men, taking care of children and parents, doing housework. We must be more sensitive to the differences in women's and men's lives and respond to these differences."[16] Both governments and companies are introducing compassionate care programs to address gender issues, such as increased leave for family and health reasons and better job protection for women returning from maternity or parental leave. But laws that guarantee women equal rights, such as the *Charter of Rights and Freedoms*, need to be put into action to achieve equal participation and compensation for men and women in the workplace.

Generational change is always full of surprises. The concept became popular with the post-war generation of the 1960s known as the baby boomers, a large mass of youth with a hunger to experience the world and establish new sets of values. It was followed by Generation X, the first wave of baby boomer offspring, and then Generation Y, also known as the Millennials, the second wave, many of whom are currently entering the workforce. Researcher Sean Foley of the Carlton University School of Business summarizes the differences this way: "Baby Boomers value experience, because that's what they have; Generation Xers value education because that's what they have, and the next generation values technological savvy, street smarts, and creativity, because that's what they have."[17] Generation Yers also possess a high degree of optimism about their abilities and their future, some of it no doubt rooted in the degree of comfort they demonstrate with adopting new technologies. They place more emphasis on self-enhancement, achievement, hedonism, and self-direction.

A massive study conducted by Linda Duxbury and Chris Higgins on work–life balance points out that traditional motivators such as pay raises and promotions are not always effective for today's young job candidates.[18] Having witnessed the diminishing rewards of work that their parents experienced, as a result of long hours, absence from family functions, and limited financial gains, this generation puts greater priority on an engaging work environment, learning, and the satisfaction of personal interests. Duxbury describes them as the "show-me-what-you-can-do-for-me" generation. Rogers Telecommunications discovered young people's changing views of the workplace when it ran a TV ad to recruit employees. Their promise of good pay and benefits did not elicit enough responses. As a test, they ran a second ad in which the boss gets a pie in the face after his pitch, while a voice-over says, "And it's fun to work here." The second ad drew more applicants and a higher calibre of employees.[19] In order to attract and retain workers, companies need to satisfy a lot more of their employees' needs than they used to.

Today's twenty-somethings are still living adolescent lifestyles, some of them even after becoming thirty-somethings. Though they are embarking on adult pleasures, they are assuming the responsibilities of adulthood later. As young people combine experimentation and education into their mid-thirties, trying out jobs, moving in and out of parents' homes, travelling, and picking up courses to add to their diplomas and degrees, the effect is like having two full decades of teenagehood. Various explanations are offered for this phenomenon—the financial difficulties of starting out in today's urban centres, the career pressures of trying to live up to their parents' demanding ideas of success, and their unwillingness to do grunt work after having had higher expectations ever since high-school graduation.

Human resources managers are puzzled by how to handle them, especially with massive skills shortages on the horizon as baby boomers head toward retirement. According to Barbara Moses, a career consultant, their values echo those of their parents and bosses: comfort, the good life, work–life balance.[20] Yet they reflect the different circumstances in which they grew up. They expect immediate feedback, having grown up on video games; they have no sense of authority, having called most of their parents' adult friends by their first names; they don't respond to weak messages, having been raised on a diet of "awesome," "cool," and "amazing." To reach this new breed, Dofasco Inc. has developed a student ambassador program, where students recruit their peers. This pays off because students trust each other more. Students have been on co-ops and internships and been disappointed by the low level of work in which they were stuck. Today they want to know how much a part of the company they will be.[21]

Still, the hiring-forecast numbers tell the tale. John Murphy, of human resources at Ontario Power Generation, stated that by 2009 his company will need to replace more than a quarter of its 11 000 employees.[22] The average age of an Ontario Power Generation worker is 45, and many of those leaving will be senior technical people who will take their skills and knowledge with them. And, according to the *Montreal Gazette*, 300 000 jobs in Quebec will be vacant because of retirement by 2007. The hopeful note in all of this is that the total size of Generation Y, or the "gamer" generation as they are also known, is already far greater than the baby boom generation ever was.[23]

Chapter 1 / The Changing Workplace

Despite the higher priority of work–life balance held by today's young job candidates, the workplace shows some alarming trends in the opposite direction. People of all ages, but mostly the older ones, are working harder than ever, and it is having an impact on their health. The Canadian Policy Research Network's study into the quality of jobs in 17 countries suggests that today's relentless work pace is a North America–wide phenomenon.[24] Canada tops the list for working the hardest, with American workers close behind.

Business Ethics

Ethics and business traditionally have been an odd couple. The famous scandals of the late 1990s and early 2000s exemplify the types of business values where the ends justify the means, where the payoffs became so ridiculously large that any risk seems worth taking, and where breaking rules is the price of doing business. Companies such as Enron, World-Com, Tyco, Baring's Bank, Hollinger, and Bre-X Mining unwittingly ushered in a watershed event of sorts: the relationship between ethics, social responsibility, and business is being closely analyzed. Today, organizations have ethics advisors and universities offer courses in social responsibility.

Emphasizing ethical practices has become attractive to business, as it can be a pathway to doing business more successfully. The basic problem with unethical business practices is that they undermine employee loyalty, trust, security, and performance. To create an atmosphere of trust and bring out the best in employees, an organization must ground everything it does in positive and sustainable values that address financial, personal, social, and environmental concerns. Unethical activity from senior managers, such as accounting fraud, theft, or dishonesty, will eventually erode all employees' values.

Today, many organizations have discovered the long-term benefits of good ethical practices. An organization develops stronger relationships with employees, customers, the community, and other stakeholders. Good ethics can also contribute to employee-empowerment strategies that aim to tap into the higher-order needs of workers for growth, autonomy, and self-development. Through empowerment, individual viewpoints based on self-interest change into shared ones based on a collective interest. Employees will more easily support organizational goals if they have confidence that their leaders are ethical and will guide them toward goals and objectives that will benefit the organization, its members, other stakeholders, and society at large. An ethical atmosphere is founded on openness and trust, two essential elements of doing good business.

The Spirit of Work

Working in an organization involves a basic conflict: workers are individuals who have a life, but when they come to work in an organization they are expected to leave their life at home. Personal characteristics, such as our unique features, idiosyncrasies, impulses, attitudes, egos, feelings, joys, and fears, cannot thrive in an organizational setting that stresses conformity, compliance, submissiveness, order, integration, and uniformity.

Addressing this basic conflict is a challenge for every manager. One common conceptual approach has been to align the values of the employees and the organization. The premise behind this approach is simple: the more an individual's values relate to the organization's values, the more employees will discover meaning and purpose in the workplace and the greater contribution they will make. An alignment of values creates an atmosphere of trust that releases energy in employees. When people believe in what they do for a living, they can tap into their deepest creative potential. So, the natural differences between the individual and the organization are not only minimized, but turned into a positive result.

What this process involves is the removal of traditional barriers to employee potential. The presence of status in the workplace has long been considered a barrier to productivity because of the energy that is used up in maintaining a command-and-control system. So, today's workplaces have adopted team structures with reduced presence of authority. Workplaces also have emotional barriers. The field of emotional intelligence trains employees to remove emotional barriers to performance in the workplace by letting their emotional life become part of the workplace instead of being left at home. Spirituality in the workplace has also been discussed as a method of incorporating a person's values and beliefs into the workplace. Overall, the trend points toward employees seeing themselves as more balanced human beings, including the body, mind, spirit, and heart in the context of the workplace. Traditional organizational values expressed the values of those in power or ownership positions. A work–life balance approach expresses the values of all organizational members.

The emphasis given to work–life balance issues today is partly a result of increasing demands on all workers. Employees have more frequent job changes and less job security, do more contract work, work longer hours, experience more stress, and are continuously faced with cost-cutting measures. Based on a survey of Canadian employees, the human resources research agency Watson Wyatt found that 46 percent were unhappy enough with their jobs to switch without a second thought, an increase of 10 percent from a similar study two years earlier.[25] The most common reasons given were:

- 60 percent of employees felt they had no opportunity for professional development;
- 40 percent said they understood the companies' goals but did not know what steps were needed to achieve them.

A 2005 study of 1400 Canadian lawyers found that about three-quarters of them rated "an environment supportive of my family and personal commitments" as an important factor in choosing an employer.[26] Susan Black of Catalyst Canada, a research group centred on the legal community, adds, "The newest generation to join the work force is demonstrating that work–life balance is of critical importance to them." Sabbaticals are working their way into the private sector as part of a company's compensation package. In 2004, Mercer Human Resources Consultants found that 25 percent of surveyed companies offered sabbaticals. Toronto-Dominion Bank, for example, gave leave to 450 people last year, or 1 percent of its staff, though it was unpaid.[27] Another avenue is a reduced workload, though many professionals warn of the pitfalls. Cutting back to a four-day from a five-day work week to spend more time raising your children, for example, sounds enticing, but the reality can often turn out to be five days of work crunched into four days of time—a recipe for burnout.

Karl Marx said a long time ago that in modern industrial organizations work has ceased to belong to the individual, that a worker does not confirm himself, but denies himself, through his work, and cannot develop mental and physical energy.[28] As individual knowledge becomes more valuable in workers, and as constant learning becomes more central to the activity of accomplishing work, people in the workplace are reconnecting to their work. This gives them an opportunity to express themselves and form self-identities through their workplaces.

What is the connection between meaningful work and communication? The same as that between a meaningful life and communication: it is through communication that meaning is created. Not only that, but communication in an organization can bring out the different aspects of its members. That is why company barbecues can be not only fun but motivating: they bring more of the whole person into the world of the workplace. People experience the power of sharing ideas, of connecting in ways either related or unrelated to work.

Organization of Work—Top-Down and Bottom-Up

A lot of effort has been put into redesigning organizations in recent years. The focus has been on "righting" wrong organizations. Organizing based on the principles of function and specialization is not effective in today's business context. So the focus has shifted from product development to process development, including:

- emphasis on flexibility rather than size and scale;
- teamwork instead of command and control;
- reliance on technology and outsourcing instead of middle management; and
- integration instead of division.

Two approaches have been commonly used: top-down and bottom-up. Top-down organizational change is referred to as *re-engineering*. It's driven by senior management and aims to achieve a radical, outcome-focused vision. Since it originates with senior management, it has the authority behind it to cut across organizational boundaries. A main goal of re-engineering is increasing shareholder value. Big increases in shareholder value require quantum leaps in performance. Thus, re-engineering often begins with employee layoffs, often in the 25 percent range. The re-engineering assault on workplaces reached its peak in the late 1980s and early 1990s, but regular trimming has been the ongoing legacy. It left no industry sector untouched, from banking to insurance, to energy, to government. Fifty percent of Canadian companies in the service sector and 25 percent in manufacturing, mostly heavy industry, re-engineered. Of all Canadian companies, 8 percent re-engineered, compared to 31 percent in the U.S. The reason cited for the difference is that Canadian companies were already more efficient than their U.S. counterparts.[29]

Thomas H. Davenport, one of the creators of re-engineering, describes it as "the last gasp of Industrial Age management."[30] The "Re-engineering Revolution" quickly turned ugly as cost reduction through massive layoffs became the singular goal, though the creators of re-engineering warned that that was not a sensible goal. "Reengineering treated the people inside companies as if they were so many bits and bytes, interchangeable parts," states Davenport. It created a survival atmosphere in organizations, filled with anxiety and fear.

The kernel of redemption in re-engineering, though, was that it focused management's attention on business processes or on the ways work is done in organizations. Davenport advises, "When the next big thing in management hits . . . start with a question: 'Would I like this management approach applied to me and my job?' If the answer is yes, do it to yourself first. You'll set a great example."

Bottom-up organizational change focuses on *restructuring* the process of the work itself. Total Quality Management (TQM) is a commonly used method. It's a bottom-up, people-driven process that integrates functions in a team-based structure that relies heavily on communication and interaction. Teams become the fundamental building blocks of an organization instead of specialized functions and departments. Restructuring also changes people's roles in organizations: employees become owners, as they manage themselves, and customers become bosses.

Authority relationships are mediated by what the Chinese call *guan xi*, a combination of social position and personal leverage.[31] In fact, Canadians find doing business with China tricky because of the Chinese emphasis on this ancient, socially established hierarchy based on understanding face and face loss, respect, and politeness, all intelligible through minute, nonverbal messages. Put simply, both money and style matter. A parallel Western business practice may be the golf game with business associates, where showing bad golf etiquette or hitting the ground on a swing and splattering your boss with dirt could damage your chances of making business contacts on the golf course.

People's individual business styles are often the basis of interpersonal relationships at the workplace that make up the informal structure of an organization—voluntary alliances that come together as needed and contain an organization's real intelligence. Though most organizations still operate on a bureaucratic model, the effective ones have learned the value of delegating authority down the ranks to the people with the knowledge of how best to do the work. To tap into the knowledge available in every organization, all members must have the decision-making freedom to choose the best actions. The bottom line is that restructuring means redistributing power from the positions along the chain of command to the operational levels. As Linda Duxbury of the Carlton School of Business says, effective restructuring is a necessary survival strategy for today's companies:

> [C]ompanies talked throughout the 1990s about being "people-focused...but it's only within the last two years [since 2002] that a lot of organizations have become serious about this. They've only become serious because we're moving into a sellers' market. They now see the writing on the wall with respect to demographics...we're facing a skilled labour shortage. All of a sudden employers are recognizing that it's not just good enough anymore to just talk about being best practice, you actually have to be best practice.[32]

Leadership styles in restructured organizations are different and new skills are required. Instead of expertise in control and command, managers need skills in team building, communication, and problem solving. Leadership in intelligent organizations exists as a service to enhance the abilities of people and teams to self-manage. A leader is a coordinator and facilitator. The connections among workers are lateral, based on skills, projects, and products, rather than vertical ones based on authority and chain of command.

Total Quality Management (TQM) in Canada was fledging as recently as 1996, with only 8 percent of companies using it in a survey of major employers such as Scotiabank, Ford, Alberta Energy, Noranda, Sears, and Hydro-Quebec. Of the 70 companies surveyed, close to half (44 percent) had either downsized or re-engineered.[33] Though TQM has been shown to improve competitiveness in international markets such as Japan, Canadian companies prefer re-engineering because it produces positive results more quickly. TQM is a long-term strategy that necessitates the creation of a culture of continuous learning, so it usually takes several years before TQM practices have any positive impact on a company's performance.

The days of simple tasks, stable markets, and unchanging technology are gone, but the management style of those times still exists. TQM requires a new management model. It involves a cultural change that breaks free of traditional ways of running an organization and doing business. It's an all-or-nothing proposition. For example, Toyota used to practise *"nemawashi,"* where if you had an idea, you presented it to your manager, who presented it to his or her manager, and so on up to the decision maker. Often ideas became distorted along this serial communication chain and also used up a lot of time. Now they use "reverse *nemawashi,"*—you take your idea straight to the decision maker, eliminating unnecessary steps and saving time.

Snapshot of Work Design in the Twentieth Century

Compared to the craftsmen age that preceded it, where workers took a product from beginning to completion, the 1900s ushered in a work style based on the division of labour. Jobs were redesigned into components that were performed repeatedly throughout the entire day by semiskilled workers. Thus, a worker became a cog in a big machine. The result was the production line and great efficiency.

But problems arose. The style of work was not motivating, causing a lot of coordination and control problems. To solve this, managers and control systems were added, but the motivation problem remained. The next solution was job enrichment, to make work more challenging and interesting. Still, the division between a worker and his or her work persisted. Managers did not realize that the problem was not in the work itself, but in the relationship between the worker and the job—the original division that had begun at the beginning of the century. Participatory work programs such as TQM became successful because they reconnected the worker to the job. They created a new social reality in the workplace by re-humanizing the organization.

In the coming chapters, we will take a closer look at what organizations are, how they have changed, and why communication is so important in them. We will begin in Part 1 by looking at communication theory and applying it to a human and organizational context. Next, we will discuss the nature of organizations. The following chapters examine different management styles that have evolved over the years and the role of communication in them, including the classical school of management, the human relations movement, the systems theory approach, organizational culture, and organizations as power structures. Each chapter connects theoretical principles with business practices from the Canadian workplace, and case studies and classroom activities highlight the application of concepts to real workplaces.

Part 2 of the book explores individual, group, and organizational activities necessary for effective workplaces. We begin with a look at how communication works in organizations, focusing on communication structures such as formal and informal networks. Next, we look at interpersonal processes for building effective relationships in the workplace. The following chapters explore the concepts and practices of teamwork, meetings, decision making and conflict management, and the role of communication in effective leadership. The section on corporate communication examines how internal and external communication strategies relate to the achievement of business objectives. Our final chapter addresses some important contemporary issues in the field of organizational communication, such as knowledge management, workplace diversity, ethics, corporate social responsibility, and work–life balance.

Essential Skills for Today's Workplace

To sum up this introductory chapter, let us look at some of the skills essential for success in today's workplaces.

- *Connection*—the workplace is built on bridges that connect people, cultures, genders, and differences of opinion. Communication connects us with our environment by creating awareness of it.
- *Collaboration and negotiation*—complex organizations are more ambiguous and require constant negotiation.
- *Bear hugging*—a common reason people stay with an organization is that they have good relationships with the people within it. Communication helps us discover and satsisfy each other's personal and social needs.
- *Continuous learning*—making sense of situations and learning from them requires an open mind and the ability to ask questions. Be adaptable.
- *Work–life balance*—a view of the whole picture is important. When we look today at people who can't balance their lives, we find that they have substantially higher levels of stress, higher levels of depression, and feel that their health is poorer than their colleagues who have achieved a balance.

From its classical management origins based on a simple relationship between owners and workers to do work for money, the organization has developed into a complex and organic workplace. Information technology has expanded the workplace beyond its physical walls and given workers the dubious ability of doing work from home. The virtual workplace has imposed new demands on workers as we attempt to satisfy the social element of the traditional workplace with virtual relationships. Diversity in organizations comes from the increasing number of differences among workers, in particular those based on gender, culture, and age. Fortunately, enlightened organizations have found ways to turn diversity into a source of positive and productive change. Ethics has become a growing challenge in modern organizations as pressures rise to continuously improve performance. And organizations are starting to realize the business benefits of acting in a socially responsible manner when it comes to policies related to the environment and social issues. Another major change involves the seemingly endless restructuring companies are going through in order to meet the challenges of a rapidly changing economic environment. The increased focus on making the most of a company's human capital has brought benefits to workers, such as greater involvement in workplace activity. It has also placed more demands on their ability to get along with coworkers, to work in self-managed teams, and to use their communication skills to maximize their contribution to their work group.

Classroom Activities

Communication and Technology

In groups, think of one particular type of communication technology that has changed your lives personally. How has it changed the way you behave and live? Do you use this technology or observe it? Are the changes positive or negative? Do you consider the technology necessary for today's workplace or society?

Business Practices

Look through the business sections of some major newspapers or through business magazines, such as *Report on Business*, *Canadian Business*, or the *Financial Post* magazine, and try to get a sense of the dominant issues with which organizations today are concerned. Discuss them in groups and then share them with the class.

Glossary

Notes

1. Scott Kirsner, "Fast Company," *Collision Course*, January 2000, 118.

2. Noreen Farooqui, "Virtual office solutions," Canadian Telework Association, *The Toronto Star*, March 5, 2005, D14.

3. Ibid.

4. Mary Campbell, "The future of work," *The Globe and Mail*, January 3, 1997, A4, quoting Jeremy Rifkin.

5. Joseph Hall, "Weaving a new Canada," *The Toronto Star*, March 23, 2005, B2.

6. William R. C. Blundell, "Prescription for the '90s: The Boundary-less Company," *Business Quarterly* (Autumn 1990): 71.

7. Brian Grow, "A Day's Pay for a Day's Work—Maybe," *Business Week* online, December 8, 2003.

8. Hall, "Weaving a New Canada," B1.

9. Richard Florida, *The Rise of the Creative Class* (New York: Basic Books, 2002).

10. Canada, *The Changing Face of Canadian Workplaces* (Ottawa: HRSDC, 2002).

11. Linda Leatherdale, "Moms make it big," *Toronto Sun*, May 5, 2005, 51.

12. Lisa Newman, "Why Professional Women Need an 'Old Girls' Network,'" *Workplace Today* (October 2003). Institute of Professional Management, Ottawa, Ontario, http://www.workplace.ca (accessed July 25, 2006).

13. Denise McLean, *Workplaces that Work*. The Centre of Excellence for Women's Advancement, The Conference Board of Canada, 2003. Ministry of Citizenship and Immigration, http://www.citizenship.gov.on.ca (accessed July 25, 2006).

14. Manitoba Women's Directorate, *About Women* (Winnipeg, Spring 2004), newsletter article, http://www.gov.mb.ca/wd/newsletter/newsletter.html (accessed May 16, 2005).

15. Omar El Akkad, "A new generation of powerful women," *The Globe and Mail*, November 24, 2005, B7.

16. Donna Wuest, "Women in Science and Engineering—Still in Search of a Critical Mass," presented at the Achieving Harmony Conference, Women in the Workplace, Vancouver, 2004, http://www.apegga.com/whatsnew/peggs/Web07-98/wiw.htm (accessed July 25, 2006).

17. Sean Foley, quoted in Anne Marie Owens, "Workplace Cockiness the way of the future," *National Post* online, January 31, 2005 (accessed May 18, 2005).

18. Linda Duxbury and Chris Higgins, *Work-Life Conflict in Canada in the New Millennium* (Ottawa: Health Canada, 2001), http://www.phac-aspc.gc.ca/publicat/work-travail/report2/index.html (accessed July 25, 2006).

19. Wallace Immen, "Shifting values: more than a pay cheque," *The Globe and Mail*, April 29, 2005, C1.

20. Barbara Moses, "Coddled, confident, and cocky: The challenge of managing Gen Y," *The Globe and Mail*, March 11, 2005, C1.

21. Virginia Galt, "Kid-Glove approach woos new grads," *The Globe and Mail*, March 9, 2005, C1.

22. Andrew Wahl, "Skills Shortage Dead Ahead," *Canadian Business*, August 25, 2004.

23. John C. Beck and Mitchell Wade, "Harness Talents of gamer generation," *The Globe and Mail*, January 7, 2005, C1.

24. Kathryn May, "Canada Home to Hardest Workers," Dec. 22, 2003, CanWest News Services, December 22, 2003, http://www.workrights.ca/News/News+122203 (accessed June 21, 2005).

25. CTV, "Many Canadian workers ready to quit," February 2, 2005, CTV.ca, HR Data Network, http://www.ctv.ca/servlet/ArticleNews/story/CTVNews/20050126/canada (accessed June 1, 2005).

26. Virginia Galt, "Professionals demanding a work-life balance—and backing it up," *The Globe and Mail*, March 17, 2005, B1.

27. Ibid.

28. Wayne Visser, *Meaning, Work, and Social Responsibility*, International Network on Personal Meaning, http://www.meaning.ca/business/index.htm (accessed April 22, 2005).

29. Sundar Magan, "Effects of Restructuring on Company Organizational Structure and Performance," from *Restructuring in Canadian Companies* (Ottawa: Industry Canada 1996), http://www.strategis.ic.gc.ca/epic/internet/ineas-aes.nsf/vwapj/wp23e.pdf/$FILE/wp23e.pdf (accessed May 10, 2005), 17.

30. Thomas H. Davenport, "The Fad That Forgot People," *Fast Company* magazine November 1995, 70.

31. Mark Kingwell, "Searching for the Future of Architecture in Shanghai," *Harper's*, February 2005, 66.

32. Linda Duxbury, "Leader Profiles: Interview with Linda Duxbury" (Social Development Canada, June 2001.

33. Sunder Magun, *Restructuring in Canadian Industries: A Micro Analysis*, Working Paper 23, Applied International Economics, June 1998, www.strategic.ic.gc.ca/epic/internet/ineas-aes.nsf/en/ra01683e.html (accessed October 27, 2006).

PART TWO

2

Communication Perspectives

The Nature of Communication

2

Tea at the Palaz of Hoon
Not less because in purple I descended
The western day through what you called
The loneliest air, not less was I myself.

What was the ointment sprinkled on my beard?
What were the hymns that buzzed beside my ears?
What was the sea whose tide swept through me there?

Out of my mind the golden ointment rained,
And my ears made the blowing hymns they heard.
I was myself the compass of that sea:

I was the world in which I walked, and what I saw
Or heard or felt came not but from myself;
And there I found myself more truly and more strange.

—Wallace Stevens

Learning Objectives

- Discover and define the nature of human communication

- Examine the stages of the human communication process

- Explore and compare the origins of communication theory by examining
  European, American, and Canadian communication studies

- Identify the perspectives of communication theory by looking at the
  rhetorical, mechanistic, psychological, interactional, and transactional
  perspectives

The Nature of Human Communication

Defining Communication

Few concepts have as many meanings as the term "communication." Its all-encompassing and constantly changing nature makes it difficult to define. On a very general level, it can be defined as a response by an organism to a stimulus. This would include communication experiences ranging from thinking processes, to workplace meetings, to watching TV, to essentially every conscious act we engage in—to life itself. From a communication theory standpoint, though, such a definition is not very useful.

To appreciate the difficulty of defining the term "communication," let's look at why it has so many different meanings. Brent Rubin summarized reasons for it.[1] One reason is its interdisciplinary nature. It has been studied for centuries by philosophers. More recently, psychologists and sociologists have examined how communication takes place among people and societies. Politicians use communication techniques to appeal to voters. Engineers use technical skills for developing electronic communication systems, and zoologists focus on communication between animals. Also, the word *communication* refers to both a field of study, such as the effects of satellite communication systems of the remote communities of the Canadian North, as well as an activity that people do. Communication also overlaps two academic domains with different theoretical traditions: the humanities, with subjects such as literature, linguistics, philosophy, visual and performing arts; and the social sciences, with psychology, sociology, and anthropology. This text adds to the mix by including management and organizational studies in the rapidly emerging field of organizational communication. The debate continues even about the name of the field. Communications (with an "s") has been used to refer to technology and mass media. Communication is typically used to describe human communication. But the two terms are increasingly being used interchangeably.

An outcome of the multiplicity of the communication field is the diversity of programs in communication offered at Canadian colleges and universities. Annette Shelby developed a useful classification of program areas for professional communication studies: business communication, management communication, corporate communication, organizational communication.[2] Virtually every college in the country offers applied communication courses, the most popular being business communication, focusing on writing and presentations. Many colleges also offer a basic course in technical communication. Advanced professional communication courses cover individual management skills in leadership, decision making, team structures, conflict management, and interpersonal skills. Organizational communication involves an understanding of practical and theoretical issues of how an organization works in terms of communication. Other applied areas common in colleges are communication media courses, such as broadcasting, journalism, advertising, and graphic arts.

Universities generally offer professional courses in communication oriented around business practices. Many offer courses in management, interpersonal, and organizational communication, often within the department of business or social sciences, since these courses rely on management studies, psychology, and sociology for conceptual foundations, or in a humanities department. A particularly large field in the universities, and very unique to Canada, is the humanities branch generally known as Communication Studies. About 30 Canadian universities offer undergraduate programs in Communication Studies, and at least 10 offer graduate programs in the field. Many other related programs are available, such as culture and communication, media studies, information technology, multimedia, writing, journalism, rhetoric, and composition.

The Human Communication Process

To achieve a more theoretically meaningful definition of communication, scholars have used more restrictive terms, often determined by purpose or the context of the area of study. A generally accepted definition of human communication is as follows: communication is the process of people using messages to create meaning within and across various channels and contexts. This definition includes both face-to-face and mediated messages (since people are at the origins of all mediated messages). The key ideas in this definition are people, meaning, interaction, messages, and context.

Let's use a typical example of human communication, that of introducing yourself to someone with a handshake, to take a closer look at the different activities involved in human communication.

- You bring everything you are to a communication activity such as a personal introduction: your memories of past introductions, expectations around meeting people, your goals and needs, assumptions about the rules people should follow during introductions, anxieties about meeting people—simply put, the entire meaning systems you have developed over the course of your life.
- Meaning is created as each person interprets the other person's symbolic behaviours during the interaction and forms responses to messages. You may perceive someone's handshake as friendly and decide to respond in kind. Your internal system of meanings would register this person positively as someone you might enjoy developing a further relationship with. If your meaning system possesses a cynical vein, you might reserve judgment, suspecting the person has a hidden agenda.
- Messages are used during the interaction, both verbal (words) and nonverbal (body language, tone of voice, facial expressions). People express themselves verbally, saying, "Hello; How are you; Nice to meet you; Hi, my name is Joe;" and so forth. Nonverbal symbols include an extended arm, a press of the hands, a smile, eye contact, a nod of the head, direct posture, and numerous other actions such as voice inflections and eye movements, many of which are tiny but noticeable. Your appearance—grooming, clothing, body shape—also speaks to the other person.
- Context provides the rules of engagement. Introductions at a family dinner or in a social environment would likely be trusting, casual, and warm. In a business setting, they could be more formal and strategic. As an exercise at the beginning of my organizational communication class, handshakes are always a lot of fun and a great way to create awareness of the numerous activities taking place during the few seconds that an introduction takes.

Can you communicate with yourself? This text includes intrapersonal communication in our definition of communication. Intrapersonal refers to communicating with oneself.[3] It's a form of self-awareness that allows you to discover yourself through experiencing your environment or the way you experience a novel, a play, or a beautiful landscape. In the poem that starts off the chapter, *Tea at the Palaz of Hoon*, Wallace Stevens describes how communication is an inner dialogue between the external and internal worlds. External reality becomes known and takes on significance through meaning structures that exist internally. The poem highlights the stages of the sense-making process: observation, interpretation, meaning, and self-discovery. As the poet says,

> Out of my mind the golden ointment rained,
> My ears made the blowing hymns they heard . . .
> And what I saw or heard or felt came not from myself.[4]

We act as the "compass" of our world, the fixed point around which everything revolves. In this way, each one of us is the creator of our own unique world.

Communication is a sense-making process in which the objective world becomes meaningful once it is apprehended and personalized by the observer. By interpreting the actions of others and events in our environment we are engaged in sense-making behaviour, in meaning creation.

What happens when it is difficult to make sense of our surroundings? Our longing for order and meaning becomes acute as uncertainty in a situation rises, such as when we meet strangers. There is so much to know about a person, yet so little comes out in a brief introduction. We deal with this by relying on generalizations. If someone smiles, makes eye contact, and has a firm handshake, we confer positive qualities on that person: decisive, confident, open, trustworthy, friendly, fun to have dinner with. In this way, the stranger fits into our comfort zone. Other anxiety-producing situations are going on first dates, job interviews, and everyone's favourite—public speaking. The high level of uncertainty in each situation—in other words, the level of difficulty in establishing meaning in the situation—makes us uncomfortable. Anxiety is reduced as situations become meaningful.

Where do these meaning systems come from? People's sense-making abilities have improved over time as systems for interpreting behaviours have been developed, not only language systems, but sets of behaviours that coincide with certain contexts and situations. As children grow, they acquire the sense-making methods of their parents and other people around them. Language, of course, is a major communication system. Other systems for interpreting communication behaviours are:

- *Paralinguistics*—voice pitch and tone, rate of speech, and other vocal qualities
- *Kinesics*—facial expressions, gestures, other movements
- *Proxemics*—space, such as how close we stand to different people during communication
- *Chronemics*—time, such as how long we spend with different people, the amount of time we give to an activity, how long we make people wait
- *Oculesics*—eye contact
- *Haptics*—touch
- *Objectics*—objects, such as uniforms, furnishings, status symbols

The list is virtually endless. The meanings we form about any particular person accumulate continually as we find out more information, such as favourite types of food, favourite movies, preferred vacation spots, and so forth.

Stages of the Communication Process

Now that we've broken down a common communication activity, the handshake, let us look at the different parts of that activity in terms of the process of communication. The key stages in the human communication process form a loop that travels in two directions, as shown in Figure 2.1.

To create shared meaning, the basic communication act consists of three stages:

1. the sender telling the receiver something;
   ("Hello, I'm Jennifer.")
2. the receiver responding to the sender;
   ("Hi, I'm Paul. Nice to meet you.")
3. the sender indicating that the message was understood.
   ("Nice to meet you.")

Next comes more verbal and nonverbal interaction as the creation of shared meanings continues. Let's look more closely at each stage in the process.

The Sender
The *sender* initiates the message. The process of creating shared meaning is started by communicating an idea or feeling in a verbal or nonverbal form, or a combination of

Figure 2.1	Two-Way Human Communication Process

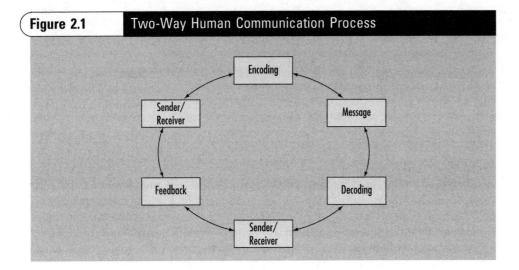

them. Since messages travel in both directions in the communication process, each person engaged in the process is both a sender and a receiver, often simultaneously, since as we are speaking to someone using verbal messages we are watching for his or her nonverbal reactions to our messages. In this way, someone could be laughing or gesturing in response to someone speaking. Through using effective listening skills, we determine how to respond to people's messages. Sometimes we need to listen for the feelings behind the words to reveal the deeper concerns of the message.

The challenge for the sender is to make sure the message is understood, so the more the sender knows about the receiver, the better chance there is for effective communication. For example, before giving a presentation, it's important to know who your audience will be—will it be made up of technicians, managers, or grade 3 students? By presenting information at the appropriate knowledge level, you ensure that it will be relevant and well understood.

Encoding

The *encoding* stage involves formulating your idea into symbols that are shared by the receiver. In our example of people introducing themselves, the sender decided to use spoken words as symbols to communicate her name. In contrast, in the game of charades, and we are allowed to use only gestures to externalize our ideas. When you encode, you decide things such as message length, tone, style, timing, and vocabulary. Since each receiver is a unique individual, you take into account people's differences and personalities. Managers, for example, use different motivational methods with employees because people react differently. Some employees might work harder if you criticize them, while others might lose confidence and quit trying. You also consider the receiver's emotional state, attitudes, and values.

Message

The *message*, which started out as an idea inside someone's mind and then became a symbol, now becomes a physical representation, a stimulus for the receiver. It can be a gesture, word, sound, electrical impulse, print, or a picture on paper. Messages themselves are not meanings, since the meaning comes from the interpretation the receiver gives to the message in the next stage, decoding. Since the context of a message also contributes meaning, messages are influenced by situational and cultural factors.

The channel used for a message has been referred to as the medium through which the message is transmitted. Sound frequency is the medium that carries words. On a telephone, electrical impulses carry words along wires or through the air. Print on paper is a medium that carries the stimulus of words or pictures. Whether it's interpersonal or mass communication, messages need a channel or medium for their journey. Mass communication, of course, involves more technology than interpersonal communication, though in today's heavily messaged world, much interpersonal communication is done electronically. The type of channel you decide to use for your message is determined by various factors. If your message is complex, a written format would be better for remembering details. Often cost is a factor, so you weigh the cost and benefits when deciding on the channel.

Decoding

Decoding is when the receiver interprets the sender's messages and assigns meanings to them. The receiver's personal characteristics, attitudes, values, and background, as well as the context of the message, will influence the interpretation of the sender's symbols. Human communication never achieves 100 percent fidelity because of the individual differences we have between us. The bigger the differences, the fewer symbols and meanings we share, and the more difficult it becomes to understand each other.

Receiver

The *receiver* needs to do two things: "listen" carefully for both verbal and nonverbal messages, and provide feedback to the sender. The process of listening involves all of the perceptual senses we used in our handshake exercise: hearing and seeing a message, touching, perhaps smelling the person's cologne. The last two stages are interpreting and understanding the messages and, finally, evaluating appropriate responses. These processes occur very rapidly as we become more skilled in social interaction.

Feedback

The receiver's stage is important because it is where *feedback* takes place. This enables the sender to know how well the message was understood. We must remember that this process is nearly concurrent—we both send and receive messages so quickly that they may seem simultaneous. In reality, each message is a response to a previous message, though, along a continuous stream of meaning.

Message Distortion—Noise

Messages can be distorted or lose information at any stage of the communication process. The two causes of *message distortion* originate in the technological channels and the perceptual senses operating. Just as telephone lines sometimes produce distortion, our senses also are not guaranteed to be perfect. We all have different levels of vision and hearing. We may experience message distortion psychologically or emotionally when we are preoccupied with a previous event instead of paying attention to the current activity. Conflict and worry are common causes of distortion. In fact, many workplaces are initiating practices that help employees deal with workplace conflict and that allow them to build harmonious relationships. Conflict and poor relationships are two major sources of noise in the communication process. Workplaces have also developed policies that allow an employee's emotional concerns to be a part of his or her professional life—changes specifically related to the creation of a facilitative communication environment for the workplace.

Communication Context

Context represents a huge source of information for communicators, including the details of time and place, the relationships involved, social and cultural rules, status of participants, our level of comfort, and our freedom to express ourselves. In fact, it

Conducting a Management Communication Seminar

You have been hired as the Communication Director for a large home building corporation that has 2500 employees. Your area is central Canada—Saskatchewan, Manitoba, and northwestern Ontario. Senior management has decided that managers in all departments need to develop more effective communication skills. Your first task in your new job will be to conduct half-day seminars for the managers from all the different departments that provide an overview of the training programs that will take place. Training in communication will be a new experience for these managers. As a matter of fact, they will be surprised when they discover that senior management thinks they need help in communication. They all have college and university degrees specific to their area: financial managers are educated in accounting; general managers and customer service in business administration; information technology managers in computer sciences; and technical managers in their specific field. You would probably divide the managers into two groups: managerial and technical. Your boss is a 35-year-old vice-president, outgoing and proactive. His office displays best-selling business books on topics such as leadership, motivation, communication, and teamwork.

Discussion Questions

1. What are the differences in the managerial and technical groups that would need to be considered in planning the content and delivery of your seminar?

2. Would you use different channels of communication for each group?

would be impossible not to have a context when communicating. Context is most pronounced in interpersonal relationships, where our communication style and messages are mainly determined by the type of relationship we have. A close friendship provides a context of trust, comfort, and openness. Meeting a stranger is more of an anxious experience. Having a conflict with a close friend can be agonizing, whereas conflict with a stranger is quickly forgotten. Context is significant in a workplace because of the closeness that is established between coworkers. In communication jargon, we express our relationships with people through "relational" messages—statements about how we feel toward one another and how other people meet our basic needs for affection and create a sense of belonging.

Origins of Communication Theory

The multidisciplinary scope of communication has over the years supported the development of many theories of communication from the fields of rhetoric, psychology, sociology, cultural studies, history, media studies, language, and mathematics. This section will discuss the major theories, their origins, and their relevance to communication studies.

Today, many theoretical perspectives have become integrated throughout research communities around the globe, but the various traditions all had their own unique beginnings. Communication thought in Canada grew out of the humanities field, focusing on the individual, social, and cultural processes that define reality and human experience. In contrast, the tradition of European communication studies emphasizes ideological theory in an attempt to discover forms of consciousness based on social and economic conditions as outlined in the writings of Marx and Engels.[5] American communication research grew out of stimulus–response psychology and the transportational models of Shannon and Weaver, in which communication was portrayed as a message travelling along a channel to a receiver, who then provided feedback. The model was based on a mechanical perspective that did not take into account the influences of human factors, such as attitudes, values, and cultural differences. These functional starting points, though, have since developed into many diverse, innovative, and comprehensive perspectives.

Why are there so many different perspectives? It depends on the theoretical traditions a researcher is building on and the circumstances that are contributing to the shaping of individual and social consciousness. We will begin with a look at our own distinctly Canadian approach to the study of communication, based on the traditions of Harold Innis and Marshall McLuhan.

In the Canadian perspective, McLuhan proposes that it is technological conditioning that is responsible for the characteristics of our consciousness. We adopt thinking patterns based on the various forms of media we use to experience reality. He proposed this theory in *The Gutenberg Galaxy*, where he states that the printing press is the reason for all psychic and social change in the Western world since the Renaissance. He proposes that "an analysis of human culture involves the retracing of the stages of human apprehension."[6] McLuhan studies the environment as if it were some type of artifact.[7] The environment is both artistic, in the sense that it is subjectively created by the observer; and structural, or architectural, in that it provides observers with a structure for thinking, which in turn becomes a part of a person's internalized sense-making system to be used for subsequent observations. He describes the process in the phrase "we shape our tools, and then our tools shape us." This view is in line with much human communication theory, which proposes that our experiences become frames of reference for understanding further experiences—a process that continually evolves through time.

The origins of the American communication model assume the direct mechanical effect of a message by the sender on the receiver, as in a stimulus–response relationship.[8] Everything except the intended message—all unintentional information—is "noise." The concept of fidelity states that noise must be eliminated for effective communication. The strength of the model is its focus on the message itself and on the function of the message. Though the model helps to explain some communication activity, it neglects the importance of the vast quantities of information that a person experiences in the form of "noise." These messages, though considered extraneous, make up the larger social and cultural context and have been shown in subsequent research to be of paramount importance in the process of making sense of reality.

The model is suitable for purposeful, linear communication; hence, its popularity in organizational communication. It is inadequate, however, for defining the comprehensive nature of individual and social reality. It originated during World War II, where it was applied spur-of-the-moment style to integrate the communication activity of the American war effort, so its functional nature is understandable. In American organizational communication research, breakthrough advances took place in human relations, systems theory, and cultural perspectives. These new directions greatly expanded the scope of investigation and gave communication studies a highly interdisciplinary character—an approach that has grown greatly in popularity. As we review organizational communication perspectives in the coming chapters, we will see this continually more inclusive trend.

The origins of communication thought in Canada are strongly connected to the founding forces that shaped this country: our climate and geography, our multiculturalism, our powerful southern neighbour, and our European roots. As a result, a national concern with the state of our being has developed through our speculations on the place of individuals or groups within the larger picture. Donald Theall states:

Following the Second World War there emerged in Canada at both a theoretical and practical level a temporary realization of the intricate inter-relations between what has come to be described somewhat awkwardly as the cultural industries, the knowledge industries, and the communication industries. This is represented theoretically in the interests of Innis and McLuhan and in a practical way through the evolution of the National Film Board, the Canadian Broadcasting Corporation, and government communications policy.[9]

Theall points out that universities played a strong influence in the development of communication studies in Canada, especially in the Innis and McLuhan years at mid-century at the University of Toronto. Their work provided Canadian communication theory with a rich diversity of disciplines—from history, philosophy, humanities, and arts—that combined with influences from European and American schools of thought. The influence of the social sciences that was a dominant approach in American communication studies had not yet reached north of the border, as Theall notes: "The climate and context for developing a theory in Canada differed from the situation in the United States because empirical and behavioural studies had not come to occupy as strong an authoritative role with regards to communication study."[10]

Robert Babe has summarized key points in the development of communication thought in Canada:[11]

- It is traditionally "critical" in nature. By applying the notion of "appraisal" to critical research, it focuses on not only revealing and explaining social trends, but also on evaluating events, activities, and policies against enduring values, such as law and order, equality, and the public interest.
- It is more inclusive and humanities-oriented, exhibiting a preference for cultural priorities and human equality over commercial interests, in contrast to much American communication discourse focusing on administrative and profit-motivated goals.
- It stresses the importance of the human imagination and studies how our imaginations are influenced and shaped by our social and technological systems.
- It emphasizes context and the mediating processes, such as institutions, technologies, mass media, and historical events we use to understand our experiences. The notion of power and control over these mediated systems and whose interests are being served is the goal of inquiry. This interest in political economy characterizes Canadian communication thought and the curriculum of many communication studies programs.

Harold Innis was a major influence in establishing the political economy approach to communication studies in Canada. Paul Heyer, author of a recent book on Harold Innis, describes the events in Innis's personal life that helped shape his communication theories. With academic roots in economics and history, Innis's approach to communication had a broad scope. According to Heyer, "The historical approach Innis employed is one in which individuals, almost in a Marxian sense, are agents of broader institutional patterns and processes."[12] Innis's familiarity with some of our staple resource industries, such as furs, fish, and pulp and paper, led the way to communication theories about our cultural and communication industries. According to Heyer, Innis followed the value chain through its stages from pulp and paper to newspapers, advertising, and books. Resource-based commodities such as pulp and paper were eventually transformed into the commodities of information and knowledge, serving the interests of those in power at every stage. These ideas were the beginnings for his two major communication books, *Empire and Communications* and *The Bias of Communication*.

The contrast between Canadian and American approaches to critical theory is evident in the social responsibilities we place on our governments. In the mass media, Canadians are comfortable with not only evaluating social and economic policies, but looking to the government for corrective action when they fail. In contrast, the American

Chapter 2 / The Nature of Communication

approach to explaining reality steers clear of pointing the finger at government—perhaps an expression of the spirit of individualism more common in American culture.

Most observers of politics would be aware of the pro-business economic policies that recent governments in the U.S. and Canada have implemented. Policies such as deregulation, outsourcing, the removal of market barriers, corporate tax reductions, relaxed labour laws, and globalization practices in general come to mind. The amount of government funding for public radio stations in the U.S. has decreased by almost 70 percent in the last two decades.[13] Though the forces of deregulation have also been felt in Canada, our impulse still is to appeal to government to make things better. As an example, consider the quickness with which Canadians criticized the Ontario government when privatized licence agencies were discovered issuing fake driver's licences in 2005. We blamed the government for letting it happen, even though the service was being administered by a private company.

The issues of political economy fit into Marshall McLuhan's framework of thinking. Dreyer Berg explains McLuhan's unique point of view by describing it as "learning about the very process of the actualization of being."[14] The human experience is imaginative and subjective. For McLuhan and Innis, communication was not simply sending messages and eliminating noise, it was an integrated and generative process of senders, receivers, messages, and media that "are simultaneously parts and products in an ongoing social order."[15]

Media and cultural studies programs in communication in Canada generally focus on the complex relationship between the individual and society. Similarly, considerable research in organizational communication focuses on the relationships between the individual and the organization. Eisenberg and Goodhall examine two opposing perspectives in terms of looking at the individual within the larger environment: a macro perceptive views people as being influenced and shaped by the forces of society; the micro perspective sees individuals as creators of the larger forces.[16] This dual approach suggests a potential common ground in social and organizational perspectives based on cultural studies. In fact, cultural studies research has contributed significantly to a major branch of organizational communication known as organizational culture. Yet the emphasis on institutions and technologies in Canadian studies focuses too much on ideals, activism, and social prescription and ventures into abstract territory too often, according to communications scholar Rowland Latimer.

> The models of research and inquiry needed are not those which lend legitimacy to social and media criticism . . . but others which value a sophisticated and detailed understanding of the nature and dynamics of the phenomenon within which they are engaged. Such an understanding would include economic, political, social, cultural, technical, and professional variables and their interaction.[17]

Lorimer's proposal for Canadian communication studies stresses more professional communication training. For his part, he helped to set up a graduate program in publishing at Simon Fraser University. Other examples are the University of Toronto, with graduate degree programs in Professional Writing and Industrial Relations, and Mount Saint Vincent in Halifax, with its program in Public Relations. For a more academic orientation, St. Mary's in Halifax has Industrial/Organizational Psychology, and Concordia University and the University of Western Ontario have graduate programs in journalism and media studies. McGill University and a joint program between Concordia, the University of Quebec at Montreal, and the University of Montreal offer graduate programs in Organizational Communication. Some certificate programs are also available, through the University of Waterloo. Most major universities offer courses in organizational communication. The colleges across the country, of course, have been providing applied communication programs since they opened. With the growing interest in workplace well-being—no doubt a result of the gradual deterioration of the health of the workplace due to increasing contract work, outsourcing, distributed workplaces, corruption, overwork, and stress—numerous subjects concerning healthy workplaces are included in college and university curriculums, among them conflict resolution, emotional intelligence, cultural diversity, group skills, and issues of social responsibility and ethics.

Perspectives on Communication Theory

History provides us with an abundance on perspectives of communication, since people have been theorizing about it from the earliest civilizations. In the following section we will describe some of the major perspectives.

The Rhetorical Tradition—Persuasive Communication

This perspective dates back to ancient Greek and Roman cultures and focuses on the art of rhetoric—the use of structure, style, and delivery in public speaking for the purposes of persuasion.[18] Aristotle defined rhetoric as the persuasive techniques known as ethos (appeals to credibility of the source), pathos (appeals to emotion), and logos (appeals to logic). A researcher in the field of rhetorical analysis would study the effects of messages on audiences by looking at the strategies used by a sender to achieve a desired effect on a receiver (see Figure 2.2). Political debates are full of examples of rhetorical strategies.

Application

Today, rhetorical techniques are used in political communication, advertising, internal and external corporate communication, and arts and entertainment. An example from advertising is the campaign in the early 2000s to bring back formal wear into the business world after years of khakis, jeans, and casual shirts—the fashion of the status-erasing trend in workplaces that has existed since the early 1990s. The ads were sponsored by formal clothing companies, the high-end Harry Rosen clothing chain among them. The message suggested a return to the traditional, professional business image that used clothing as a status distinction in the workplace—with, of course, the intended goal of selling more suits and ties. Today's media-trained generations could no doubt with a quick examination of any television ad pick out the persuasive techniques used, especially the major-label commercials usually dominated by the sure-fire but unsophisticated appeals to security, status, and sex.

The Mechanistic Perspective—Flowing along the Channel

A major area of communication theory begins with the mechanistic perspective, based on the linear model of communication created by Shannon and Weaver in 1947.[19] The highly influential model describes messages flowing along channels, as though they were items on a "conveyer belt." The mechanistic perspective, also called transmissional, follows the stages outlined in Figure 2.3: sender → encoding → message → decoding → receiver → feedback. The model was developed to separate noise from information-

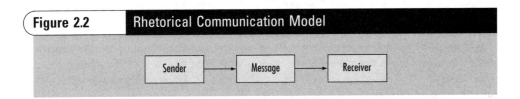

Figure 2.2	Rhetorical Communication Model

Sender → Message → Receiver

Figure 2.3	Mechanistic Communication Model

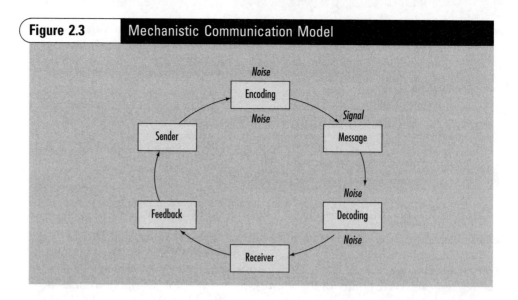

carrying signals. Noise that exists at every stage of the process affects the message's fidelity—its accuracy of reproduction. If a person is telling a joke and forgets certain details, the message loses fidelity. Similarly, fidelity is lost if a receiver defines words differently than a sender. Fidelity refers to the extent to which the message is the same at two points between the sender and receiver. Anything that reduces fidelity by interfering with the process is called noise.

Noise

Losing information in the communication process is a normal occurrence. As communicators, we take this into account. For example, in a room full of loud voices, we speak up to be heard. In the classic telephone game, an example of serial communication, people in a line whisper the same message to each other. The message gradually becomes distorted and loses fidelity. Shannon and Weaver's model is useful because it identifies specific factors that can be controlled to increase fidelity—in particular, redundancy and repetition. Encoding strategies that use redundancy or repetition help overcome the loss of message fidelity. Teachers often use repetition as a way of helping students understand key ideas in a lesson. Face-to-face communication, typically employing nonverbal messages to support verbal messages, also shows the uses of redundancy for message clarity, as when a person smiles when making a happy statement.

Channel

Channel capacity is also viewed in mechanistic terms, such as the carrying capacity of a telephone line. A channel is any medium that carries messages, such as air, for face-to-face conversations, radio frequencies, synapses in the nervous system, or a written letter. Too much information can cause information overload, which leads to a breakdown in communication. The ideal formula would include enough redundancy to ensure fidelity but not so much as to cause overload. The information provided by a clear message would have the effect of reducing uncertainty in the receiver.

Feedback

The concept of feedback, referring to messages sent from the receiver to the sender, indicates how clearly the message was received. A sender can modify a message to improve its fidelity based on feedback from the receiver. Effective listening skills, useful in discussions involving differences of opinion or conflicts, are methods of offering

A husband and wife were having some problems at home and were giving each other the silent treatment. Suddenly, the husband realized that the next day he would need his wife to wake him at 5 a.m. for an early morning business flight. Not wanting to be first to break the silence, he wrote on a piece of paper, "Please wake me at 5 a.m." He left the note where he knew she would find it.

The next morning the husband woke up to discover that it was 9 a.m. and he had missed his flight. Furious, he was about to go and see why his wife had not woke him, when he noticed a piece of paper by the bed. On it was written, "It is 5 a.m. Wake up."

feedback to unclear messages to elicit more complete and accurate information from the sender.

Conclusion and Critique

The strong linear or directional connection between communicators in the mechanistic perspective implies that a message from a source has an impact, or an effect, on the receiver. Its simplistic framework depicts the sender as an active creator of messages and the receiver as a passive recipient, in a cause-and-effect relationship. A quick look at how we use language, though, shows that there is more to this process. Today, you can hear people describe having a conversation as "talking with" someone instead of "talking to" them. "Talking to" is mechanistic, suggesting a one-way linear flow of information, whereas "talking with" suggests an interactive process, much more conducive to the way meanings are shared as we talk together. The linear model was developed in an era when information theory was popular, so it applies more to mechanical situations. Human communication is often more concerned with sharing meaning. Instead of simply receiving a signal, the process of human communication involves messages jointly created by senders and receivers.

In terms of defining our social and organizational realities, the linear model is incomplete because it filters out as "noise" a lot of information that is potentially important. Organizational reality can be based on behaviour that is irrational or unintentional. And many activities in the workplace occur through random, informal interaction. Often we end up with a different reality than we set out to create, once the human negotiation process begins.

Application

The mechanistic approach is still widely used today because of the purposeful nature of organizations—everything not related to achieving the goal is regarded as "noise." This perspective can be valuable for designing communication networks and channels to improve fidelity of communication by removing barriers to the understanding of messages and eliminating information overload. Typical areas of research in the mechanistic perspective have focused on direction of information flow, informal and formal networks, and types of information channels in organizations.

Psychological Perspective—Conceptual Filters

The psychological perspective shifts the focus of communication from the communication channel to the cognitive processes occurring in people's minds during communication (see Figure 2.4). To understand how communication works, we must analyze how an external stimulus is perceived through our senses and processed by conceptual filters

Figure 2.4   Psychological Communication Model

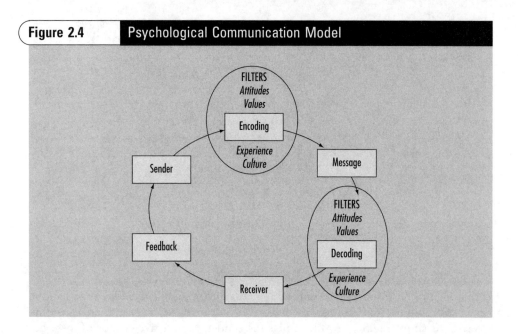

such as attitudes, values, beliefs, and psychological and emotional needs—mental constructs referred to as an individual's "black box."

To develop a clear idea of what we mean by a "stimulus," let's look at three conceptualizations.[20] First, a stimulus can be a person or object that exists in the environment that has an influence on a person. In our handshake example, each person's behaviour would be explainable as a response to the other person's actions—one smiles, and it causes the other to smile. This is the classic stimulus–response formula.

The second conceptualization internalizes the experience of a stimulus by examining the impact on the senses. The stimulus becomes an object expressed through physiological sensations, such as patterns on the eye, vibrations in the eardrum, dilation of pupils, breathing and heart rates, and sweating. The area of study is the apprehension of an object by a sensory receptor.

The third conceptualization goes one step further by integrating a person's response to an object with his or her understanding of it. So, we see an object as something that is meaningful to us after interpreting it. This step allows us to infer a cultural or social meaning instead of a literal one when, for instance, we ask "How are you?" while shaking hands. In a different situation, though, if it were a police officer questioning a victim at an accident scene, the message would be interpreted in a literal sense. The victim would respond by indicating whether or not he or she was injured. The important point here is that communication takes place on different levels, and all three conceptualizations are often working in combination.

Application

Theories of communication from the psychological perspective attempt to explain the effects of communication based on the cognitive processes taking place during observation and interpretation. A common function of communication is to shape or change a person's attitude, defined as a predisposition to choose one stimulus over another. Choosing a beef burger over a veggie burger would show a more positive attitude toward one than the other. Communicators in this area try to shape people's attitudes to achieve a certain objective, such as selling products or services. Political campaigns based on free markets or tax cuts, for instance, attempt to change people's attitudes about these issues in order to change their voting behaviour.

In organizational communication, the psychological perspective is important because it emphasizes the treatment of communicators as human beings—signalling a return to humanistic principles. Research in the area of communication climate in organizations, which focuses on how it feels in a workplace based on levels of trust, openness, and supportiveness, hinges on psychological principles. The human relations approach in management studies relies considerably on this perspective of communication.

Interactional Perspective—The Social Nature of Communication

If the mechanistic perspective can be seen as a "monologue" approach to communication, suggesting the idea of someone doing something to somebody, the interactional perspective can be regarded as a "dialogue." So, communication is seen as a *dialogic* activity (see Figure 2.5). Through social interaction, mutual understanding is created and the self is expressed and developed. The principle characteristic of the perspective is the emphasis on the human self, representing the heart of both meaning and interaction. As Stephen Littlejohn states, "Meaning is a product of social life. Whatever meaning a person possesses for a thing is the result of social interaction with others about the object being defined. A person has no meaning for something apart from the interaction with other human beings."[21]

The unique aspect of interactionism is that meaning comes from conscious interpretation—something becomes meaningful to a person when he or she consciously thinks about it. The process of managing meanings is simply an internal conversation with the goal of making sense of things. We are now talking about something similar to the meanings and self-identity expressed in the poem at the beginning of the chapter, where every experience of the environment creates a new meaning and leads to new self-discovery. As Wallace Stevens says in the last verse of *Tea at the Palaz of Hoon*:

I was the world in which I walked, and what I saw
Or heard or felt came not but from myself;
And there I found myself more truly and more strange.

The interactional view offers an interesting answer to an old question: if a tree falls in the forest and nobody sees it, did it really fall? Without anybody there to *see* the tree fall, no conscious interpretation of the event could happen. The tree could very well have fallen,

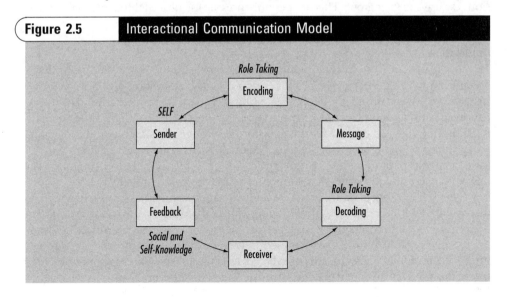

Figure 2.5   Interactional Communication Model

Chapter 2 / The Nature of Communication

but the event will not exist in anyone's meaning system. It would be like a rock falling off a hill on Jupiter—it's meaningless until it's experienced.

Role Taking

The objective of dialogic communication involves reaching out to someone in order to experience somebody else—a "going outside of self." In order to achieve this, role taking, one of the two main theoretical foundations of this perspective, is required. Role taking allows a person to see himself or herself through the eyes of others. It is also referred to as empathy and sensitivity in terms of communication skills, qualities not found in the mechanical models. If you want to ask your boss for a raise, you put yourself in his or her place to imagine what the answer might be. You design your question according to the answer you think you will get. So, role taking involves learning how to effectively interact in social situations.

Symbolic Interaction

The achievement of self-understanding is made possible through symbolic interaction, a communication perspective based on the tradition of symbolic interactionism developed by sociologist George Herbert Mead.[22] A person can achieve self-development only through interaction with other people. As years go by, a person develops a catalogue of responses and interpretations from observing his or her own actions and those of others. The perspective is different from the psychological one because it does not rely on the concepts of filters. Behaviour is not a response; it is a part of the process of interpretation, self-expression, and self-creation. People act both creatively and routinely toward their surroundings instead of merely existing as sensory receptors in a field of stimuli.

The ability to play different roles lets a person navigate through communication situations more effectively, from something as simple as how to approach people at a party to conducting yourself at a business meeting. We make communication choices by envisioning how others would respond to such a message based on accepted norms and expectations. Having communication skills, then, can be said to give a person the capacity for learned social interaction. As we gain experience in life, we are able to visualize and perform a growing number of roles. The sociologist Erving Goffman developed a drama theory of human interaction.[23] If social interaction is role playing, then it can also be performance. This drama metaphor for communication becomes evident when you observe close friends or brothers and sisters going through their routines, punching each other or using expressions exclusive to their group. Effective performances are established through social consensus and continue to be played as roles are constructed and reconstructed.

Application

The implications of the interactional perspective for organizational communication are enormous. The perspective proposes that a single external reality doesn't exist; instead, reality is continually being created by many groups within an organization. An organization's reality would be the accumulation of all its communication behaviours. In this view, an organization is transformed from a physical place that contains its members to the ongoing activity represented by the interaction of its members. Researchers in organizational culture study, for example, orientation programs for new employees and the stages of assimilation as an employee gradually integrates himself or herself into organizational life. Mainly, the approach has given us a new way of discovering and understanding the different values that exist in organizations—some organizations value competition, others customer service or quality, or meeting deadlines. Some organizations have attempted to create values in their workplace through internal communication programs or even advertising slogans. This type of effort combines the interactional perspective with the mechanical one in an effort to create culture, a risky business in which the results can be unpredictable, as we will see in our section on organizational culture in Chapter 7.

Transactional Perspective—Recurring Patterns of Communication

Though the emphasis is still on interaction, it has shifted with the transactional perspective from the self to the relationships that develop as a result of communication and the actions performed by people who are part of a communication system. It is important to note that the transactional perspective examines recurring actions; isolated actions are insignificant. Communication, then, is not something that someone does, but a system in which one participates in repetitive fashion (see Figure 2.6).

Structure and Change

Repetition in a system creates constraint by limiting choices. The result is that relationships form and structure is established. Choosing certain people to develop relationships with involves a repetition of social activities, which in principle limits choices and increases structure and stability. A classic example would be getting married. You make a choice to give up other choices on the basis that the deeper and more joyful experiences of life are unachievable by hanging onto everything. So, our different relationships represent open and closed systems in varying degrees.

The opposing force to structure—change—is also necessary for successful relationships as they evolve over time, whether in the home or workplace. Structure is essential for an organization to create stability, but too much can be suffocating. In organizational life, the more structured a system is, the less adaptable it is to changes in the environment.

Much research in organizational communication—for example, that of Henry Mintzburg in *The Nature of Managerial Work*—has focused on developing an organizational structure that is compatible with the level of uncertainty, or change, in the environment.[24]

The origins of the transactional perspective are in Bertalanffy's General Systems Theory, a multidisciplinary set of assumptions that provides a framework for studying many different areas of inquiry. Subsequent research has focused on human systems. Families or work groups establish patterns of interaction. Relationships then develop, systems of communication form, and stability, or homeostasis, is created. When change enters the system, it affects the entire system because of the interdependence of all parts. A system that is disturbed from its normal patterns seeks to restore the balance that existed previously.

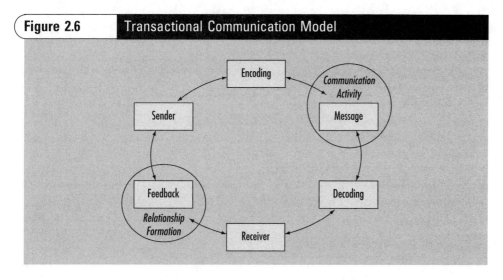

| Figure 2.6 | Transactional Communication Model |

Application

The transactional perspective is useful for examining relationships in general or in an organization. Interaction patterns provide a way of analyzing communication problems, since the main outcome of communication is the relationships that develop. The transactional perspective points out the two kinds of information that exist in every social communication act: content and relational messages.[25] The point is that the types of relationships we have influence both what we say and how it's interpreted. For example, in the workplace where superior–subordinate relationships are common, relational factors may discourage a subordinate from reporting a problem to the superior. The subordinate might feel that it's inappropriate because it might imply a criticism of the superior. In families, often things are "better left unsaid," as the saying goes, so that relationships are not disturbed.

We began the chapter with an examination of the nature of human communication and we used the introductory handshake as a working example to illustrate the stages of the communication process and how meaning is created between people through the use of symbolic behaviour. We also discussed the cognitive and perceptual processes operating when we encounter our environment, people, and ourselves. The chapter defined communication by referring to various scholars.

We compared the European, American, and Canadian approaches to communication studies. The European tradition focuses on the writings of Marx and Engels in an attempt to portray forms of consciousness based on social and economic conditions. The American school began in pragmatic and mechanistic models of stimulus–response relationships between senders and receivers of messages and has evolved to include more comprehensive approaches such as systems and cultural models. The Canadian tradition blends social and critical perspectives on communication with more applied areas that focus on specific human interaction.

Our final section looked at the major theoretical perspectives of communication theory. The rhetorical perspective focuses on persuasive speaking. Communication studies had its American beginnings with the mechanistic perspective, based on a linear model of communication. The psychological perspective introduced cognitive processes, such as attitudes, emotions, and values to communication studies. The interactional perspective shifted the focal point again, this time to communication activity as a social construction of meaning that creates relationships and self-identity. The transactional perspective looks at systems theory and explains how communication works along networks of people.

Walking the Talk of Employee Value

The three-week winter strike by college faculty was a friendly, polite affair. The new college president stuck by the message she had been promoting for the past year: "The team is at the heart of everything we do." She opened the doors of the college for washroom breaks and free coffee. She spoke in the media about the irreplaceable value teachers bring to the classroom. In her messy-haired, informal, personable style, she managed to convince many employees that a new beginning might be happening and that she should be given a chance. She began holding regular staff meetings that advocated a spirit of teamwork, excellence, and the importance of people in the college's activities.

It took only a few weeks after the strike before big changes starting taking place. Instead of making class sizes smaller and turning more part-time teaching positions into full-time ones, the very demands the union went on strike for, the opposite happened: class sizes doubled and all part-time teachers were fired. In all, 300 members of "the team," representing 40 percent of the faculty, would not be coming back for the fall semester.

This about-turn in policy was a communication challenge for the chairs of departments, who had all along been wholeheartedly passing along the president's positive attitudes to their staff. The news came out in a group e-mail that began innocently with, "Here is some information about fall teaching assignments." The message was sprinkled with the usual management jargon, such as "fiscal realties" and "work assignment efficiencies." Finally, the doubling of class sizes was announced, with the closing thought that it was not known how this would all work out in the end. The indirect writing structure of the message tried to de-emphasize the impact, but the faculty was shell-shocked.

Full-time staff members were concerned about the large increase in class size and exchanged e-mails on the staff network. Part-time staff members were worried about the impact of bigger class sizes on their jobs and called for a meeting, but no one knew anything for sure. Anxiety was growing around the water cooler, and no one was providing answers. People complained about the silence of senior administration, and rumours flourished in the absence of facts. Normally respectful and professional people saw their frustration turn to anger and even to shame. Then came sarcasm and satire as anonymous, vindictive messages began to appear in people's mailboxes. Union reps and staff members tried to keep a lid on things as accusations flew about who the composers of these messages were.

The staff union called a meeting, but by then people had put the message together: part-timers knew they would not be coming back, some of them after more than 10 years of service. At the meeting it was announced that full-time staff members would receive $1200 for return-to-work pay for planning and condensing the semester. Part-timers would receive a percentage of their earnings. Full-time staff expressed disgust that part-timers were being fired after walking arm in arm with them for three weeks on the picket line. And part-timers expressed their anger in direct ways by complaining about the lack of recognition they received, in statements such as "We're human beings with feelings and pride in our work; at least recognize what we've done before we go."

Official word from the chair finally arrived in an e-mail stating what everyone had already pieced together for themselves, along with the announcement of a staff meeting. The chair expressed sadness for those who would not be returning.

At the meeting, the president starting describing the new organizational structure. After 20 minutes of administrative chatter, faculty members got to the purpose of the meeting: to answer faculty members' questions about layoffs and doubling of class sizes. The arms began going up. Some members were alarmed at the context of the announcement—so close after a strike—and the method—indirect, almost cowering. The president realized she wouldn't be able to answer all the questions, so she announced that her assistant would write them down and she would get back to faculty with answers. The rest of the meeting was pretty much all questions.

After the meeting, faculty members fired up the intranet. One member complained that his message was deleted before people could read it, and the issue now touched on censorship and who owned the faculty intranet. Obscenities had been used. Some had read it before it was deleted. The censored writer was outraged. He challenged people to a bet that there would be no reply. Faculty are still waiting.

Discussion Questions

1. Describe how the context of the e-mail from the chair influenced the way it was understood by faculty members.

2. Describe the sources of "noise" in the communication activities taking place.

3. Describe the channels being used. Are they effective?

4. Describe the role of organizational factors in the communication activities that took place. Was there effective two-way communication? Did status play a role in the type of communication used?

5. Which of the five communication perspectives best explains the communication style practised by the college? Why?

6. Which perspective would help create a more participative, two-way communication style?

Classroom Activity

Getting to Know You

As a way of getting to know each other and demonstrating some common communication behaviours, students will have the opportunity of meeting each other by walking around the room and introducing themselves to each other. After everyone has finished, discuss verbal and nonverbal communication in terms of the messages exchanged in the student introductions. On the board, list the specific messages students used to greet others. Chances are your nonverbal list will be much longer. Discuss whether verbal or nonverbal messages carry the most meaning when we meet people and in communication in general. Bring other concepts into the discussion from the chapter, such as our need to organize our surroundings and whether meanings originate in internal or external realities, or a combination, or both.

Glossary

Paralinguistics, p. 22
Kinesics, p. 22
Proxemics, p. 22
Chronemics, p. 22
Oculesics, p. 22
Haptics, p. 22
Objectics, p. 22
Sender, p. 22
Encoding, p. 23

Message, p. 23
Decoding, p. 24
Receiver, p. 24
Feedback, p. 24
Message distortion, p. 24
Context, p. 24
Dialogic, p. 33

Notes

1. R.B. Rubin, E.M. Perse, and C.A. Barbato, "Conceptualization and Measurement of Interpersonal Communication Motives," *Human Communication Research* 14 (1998): 602–28.
2. Annette Shelby, "Organizational, Business, Management, and Corporate Communication: An Analysis of Boundaries and Relationships," *Journal of Business Communication* 30, no. 3 (1993): 241–67.
3. Rubin, Perse, and Barbato, "Conceptualization and Measurement."
4. Wallace Stevens, *The Palm at the End of the Mind* (New York: Vintage Books, 1972).
5. Dreyer Berg, "Cambridge and Toronto: The Twentieth Century Schools of Communication," *Canadian Journal of Communication* 11, no. 3 (1985): 251–57.
6. Marshall McLuhan, *The Interior Landscape: The Literary Criticism of Marshall McLuhan, 1942–1963*, ed. Eugene MacNamara (Toronto: McGraw-Hill, 1969).
7. Berg, "Cambridge and Toronto."
8. Claude Shannon and Warren Weaver, *The Mathematical Theory of Communication* (Urbana: University of Illinois Press, 1949).
9. Donald Theall, "Communication and Knowledge in Canadian Communication Theory: The Context of the University and the Academy," *Canadian Journal of Communication* 8, no. 1 (1981): 1–13.
10. Ibid.
11. Robert Babe, "Foundations of Canadian Communication Thought," *Canadian Journal of Communication* 25, no. 1 (2000).
12. Paul Heyer, *Harold Innis* (Lanham, MD: Rowman and Littlefield, 2003).
13. Harper's Index, *Harper's* magazine, June 2006, 13.
14. McLuhan, *The Interior Landscape*.
15. Babe, "Foundations."
16. Eric M. Eisenberg and H.L. Goodhall, Jr., *Organizational Communication, Balancing Creativity and Constraint* (Boston: Bedford/St. Martin's, 2004).
17. Rowland Latimer, "Introduction: Communications Teaching and Research—Looking Forward from 2000," *Canadian Journal of Communication* 25, no. 1 (2000).
18. Stephen W. Littlejohn, *Theories of Human Communication*, 2nd ed. (Belmont, CA: Wadsworth, 1983).
19. Shannon and Weaver, *The Mathematical Theory of Communication*.
20. B. Aubrey Fisher, *Perspectives on Human Communication* (New York: Macmillan, 1978).
21. Littlejohn, *Theories of Human Communication*.
22. George Herbert Mead, *Mind, Self, and Society*, ed. C.W. Morris (Chicago: University of Chicago Press, 1943).
23. Erving Goffman, *The Presentation of Self in Everyday Life* (New York: Doubleday Anchor, 1959).
24. Henry Mintzberg, *The Nature of Managerial Work* (New York: Harper Collins, 1973).
25. P. Watzlawick, J. Beavin, and D. Jackson, *Pragmatics of Human Communication: A Study of Interactional Patterns, Pathologies, and Paradoxes* (New York: Norton, 1967).

Chapter Three
Theoretical Perspectives

Imagine a termite colony somewhere in the tropics. There are thousands of termites milling around. The ground on which they start to build their nest is quite flat. The termites begin their work by moving earth in a random fashion. Gradually, distinct piles of earth begin to emerge. These then become the focus of sustained building activity, resulting in columns located in more or less random positions. These are built to a certain height, then construction stops. When columns emerge that are sufficiently close together, building resumes until they are joined at the top to form a rounded arch. In this way, the termite nest evolves into an increasingly complex structure, with the arch as the basic unit. The approach eventually results in a kind of free form architecture, comprised of interlocking caverns and tunnels that are ventilated, humidity-controlled and beautifully formed. African termite nests may rise twelve feet high and measure a hundred feet across. They can house millions of termites. In terms of scale, they're equivalent to human beings creating a building over a mile high.

—Gareth Morgan, Imaginization[1]

Learning Objectives

- Analyze the nature of organizations
- Examine theoretical approaches to organizational communication, specifically the functional, interpretive, and critical approaches, as well as some emerging approaches
- Define organizational communication
- Explore organizational communication studies in Canada
- Identify the principles of organizational communication

What Is an Organization?

The termite story is from Gareth Morgan, a leading researcher in organizational studies from the Schulich School of Business at York University. Morgan raises some intriguing questions about the termites' activity:

- If there is a plan for this structure, where does it come from?
- How do termites direct and coordinate their activity?
- How do they acquire the ability to repair parts of the nest to make them as good as new?

The answers are not easy to find, but one thing is clear: termites don't build their nests the way humans build their houses or office towers because they don't follow a predetermined plan. Morgan's research suggests a new theory emerging from the study of termite behaviour: that work in the termite colony is based on a self-organizing process where order emerges out of chaos. The creation evolves from random, chaotic activities guided by a seemingly overall sense of purpose, but without specific direction.[2]

In this section we will attempt to answer the question: How do people get things done in an organization? The important factors to keep in mind are:

- we all begin with different reactions to things in our environments; and
- these differences are based on people's experiences, which are characterized by an individual rather than a collective sense of reality. Through communication a collective sense of reality begins to emerge.

Also important to remember is the two-sided nature of human experience. As Eisenberg and Goodhall express: "Individuals are molded, controlled, ordered, and shaped by society and social institutions; individuals also create society and social institutions."[3] This view is referred to as the duality of structure. Both of these are central processes in human communication, as we create relationships and events through a culturally dependent process of assigning meanings to symbols.

In the previous chapter we looked at perspectives of communication theory, representing different views of how to study communication. In this section we will examine the three main approaches to studying organizational communication. Many of the same issues will be relevant. We will apply the termite-colony example to illustrate concepts in each approach.

Theoretical Approaches

Organizations are not only complex structures, they also come in endless varieties, from governments, to corporations, to small businesses, to volunteer groups. Each one has a unique purpose, and it designs it structure to best meet its purpose. The 314-year-old Lloyd's of London Insurance, though one of the best names in finance, is not just one company. Rather, it is a marketplace where 62 syndicates of underwriters congregate who are independent but subject to the broad rules set down by Lloyd's authorities.[4] A minor-league hockey team will have a head coach, assistant coaches, a trainer, a manager, a captain, and two assistant captains—a considerable structure for an organization of less than 20 people.

The three approaches for analyzing organizations—functional, interpretive, and critical—enable us to analyze organizations from a communication perspective. By using these approaches, we can better understand how organizations work and develop methods for improving organizational performance. Each perspective when applied to the analysis of an organization will reveal a unique view.

As we saw in our discussion of perspectives on communication theory, the field of communication is so broad a concept that it is difficult to develop one comprehensive theory. The types of theories that have been developed often reflect a person's fundamental views of life. For example, people have different views on capital punishment depending on the beliefs they hold about life and death. Current debates about the pros and cons of globalization also bring out people's different beliefs about how society should be arranged and who should be making the rules. The purpose behind the research will also influence the theories that are developed. If the purpose, for instance, is to improve communication flow in an organization, a functional approach may be useful. However, if the purpose is to understand the feelings people in an organization have or the values they hold about quality, working overtime, or taking on increased responsibility, an interpretive, or meaning-centred, approach may be more revealing. A critical approach may be appropriate to uncover feelings of unfairness, exploitation, or imbalances of power.

This chapter will allow you to address issues and questions about the functional approach, the interpretive approach, the critical approach, and some emerging approaches.

Functional Approach

Operational Aspects

The *functional approach* and focuses on the operational aspects of structures and positions of authority, communication channels, and message flow. This approach is rooted in the mechanistic and transactional perspectives. It focuses on what messages do, how they move though organizations, and how they contribute to the overall functioning of the organization.

Messages have task functions and relationship functions. Task functions focus on providing employees with the directions needed to get the work done, such as procedures, policies, handbooks, newsletters, and training manuals—anything that defines work tasks and provides instructions and evaluation methods. Task messages are also used in decision making, problem solving, and research activities.

The relationship functions of messages in organizations help members create social relationships within the organization through informal conversations. Relationship messages also establish status differences through awards, job titles, office space, and other ways that signify the person's relationship to the organization.

How Communication Works

The functional approach asks how and why communication works. Messages flow along channels between networks of people. Examples of channels are numerous: face to face, group meetings, presentations, memos and letters, reports and proposals, and mediated channels, such as teleconferences and websites.

Messages usually flow in one of three directions in a workplace: downward, upward, and horizontally.[5] Downward communication describes messages from a superior to a subordinate, with authority defined by the chain of command. Downward communication is usually concerned with task messages. Upward communication describes messages from subordinates to superiors, or up the chain of command. Horizontal messages take place among coworkers on the same level of authority.

The functional approach also includes a systems perspective of organizations. An organization is an information-processing system made up of formal and informal communication networks that operate interdependently within the organization. Through the use of information inputs and outputs, an organization interacts with its environment. Inputs are essential for providing information used in decision making to adapt to events and changes outside the organization. For example, customer service departments make use of feedback from customers about products in order to improve their quality. Outputs are messages going back to the outside environment. Organizations that have effective information processing through continual interaction with their environments are described as open systems. In contrast, closed systems fail to incorporate new information. In today's hi-tech business world, not knowing what's happening with your customers or competitors can be harmful.

Position vs. Individual
The functional approach places emphasis on a position instead of an individual. This perspective is strongly associated with a management orientation, since its concern is organizational performance. Human diversity causes problems of control, and therefore individuality is discouraged; professionalism and specialization, linked to a position, are desirable goals.

Efficiency and Productivity
Making an organization efficient and productive is a focus of the functional approach. This pragmatic perspective is concerned with ways to improve communication systems and behaviours in an organization. A message has a specific function intended to help the organization achieve its goals. The functional perspective has been influential in organizational communication because of its usefulness in improving the performance of organizations.

Interpretive Approach

The *interpretive approach* focuses on the meaning or symbolic significance of organizational structures and positions of authority, communication channels, and message flow. Instead of managing the organization, the interpretive approach strives to understand communication from the individual's point of view. Where functionalists view organizational reality as objective and orderly, interpretivists see it as being constructed through the subjective experiences of organizational members.

What Is Communication?
The interpretive approach asks what communication is and what it means. To understand human communication in organizations, researchers analyze content and meaning of conversations, as well as stories, fantasies, myths, and metaphors. Often these studies focus on "organizational culture." Analyzing the communication climate of an organization reveals how people feel about the organization in terms of levels of trust, openness, and supportiveness—what is known as communication climate.[6] Charles Redding proposed that in a supportive and participative communication environment, employees will have a more positive attitude about the atmosphere within the organization, an ingredient that ultimately leads to greater job satisfaction.

Significance of the Individual
The individual as the centre of significance in the organization is emphasized in the interpretive approach. All human interaction is regarded as communication, and an organization is the sum of its communication activities. Karl Weick, a noted researcher in organizational studies, proposes that organizations do not exist, but are constantly being brought into existence through human communication—people "enact" organizations. And this enactment differs from person to person, creating a diversity of meanings. These dynamic social processes lead to the construction of

self-identity, a sense of belonging, and some degree of compatibility between individual and organizational goals.[7]

Understanding the Individual

The interpretive approach is concerned with understanding the feelings, attitudes, and values of organizational members. This approach, also described as a "meaning-centred" approach in a popular textbook by Pamela Shockley-Zalabak, shifts emphasis from the strictly administrative concerns of traditional organizational communication in order to capture the human experiences of people in the organization.[8] But this raises a question: Is a meaning-centred approach useful for an organization seeking to improve performance? The field of organizational culture has spawned numerous consultants. We will take a closer look at this area in the section on organizational culture.

Critical Approach

The *critical approach* focuses on the use of communication to express and maintain power in structures and positions of authority, communication channels, and message flow. The roots of the critical approach are in the European school of thought known as critical theory. Borrowing significantly from a Marxist analytical framework, the critical approach is concerned with issues of power, control, and the distribution of economic rewards in organizations. It views organizations as systems that manipulate communication to achieve power.

Communication Methods

The critical approach asks what communication methods are being used in the development of power structures. Power in organizations is exercised through communication activities that are hidden rather than open and explicit. As a result, over time structures of power become invisible to people and are ultimately accepted as normal. Critical theory examines how organizational practices can be changed to reflect more equally the interests of all organizational members.

Individual Freedom

The critical approach emphasizes individual freedom and creativity over organizational conformity. As hidden communication practices are exposed, improvements in organizational conditions can be achieved. The unmasking of methods of domination by those in power is intended to create opposition against existing power structures for the purpose of bringing about change.

Who Benefits?

Who benefits from gains in organizational efficiency and productivity is a concern of the critical approach. The main issue for critical theorists is to create a balanced system of rewards for all stakeholders and make possible new systems of organizing. As Stanley Deetz explains:

> The central goal of critical theory in organizational communication studies has been to create a society and workplaces that are free from domination and where all members can contribute equally to produce systems that meet human needs and lead to the progressive development of all.[9]

Emerging Approaches

Emerging approaches focus on the use of communication to express and maintain power in structures and positions of authority, communication channels, and message flow, especially in the areas of gender equality, ethics, and social responsibility. Emerging approaches are various. One major field is feminist theory, which directs the critical approach specifically on domination and the devaluing of females in the workplace. Feminist theory attempts to advance beyond the patriarchal style of organizations and society by promoting greater equality between the sexes. Studies in ethics and social responsibility combine the interpretive approach—communication as a process of meaning development—with a critical approach, in the sense that it calls for greater emphasis on ethics, social responsibility, and open participation in the process of defining social and political experiences. As Deetz explains:

> Open participatory democracy supersedes all other goals of communication. From a communication perspective, efficiency, effectiveness, and information transfer cannot stand alone, but are interpreted within the promotion or demise of participation. Communication research thus is about the creation of more participatory communication practices and the critique and/or deconstruction of control processes.[10]

Communication Methods

Emerging approaches ask what communication methods are being used in the development of power structures and recommends alternatives. The focus is on communication practices that maintain an undesirable status quo.

Equality in Decision Making

Equality of gender, openness, and participation in decision making about resources is emphasized in emerging approaches. Revealing the barriers to equality and openness promotes their removal.

Development of the Individual

Emerging approaches are concerned with equal opportunity, ethics, social responsibility, and participation. Individuals will develop personally, socially, and professionally when traditional assumptions about gender status and power-based organizational structures are changed. Communication as an interactive meaning-construction activity will enable the development of the self and effective social systems.

Defining Organizational Communication

Concepts of Organizations

Now that we've looked at various perspectives on human communication, we can apply them more closely to an organizational setting to examine how communication influences organizational processes. An organization is commonly defined as a group of people that form a network of interdependent relationships assembled to achieve a common goal. This definition is suitable for any type of organization, from a minor-league hockey team to a government department. To help achieve its goals, an organization develops a strategy that includes:

- *Vision*—a specified goal that indicates peak performance
- *Mission*—an overall operating purpose
- *Values*—these establish priorities in the carrying out of activities
- *Strategic goals*—steps along the way to mission accomplishment
- *Operating processes*—repetitive activities for achieving objectives
- *Systems*—integrated collections of objects or people operating within the overall organizational system

An organization should be designed in a way that best achieves its goals. No one structure exists that works for all organizations. An organization's structure is determined by the variety found in its environment, in particular the complexity in the environment and the pace of change.[11] Key concepts in the operational design of an organization are:

- *Span of control*—the number of employees reporting to a superior
- *Authority*—the degree of power of a formal position
- *Delegation*—assigning tasks to subordinates
- *Chain of command*—the formal lines of authority
- *Accountability*—responsibility for the outcome of operational activity

An organization also has a structural design, referring to how departments are arranged and how operational activities are carried out. These include:

- *Centralization/decentralization*—the extent to which control of operations is dispersed throughout the organization
- *Formalization*—the extent of policies and procedures in an organization
- *Hierarchy*—the number of levels of authority
- *Routinization*—the amount of standardization of processes
- *Specialization*—the extent to which tasks are distinguished from each other
- *Training*—activities that equip members with knowledge and skills

The parts that make up organizations have been described by many scholars. Katherine Miller lists five features found in all organizations: two or more people, goals, coordinating activity, structure, and environmental embeddedness.[12] Amitai Etzioni has described organizations as groupings of people deliberately constructed and reconstructed to strive for specific goals.[13] Gerald Goldhaber advances the discussion with a stronger emphasis on information, relationships, and the process of change as he describes an organization as "a living, open system connected by the flow of information."[14] Research has also distinguished between an organization and the acts of organizing. The traditional view sees an organization as a piece of physical geography, an approach known as the "container" view. The organization is an objective thing. The subjective approach, on the other hand, states that an organization is created and maintained through the continual interactions of its members. An organization does not exist separately from its members. This points to a major difference in these views: from the objective view, an organization means structure; from the subjective view, an organization means process.[15]

Highly interactive organizations strive to be more open and receptive to information from the environment and more adaptive to change. They are characterized by:

- *Strong employee involvement*—employees are empowered to make decisions contributing to organizational objectives
- *Organic*—less reliance on routine procedure, more acceptance of flexibility
- *Capability-based authority*—authority based on knowledge and skills instead of formal positions
- *Alliance formation*—large use of collaborations, networks, mergers
- *Team structure*—sharing of activities to ensure full involvement of members
- *Flat structures*—more direct interaction between top management and operational levels
- *Learning orientation*—priority on inquiry and feedback to enable quick adjustments to internal and external changes

As well as focusing on increases in capability, organizations are beginning to consider the social effects of their decisions and operations. As Stanley Deetz states: "Corporate practices pervade modern life by providing personal identity, structuring time and experience, influencing education and knowledge production, directing artistic expression, and instituting particular structures of family life."[16]

All modern organizations are a mix of these characteristics. By becoming organizations, they establish structures to enable them in their activities. These structures are based on groups of people engaged in the process of communication. So, understanding what an organization is and how it works requires an understanding of how communication is done within it. That is the subject matter of organizational communication. In the following chapters, we will examine different types of organizations, from the traditional to the contemporary, with the goal of understanding the central role that human communication plays in their creation, maintenance, and regeneration.

Metaphors of Organizations

A useful way of understanding organizations is through the use of metaphors, discussed by Gareth Morgan in *Images of Organization*. According to Morgan, we use metaphors to explain reality. They give us new ways of looking at things. Morgan uses the following metaphors to analyze organizations:[17]

Organization as machine. This way of thinking underpins the classical style of management. It emphasizes efficiency, order, standardization, measurement, control, and production. According to Morgan, "The mechanical way of thinking is so ingrained in our everyday conceptions of organization that it is often very difficult to organize in any other way."[18]

Organization as organism. The metaphor of a living system sees an organization in terms of environmental relations, adaptation to different conditions, maintaining a balance of inputs and outputs, seeing one system in terms of smaller and larger systems related to it, evolution, health, and life cycles of an organization. As Morgan says, the organism metaphor places importance on an organization's ability to "innovate and evolve and thus meet the challenges and demands of a changing environment."[19]

Organization as brain. This view focuses on information processing, learning, intelligence, knowledge management, and feedback. The emphasis on learning is expressed by Morgan: "Innovative organizations must be designed as learning systems that place primary emphasis on being open to inquiry and self-criticism."[20]

Organization as culture. This metaphor explains organizations in terms of their social characteristics, such as values, beliefs, traditions, rituals, norms, stories, and history. Through communication, these characteristics become patterns of shared meaning among organizational members. It is generally agreed that a strong corporate culture makes an effective organization. As Morgan says, "In talking about culture we are really talking about a process of reality construction that allows people to see and understand particular events, actions, objects, utterances, or situations in distinctive ways. These patterns of understanding also provide a basis for making one's own behaviour sensible and meaningful."[21]

Organizations as political systems. The political view explores organizations in terms of their power structures, conflicts, and interests. It looks at how organizations maintain order and legitimize their authority, often through hidden rather than open communication activities. It also examines, as Morgan states, "how divergent interests give rise to conflicts, visible and invisible, that are resolved or perpetuated by various kinds of power play."[22]

Organizations as psychic prisons. This abstract metaphor focuses on the psychological processes and effects of being trapped in repressive and confining ways of thinking.

Often, the realities people exercise have a measure of control over them. As Morgan says, in psychic prisons, "members become trapped by constructions of reality that, at best, give but an imperfect grasp on the world."[23]

Organizations as flux and transformation. Organizations are self-recreating systems, continuously, through each interaction, evolving into a variation of their previous forms. They fluctuate between order and chaos as they seek a dynamic equilibrium. This view proposes a daring and intriguing explanation of the "logic of change." As Morgan says, "the aim of such systems is ultimately to produce themselves: their own organization and identity is their most important product."[24]

Organizations as instruments of domination. This view explores the capacity of organizations to exploit people and things for selfish purposes and impose their will on others. According to Morgan, this metaphor is useful "for understanding organizations from the perspective of exploited groups, and for understanding how actions that are rational from one viewpoint can prove exploitative from another."[25]

You could add to Morgan's list of metaphors. How often have you heard someone describe their workplace as a zoo or a circus, or their workday as "a walk in the park"? Let's take what we've learned from applying metaphors to organizations as we attempt to form a definition of organizational communication.

Definitions of Organizational Communication

Though the field of organizational communication is growing rapidly in Canadian schools and can be found across the country, its roots and most of its research are uniquely American. Some scholars have attempted to apply an "organizational" perspective to the writings of Innis, McLuhan, and others with useful results, especially in terms of the interactive, critical, and systems perspectives. Canadian scholarship has never really developed a tradition in the functional areas of organizational communication studies, other than professional writing and public speaking programs, though some effort has been made in this direction.

Gerald Goldhaber, whose first-edition textbook dating back to 1974 makes him one of the pioneers in the field, offers this definition: organizational communication is "the process of creating and exchanging messages within a network of interdependent relationships to cope with environmental uncertainties."[26] Goldhaber's definition fits well with a functional, transactional perspective, in that it focuses on systems of communication that bring information from the environment to fulfill organizational purposes. He focuses on seven key concepts:

1. *Process*—communication in an organization is continuous and reciprocal. Because the process is ever-changing, it has been described as evolutionary and culturally dependent.
2. *Message*—communication uses verbal and nonverbal symbols to create messages that are different for all members of an organization. Through communication, multiple perceptions are negotiated to form shared realities.
3. *Network*—communication takes place along sets of pathways made up of people who over time form personal relationships and workplace networks.
4. *Interdependence*—all parts of a system are affected by each other.
5. *Relationship*—communication networks are made up of interpersonal relationships.
6. *Environment*—an organization interacts with its environment by importing information, processing it, and exporting it back into the environment.
7. *Uncertainty*—communication reduces the uncertainty caused by changes in the environment

Eisenberg and Goodhall provide us with a concise definition of organizational communication as a starting point for our discussion: organizational communication is "the interaction required to direct a group toward a set of common goals."[27] The key ideas, interaction and common goals, emphasize human communication and the interdependence essential in an organizational context. Eisenberg and Goodhall give us four approaches to defining organizational communication:

1. **Communication as information transfer.** A message follows a "pipeline" from one person to another, usually from superior to subordinate. The meaning of a message belongs to the sender who tries to convey it to a receiver as accurately as possible. Through feedback, the sender discovers how accurately the meaning was received. Though overly simplistic, the unwillingness in business culture to accept a two-way flow of information makes this approach common even in today's organizations.

2. **Communication as transactional process.** Communication is a process that creates relationships as people develop shared meanings for organizational activity. Meanings exists in people, not in words travelling along channels as the information transfer view states, so the meaning of a message is not received but constructed by a person. As a result, miscommunication is normal, and shared understandings are not immediate but emerge over time.

3. **Communication as strategic control.** Communication in organizations is a process with multiple goals. An employee may be concerned with expressing a message clearly to his or her boss to get a task accomplished properly while wanting to be respectful. In order to avoid a condescending tone in a message and maintain a positive atmosphere, relationships in the workplace usually aim for an adult-to-adult level of communication. People may communicate unclearly or incompletely on purpose and still accomplish their goals by learning to use the appropriate level of ambiguity. For example, if an employee is doing a job incorrectly, you can avoid talking down to him or her by suggesting a corrective action without being too explicit. In this way, shared meaning is created and relationships remain positive and on an equal level. A major advantage of this approach is that it promotes diversity of interpretations or organizational events by allowing people to define organizational goals in personal ways. The results can increase employee commitment by bringing the goals of the employee and the organization closer together. The opposite can also happen—strategic ambiguity can be used to escape blame, since a problem can be blamed on the unclear language of a message.

4. **Communication as a balance of creativity and constraint.** Communication is a circular process. We construct our social reality by establishing ways of doing things and patterns of behaviour, and then we are constrained by those established patterns as conditions change over time. When this happens, we usually abandon the old ones and construct new ones. Eisenberg and Goodhall's more complete definition of organizational communication includes these ideas: organizational communication is the moment-to-moment working out of the tension between individual creativity and organizational constraint. Communication has the ability to be enabling, giving people the opportunity to create necessary realities and new patterns of behaviour, as well as to be constraining, providing people with structures for accomplishing things, such as procedures or methods. This approach recalls Anthony Gidden's theory of structuration: an organization is a "duality of structure," based on the oppositional forces of the need to maintain order and the need to promote change.[28] We will return to this approach in our discussion of Canadian organizational communication studies, below.

Other researchers have expressed similar ideas in terms of independence (creativity) and interdependence(constraint). As Charles Conrad states, cultures face a central dilemma: they must meet their needs for coordination and control while simultaneously

The Communication Manager

You've just been promoted to the position of manager of a customer service department at a software company with 800 employees. During the past few years, the previous manager's communication style created an atmosphere of mistrust and secrecy. Employees were afraid to share ideas and experiences out of fear of being singled out as being the cause of problems or being accused of whining. So, most employees just did their work and stayed to themselves. This prevented employees from learning from each other's experiences. What's worse is that feedback from customers usually did not travel upward to the manager, so valuable product information was never received by decision makers.

As the new manager you want to break with the past and create an open door policy to create a more positive and productive workplace atmosphere. You want communication to be a priority at all levels of the organization. To do this you will have to eliminate barriers to communication that have existed for years. You must engage in direct and timely communication to employees, and be receptive to feedback.

Discussion Questions

1. Discuss how the principles of organizational communication mentioned above—process, message, network, interdependence, relationships, environment, and uncertainty—apply to the challenge you face as a new manager.

2. What difficulties would you face in creating an open communication workplace and what strategies would you use to overcome them?

meeting their employees' needs for creativity, autonomy, and stability.[29] A culture is a system of shared meanings that are expressed through symbolic forms and hold a group of people together. Employees differ from people in society because an organization is a much more powerful and immediate context than society in general. Thus, our relationships at work have both an interpersonal and an organizational dimension.

Daniel Modaff and Sue DeWine propose the following definition: organizational communication is the process of creating, exchanging, interpreting (correctly or incorrectly), and storing messages within a system of human relationships. In contrast to Eisenberg and Goodhall, their focus is more on how humans use messages, because, as they say, "the focus on language [message] use becomes important as a means of differentiating the study of organizational communication from related fields such as management and industrial psychology."[30]. The process of employees identifying with their organization has also appeared in the literature. Cheney and Tompkins suggest that the communication of shared organizational interests develops a linkage between the individual and the organization. Identification has been correlated with several relevant workplace outcomes, including motivation, performance, job satisfaction, effective conflict management, and length of service.[31]

Organizational Communication Studies in Canada

The focus on language—specifically, how organizations are structured through discourse—has proven to be a point of connection between the Canadian communication traditions and organizational communication. James R. Taylor states, "The result [of the Canadian perspective] is an attention to language and discourse, and a commitment to naturalistic studies using qualitative methods that is singular within the larger field of organizational communication studies."[32] Taylor, who spent his academic career at the University of Montreal, also states that the European influence on the Canadian approach is more strongly demonstrated in French-language research. This research trend is supported by Dennis Mumby and Linda Putnam. They suggest that contemporary directions of research "focus on discourse and linguistic patterns as the institutional practices that shape rationality, construct power relationships, and enact member identities."[33]

A thought-provoking application of the work of Harold Innis is made by Charles Taylor in an article called "Is There a Canadian Approach to the Study of Organizational Communication?"[34] He proposes that Innis's *Minerva's Owl* articulates a theory of organization based on his ideas of space-binding and time-binding technologies. An organization contains both. Time binding is expressed in the "oral tradition" or the "vernacular" and exists in the ongoing conversations of organizational members; space binding exists in the "systems of writing" that become established in the meaning system of the organization. Systems of writing lead to specialization, hierarchies, technical jargon, and an increasing difficulty in communicating in everyday language. Thus a barrier is created between the rigid, mechanical systems of knowledge contained in the formal organization, in the form of programmed activities, rules, policies, and procedures; and the flexible, organic knowledge activities taking place among members on the floor of the organization. So even though Innis's work focused on the much larger scope of growth and collapse of historical empires, such as Rome, Egypt, and Britain, there are some conceptual frameworks to use for analysis of organizational life—and maybe even termites, if we ever figure out how they do it.

This hypothesis can be further supported in Innis's book *Empire and Communication,* as Taylor points out, because organizations that emphasize space favour centralization—systems for control and order—while organizations that emphasize time favour decentralization—systems for change and adaptability. Thus, the more an organization relies on codified systems of knowledge, the less effective it becomes in making sense of uncertain or incomprehensible environments. The "freshness and elasticity" (in Innis's words) of organizational conversation is the ultimate resource for coping with uncertainty and solving problems effectively.

Taylor also refers to the influential book by Karl Weick, *The Social Psychology of Organizing,*[35] which describes a similar approach. Weick discusses two types of knowledge in organizations: symbolic, explicit knowledge that is used for establishing procedures and organizational understandings, and sub-symbolic, tacit knowledge, which is practical and is used and regenerated in conversations. For a simple contrast of explicit and tacit knowledge, think about the things you learn in college or university on a daily basis. They represent your explicit knowledge—a collection of details. Now think about the things you learn that you will take with you after graduation—the thinking methods, problem-solving systems, the perspectives and approaches. These represent your tacit knowledge. So when somebody asks you "What did you learn in college or university?" your answer will focus on tacit knowledge. It's a little like asking Wayne Gretzky how to be a good hockey player—it's a lot harder to explain than to do.

Describing organizations is difficult because of their endless variety. We use a word such as "organization" as an abstraction to describe an extremely elusive concept. We group all these structures we call organizations together to define them, yet we know that every organization is different and unique. Our impulse is to make them into identifiable structures—to reduce the differences among them. But this leads to the danger of oversimplification, of reducing complex activities into routine ones. And most traditional definitions of organizations remove the human element, as if an organization were merely a collection of inanimate objects and rules. One way that organizational communication studies has contributed to our knowledge of how organizations work is the emphasis it puts on the process of communication. Contemporary definitions of organizations have emphasized communication activity to the point that it represents the common essence found in all organizations. Charles Taylor states that organizations are ultimately a phenomenon generated through the act of people communicating:

> An organization is thus fundamentally a construction enabled by a particular property of language. There is, therefore, no single reality, no independent entity, that corresponds to an organization, but, rather, an abstract object that has as many possible points of reference as there are people to imaginate it. The organization is forever being recreated in the ongoing conversations of people.[36]

Organizations as Dialogues

A great amount of interest in the study of organizations as dialogues has recently developed. According to Eisenberg and Goodhall, the critical issues of organizational communication revolve around identity and community, specifically self, other, and context. The self is described as dialogic—it is made in concert with others. This approach is similar to dialogic approaches to effective listening skills. We don't *talk to* someone, as if we were transporting a message. Instead we share meanings and construct a mutual interpretation. The receiver's meaning is not the sender's—it belongs to both of them and is created dialogically. Through interaction with others, we also construct our self-identity, and, finally, we construct conceptions of other people based on our self-identity. If our self-identity is a positive one, for example, the perceptions we make about others will generally be positive, and vice versa. In organizations, employees are often treated by managers as receivers who need to be communicated to, to be ordered and controlled, rather than as participants in an organizational dialogue. Earlier communication perspectives, such as the mechanistic model, represent this position (see Figure 3.1).

Context refers to where communication takes place and the relationships of the people communicating. You might be alarmed if, for instance, you see two guys wrestling in a parking lot, but after finding out they are friends who like to play rough, your feeling of alarm would stop.

Organizational context is complex because many factors influence the interpretation of a message—authority, personal relationships, cultural factors, politics, self-identity, and business attitudes. Our previous discussion about duality of structure applies here, since context limits or constrains our interpretations, and yet we define our contexts through our past behaviours. So a large part of working life involves interpreting and recreating contexts.

The dialogic approach has huge potential for organizations in its power of creation (see Figure 3.2). This is true in both a practical sense, since every conversation creates a shared understanding; and in a larger, perhaps spiritual and emotional, sense: true dialogue, which requires mutual respect and openness, can lead to self-discovery, or, to put it simply, "being the best that you can be." It represents the highest point of self-development, similar

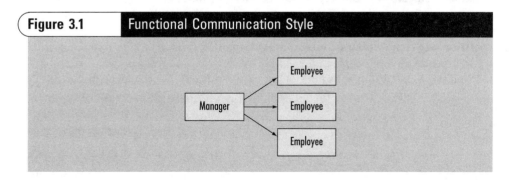

Figure 3.1 **Functional Communication Style**

Figure 3.2 Dialogic Communication Style

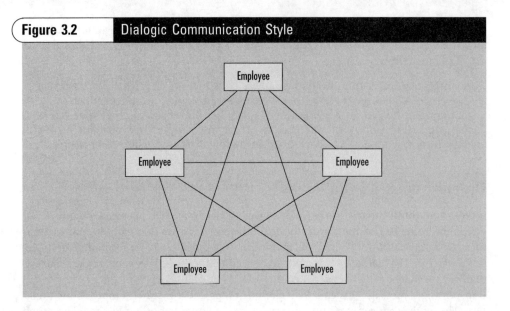

to self-actualization on Maslow's hierarchy of needs, though the road for getting there has not been totally mapped out yet. In social and political terms, it could represent the equivalent of a true participatory democracy, as outlined in theory, not in practice.

Principles of Organizational Communication

As a way of bringing our ideas together, five principles of organization communication summarized by William Neher[37] are offered below.

1. **Communication is the fundamental process of organizing.** Many researchers have concluded that a manager's work is primarily communication, including verbal and written messages, such as meetings, interviews, announcements, e-mail, and reports.

2. **Understanding organizational communication helps us understand how organizations work.** Thinking about an organization as a collection of ongoing communication activities helps us to understand how it works. We could think of an organization as a machine, a culture, a system, a brain, or a prison—all these different points of view can be illuminating.

3. **Communication skills are the basis for effective leadership in organizations.** Very much of what we call leadership is communication behaviour, such as asking questions, summarizing ideas, helping people understand each other by resolving conflict, and being friendly and open.

4. **Communication is the key to sound decision making within organizations.** Good decision making involves people understanding each other and working together to solve problems.

5. **Diversity characterizes contemporary organizations.** In addition to the normal differences among people in the workplace, such as age, gender, level of education, and status, today a major source of diversity is cultural. The challenges involve both face-to-face local interaction and long-distance, mediated communication.

Our common definitions of an organization come from the traditional perspectives we've developed over time. Organizational communication offers new ways of defining organizations. In fact, a lot of our organizational activity is similar to the termites, as we negotiate our way with fellow workers. Human organization, however, leans heavily on planning. Organizational communication looks at alternatives to traditionally ordered work processes.

Various approaches are used in studying organizational communication. The functional approach focuses on messages travelling through the organization. The interpretive approach looks at how meaning is created and shared by people through communication. The critical approach focuses on how communication is used to exercise power in organizations. Emerging approaches look at feminist issues and more socially responsible and participative styles of organizations.

The common elements in definitions of organizational communication are the creation and exchange of messages, the creation of shared meanings, interdependent relationships, environmental uncertainties, interpretation of messages, and a focus on language and discourse. Organizational communication in Canada is quickly growing in the direction of language and discourse, a major branch of research.

Critical issues of organizational communication revolve around identity and community, or a sense of self and a context. Through communication in the workplace, our sense of self develops.

Communication is the fundamental process of organizing, so if we can understand how it works we will understand organizations better. Communication is also the means through which leadership and decision making are accomplished. The growing diversity in today's workplaces also emphasizes the importance of effective communication.

Wikipedia—The Free Encyclopedia[38]

Since 2001, Wikipedia (www.wikipedia.com) has become the world's largest reference work. In February 2005, it had 1.3 million articles in 200 languages, with 1000 new articles being added each day. Though more than 30 000 people have written or edited articles for the database, it remains an all-volunteer organization.

Wikipedia started as an open-source encyclopedia with a few basic rules: whenever someone contributes or edits an article, a new version of it is created and saved, so new articles are continually being created and added to existing ones. The name Wikipedia comes from "wiki," the name of the collaborative software that runs the website. Contributors are motivated to submit material by the recognition they receive as authors, and these submissions, no matter how small, are saved and retrievable.

Each article also includes a chat page where authors can discuss different views of the article.

Critics complain that Wikipedia's authors have no professional or academic authority and that no standards of grammar, writing style, or fact-checking exist. Wikipedians reply that although articles may start out rough and incomplete, they improve over time, as the multitude of contributors sharpens the ideas and fills in the details. For example, Wikipedia's entry on the Indian Ocean tsunami disaster in December of 2004 includes animations, geological information, figures on the international relief effort, and numerous external links to websites, videos, and photographs. The quantity, quality, and diversity of coverage would be next to impossible for a traditional encyclopedia to provide.

What about mistakes? The system's power to correct mistakes makes it almost mistake-proof. Often within a matter of days, errors are removed. A paper-based encyclopedia would need to wait until the next edition was printed—usually years. Generally, the criticisms of Wikipedia amount to a lament for a long-established practice that was suddenly overwhelmed not just by a newcomer, but by a new way of collecting and organizing information. Instead of relying on standards and conventional systems where information is provided to users by specialists, Wikipedia exploits the collective resources and evolving knowledge base of all participants in the system. Users become contributors, contributors are users in an ongoing, integrated effort, which seems to have no real organizing principle other a few basic rules. Instead of producing a book of final answers based on the views of experts, Wikipedia provides us with ongoing provisional understandings, reflecting the multiple contexts and situations in which people make meanings. Thus, contributors are encouraged to ask questions and invite others into the dialogue.

What advantages does Wikipedia offer? First, staying up to date with the rapidly growing mass of information, from science and technology, to economics, to pop culture, to current events, is becoming more difficult for traditional encyclopedias. For Wikipedia, it is no problem. Second, the Internet has enabled the "leeching" of information from specialists, who have spent long years studying their subjects, by non-experts who can reproduce it in a Wikipedia entry in a few hours. The effect is not that much different from normal journalism. Third, and perhaps best of all, Wikipedia is free.

Discussion Questions

1. Compare the process used by Wikipedia to organize and create itself with the termite strategy described at the beginning of the chapter. What are the similarities in the ways they get things done? What are the differences?

2. How are both different from a traditional business organization?

3. How do the coordinating efforts exhibited by Wikipedia and by traditional business organizations help us to define what an organization is?

4. Relate the activities in Wikipedia and traditional business organizations to the theoretical perspectives discussed in the chapter. Which one do they fit in best with?

Classroom Activity

Form groups of four or five and take about 10–15 minutes to organize yourselves in any way you want. There are no rules. Two students per group will play the role of observers and record the organizing activities of their group. They will note who initiates any organizing activity, how it is done, what messages are used, what purposes they serve, who participates, who doesn't, how long it takes to do anything, the clarity of objectives, and how organizing is completed. When all groups are organized, the observers will describe the process they observed to the class. As a class, discuss some common organizing methods used by all groups.

Glossary

Functional approach, p. 43
Interpretive approach, p. 44

Critical approach, p. 45

Notes

1. Gareth Morgan. *Imaginization: New Mindsets for Seeing, Organizing and Managing,* (Newbury Park and San Francisco, CA: Sage Publications, 1993), 59.

2. Ibid.

3. Eric M. Eisenberg and H.L. Goodhall, Jr., *Organizational Communication, Balancing Creativity and Constraint* (Boston: Bedford/St. Martin's, 2004).

4. Charles Fleming, "Archaic, costly ways at Lloyd's give edge to its insurers," *The Globe and Mail*, May 16, 2005, B10.

5. Gerald Goldhaber, *Organizational Communication*, 6th ed. (Dubuque, IA: Brown, 1993).

6. W. Charles Redding, *Communication within the Organization* (New York: Industrial Communication Council, 1972).

7. Karl Weick, *Sense Making in Organizations* (Newbury Park, CA: Sage, 1996).

8. Pamela Shockley-Zalabak, *Fundamentals of Organizational Communication, Knowledge, Sensitivity, Skills, Values,* 5th ed. (Boston: Allyn and Bacon, 2002).

9. Stanley Deetz, "Conceptual Foundations," in *The New Handbook of Organizational Communication: Advances in Theory, Research, and Methods,* eds., F.M. Jablin and L.L. Putnam (Thousand Oaks, CA: Sage, 2001), 3–46.

10. Stanley Deetz, *Transforming Communication, Transforming Business: Building Responsive and Responsible Workplaces* (Cresskill, NJ: Hampton Press, 1994), 108.

11. Henry Mintzberg, *The Nature of Managerial Work* (New York: Harper Collins, 1973).

12. Katherine Miller, *Organizational Communication, Approaches and Processes* (Belmont, CA: Thomson Wadsworth, 2003).

13. Amitai Etzioni, *Modern Organizations* (Englewood Cliffs, NJ: Prentice Hall, 1964).

14. Goldhaber, *Organizational Communication.*

15. Wayne R. Pace and Don F. Faules, *Organizational Communication*, 3rd ed. (Englewood Cliffs, NJ: Prentice Hall, 1994).

16. Deetz, *Transforming Communication*, 108.

17. Gareth Morgan, *Images of Organization* (Thousand Oaks, CA: Sage, 1997).

18. Ibid., 14.

19. Ibid., 105.

20. Ibid., 105.

21. Ibid., 128.

22. Ibid., 148.

23. Ibid., 200.

24. Ibid., 236.

25. Ibid., 15.

26. Goldhaber, *Organizational Communication.*

27. Eisenberg and Goodhall, *Organizational Communication*, 4.

28. Anthony Gidden, *The Constitution of Society: Outline of the Theory of Structuration* (Berkeley: University of California Press, 1984).

29. Charles Conrad, *Strategic Organizational Communication: Toward the Twenty-First Century*, 3rd ed. (Fort Worth: Harcourt Brace College Publishers, 1994).

30. Daniel Modaff and Sue DeWine, *Organizational Communication, Foundations, Challenges, and Misunderstandings* (Los Angeles: Roxbury Publishing, 2002).

31. G. Cheney and P.K. Tompkins, "Coming to Terms with Organizational Identification and Commitment," *Central States Speech Journal* 38 (1987): 1–15.

32. Charles Taylor, "Is There a Canadian Approach to the Study of Organizational Communication?" *Canadian Journal of Communication* 25, no. 1 (2000).

33. Dennis Mumby and Linda Putnam, "The Politics of Emotion: A Feminist Reading of Bounded Rationality," *Academy of Management Review* 17 (1992): 465–86.

34. Taylor, "Is There a Canadian Approach?"

35. K. Weick, *The Social Psychology of Organizing*, 2nd ed. (Reading, MA: Addison-Wesley Publishing, 1979).

36. Taylor, "Is There a Canadian Approach."

37. William W. Neher, *Organizational Communication: Challenges of Change, Continuity, and Diversity* (Boston: Allyn and Bacon, 1997).

38. *Case Study based on Wynn Quon, "The New Know-it-all," National Post, February 26, 2005, FP19.*

PART THREE

Traditional Approaches

4

Chapter Four

Classical Management Approach

We are not running a Christian Scientists' meeting here, where we all have to sing from the same hymn sheet. Anybody who complains about it can take a hike.

—Conrad Black, outlining his plan to deal with pesky
shareholders demanding a fair deal[1]

Learning Objectives

- Review the principles of classical management—the origins of management in the modern workplace

- Examine the scientific management of Fredrick Taylor

- Explore the administrative theory of Henri Fayol

- Review bureaucratic theory

- Identify the practices of classical management in today's organizations

- Explore classical management and its effects on communication

Classical Management Theories

In this chapter we will look at classical management theories of organizations; specifically, scientific management, administrative theory, and bureaucratic theory, and the influence they have on communication in the workplace. Classical management best represents the functional perspective of organizations and communication. It focuses on the formal structure of a workplace, represented by the *chain of command,* and on how to design operations and train workers for maximum efficiency by employing division of labour strategies.

Anyone with work experience will realize that classical management methods based on control and command are still dominant in today's workplaces. The opening quote by Conrad Black expresses a type of controlling attitude that grew out of classical management perspectives. The fast-food industry, with its dependence on low-skilled, low-paid, and non-permanent workers, is an example of how prevalent the mechanically designed workplace is. Becoming familiar with traditional approaches will help us to appreciate the contemporary approaches discussed in the following chapters.

The roots of classical management are many, and they reflect the particular historical circumstances of their time. The division of labour as an organizing principle in the workplace was mentioned by Adam Smith in *The Wealth of Nations* in 1776. Smith admires a pin-making assembly line, which increased a person's pin-making production capacity from 10 pins per day to 4800.[2] Karl Marx, however, with a different point of view of the emerging classical management form, expresses alarm at the separation of the worker from his or her tools and from the final product. Marx recalls a time when craftspeople owned their own tools, made the complete product, and personally sold or traded it. Marx also pointed out the growing rift between the roles of labour and management.

Management in the Modern Workplace

I can no longer obey; I have tasted command, and I cannot give it up.

—*Napoleon Bonaparte, 1769–1821*

People have been organizing themselves throughout history. The point in time at which we will start our discussion is unique because of a few major factors. Technological breakthroughs and social changes in the seventeenth and eighteenth centuries that led to the Industrial Revolution secularized people's thinking. A belief in science and the use of scientific methods replaced the leadership and authority of religion in society. The Industrial Revolution brought new ways of organizing, used to develop systematic modes of production based on scientific methods. The resulting concepts are familiar today: division of labour, job specialization, standardization of methods, and the application of mechanical principles to the design of the workplace.

Classical management is made up of three branches of study: operational, administrative, and organizational. Fredrick Taylor wrote *The Principles of Scientific Management* to provide a method for designing and measuring the performance of tasks at an operational level. Henri Fayol focused on designing the administrative structure of an organization, and Max Weber contributed a bureaucratic model that established a rational basis for rules and procedures.

Using different perspectives to understand organizations is more complicated than having one all-encompassing theory, but it has its benefits. We begin to realize that one perspective produces only part of the story, so we grasp a more complete understanding of an organization using different ones. Different theories also reflect the biases of the observer. In organizational communication, academics often favour the conceptual side of research, whereas managers prefer the practical side. When it comes to an issue such as environmental responsibility, for instance, priorities are different: academics promote long-range alternative energy systems, suggesting an integrated view of communication. Managers, on the other hand, focus on short-term financial issues, advocating a functional view. In the workplace, different priorities have over the years led to tensions between owners and employees, with workers stressing human interests and owners keeping a firm grip on the company's interests. Eisenberg and Goodhall have referred to these as narratives of domination and narratives of resistance.[3] These usually take the form of stories or songs of the powerful and the powerless. Typically, because of greater access to communication channels, the stories of the powerful become public; those of the powerless remain mostly private. Resistance themes have often found a voice in music, from the blues, to rock and roll, to rap music. The lyrics for "The Puddler's Tale," about working-life experiences in a steel mill from Canadian folk music legend Stan Rogers, are an example.

The Scientific Management of Fredrick Taylor

Fredrick Taylor, author of the groundbreaking *The Principles of Scientific Management*, published in 1911, was an engineer at the Midvale Steelworks in Philadelphia in the late 1800s. His book proposed a solution to a problem that has been an ongoing issue in industrial workplaces even to the present day: how to design a workplace to elicit the maximum performance from workers. His solution was based on the assumption that management can be organized as a science based on clearly known laws, rules, roles, and methods.[5]

Taylor referred to the main problem of productivity in the workplace as *systematic soldiering*. Employees' work output rarely reaches their maximum capacity and often is closer to their minimum. Expending as little effort as possible to get the job done was

---

Ped Box   **The Puddler's Tale**

by Stan Rogers[4]

They neither know of night or day,
They night and day pour out their
   thunder,
As every ingot rolls away,
A dozen more are split asunder.
There is a sign beside the gate,
"Eleven Days" since a man lay dying,
Now every shift brings fear and hate
And shaken men in terror crying.
The molten rivers boil away,
A fiery brew hell never equaled.
To their profits the bosses pray,
And Mammon sings in his grim
   cathedral.
His attendants join the choir,
And heaven help us if we're shirking,
Stoke the furnace-altar fire,
And just be thankful that we're working!

Do this, then, charge the hoppers high
Lest you endure the foreman's choler,
Do this, then, drain the tankards dry,
And let us toast the almighty dollar,
That keeps us chained here before the fire
Where heat and noise set the weak
   a-quaking.
At the siren's infernal cry,
The open hearth sets the ground to
shaking.

Do this, then, raise the babies high
And make them shriek with love and
laughter!
Do this, then, kiss your woman's eyes
And raise a song unto the rafters!
Wash the steel mill from your hair,
Heap the table 'til it's breaking,
'Nor let terror enter there.
And in hearth set the glasses breaking.

---

an individual goal, the soldiering part, and benchmarking this goal was a group deter-
mination, the systematic part.

According to Taylor, systematic soldiering was caused by three things:

1. Workers felt that increasing their output would cause layoffs, so they controlled
   output as a way of achieving group job security. Taylor countered their fears with
   the promise that increased productivity would lower prices, which would increase
   demand for their products and result in new hiring.
2. In the system of pay known as piecework, the amount of pay is based on a worker's
   output. If a worker exceeds the output, the benchmark is raised, with the result that
   workers are producing more for the same pay. Knowing that the company will
   lower pay levels if work increases, workers maintain output levels at the rate of the
   slowest worker so the rate of pay will not be changed.
3. The third reason focused on the informal training methods in use at the time.
   Workers learned how to do their jobs by observing other workers, so inefficiencies
   were passed down the line. Taylor's scientific principles modernized training
   methods, an area in which significant progress was made.

Principles of Scientific Management

Taylor's aim was to transform the workplace into an efficient machine. He believed that
establishing a scientific basis for operations would remove potential problems between
workers and managers. His theory was based on four principles:[6]

1. **Every task was broken down into minute, mechanical steps that could be described,
   timed, and measured.** To eliminate informal and unspecific training methods, Taylor
   initiated time and motion studies. The procedure involved, first, finding the most
   skilled available workers to serve as models for the task to be analyzed. Second, the
   sequence of motions each worker used was studied. Third, each motion was timed and
   the fastest was selected. Fourth, all unnecessary movements were eliminated. And, fifth,
   one composite model of all the best motions was constructed.
2. **Workers capable of performing the task at a maximum output were carefully
   selected and trained.** Since most work was simple and physical, workers were not
   selected for their intelligence. It was the responsibility of the manager, deemed to be
   of higher intelligence, to train workers. In fact, Taylor regarded intelligence as a
   disqualifying factor in employee selection. As Gareth Morgan states, managers were
   paid to think and workers to work.[7] Notions such as these would be shunned today
   for their callous stereotyping of people, but Taylor's intentions do not appear to be
   deliberately cruel. In subsequent years, though, it was seen that an overly scientific
   system employing a mechanical style of operations can easily become inhumane.
   One negative result was an increased sense of status distinctions, which created
   more conflict than harmony, as history shows. The ultimate goal of scientific
   management was to create repetitive operations that required neither decision
   making nor initiative—essentially no human input.
3. **Higher wages for maximum output.** Taylor believed that workers were motivated
   by financial rewards only. If they surpassed a predetermined maximum output level,
   they would be given a bonus for the extra output. If they underperformed, they were
   notified and given additional training. If, after this, they still did not meet output
   goals, they were transferred to another task.
4. **Equal division of work between worker and supervisor.** Taylor's emphasis on
   management increased the role of managers in the workplace. They were in charge
   of the tasks of planning, training, and evaluating each worker. Before Taylor,
   workers made more decisions about how to accomplish a task. The increased role of

the manager in scientific management created the profession of management and set the roots for a work system that was not disturbed until teamwork practices appeared, about three-quarters of a century later.

Scientific Management in Today's Organizations

"Listen, dammit, I am deadly serious. Your damn bonus next year won't even buy you a cheese sandwich if production doesn't turn around."[8]

The principles of scientific management quickly spread to non-industrial workplaces that required standardization of quality, coordination of large numbers of workers, and a more specific way to measure performance. In Chapter 3, it was mentioned that the operations of the fast-food industry are formatted on a mechanical model that has broken down, using time and motion studies, all the actions required to make an endless series of identical tacos or hamburgers. Even independent pizza restaurants that existed for years on unique styles and recipes began mechanizing their operations by pre-dressing pizzas to compete with the quick delivery times advertised by the large chains—unfortunately, though, in a losing battle.

Public agencies such as medicine and education have also begun marching in unison. In search of accountability to industry and taxpayers, education systems since the 1990s virtually across Canada have been conforming to increasingly explicit instructions from provincial ministries to standardize curriculums and tests and create greater specialization of courses for the sake of large-scale efficiency. Hospitals have adopted similar time-saving and methodical practices. Critics of standardization responded by suggesting our schools were becoming career factories and our hospitals, assembly lines of medical care.

As a triumph of reason over randomness in the workplace, scientific management principles were highly efficient in theory, but have created problems in practical areas in today's workplaces. As companies quickly realized that efficiencies meant profitable returns to investors, the push for productivity began. Managers became micro-managers, breaking down jobs into tiny components to standardize processes and eliminate the chance of error, much like the fast-food industry assembly line. The excessive use of scientific management methods was satirized in Charlie Chaplin's classic movie *Modern Times*, which depicted a workplace where people took on the motions of the machines they used. Managers even resorted to extreme measures such as bullying and threatening employees to maximize output.

Today, insensitive, production-driven bosses are a common cause of stress, low morale, and high turnover. About 20 percent of a typical company's payroll goes toward dealing with stress-related problems such as absenteeism, employee turnover, disability leaves, counselling, medicine, and accidents, according to the Canadian Mental Health Association.[9] And work stress is a key factor in the onset of mental illness, a leading cause of worker disability. As the old saying goes, people don't quit jobs, they quit bosses.

Highly controlling and non-supportive bosses produce a condition called *presenteeism*, where employees show up for work in body but not in mind. Studies done in 1991 and 2001 by Linda Duxbury of Carlton University showed a long-term trend of rising levels of stress in workers as employers downsized staff and restructured their organizations, resulting in bigger workloads and longer work days.[10] Presenteeism can be traced back to the separation in scientific management between brain and muscle—managers were paid to think and direct, workers were paid to work and follow. In today's workplace, this separation between thinking jobs and labour jobs has led to the stereotyping of blue-collar jobs as less prestigious than white-collar jobs, resulting in a shortage of skilled tradespeople, even though pay scales for skilled workers are substantial. Micromanaging methods have expanded to include surveillance cameras in the workplace, even in areas where they could be perceived as an invasion of privacy, such as bathrooms and employee lounges.

Scientific management practices when taken to the extreme have created some well-known yet disturbing communication behaviours. To squash staff dissension, bad bosses have been known to use threats such as distributing employment statistics and news stories describing the plight of the jobless and telling employees they could never get jobs anywhere else. The snapping of fingers to summon support staff is used to put employees in their place, and when they're not at their work sites, male bosses have been known to bang on the women's bathroom door, calling out their names. Usually, these behaviours are intended to humiliate employees to discourage them from challenging the boss's power. Sexual harassment is still around though it is more indirect, since there is now legal protection against degrading statements.

To emphasize the distinction between themselves and their workers, some bosses seldom venture out of their office. When they pass employees, they look away. When approached with issues, they become impatient; when not informed of something, they are quick to anger. When they need an employee, right now is not soon enough. When bosses who abuse their minions get into trouble, such as Conrad Black, Martha Stewart, or the Enron gang, typically nobody stands up to speak for them. This is the time for *schadenfreude*—the delicious sense of pleasure we feel in someone else's bad fortune. Unfortunately, bad bosses, especially bully types, for a time are successful and make a lot of money, and their bullying behaviours are positively reinforced by the immediate reaction that yelling or name-calling evokes.

Two other classical theorists who expand on Taylor's management views are discussed below. While Taylor focused on the performance of specific tasks and on the relationship between a superior and subordinate, Henri Fayol and Max Weber were concerned with a larger organizational perspective. Both developed management systems that are also prevalent in today's workplaces.

The Administrative Theory of Henri Fayol

An engineer by profession, like Taylor, Henri Fayol developed a scientific system of management that described the management activities required to achieve the goals of the organization. Fayol's system was based on the hierarchical chain of command that connected the whole organization and all its departments (see Figure 4.1).

This structure provided a clear line of responsibility for direction and planning.[11] Fayol addressed the question of what it is that managers actually do, a question also

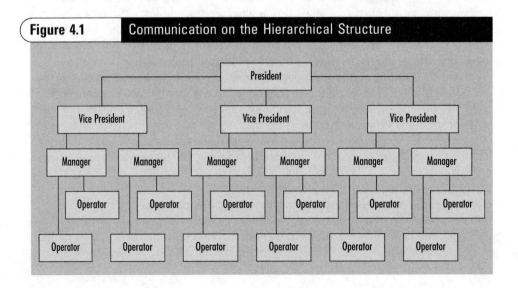

| Figure 4.1 | Communication on the Hierarchical Structure |

posed many years later by Henry Mintzberg in *The Nature of Managerial Work*. Fayol's practical answer includes the five following tasks:

1. Planning and setting goals
2. Organizing people and equipment
3. Directing and motivating people
4. Coordinating organizational units
5. Controlling and feedback

These five tasks were supplemented by the following list of organizing principles arranged into four categories by Katherine Miller:[12]

1. Structure
   - *Scalar chain*—messages would move vertically and horizontally through the organization.
   - *Unity of command*—employees have only one boss.
   - *Division of work*—similar work is arranged in groups or departments.
2. Power
   - *Centralization*—decision making is the right of management and is not distributed throughout the organization.
   - *Personal authority*—in contrast to position authority, personal authority is based on intelligence, experience, and character.
3. Rewards
   - *Pay*—monetary rewards should be seen as fair and motivating so that workplace stability is established.
4. Attitude
   - *Fairness and equity*—workers should support the reward systems of the organization to enable them to subordinate their interests for the good of the group and to develop commitment to their work.
   - *Esprit de corps*—a strong organization possesses a unity of purpose and encourages initiative to establish a positive work climate.
   - *Horizontal communication*—Fayol recognized the importance of horizontal communication between coworkers that would by necessity bypass the chain of command. This was called "Fayol's gangplank," representing a bridge across the chain of command (see Figure 4.2) that could prove to be useful in certain situations.

Figure 4.2	Fayol's Gangplank

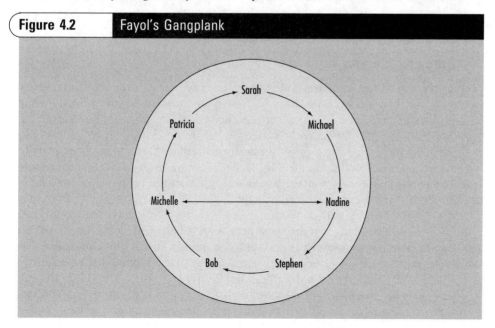

Some of the first references to communication as a management process can be found in Fayol's work. He suggested that overuse of written communication can create barriers between workers and managers and lead to negative attitudes. Furthermore, misunderstandings can be more easily cleared up in conversations than in written messages, stressing the importance of face-to-face communication.[13] Though Fayol's five management activities were mechanical in design, they introduced concepts of motivation, commitment, and job satisfaction. The numerous principles that supported the manager's basic functions opened up areas in communication that were new to the field of management.

Administrative Theory in Today's Organizations

Fayol's essential principles still form the framework of many contemporary organizations, though changes in social values have evolved and influenced the workplace over the decades. Today's managers are less directive and more cooperative—the focus is more on communication and human relationships than control and technical expertise.[14] The emphasis on participation and teamwork in today's workplace has increased the involvement of workers in the central management activities of planning, organizing, and controlling. Workers are included in planning discussions, their skills and knowledge are considered in organizing work tasks, and they are often responsible for monitoring their own quality standards.

In times of crisis, though, organizations generally revert to strong management directives and singular goals. CAE of Montreal, a world leader in flight simulation equipment and training, recently restructured. The plan included 450 job cuts (out of 5000 worldwide) and an overhaul of internal operations. CAE chief executive Robert Brown, former executive at Bombardier and Air Canada, said in answer to a question about the state of CAE when he took over,

> I'm impressed with the technology that's here. I'm impressed with the talent of the people and the passion the people have here for the product. When you look at the customers, the reputation we have, it's very, very good. But on the other side of the equation, it's been a culture that really has not been oriented toward finding a way to make money. It's been very technology-oriented as opposed to being entrepreneurial and concentrating on making money and a return to shareholders.... You're going to see an organizational structure that has clear profit and loss responsibility and accountability. You're going to see a new management team that is very, very focused on restoring shareholder confidence and returns.[15]

The Bureaucratic Theory of Max Weber

Most workers today are familiar with the practice of bureaucracy even though they may not know the theory behind it. That's because many modern organizations operate according to rational bureaucratic principles. Before we explain what bureaucracy is, let's discuss its origins. Bureaucratic structures caught on quickly in North America and became a standard part of classical management theory after Max Weber's major works were published in English in 1948. Weber's idea was an organizational structure based on rational authority. Workers would accept this authority and allow their managers to direct them in organizational activity.[19]

Of the three types of authority outlined by Weber—charismatic, traditional, and rational—rational authority was the most persuasive. Charismatic authority, based on a manager's personal characteristics and attitudes, leads to instability and disorder. A bureaucratic organization values professional rather than individualistic leadership styles. Traditional authority, based on personal loyalty and not on the ability to lead, would not benefit an organization. An example of traditional authority is the British monarchy in Canada, an authority based on long-standing loyalties that is no longer

Tough Competition Leaves No Room for Wimps

Although excellent managers need a range of skills, both administrative and human resource, success is usually measured by the financial bottom line. The big names in Canadian business became either heroes or villains, depending on your point of view, by using tough, ruthless strategies for success. Though employees may prefer the touchy-feely management style that achieves success through participative effort, investors get excited when jobs start getting slashed and the intimidation strategy goes into full swing. Let's look at a few examples.

After instructions from then Prime Minister Brian Mulroney to "go down there and clean the place out," Paul Tellier became CEO of Canadian National Railways (CN). From 1992 to 2002, he slashed half its work force, turning it from a money-losing Crown corporation into one of North America's most profitable railways. In his first few months on the job, 11 000 employees were laid off. While slashing costs, he also expanded, buying up U.S. lines that now make CN the only railroad that connects the Atlantic, Pacific, and Gulf of Mexico. Of course, the company's share price has climbed steadily upward. In his last month on the job, he axed 1150 more workers, saying, "We take no joy in announcing these permanent job reductions, but CN must leave no stone unturned in this productivity initiative." In 2003, Tellier was rewarded with a new job—CEO of Bombardier Inc.[16]

Domenic D'Alessandro, CEO of Manulife Financial Corporation since 1994, believes in company growth, and he doesn't like to compromise. "That's part of the problem with a lot of business executives. Everybody wants to be consensual, always judging as to what is politically expedient or what's going to fly." To back up his words, he tried to buy the Canadian Imperial Bank of Commerce in 1992, despite laws forbidding banks and insurers to join in business. John Manley, then finance minister, killed the plan. In his $25-billion company, D'Alessandro sets high goals for his workers, and then when they achieve them he sets higher ones. "I've dismissed people that I wish I didn't need to, because I liked them personally. But professionally, you have to make that separation."[17]

Robert Milton took over Air Canada in 2001, after it had lost $1.25 billion. Thousands of layoffs followed. He cut costs by cancelling flights at the last minute if enough seats were not sold and using a classic union-squeezing tactic: shifting operations from Air Canada to so-called new companies, such as Zip, Jazz, and other discount carriers that pay lower wages and benefits than the parent. "It's hard to let people go," says Milton, "knowing the impact it has on their lives, families and children, but you have to decide with your head and not your heart." After the layoffs, Milton sustained the pressure. He sent a letter to employees saying they weren't smiling enough.[18]

Discussion Questions

1. How are principles of classical management expressed in the actions of the managers in this case?

2. Discuss the impact of these management styles on communication in these organizations.

3. Is single bottom-line thinking, where the financial picture is the only one that is important, necessary for successful business operation?

rooted in the power to govern. Rational authority, based on the logical application of rules, carries the most promise of bringing order and stability to an organization.

The working conditions of the early 1900s were characterized by a lack of job security, employee protections, and decent wages. Often workers were fired for personal reasons based on culture, family ties, gender, or attitude. This style of management has been called *particularism,* an expedient but arbitrary and abusive form of managing workers. Weber's bureaucracy is based on the principles of *universalism*, which promoted equal treatment of workers according to work-related skills and abilities.[20] Though decision making is inconvenient in bureaucratic structures because of the abundance of regulations and levels of authority, the regulations contain protections that are designed to protect all workers from unfair treatment.

As well as embodying principles of classical management, such as division of labour and a hierarchical chain of command, bureaucracy contributed these major characteristics:

- A rigid separation of personal life from work life—personalizing a job could introduce non-rational application of rules and contaminate the purity of the rational system, so workers were discouraged from developing a sense of ownership of a position.
- Written rules of administration for clarity and to prevent deviation.
- Selection of workers on the basis of established standards of training and qualifications—workplace credentials take the form of educational diplomas and degrees, or professional or technical licenses used by accountants and carpenters.
- A view of employment as a lifelong career, advancing "up the ladder" over time, and including job security, benefits, pensions, and other benefits (though these benefits didn't always extend to operational-level workers, whose benefits often came from union contracts).

Weber's notion of authority poses some interesting questions for our discussion in the previous chapter about Harold Innis's theory of organization. We can now connect the types of authority—charismatic, traditional, and rational—to time-binding and space-binding communication systems. Space-binding systems are expressed in written form, as in an organization's set of rules and policies. The chain of command represents the formal network that reaches all corners of the organization. Time-binding systems are represented by charismatic and traditional types of authority, based more on individual characteristics and personal relationships. In organizations these would be found in the informal networks of members that exist outside of the formal chain of command in separate but linked clusters. Bureaucracy supports the spacial, uniform system, focusing on control, order, and routine. The diversified, tribal groups that bureaucracy seeks to eliminate represent the non-rational, elastic-natured aspects of an organization.

Bureaucratic Theory in Today's Organizations

The federal government is perhaps the quintessential example of bureaucracy, but that is starting to change as Ottawa considers flexing its purchasing muscle to get better deals from suppliers. "What we're doing as a government is what large companies did 20 years ago," says Scott Brison, Minister of Public Works. "We can't defend antiquated, expensive, inefficient practices to our neighbours and friends outside of government."[21] Other planned fundamental changes to the way government goes about its business include reducing the amount of paperwork businesses file with bureaucrats, maximizing the value of its real estate properties, and rebuilding a regulatory system to bring it into harmony with other departments, provinces, and trading partners. The moves will involve structural and cultural changes. Overall, the strategy seeks to embrace Bay Street–like tactics as it applies changes that will simplify business operations by reducing red tape.

Organizational Communication and Classical Management

What effects has classical management had on communication in organizations? It has been substantial, to say the least. The practical and functional nature of classical management and its status as a pioneer in the field gave it deep roots in the business

Linda Cook Meets the Good Old Boys[22]

Maybe it's her technical background or that she's a woman in an industry that's never had a female as a CEO, but Linda Cook's rise from newly graduated petroleum engineer to head of Shell Canada was a model of efficiency and professionalism. Along with her recent appointment of Cathy Williams as Chief Financial Officer, the number of top female officers will jump from zero to two in Alberta's oil patch, where the Calgary Petroleum Club barred women until 1989. As an example of her efficiency, managing director of the $300 billion Royal Dutch/Shell Group, Malcolm Brinded, says, "she is famous for running meetings with a timekeeping bleeper that is 100% oblivious to appeals for latitude."[23] Linda adds, "my sisters will tell you that when I was in charge I was a real slave driver," as kids in their family's dairy operations. Linda is known in oil circles for her energy, perseverence,

abilities in dealing with customers, and completing complex projects on time and on budget. She is quick to offload faltering assets. In the past two years, she closed offices, cutting overhead by 40%, and restructured the company's equipment portfolio. As Cook says, "There's no substitute for hard work and delivering on promises. I always think of the Chinese proverb that says, 'I got where I am because of luck and the harder I work the luckier I get.'"[24] She was directly involved in Shell's huge Sakhalin project, the largest oil and gas project ever built and the biggest foreign investment ever made in Russia. Cook supervised plant design and lined up long term contracts with Japan, China, Korea and Taiwan, earning her the nickname 'Sakhalin Linda.' In Canada, she will oversee the Athabasca Oil Sands Project, Shell's offshore gas wells off the east coast of Nova Scotia, and the development of the Mackenzie Valley Pipeline, along with Shell's regular operations.

world. Communication according to this perspective is a tool that helps management execute its normal business responsibilities.

The Purposes of Communication

- By introducing formal networks and hierarchical structures of authority, Weber and Fayol created the structure through which communication would move in organizations. As organizations grew and formal networks multiplied, this system of communication became bogged down and slow to respond.
- A person's communication behaviour is determined by his or her place on the hierarchy.
- Communication activities are specialized according to tasks and positions along the hierarchy.
- Communication is a variable of the organization that is controlled by management to reduce uncertainty.
- Taylor's concept of "soldiering," meaning that workers will do as little as possible to get by, removes the need to motivate workers through communication. Monetary rewards are the only source of motivation provided.
- Since classical management emphasizes the use of communication to achieve organizational goals and administrative objectives, it fits in best with the functional perspective on organizational communication discussed in the previous chapter.

Types of Messages and Message Flow

- Messages move along the formal channels on the chain of command mainly in a downward direction.
- Upward communication is discouraged, as is horizontal communication, except in rare situations (Fayol's bridge).
- Informal communication networks are discouraged because they bring out the personal characteristics of employees.
- Fayol and Weber stress the importance of record keeping using written communication. The volume of written records and memos over time eventually became time-consuming and unmanageable, until computers came along.
- Face-to-face communication was important for Taylor in providing training and feedback to employees.

Context of Communication

- Managers assume their role as legitimate authority without question.
- Since management makes all the decisions, there should be no sources of conflict over organizational goals, nor any input needed from workers.
- The era of management as a profession begins, and the role of the worker as a non-thinking subordinate is entrenched.
- The organization as a context exists within its physical walls and did not extend into the environment.
- The separation of thinking work and physical work took place within the larger social context of a large influx of immigrant and rural workers into manufacturing operations in the early 1900s.[25]

The development of modern organizations began with the Industrial Revolution. By the 1900s, organizations had adopted the rational structures of organization, based on management theories proposed by Fredrick Taylor, Henri Fayol, and Max Weber. The foundations of scientific management shared by all three theorists are the following:

- a focus on improving organizational efficiency by increasing management's ability to control and predict the behaviour of workers.

- a reliance on formal structure based on hierarchy, rules, and chain of command

- a downward flow of task-oriented communication from superiors to subordinates and an emphasis on written messages

- almost a total absence of attention to social and relational messages

Classical management is still a dominant management style today, though it has been streamlined in numerous ways to make it more adaptable to faster styles of doing business. Rigid, formal systems of communication have been loosened up to incorporate a wider forum of decision making and participation. Humanistic principles have been given greater consideration by organizations both as motivating techniques and out of a sense of social responsibility. In the next chapter, we examine some of the humanistic perspectives on organizations. First, though, read the case study below for a contrast in management styles, one classical and authoritarian, the other progressive and flexible.

A Tale of Two Steel Giants

Bureaucracy is hazardous for individual and organizational health

When Frank A. Sherman, legendary president of Dofasco Inc., drew up the company's first organizational chart in 1952, he had two goals: to clarify and coordinate functional relations over a rapidly growing number of departments and production processes, and to preserve the company's tradition of open and informal communication. The memo attached to the chart stated:

> The issuing of this chart does not mean that our long established policy of free interchange of ideas and opinions between [people] anywhere on the chart is to be altered in the slightest. The last thing we want is to become entangled in red tape.[26]

Open communication and informal administrative structures had been part of the corporation's culture since the 1930s, when management and the 1600 workers worked closely together in one plant. Though the chart specified hierarchical positions, Sherman emphasized "general relationships" and "general spheres of activity" to maintain organizational flexibility and multidirectional reporting flows—downward, upward, and lateral. Though formal in structure, in practice Dofasco exhibited extensive lateral relationships. According to research, steel makers face a common dilemma: though complex operational requirements demand a bureaucratic structure, this formalization also stifles innovation and de-motivates workers.[27] Open communication has had many benefits for Dofasco. It facilitated the flow of ideas from the shop floor. The company has operated a suggestion box since 1936. Awards (up to $50 000 per idea) are based on the savings the idea produces. In 1987, about one in four employees made suggestions, lowering production costs by $1.7 million.[28] An employee profit-sharing plan has been in place since 1938 and regularly yields healthy bonuses.

Yet the Dofasco family has also experienced upheaval over the years. In 1982, a recession that drove colossal steel makers like Bethlehem Steel of Buffalo into bankruptcy and vaporized steel making in the U.S. Northeast also forced Dofasco to lay off 2000 workers. This was followed by the disastrous purchase of Algoma Steel in 1991, resulting in a write-off of $700 million and a reduction in the work force from 12 000 to 7000 (most workers, though, left voluntarily, through attrition, or retirement and severance packages). Aside from these major hurdles, the "our strength is people" motto has persevered over the years. Seven out of eight senior managers have been with the company over 25 years, and its employee turnover is the lowest of any Canadian steel firm (less than 2 percent). The key to Dofasco's long-term prosperity has been its ability take a proactive approach to the huge impact of globalization and to "maintain the old, worker-centered philosophy of the founding Sherman family, while at the same time adapting to a shifting business environment."[29]

When steel production boomed after 1945, Dofasco's long-time Hamilton neighbour Stelco was also developing a more elaborate, bureaucratic structure. Though larger and more profitable than Dofasco at the time, the principles of open communication and cooperation were not a part of Stelco's workplace. It was always a purely production-driven operation. In 1945, two-thirds of employees voted to join the United Steelworkers of America, and the next year, Stelco had its first strike, lasting 81 days. Labour–management problems and work stoppages were to become Stelco's trademark. Strikes of similar duration took place every decade that followed, the last one in 1990, the year company shares fell from $26 to 98 cents. Stelco had one effective formula for success: capitalizing on the booming economic waves of the mid-twentieth century, particularly the decades following World War II. It overcame both the competition and labour strife with rapid expansion and technological excellence, breaking its own production records as it charged forward. The City of Hamilton, at the time Canada's fourth-largest city and nicknamed the "lunchbucket" city, was also booming. International Harvester was there, along with Westinghouse, Firestone, and Proctor & Gamble, and the CFL Tiger-Cats were perennial champions. For a long period you could sell everything you produced. Stelco's singular business strategy worked for decades, despite its highly antagonistic relationship with its employees.

The highpoint of its unbridled expansion was the opening of its Lake Erie Works at a cost of $870 million in 1980. To symbolically top off its success, Stelco moved its head office from Hamilton to Toronto. But crisis was looming—the recession, competition from overseas, and the 125-day strike of 1981 alarmingly brought it to its knees. In 1981, the company suffered its first net loss. Today, bankruptcy has forced it into restructuring. According to the CEO during the early 2000s, Courtney Pratt, a veteran of human resources management with no steel-making experience, the desperately needed reinvention of Stelco had been blocked by a decades-long culture of mistrust between company and union.[30]

Dofasco benefited in two ways from the fact that it never had a union. (Though many organizing efforts had been tried, none succeeded. Dofasco's long-time strategy had been to immediately give any wage and benefit increases Stelco workers received to its own workers—without a strike.) Unions often double the bureaucracy in an organization. In addition, a union's character usually reflects that of management. They fight with the same intensity, and they protect themselves with parallel rules and restrictions. The lack of cooperation in Stelco's management style was matched by the union's. Did these added bureaucratic structures hurt Stelco's success? Dofasco's non-union environment gave it the flexibility to deal with change quickly. It reduced conflict over job divisions, increasing staff mobility and cooperation. And it allowed employees to participate in improving operations.[31] In contrast, at Stelco, rigid job divisions evoked the standard phrase "It's not my job" from both workers and managers.

Management–employee tension in the workplace has a strong influence not only on organizational health, but also individual well-being. Feeling devalued or frustrated usually decreases communication. According to research, "at the root of workers distress are the traditional bureaucratic, top-down organizational structures that continue to dominate our workplace."[32] The traditional costs of bureaucracy are absenteeism, high turnover rates, and sub-par performance. A tightly managed organization such as Stelco treats its employees as replaceable parts. On the other hand, a loosely managed organization such as Dofasco sees employees in terms of their skills, not their positions. It has been known for some time that loosely managed organizations are more productive. Oil giant Syncrude Canada, for instance, emphasizes equalizing power across all levels and sharing decision-making authority with lower-level employees.[33] Many factors contribute to the health of individual workers, and clear links have been established between individual worker health and overall organizational success.

Discussion Questions

1. Discuss the benefits and drawbacks of bureaucracy for an organization.

2. Compare the workplaces of Stelco and Dofasco in terms of their levels of bureaucracy. How do they help or hinder each company?

3. What role did the union play in Stelco's problems? Was Dofasco's nonunion status the reason for its success? What other elements contributed to its success?

4. Discuss the elements of bureaucracy that affect workers on an individual basis. Are there connections between individual health and organizational health?

1. Think of organizations you have been a member of—workplaces, athletic teams, volunteer groups, or even your family. Discuss the ways these organizations operated. Were there elements of scientific management used? Was it organized in a bureaucratic way? What are some examples?

2. How easy or difficult was it to communicate in the group? Was communication two-way or one-way? How did you feel as a member of the group? Were you involved, respected, alienated, comfortable, inspired?

3. Discuss the benefits and drawbacks of scientific management in terms of your own experiences. When would scientific management principles be effective and ineffective?

4. What are the ethical concerns raised by scientific management practices?

Glossary

Chain of command, p. 62
Systematic soldiering, p. 64
Presenteeism, p. 66
Schadenfreude, p. 66
Scalar chain, p. 67
Unity of command, p. 67
Division of work, p. 67
Centralization, p. 67

Personal authority, p. 67
Pay, p. 67
Fairness and equity, p. 67
Esprit de corps, p. 67
Horizontal communication, p. 67
Particularism, p. 70
Universalism, p. 70

Notes

1. Peter C. Newman, "A titan under fire," *National Post*, March 29, 2005, A20.

2. Adam Smith, *An Inquiry into the Nature and Causes of the Wealth of Nations*, vol. I. (London: Methuen & Co., 1925).

3. Eric M. Eisenberg and H. L. Goodhall, Jr., *Organizational Communication: Balancing Creativity and Constraint* (Boston: Bedford/St. Martin's, 2004).

4. Stan Rogers, "The Puddler's Tale," *From Coffee House To Concert Hall* (Fogarty's Cove Music, 2000).

5. Fredrick W. Taylor, *The Principles of Scientific Management*. (Minneola, NY: Dover Publications, 1911).

6. Ibid.

7. Gareth Morgan, *Images of Organization* (Newbury Park, CA: Sage, 1986).

8. David Molpus, "Who's the Worst Boss?" National Public Radio broadcast, June 18, 2002.

9. Andy Riga, "Business Awakes to Cost of Stress," *Montreal Gazette*, February 27, 2006, http://www.canada.com/montrealgazette/story.html?id=eb9c321c-364e-4435-adbc-7b781d041fcb&k=22077 (accessed May 14, 2006).

10. Ibid.

11. Henri Fayol, *General and Industrial Management* (London: Pitman, 1948).

12. Katherine Miller, *Organizational Communication*, 3rd ed. (Belmont, CA: Thomson Wadsworth Learning, 2003).

13. Pamela Shockley-Zalabak, *Fundamentals of Organizational Communication: Knowledge, Sensitivity, Skills, Values*, 5th ed. (Boston: Allyn and Bacon, 2002).

14. Daniel Modaff and Sue DeWine, *Organizational Communication* (Los Angeles: Roxbury Publishing Company, 2002).

15. Sean Silcoff, "CAE: 'No magic, just hard work,'" *National Post*, February 14, 2005, FP3.

16. John Daly, "The Toughest Bosses in Business," *The Globe and Mail*, Report on Business, February 2003.

17. Ibid.

18. Ibid.

19. Max Weber, *The Theory of Social and Economic Organization*, trans. A.M. Henderson and T. Parson (New York: Free Press, 1948).

20. Eisenberg and Goodhall, *Organizational Communication*.

21. Paul Vieira, "Bureaucracy's radical reno," *National Post*, March 3, 2005, FP3.

22. Ann Walmsley, "Introducing Linda Cook," *The Globe and Mail*, Report on Business, July 2003, 27–30.

23. Ibid.

24. Ibid.

25. William W. Neher, *Organizational Communication: Challenges of Change, Continuity, and Diversity* (Boston: Allyn and Bacon, 1997).

26. Gordon Boyce, "Continuity and Transition in Corporate Capability: Incentives, Management, and Innnovation at Dofasco, Inc.," in *Business and Economic History*, ed. William J. Hausman, 2nd ser., vol. 19, The Business History Conference (ISSN 0849-6825, 1990).

27. Leonard Lynn, *How Japan Innovates: A Comparison with the U. S. in the Case of Oxygen Steelmaking* (Boulder, CO: Westview Press, 1982); Roger Emile Miller, *Innovation, Organization, and Environment: A Study of Sixteen American and West European Steel Firms* (Sherbrooke, QC: Institut de recherche et de perfectionnement en administration, 1971).

28. Boyce, "Continuity and Transition."

29. Stephen Brunt, "Heavy Mettle," *The Globe and Mail*, May 28, 2004, http://www.workopolis.com/servlet/Content/qprinter/20040528/R06DOFASCO (accessed February 4, 2006).

30. "People to Watch in 2006," *The Toronto Star*, http://www.yorku.ca/ylife/2006/01-09/media.htm (accessed March 29, 2006).

31. Boyce, "Continuity and Transition."

32. Henry A. Hornstein and Donald W. de Guerre, "Bureaucratic Organizations are Bad for our Health," *Ivey Business Journal* (March/April 2006): 1–5.

33. Ibid.

Chapter Five

Human Relations and Human Resources Approaches

I'll give you all I've got to give
If you say you'll love me true
I may not have a lot to give
But what I've got I'll give to you
I don't care too much for money,
Money can't buy me love.

—"Can't Buy Me Love," The Beatles

Learning Objectives

- Explore the origins of the human relations movement

- Examine the principles of human relations theory

- Identify the theories and practices of human resources

- Analyze the impact of human relations on organizational communication

- Explore the elements of the communication climate in organizations

The Human Relations Movement

The fact that we often end up with something we never intended explains the ironic origins of human relations theory. What started out as a series of studies to confirm the views of classical management turned into a landmark discovery that is in direct opposition to many classical management principles. Human relations shifts the focus from a classical, machine-like design of the workplace to a radically humanized one. It focuses on encouraging two-way communication up and down the ranks, creating participative systems that address the social, psychological, and emotional needs of workers. It employs concepts of human motivation, and recognizes that communication and social relationships are at the heart of organizational life. The quote from the song by the Beatles is appropriate to a human relations perspective because it expresses the limitations of money in satisfying the many needs that people have. In this section we will review the major human relations theories. Next, we will examine how they were adapted to the more practical and systematic applications of the human resources approach.

During the 1920s and 1930s, managers began to question the traditional methods of coercion and control. The great social events of the time—the Depression, World War I—created a growing interest in a more humanistic approach to the workplace and society in general. Unemployment in Canada surged so high that urban migration reversed, and people returned to farms to find work. In response to impoverished working conditions, the working class adopted a more militant posture, labour unions rapidly grew in popularity, and faith in market factors diminished. If one was lucky enough to find a job, the punishing working conditions—typically a 12-hour workday, six days a week, with a half-hour lunch—contributed to the discontent of workers and the growing division of interests between labour and management.

Academically, this time period was fruitful. New ways of understanding human behaviour were introduced, particularly as alternatives to the behavioural school on which classical management was based. Symbolic interactionism, a school of thought that draws on a number of social philosophers of the time, including William James, John Dewey, George Herbert Mead, and Sigmund Freud, proposes that in making sense of our experiences we rely on the individual meanings and interpretations we have for things. So, the direct *stimulus* Π *response* path of the behavioural approach now had a third stage: the process of interpretation that happens between the stimulus and response stages. The process now looked like this: *stimulus → interpretation → response* (see Figure 5.1). And so, a meaning-centred approach to understanding human behaviour, in addition to a behaviour-centred one, came into being.[1]

The Origins of Human Relations—The Hawthorne Studies, 1924–1932

The Hawthorne Works of the Western Electric Company near Chicago was experiencing employee dissatisfaction, high turnover rates, and reduced efficiency. To explore ways to improve productivity at the plant, researchers Elton Mayo and F.J. Roethlisberger began

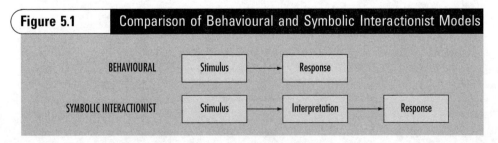

Figure 5.1   Comparison of Behavioural and Symbolic Interactionist Models

BEHAVIOURAL   Stimulus → Response

SYMBOLIC INTERACTIONIST   Stimulus → Interpretation → Response a series of studies that became the foundation of the human relations movement. Many efforts to fix these problems had already failed. Following the methods of scientific management, the researchers attempted to isolate physical conditions, such as lighting, ventilation, job and workspace design, rest periods, and hours of work to determine which ones could be manipulated to increase employee output. Their theory was based on the stimulus–response model of human behaviour: external conditions determine human actions.[2] Workers exercised certain behaviours in the expectation of a reward, which, according to classical management, was money.

The Illumination Study, one of four studies conducted at the plant over eight years, examined the effect of lighting intensity on productivity. The prediction was that a certain level of illumination would produce a maximum level of worker output. One group of workers, the test group, worked under brighter lighting, and productivity went up. The second group, the control group, worked under normal lighting levels, and productivity also went up. Even more amazing, output continued to go up when the lighting levels for the test group were lowered back to normal. When the researchers lowered light levels to below normal, output went up again, and did not stop rising until illumination was at the level of bright moonlight. Researchers became puzzled that a specific level of illumination for maximum output could not be found. In all four studies, output continued to rise in spite of the variety of conditions imposed by the researchers. The absence of a correlation between the different working conditions and rising output led to the conclusion that physical conditions alone could not explain the changes in output.

Eventually, the researchers realized that the changes in output were being caused not by physical changes but by a change in supervisory practices. Because of the experiment, supervisors were consulting with workers, asking them for feedback about working conditions, and allowing workers to talk to each other while working. The researchers concluded that social activity and relationship building could be an important factor in the productivity equation. The implications of the *Hawthorne Studies* for management were considerable:[3]

1. A supervisory style based on paying attention to the concerns and needs of employees, including giving recognition for a job well done, increases employee satisfaction and output.
2. Relationships among employees, once considered to be insignificant except for the accomplishment of tasks, play a strong role in increasing employee morale and participation in the workplace and in creating supportive and caring attitudes among employees.
3. Upward communication—asking employees for their opinions—has a strong influence on developing positive attitudes toward the organization.
4. Interpersonal relationships formed through informal communication are a major determinant of worker efficiency, perhaps even greater than the physical conditions of a workplace.

The shift in emphasis from the task-driven relationships between bosses and workers in the classical structures to the personally and socially oriented relationships of the human relations school of thought laid the foundation for much of today's thinking about management and leadership.

Several other researchers contributed to the development of the human relations approach. Mary Parker Follett (1868–1933), a social worker who became a lecturer on management, stressed the importance of psychological factors such as employees' needs and motivations.[4] As an alternative to a downward flow of messages along a formal chain of command, Follett suggested a different set of priorities: only by people cooperating and working together in groups under effective leadership could excellence

Chapter 5 / Human Relations and Human Resources Approaches be achieved in the workplace.[5] In a pioneering stroke, she promoted employee empowerment through the sharing of information, a cooperative approach to problem solving, and teamwork—processes that integrate employees and awaken their capabilities. In contrast to economic rewards, human relations motivated workers by providing individual, emotional, and social growth. Follett's view of power in organizations describes managers, workers, and other stakeholders working together. She distinguished between power-over, or coercive power, and power-with, as in coactive power:

> What is the central problem of social relations? It is the question of power . . . [b]ut our task is not to learn where to place power; it is how to develop power. . . . Genuine power can only be grown, it will slip from every arbitrary hand that grasps it; for genuine power is not coercive control, but coactive control. Coercive power is the curse of the universe; coactive power, the enrichment and advancement of every human soul.[6]

Chester Barnard's work supported this direction of thought by emphasizing the importance of communication processes in management. The organization leader is a communication link among organizational members who uses communication to facilitate cooperation.[7] Barnard also highlighted the differences between the formal and informal organization. Whereas the formal organization has enduring structure, specific rules, and a line of authority, the informal one, eventually known as the "grapevine," has an indefinite and changing structure with no established lines of authority—it exists according to practices established by members in the course of normal activity. Yet it must be recognized and understood by managers, so the formal organization may run properly. Thus, Barnard's work can be seen as a bridge between classical theory and human relations. Though he supported traditional notions of authority and formal structure, he also stressed the importance of a two-way communication system with employees and cooperative approaches between managers and workers.

The growing interest in the human infrastructure of an organization, namely, the personal and informal activities that make up organizational life, continued into the 1950s. A book that became a standard in management studies was Abraham Maslow's *Motivation and Personality*. It has been widely used to understand the behaviour of employees, in terms of their needs and what motivates them, and consumers, in terms of why people buy things—an obvious area of interest for salespeople. Maslow defined five areas of needs, as shown in Figure 5.2, along with their accompanying sources of satisfaction in the workplace. The lowest level is at the bottom of the hierarchy. According to the hierarchy, a person must satisfy lower level needs before moving on to higher ones.

Maslow's *hierarchy of needs* is useful for comparing the classical with the humanistic system of management: classical managers motivated workers with the lower levels—money and secure employment. Human relations managers, on the other hand, appealed to workers' higher level needs—social relationships, recognition, a sense of accomplishment, and personal growth. So, two clearly distinct directions of management were forming: one focused on workplace conditions and monetary rewards; the other, on human relationships, affiliation, and communication activity.

Human Relations in Today's Organizations

The human relations movement launched a great deal of interest in people-oriented management styles. The assumption was that low morale and poor productivity were caused by management's failure to treat employees as complex and sensitive individuals. So, the humanistic approach was adopted. To overcome their prevailing task orientation rooted in classical management, managers were trained in participative methods and

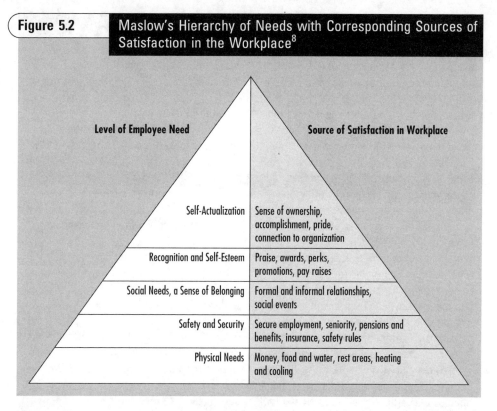

Figure 5.2 Maslow's Hierarchy of Needs with Corresponding Sources of Satisfaction in the Workplace[8]

Level of Employee Need	Source of Satisfaction in Workplace
Self-Actualization	Sense of ownership, accomplishment, pride, connection to organization
Recognition and Self-Esteem	Praise, awards, perks, promotions, pay raises
Social Needs, a Sense of Belonging	Formal and informal relationships, social events
Safety and Security	Secure employment, seniority, pensions and benefits, insurance, safety rules
Physical Needs	Money, food and water, rest areas, heating and cooling

relationship building—a set of skills that over time became associated with "charm school" or "the happiness boys." Higher morale resulted, but, unexpectedly, the increase in output did not. A couple of reasons have been cited for this shortfall. First, even today, though it goes against popular thinking, not much hard research supports the hypothesis that positive employee morale cultivates productivity—in fact, happy people are sometimes not the most productive. Second, in an effort to avoid appearing too directive or coercive, and as a result insensitive, managers let problems go for the sake of keeping good relations. "Comfort won out over consistency, personal indulgence over organizational perseverance, and so on to the point that the humanistic approach allowed individual needs to supercede the needs of the organization."[9]

Though critics generally agree that the principles of human relations are sound, the efforts to apply them were inconsistent and counterproductive. It was a classic case of saying one thing and doing another. Upward communication was encouraged but perceived as cosmetic by employees because it was not truly valued by superiors. Employees were told they were important, but they perceived it as manipulative because they were not treated accordingly. The superficial style of application of human relations principles in some cases actually decreased employee performance.[10] These shortcomings were addressed by the human resources theory of management discussed in our next section.

Human Resources Theories of Management

The theories of the human relations movement were applied ineffectively and with disappointing results for some interesting reasons. First, human relations never became a sincere effort. Gary Kreps states:

> Even when these managers were required by their organizations to institute human relations programs to increase worker involvement and satisfaction, their

In spite of the poor track record of human relations, many organizations today are designing reward programs based on face-to-face feedback in the form of praise as a way of creating positive feelings and relationships in the workplace. The public accounting firm KPMG operates a "thank-you culture," where managers recognize good work as a means of "reinforcing our corporate values," says Val Duffey, the firm's Toronto-based human resources director.[11] Such practices are not that common. According to a *Globe and Mail* Web poll, 27 percent of 2331 respondents reported they had never received a compliment from their boss. But surveys confirm that acknowledgment for good work is important to employees. And nearly 89 percent of 762 employees across North America ranked recognition from managers as extremely or very important.[12] Shawn Cornett, general manager for organizational effectiveness at Calgary-based Nexen Inc., says it doesn't matter if it's coming from your boss or your subordinate: "I like to know there's value in what I'm doing, so getting recognition from others for doing something they believe is worthwhile is very important to me."[13]

Various reasons have been cited for the absence of praise in the workplace. First, bosses are pressed for time and focus on what is going wrong instead of what is done right. Second, today's business culture is more unpredictable. Everyone's job is more conditional, so workers may not feel connected enough to offer compliments. Third, bosses may be cautious about putting praise in writing because it will become part of the employee's record and cause difficulty in case of termination. Finally, managers may have come from environments where praise was not given out and so they simply perpetuate the dysfunctional cycle.[14]

The use of praise in a workplace is a functional form of communication—it is a message with a specific purpose directed at a certain individual. The process can be as simple as saying "Good job" and giving a pat on the back. Or it can be more complex: you may need to decide whether your praise should be public or private, or whether it should be accompanied by a material reward. You may have to practise being sincere, or determine context issues such as the amount of conflict in a situation. Cindy Bordin, director of human resources at Torys LLP, one of Canada's largest law firms with 280 administrative staff at the company's Toronto head office and in New York, likes to praise her staff personally. To reach the New York staff, she'll pick up the phone because "the personal touch is really important. You can hear the sincerity in someone's voice."[15] And it also helps to develop open and honest relationships.

Discussion Questions

1. Discuss the benefits of personal praise for maintaining good relationships and good employee performance in the workplace.

2. Discuss some of your own experiences of both giving and receiving praise. What effects did it have on your relationships or task outcomes?

implementation of human relations principles was often superficial, giving workers the guise of increased participation.[16]

Thus, though managers showed concern for workers' needs and feelings, this superficial application simply substituted different behaviours into the old stimulus–response model. If a smile or a compliment is the stimulus, the appropriate response from a worker would be a positive feeling, and the result would be more work. This type of application is essentially classical management practice with new variables. Second, the interpretation stage of the stimulus-response model, containing the critical communication elements of human relations theory, was never developed enough to create the necessary two-way, participative relationships for meaningful interaction. Third, managers came to human relations with new behaviours but still hanging on to old conceptualizations of workers as cogs in a big organizational machine—a fundamental classical management attitude. Finally, over-reliance on authority as a means of organizational control, again a building block of classical management, excludes the formation of a collaborative atmosphere in a workplace. Many managers, today as then, feel nervous about handing over the reins of control to workers. And their training in the principles and practices of classical management made them uncomfortable with the participative nature of human relations. Ultimately, neither scientific management nor human relations proved adequate as a system of management. Scientific management was too tightly controlled to bring out worker potential, and human relations gained a negative reputation as a manipulative strategy that discouraged workers instead of motivating them.

In response to these shortcomings, researchers developed human resources theories. Much more than just trying to make workers happy, human resources developed systematic applications to increase worker productivity based on an awareness of human needs. In addition, researchers attempted to understand human behaviour, in particular the behaviour of managers toward workers, from the point of view of managers' attitudes and assumptions about people. As a starting point for discussing human resources theories, we will begin with Douglas McGregor's Theory X and Theory Y, from his book *The Human Side of Enterprise.*

Theory X and Theory Y—Douglas McGregor

... [he] kept a copy of a famous early nineteenth century manual on industrial relations and regularly recited the opening sentence, which asserted that any such study must start from the premise that employees are slothful, incompetent, and dishonest.

> —*Conrad Black's description of his partner, David Radler, then manager of the Sherbrooke Record daily newspaper*[17]

McGregor argued that a manager's style comes from the beliefs he or she has about human nature.[18] In the above quote, then, David Radler's assumptions that all employees are slothful, incompetent, and dishonest will have a strong influence on his management style. These assumptions help managers predict the outcomes of their workers' activities. For example, if Adam is lazy, and he is allowed to set his own deadlines, nothing will ever get done. The methods managers use to accomplish tasks, such as using rewards, threats, or punishment, also serve to control the behaviour of workers. The problem McGregor saw was that existing managerial theory was inadequate in addressing a true human relations perspective because of negative assumptions about workers' abilities and its overemphasis on authority and control. To create a collaborative work style that tapped a worker's potential, different forms of authority and control needed to be established. Since the various forms of control used by managers originated in their philosophies about people, McGregor attempted to understand managerial behaviour by examining these fundamental perspectives. He called them Theory X, representing the classical school of management founded on formal authority structures, and Theory Y, representing the human relations school of thought (see Figure 5.3).

If the pessimistic descriptions about human nature of Theory X were true, all workers would be lazy, unimaginative, irresponsible, greedy, untrustworthy, and

| Figure 5.3 | Douglas McGregor's Theory X and Theory Y[19] |

Theory X Assumptions	Theory Y Assumptions
1. People do not like work and will avoid it whenever possible.	1. People think work is as natural as play.
2. Workers must be controlled and directed.	2. Workers are capable of self-direction.
3. Workers avoid responsibility and have little ambition.	3. Workers desire responsibility and are ambitious.
4. Workers must be threatened with punishment to get their job done.	4. Workers are capable of self-motivation.
5. Workers have low levels of intelligence and creativity.	5. Workers have potentially high levels of intelligence and creativity.

unenterprising. It would be the job of a manager to force workers to behave appropriately using the blunt instruments of punishment and money. It's obvious from these assumptions why authority and control are such central principles of classical theory. McGregor disagreed with these assumptions. His opinion was that they describe a management style; they do not describe human nature. With this in mind, he outlined an alternative set of assumptions that characterized human nature more accurately, and called them Theory Y.

Theory Y depicts organizational conditions that allow workers to bring out their capabilities. In contrast to Theory X, the assumptions of Theory Y proclaim that work can be enjoyable, that workers can show initiative, responsibility, and imagination, and that they can be committed to and participate actively in reaching organizational objectives. The matter of control under Theory Y is addressed by integrating individual and organizational goals: the more workers' goals are satisfied, the stronger their commitment to the goals of the organization, and the higher their production levels. So, coercion, punishment, and financial reward would no longer be the only methods available to managers for controlling workers in order to achieve organizational goals. With a far more positive view of human nature, Theory Y leads to greater respect for and confidence in employees and a more personal and human approach to management. In terms of communication, starting with Theory X or Theory Y assumptions can make a big difference in how people communicate with each other. Think back to communication experiences with people you've known or bosses you've had. If they made you feel like a person, a human relations perspective was evident; if you felt like an object being talked at, it was probably based on Theory X assumptions.

Four Systems of Management: Rensis Likert

Human relations theories were further developed into human resources applications by Rensis Likert in two influential books, *New Patterns of Management* and *The Human Organization*. Likert's human resources theory exhibits similar basic principles to those outlined by McGregor in Figure 5.3. Figure 5.4 describes how human resources developed the idea of human relations. In designing a set of management systems, Likert embraced principles that spread along a continuum from classical styles (Theory X) to human resources (Theory Y). Though the four systems include classical approaches, the participative system is the most progressive, emphasizing the importance of managing the human component of an organization. Below is a brief description of the four systems.[20]

Figure 5.4 — Comparison of Human Relations and Human Resources Perspectives of Management[21]

Human Relations

1. People need to belong, to be liked, to be respected.
2. A manager must make workers believe they are an important part of an organization.
3. A manager should make routine decisions with subordinates and discuss their objections.
4. Within narrow limits, workers should be allowed to exercise self-direction.
5. Involving employees in decision making will help satisfy their needs for belonging and recognition.
6. Higher employee morale should lead to improved performance.

Human Resources

1. In addition to these needs, people want to contribute effectively and creatively to the accomplishment of goals.
2. A manager must create an environment in which all workers can contribute their full range of talents.
3. A manager should encourage subordinates to participate in decision making—the more important the decision, the greater the need for employee input.
4. A manager should continually expand an employee's amount of self-direction according to the level of ability he or she has demonstrated.
5. The quality of decision making will improve as a manager makes full use of each workers' potential.
6. Employee morale will increase as a result of improved performance and the opportunity to be involved in it.

System I—Exploitative Authoritative

This system is your typical scientific management style, based on orders from superiors, the use of punishment and fear as persuasive techniques to accomplish tasks, a top-down decision-making style, and employees who are uninvolved mentally and emotionally in workplace activity. Productivity is usually low.

Communication in System I. Communication is one-way—downward. Upward, two-way communication is discouraged, as it cuts into work time. The atmosphere is impersonal and uncooperative, resulting in high levels of distrust among workers and bosses that creates frequent distortion of messages. Messages from superiors revolve around threats and rewards based on physical needs.

System II—Benevolent Exploitative

The second system is slightly more humanistic, as the name implies. There is more emphasis on rewards as motivators, and some decision-making activity may trickle down to workers, suggesting the beginnings of participative activity. Workers, though, show virtually no involvement or responsibility for organizational goals.

Communication in System II. Communication is mostly downward, and these messages are often incomplete, causing confusion and frustration among employees. The irregular reliance on upward communication creates a suspicious, even hostile, workplace atmosphere. The result is a generally dissatisfied workplace, with productivity and morale leaving a lot to be desired. The communication priorities of managers are in *saying* the right things, instead of *doing* them.

System III—Consultative

Workers are motivated through some use of rewards and punishments and partial involvement in decision making, usually on specific operational issues. Subordinates contribute to goal setting as consultants—as "outsiders"—and therefore may not feel genuine commitment to organizational goals.

Communication in System III. Upward communication increases in System III, though not to the level of downward information flow. A generally satisfying work atmosphere exists, and productivity is usually good. Along with greater upward communication, there is also more horizontal message flow, which opens up the process of relationship building and meeting social needs.

System IV—Participative

System IV represents the human resources principles of participation in decision making, involvement in goal setting, open communication, and the full opportunity for employees' creative resources to be released—ingredients that Likert considered the most effective for management. The beauty of this system is that the participative methods become motivators, in addition to the economic rewards provided in the previous three systems. Good work performance brings an invitation for greater involvement.

Communication in System IV. Since communication is the essential means of integrating individual and organizational activity in a participative system, it flows in all directions and can be initiated at any level. Openness of communication reduces message distortion and creates favourable attitudes and high levels of trust among workers. Productivity and job satisfaction are highest in System IV.

The comparative analysis of different management styles offered by Likert was an attempt to show the superiority of participative management (System IV). His findings establish a connection between levels of productivity and levels of employee participation. In contrast to Taylor's scientific management, which dealt with variability in output of different workers by designing standardized procedures, Likert called for more participation and communication. Likert's emphasis on communication was made clear in the following statement: "Communication is essential to the functioning of an organization. It is viewed widely as one of the most important processes of management."[22]

The following human resources principles show the importance of communication for Likert's participative style of management:

- An organization must develop a system of networks that provide upward, downward, and horizontal communication.
- Employees should actively and genuinely participate in the establishment of organizational goals.
- An environment of trust and respect enables employees to contribute to organizational dialogue in open and meaningful ways.
- Interpersonal communication is vital for the formation of supportive workplace relationships that facilitate the accomplishment of organizational goals.
- Group decision making becomes an interlocking process in the overall organization through the work of *linking pins*, people who have multiple group memberships and carry information from group to group.

A similar approach to Likert's was found in *The Managerial Grid*, by Robert Blake and Jane Mouton. The managerial grid was a tool for diagnosing a manager's orientation toward the two central variables of the workplace: production and people, or task

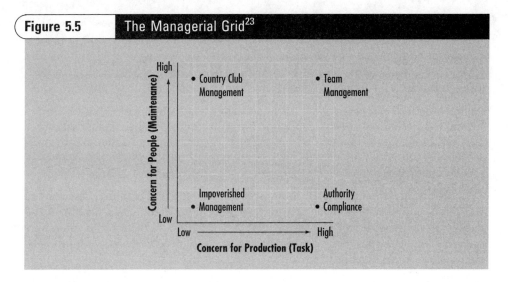

Figure 5.5 | The Managerial Grid[23]

Concern for People (Maintenance) — High / Low

• Country Club Management

• Team Management

• Impoverished Management

Authority • Compliance

Concern for Production (Task) — Low → High

and maintenance. Communication in a group can serve two purposes: the social purpose of improving relationships and the production purpose of advancing the group's progress toward the task. On the grid (see Figure 5.5), a grid point of 1,9 would fall into the Country Club Management section, characterized by a strong attention to people and very little on task accomplishment, as the name suggests. The opposite end shows a 9,1 point, described as having a strong concern for efficiency and little for people, reminiscent of the classical management style. Likert's participative system would be in the 9,9 position.

The human relations and human resources theories developed by Maslow, Likert, McGregor, and Blake and Mouton contributed significantly to the growing management movement toward participative decision making and free-flowing communication. In our next section we will examine communication climate, a branch of study specific to organizational communication based on the field of human relations.

Communication Climate in Organizations

Any situation that leads employees to believe that their sense of justice and fair treatment is violated increases the likelihood that some employees will react with dishonest behaviour against their employer.

—*Joerg Dietz*, explaining employee responses to wage cuts[24]

Metaphors are often used in organizational studies to provide different ways of looking at a workplace. We referred to a workplace as a machine in our discussion of classical management. The machine metaphor emphasizes formal structure, efficiency, repetition, routine, and uniformity—all characteristics of a classically managed workplace. You might have heard people refer to their workplace as a "jungle," suggesting unpredictability, disorder, messiness, and coincidence. A "prison" metaphor would suggest a dead-end job with no hope of improvement or advancement.

Using the "climate" metaphor to refer to a workplace emphasizes people's feelings and social relationships. A workplace can be said to have an "atmosphere" that feels cold, meaning unfriendly and hostile, or warm, meaning pleasant and open. Workplaces could be described as stormy, unsettled, tranquil, breezy, invigorating, chilly, threatening, or stifling—the same words used to describe the weather can be used to describe how the atmosphere feels inside an organization. And, in the same way that we perceive weather characteristics as either positive or negative—sunny and calm is generally more favourable than stormy and cold—we perceive a workplace climate as having a positive or negative influence on organizational activity. A stormy workplace climate would make it more difficult to do your job effectively. Research in communication climate is concerned with

> improving superior-subordinate communication through openness, trust, and mutual respect; for establishing supportive organizational climates; and for sharing power through participatory decision making. Theorists reasoned that improving relational communication would increase job satisfaction and worker involvement thus leading to higher productivity.[25]

In the opening quote, Joerg Dietz is discussing two different employee responses to wage cuts found in a study of manufacturing plants. In the first, management fully and sensitively explained the reasons for the cuts. As a result, rates of employee theft were lower than in the second case, where management announced wage cuts with no explanation. The bottom line: mistreatment breeds mistreatment.

Origins of Communication Climate

The study of communication climate grows out of field theory studies of Kurt Lewin, who observed that "behaviour is a function of 'life spaces,' the interaction between person and environment."[26] In other words, people's experiences take on meaning in relation to the setting, or field, they occur in. The field provides a context for interpreting our experiences. So, a fight between two players on the ice during a hockey game is experienced differently than a fight around a dinner table. In the workplace, the issue of sexual harassment invites different interpretations: sexual joking may be seen by men in one way and by women in a very different way. The significance of field theory for communication climate is that it recognizes the importance of the environment in which communication is taking place. The environment is relatively stable and influences people's behaviour.

A weakness in human relations theories was that they were based on people's feelings, and it was difficult to establish a relationship between people's feelings and conditions in the workplace. In terms of the climate metaphor, sunny and warm weather will not always make people happy. Many other factors can play a role. Communication climate argues that, although climate is something that is experienced on an individual basis, people's experiences are influenced by enduring characteristics of an organization. In this way, individual feelings do reflect conditions in the workplace. The next step was to identify characteristics of a positive and productive communication climate and implement them in the organization in the hopes that they would motivate workers—an application of the functional perspective of organizations.

Characteristics of Communication Climate

Communication climate focuses on how people perceive the communication activities in their organization. Charles Redding identified the following five factors necessary for an ideal communication climate:[28]

1. *Supportiveness*—communication that is genuine, respectful, constructive, alert to the human needs of employees
2. *Participative decision making*—communication that shows meaningful contribution from bosses and workers to the decision-making process
3. *Trust, credibility, and confidence*—communication that expresses a belief in the good intentions and work practices of all members

The website for Applecore Interactive, a St. John's marketing agency, shows a green Granny Smith apple surrounded by oranges. Underneath is the company's slogan—Dare To Be Different. The vibrant work environment, with its vivid yellow, tangerine, and lime colour scheme, emphasizes to both employees and customers Applecore's commitment to providing a fresh approach to clients' communication needs.

The work style at Applecore aims to create a balance between delivering amazing results for clients—the company showcases the client "WOW" factor on their website as its ultimate goal—while striving to retain a relaxed and respectful workplace atmosphere. As founders Wilma Hartmann and Deborah Bourden say, "We were committed to creating a company that was both a great place to do business and a great place to work."

An amazing challenge was indeed the order when a prominent politician needed a website developed and live on the Internet within 36 hours. To meet the challenge, the team rallied, armed with the "No task is ever impossible" company motto. They even pulled an all-nighter, a practice Hartmann tries to avoid because it saps employees' creativity, but the job was up and running on time. The client, needless to say, experienced the "WOW" factor.

Success at Applecore relies on certain key elements. Employees share a familial atmosphere based on easy-going camaraderie and a strong dose of mutual respect. The company not only strives for superior work but also invests effort into making the world a better place. They support literacy programs, non-profit organizations such as the Association for New Canadians, and the St. John's Women's Centre. The company compensation plans recognize employees financially and personally, providing flexible staff schedules for those with child-care responsibilities. And to work out the wrinkles of a stressful day, there's a Ping-Pong table in the middle of the office. Annual awards for individual contributions, such as "Baby Duck," "Rock of the Rock," and "Sour Puss," reflect the sense of humour that connects the challenging deadlines with the rigorous details to create a balance that works.

4. *Openness*—communication that is complete, objective, honest, delivered without fear
5. *High-performance goals*—communication that will give employees an opportunity to accomplish something meaningful to them and the organization

A workplace that contains Redding's five factors will be more personally satisfying to employees and more productive as an organization. The absence of these factors will produce a climate that wastes energy on correcting misunderstandings in communication. Genuine, participative decision making is regarded as a motivating factor that brings out a feeling of involvement in workers. Research also shows that organizational commitment is strengthened when employees are satisfied with their communication experiences.

The Impact of Human Relations

The human relations movement has had a major impact on how employees communicate with each other in the workplace. The following areas are of particular significance.

Purpose of Communication
- communication develops feelings of trust in order to encourage open discussion between superiors and subordinates
- horizontal communication among coworkers has a positive effect on productivity and develops feelings of connection with the organization and its members

- through open communication, employees contribute to decision making, signifying the belief that workers are capable of effective organizational input

Types of Messages and Message Flow
- messages move in all directions, up to superiors, down to subordinates, and across to coworkers, with more emphasis on two-way communication
- messages move along formal and informal networks carrying work-related and personal messages
- greater frequency is found in face-to-face interpersonal messages, as opposed to written ones
- since a free-flowing communication style is desirable, the volume and variety of messages is high

Context of Communication
- communication takes place within the organization and within each members' psychological and emotional experiences
- communication takes place within a hierarchical structure, but it is less rigid, more compassionate, and places more importance on the human element
- an open and supportive communication climate is believed to promote productivity
- group discussions are a common method of communication

Human Relations in Today's Organization

Dave Mowat, CEO of VanCity Credit Union in British Columbia, says, "It is a fact that the higher the morale of your organization, the more money you make."[29] Mowat has credibility in both the financial and human elements of the picture, as VanCity is the country's largest credit union ($10.5 billion in assets and 16 000 employees) and was acclaimed in 2004 by *Maclean's* magazine as the best to place to work in Canada.

The study of happiness is a growing interest among economists. John Helliwell of the University of British Columbia, author of *Globalization and Well-Being*, has done research in the area of social capital, which represents the networks of trust and commitment generated through communication activities.[30] Helliwell, in collaboration with Statistics Canada, focuses specifically on the social capital of the workplace. He has identified five factors responsible for happiness in the workplace. The most important one is trust. Next comes variety of tasks, followed by the level of challenge in a job. The final two are a workplace free of conflicting demands, and having enough time to do the work. Mowat says VanCity is successful because of its ability to link economic goals with social goals.

The criteria used by *Maclean's* to pick the best workplace were similar to Helliwell's. Organizations were reviewed on their work and social atmosphere; health, financial, and family benefits; vacation and time off; employee communication; training and skills development; and community involvement.[31] VanCity's commitment to employees was recognized in the same year by the American Psychological Association for its innovative programs to create psychologically healthy workplaces—the first Canadian company to receive this distinction. According to Mike Harris, a 27-year-old employee who directs customers as they enter the branch, the main issue is trust. VanCity lets him makes decisions such as reversing a customer charge without consulting a superior. Economic rewards are also substantial: Harris's bonus was 16 percent of his salary.

Employee Engagement
The VanCity formula links employee engagement with pay successfully, but it's not easy in all companies to do this. Higher engagement levels, according to research, result in

less employee turnover and higher productivity. Finding the right formula requires the right organizational culture. CEO Dave Mowat stresses the importance of high employee engagement for organizatuions in the service industry: "We're a service business. We can have the best products in the world, but if everyone on the front line is deadpan, we wouldn't sell or keep much business. Making sure those people are engaged is super critical to us."[32]

The concept of engagement at VanCity is innovative for another reason: it extends beyond the office walls. Holders of VanCity Visa cards can donate points they earn to charity. In 2004, VanCity gave out $5.2 million in community donations, 13.5 percent of its earnings. In comparison, Canada's largest banks averaged just 1 percent of earnings in charitable donations, though that is still a fairly substantial amount considering the enormous revenues they generate. The spirit of human relations is growing in the attitudes of workers and businesses in general. Acsenta Health Ltd, creators of NutraSea, a top-selling nutritional fish oil supplement in North America, Europe, and Asia, is based in Dartmouth, Nova Scotia. Its president, Marc St. Onge, states: "What motivates me? At the top of the list are people we have helped. Being an entrepreneur was never about big cars or fancy homes (of which I have neither). It was about helping people. Great ideas don't make a lot of money; they help a lot of people. And if you do that, you may be lucky and make a lot of money too."[33] We will discuss this theme in more detail in our section on corporate social responsibility later in the book. John Restakis, of the B.C. Co-operative Association, which represents the credit unions in the province, sees social capital as a prime reason for the success of cooperatives. Cooperatives, he says, generate social capital rather than consume it.

> Traditional investor-owned firms are consumers of social capital. If we start a company and issue stock, we will consume social capital, using trust to support our financial objectives. Co-operatives, on the other hand, are generators of social capital. Because of the way they're structured, and the way people engage with each other in economic activity, they create more trust.[34]

Outside North America, cooperative economies are more widespread. Italy's Emilia Romagna region, comprising an array of social and industrial enterprises, has one of the best economies of the European Union based on a cooperative structure. And on a national scale, the government of the tiny Buddhist kingdom of Bhutan in the Himalayas has declared that happiness is more important than economic wealth. In Bhutan, as in Helliwell's studies and the example of VanCity, happiness arises from the basics of society, such as education, health, family, friends, culture, and the environment—communication networks form around these social elements and social capital becomes generated. Helliwell claims his work can establish which happiness-producing initiatives governments can promote, such as raising literacy levels in certain regions of the country.

The theories of the human relations movement represent a paradigm shift in management thinking. In sharp contrast to classical management, the human element becomes the focal point of management studies. Both human relations and human resources theories elevated the importance of human interaction, relationships, and communication activities in the organization to promote an atmosphere of trust, respect, and openness in the workplace. The most effective organizations exercised group involvement and supportive relationships to establish a participative style of organization. This represents the main difference between human relations and classical management.

Surprisingly enough, though, human relations theories share some points in common from an overall perspective with classical management. Both human relations and classical management share a common goal: to make the organization more productive. The theories of both provide methods to make managers more effective, one through efficient task design, the other through effective management of people. Both human relations and classical management also rely on the empirical methods of the social sciences to develop theoretical foundations for their principles.

Case Study

Pigeon Park Savings Company: Good Business and Social Responsibility Converge

"In the end, I saw it as a broad social opportunity instead of a tiny business opportunity," says Lydia Johnson, VanCity's VP of sales and service. She's referring to Pigeon Park Savings Company, an innovative new enterprise opened in 2004 by VanCity on Vancouver's East Hastings Street. The building was once a Scotiabank and, more recently, a pawn shop. It was a vacant mess when volunteers from VanCity, including CEO Dave Mowat, pitched in with personal effort, a $200 000 corporate donation, training to Pigeon Park employees, used furniture, and an ATM. Community activist from the Downtown Eastside and Pigeon Park manager Kerstin Stuerbecher says, "As a non-profit, we're used to people saying they want to partner with us, but we end up doing all the work. This, with all the VanCity people who showed up, was a true partnership."

Most local residents are low-income earners, many of them battling drug addiction, mental illness, and homelessness. The financial services in the neighbourhood were limited to a costly cheque-cashing business, and without proper identification to open an account or enough money to keep it going, that was the only choice for many residents. Pigeon Park Savings offers a variety of financial services at specially reduced fees. VanCity provides all technical support, administrative services, training, and security.

"A key part of our triple bottom-line approach has always been to help people thrive and prosper," says Dave Mowat, CEO of VanCity. A triple bottom-line approach focuses on the interests of the company, its employees, and the community as equal priorities. "I can think of no better example than Pigeon Park, where our focus is not solely on profit, but on fulfilling our commitment to build better communities." VanCity is responding to a growing workplace trend: not only are workers fed up with the financial scandals that have plagued corporations in the last decade, but the new generation in the workplace is seeking more than just a good paycheque. Pigeon Park's goal is to become a self-sustaining operation, providing low-cost, reliable financial services in a supportive environment that otherwise might not be available to Vancouver's Downtown Eastside residents.[35]

Tradionally, corporate reports would include environmental or social stories as dressing to make their company look good in the eyes of investors and the community. As CEO Dave Mowatt says, "In the past, the process was 'We need to get out a few environmental or health and safety statistics, so let's just package them up and ship them out in a public report.' Now they're actually engaging their operations people and management at looking at what those numbers mean. And it's starting to drive performance."[36]

According to George Greene, president of Ottawa-based consulting firm Stratos Inc., VanCity has done "a lot of work among their clientele to understand what they're looking for in terms of good, responsible behaviour, and they've integrated that into their business objectives." The trend is growing. In 2001, 35 percent of companies listed on the Toronto Stock Exchange had some sustainability information—discussion of environment, employee well-being, or social practices—in their annual reports. By 2005, the number had grown to 70 percent. The sectors with the biggest participation in sustainability efforts are financial services and utilities. The oil and gas sector shows weaker participation, with only 10 companies out of 165 listed by the Canadian Association of Petroleum Producers including discussions of sustainability in their reports. But Dave Mowatt feels a change coming. "I think the next generation—the kids coming out of colleges and universities now—are going to put pressure on all of us as employers to be much more transparent on what our strategies are and what we're doing on a variety of fronts, more than just making money."[37]

Discussion Questions

1. Discuss VanCity's reasons for opening Pigeon Park Savings. How do they fit in with human relations principles?

2. Is there a role for human resouces theories in the Pigeon Park Savings enterprise?

3. What specific theories are applicable in your discussion?

4. Discuss how VanCity links economic success with personal satisfaction.

Participation or Else

When organizations try to initiate human relations and human resources practices in organizations, the obstacles are many. Managers often are unwilling to give up their hard-won authority by consulting with their subordinates about how work should be done. Many managers are also trained to be adversaries of unions that represent their employees, further enlarging the division between managers and workers. But resistance can also come from deeply ingrained attitudes in workers. Consider the following conversation:

Manager: "How can we cut the waste on this production run?"

Worker: "That's not my job."

Manager: "Why not?"

Worker: "It just isn't."

Classroom Activity

Manager: "But I need your help. How can we have participative management if you won't participate?"

Worker: "I don't know. That's your job."

After decades of learning to follow orders, workers grew to like the arrangement where they did the working and managers did the thinking. They liked the good wages and benefits, but did not want the headaches of increased responsibility. So what is a manager to do when increased employee participation is the goal?

Form groups of from four to six people. Half the group will be managers and the other half, workers. The managers will take a few minutes to develop reasons to try to convince the workers to accept participative management practices and then present them to the workers. At the same time, workers will prepare their own arguments against adopting a participative workplace. Workers will resist until they are won over with clearly beneficial reasons and an acceptable strategy.

Glossary

Stimulus → response, p. 78
Stimulus → interpretation → response, p. 78
Hawthorne Studies, p. 79

Hierarchy of needs, p. 80
Communication climate, p. 88

Notes

1. Eric M. Eisenberg and H.L. Goodhall, Jr., *Organizational Communication: Balancing Creativity and Constraint* (Boston: Bedford/St. Martin's, 2004), 70.

2. G.C. Homans, "The Western Electric Researches," in *Management and Organization Behaviour Classics*, ed. M.T. Matteson and J.M. Ivancevich (Homewood, IL: BPI-Irwin, 1989).

3. Daniel Modaff and Sue DeWine, *Organizational Communication: Foundations, Challenges, and Misunderstandings* (Los Angeles: Roxbury Publishing, 2002).

4. Pamela Shockley-Zalabak, *Fundamentals of Organizational Communication: Knowledge, Sensitivity, Skills, Values*, 5th ed. (Boston: Allyn and Bacon, 2002).

5. Mary Parker Follett, *Creative Experience* (New York: Longman Green and Co., 1924; repr., Peter Owen, 1951), xii-xiii.

6. Ibid.

7. Gary L. Kreps, *Organizational Communication Theory and Practice*, 2nd ed. (New York: Longman, 1990).

8. Abraham Maslow, *Motivation and Personality* (New York, Harper and Row, 1954).

9. Thomas E. Harris, *Applied Organizational Communication, Perspectives Principles, and Pragmatics* (Hillsdale, NJ: Lawrence Erlbaum Associates, Publishers, 1993), 50.

10. Peggy Yuhas Byers, *Organizational Communication Theory and Practice* (Boston: Allyn and Bacon, 1997).

11. Jeff Buckstein, "In praise of praise in the workplace," *The Globe and Mail*, June 15, 2005, C1.

12. Ibid.

13. Ibid.

14. Judith Timson, "Try thank you, instead of spank you," *The Globe and Mail*, June 15, 2005, C5.

15. Buckstein, "In praise of praise."

16. Kreps, *Organizational Communication*, 85.

17. David Olive, "Say this for Radler—he's got nerve." *The Toronto Star*, August 23, 2005, D1.

18. Douglas McGregor, *The Human Side of Enterprise*, 2nd ed. (Boston: New York: McGraw-Hill, 1960), 33–34.

19. Ibid.

20. Rensis Likert, *New Patterns of Management* (New York: McGraw-Hill, 1961); Rensis Likert, *The Human Organization* (New York, McGraw-Hill, 1967)

21. R.E. Miles, "Human Relations of Human Resources," *Harvard Business Review* 43 (1965): 151.

22. Ibid.

23. Robert Blake and Anne Adams McCanse, from *Leadership Dilemmas—Grid Solutions*, The Leadership Grid Figure, formerly The Managerial Grid Figure by Robert Blake and Jane S. Mouton (Houston: Gulf Publishing Company, 1964), 29–30.

24. Randy Ray, "Truth about time theft," *The Globe and Mail*, June 22, 2005, C1.

25. Nancy A. Euske and Karlene H. Roberts, "Evolving Perspectives in Organization Theory: Communication Implications," in *Handbook of Organizational Communication*, eds. Fredric M. Jablin, Linda L. Putnam, Karlene H. Roberts, and Lyman W. Porter (Newbury Park, CA: Sage, 1987), 45.

26. Raymond L. Falcione, Lyle Sussman, and Richard P. Herden, "Communication Climate in Organizations," in *Handbook of Organizational Communication*, eds. Fredric M. Jablin, Linda L. Putnam, Karlene H. Roberts, and Lyman W. Porter (Newbury Park, CA: Sage, 1987), 195.

27. Ann James, "Core Strength," *Atlantic Business Magazine*, August 31, 2005, http://www.atlanticbusinessmagazine.com/more.php?id=A78_0_1_0_C-40k (accessed November 12, 2005).

28. Charles Redding, *Communication within the Organization: An Interpretive Review of Theory and Research* (New York: Industrial Communication Council, 1972).

29. Jill Lambert, "The Economics of Happiness," *Canadian Business*, Summer 2005, 184–187.

30. Ibid.

31. "Best Places to work in Canada," *Maclean's*, October 11, 2004, http://www.macleans.ca/top100/ (accessed June 16, 2005).

32. Ibid.

33. Roynat Capital, "A Day in the Life," *National Post*, January 9, 2006, G3.

34. Lambert, "The Economics of Happiness," 187.

35. Case Study adapted from Pigeon Park Savings story on VanCity website, https://www.VanCity.com/MyCommunity/CommunityInvestment/AccesstoFinancialServices/PigeonParkSavings/ (accessed June 15, 2005).

36. Janet McFarland, "Are you making yourself accountable?," *The Globe and Mail*, April 20, 2006, B12.

37. Ibid.

Contemporary Approaches

6

Chapter Six

Communication and Systems Theory

It is fearfully simple: The incomplete individual cannot stand on his own, cannot make sense by himself. He is a part and not a self-sufficient whole. He can make sense, have a purpose, and seem useful when he becomes a part of a functioning whole.

—*Eric Hoffer*, The True Believer[1]

The quantum world has demolished the concept of the unconnected individual.

—*Margaret Wheatley*, Leadership and the New Science[2]

Learning Objectives

- Review the origins and characteristics of systems theory

- Compare systems theory to classical and human relations approaches to organizational communication

- Explore the importance of systems theory for understanding communication in organizations

- Analyze the importance of communication and the concept of environment in systems theory

- Examine contemporary applications of systems theory in the workplace, focusing on learning and self-renewing organizations

What Is the Systems Perspective?

This chapter on systems theory takes us in a new direction in organizational communication, one that focuses on the patterns of communication that are formed in organizations. Let's quickly review classical management and human relations approaches to appreciate the full impact of this change in direction.

Classical management emphasized structure and order, above all. The rapid and unexpected changes arising from the Industrial Revolution caused chaos in the workplace, and a rationally organized workplace was the solution. Scientific principles were applied from the micro level of the superior–subordinate relationship, Fredrick Taylor's Scientific Management, which focused on the isolated routines of individual operations; to the macro level, the administrative and bureaucratic theories of Henri Fayol and Max Weber, which examined ways of ordering the activities of the overall organization. From top to bottom, structure was supreme. Finding the best possible system of organizing was the objective.

Human relations, in an effort to counteract the mechanical and impersonal approaches of classical management, concentrated on the psychological and emotional processes of each unique individual. It was discovered that workers could be motivated through personal involvement in the workplace. Both approaches, though, had more in common than it would first appear. William Neher describes their similarities this way:

> ... [T]hey both characterized the organization as having a single goal or purpose, determined by the "owners" or management; they both emphasized the rational and scientific nature of management; they both accepted the idea that the purpose of organizational theories was to develop principles for more effective administration that could be generalized and applied to any kind of human organization.[3]

Simply put, though their areas of concern were different, both classical and human relations approaches assumed that all organizations had a single goal, the one held by the owners. They both employed scientific methods to achieve that goal. Communication served the functional purpose of assisting with the achievement of organizational goals.

Systems theory takes a different route: instead of prescribing structures and behaviours that will make the organization more effective, systems theory provides a framework for analyzing and understanding an organization. Instead of focusing on individuals and their specialized tasks, systems theory examines the totality of interlocking relationships that makes up the organization. Systems theory holds that there is not only one reason why things happen, as in classical management, but many, because organizational systems are complex structures.

Furthermore, a systems approach brings a new entity into the discussion—the outside environment. For the first time, the environment of an organization is seen as playing a significant role in shaping the organization. And what makes a systems approach important for organizational communication is that, in systems theory, communication activity begins to play an increasingly central role in organizational achievement.

In this chapter, we will discuss the approach to organizational communication known as systems theory. We will end by highlighting some intriguing contemporary outcomes of the systems approach to organizational communication.

The Systems Theory Approach

In Chapter 4, we used the "machine" metaphor to describe classical management. Workers were cogs that had specific and repetitive functions in the large machine of the organization. Systems theory uses a different metaphor: an organization is a "living organism," and workers are small organisms within the larger whole. In terms of the environment, the organization becomes a smaller organism or sub-system within the environment, which encompasses many other organizations, and so on. All systems are sub-systems of a larger system. An organization *is* an environment for its members, and it also exists *within* a larger environment made up of its business, social, and political communities. We will see in the discussion of contemporary approaches later in the chapter that systems theory can also include emotional and psychological systems of meaning. In human relationships, in organizational activity, and in individual thinking processes, everything is understood in patterns of meaning. System theory, then, focuses on the following two aspects of an organization: the relationships among the sub-systems of the organization and the relationship of the organization with its environment. Let's start with the relationships within organizations.

The groups that form an organization become a system when they process information together, since that is how they interact. Systems in organizations are defined by their patterns of interaction, or by the relationships they create through information processing. For a simple example of a *system*, let's take the human body. It is made up of numerous interrelated sub-systems, such as the circulatory system, the nervous system, and the respiratory system, all of which must coordinate their functions so that the whole body operates effectively. If one system breaks down, the others will be unable to function normally and may eventually break down themselves. A car is another example of a system, which is made up of many sub-systems. Let's say the cooling system on a car stops working because of a broken water pump. The warning lights on the instrument panel will flash, indicating that the engine is starting to overheat and it is time to turn the car off. Once a new water pump is installed, the system should function normally again. The basic advantage of systems structures is the concept of wholeness, which simply means that an effective system is more than the sum of its parts. For example, a football team working as a unit functions better than 12 unorganized football players. In any group of people—a family, a business, a planet—it is the types of relationships that determine whether they are working separately or together as a whole. Systems theory provides ways of analyzing organizations to determine how effectively all the parts are working together.

The other distinguishing feature of systems theory is the emphasis on an organization's relationship with its environment. The environment was never an issue with the classical and human relations approaches because they both dealt with the fixed individual qualities of their workers and particular working conditions within the boundaries of the organization. But all systems exist within an environment that affects them in many ways. For instance, the human body reacts to changes in temperature by sweating when hot or shaking when cold. In the same way, poor sales or negative customer feedback may cause a business to change its strategy. Both examples involve interaction between a system and its environment.

Open and Closed Systems

What distinguishes a system that is working as a whole from one that is working as a collection of separate units? When an organization interacts with its environment by receiving outside information, it is acting like an *open system*. An effective and efficient organization is capable of processing information from the environment quickly, indicating a large degree of openness to the environment. The degree of openness is measured by the organization's ability to receive and make meaningful the *feedback* it is receiving from the environment. If a business's sales are down, it can use information that comes into the system as feedback to restore desired sales levels. If salespeople are not working hard enough, a more aggressive sales approach may be needed. If, however, customers are turning to the competition, a product makeover may be required.

To stay alive, Winnipeg-based Western Glove Works has had to reduce its work force from 1200 to 250 and focus its energy on design and brand promotion. Most of its manufacturing jobs have been outsourced to plants in China, Bangladesh, Mexico, and Macau. The company is responding to the lifting of 40-year-old import quotas imposed by the World Trade Organization on countries such as China and India. It was expected that China's stake in the global textile market would increase to 50 percent from 17 percent in 2003. Says Bob Kirke, executive director of the Canadian Apparel Foundation, "The bottom line is I regard this as inevitable. The rules of the game have changed." To adapt, the industry has refocused its energy on designing, marketing, and merchandising. Utex, a Montreal-based suit maker, closed its only Canadian factory in Victoriaville in 2002 and shipped its manufacturing to foreign plants when it became too expensive to remain in Canada. Another company,

Peerless Clothing Co. of Montreal, managed to keep jobs in Canada by improving the quality of its product. Elliot Liftson, vice-chairman of Peerless, says Canadian companies can maintain low costs and still make higher-quality products than foreign companies. Mr. Silver of Western Glove Works says Canadian clothing makers should now focus on brand building and "made-in-Canada" designs: "The last thing we want to do now is lose our design talent, because those are the creators of the product."

Discussion Questions

1. What are the key sources of feedback in the above case for the companies involved?
2. How have the companies applied open systems concepts successfully or unsuccessfully?
3. Discuss your own experiences in organizations in terms of systems concepts.

Today's business environment has been described as turbulent, meaning that it changes rapidly. To keep up, organizations need to develop open relationships with their environment and quick information-processing systems for faster decision making. So, in contrast to the classical approach, which responds to a turbulent environment with increased structure and more specialized training, and the human relations approach, which responds to change by coping with its psychological and emotional effects, the systems approach deals with change by examining an organization's systems to identify the places where effective information processing and interaction with the environment is not taking place—or, in other words, where the characteristics of a closed system are identified.

A *closed system* is the opposite of an open system, in that it fails "to recognize fully the dependence of organizations on inputs from their environment."[5] Organizations rely on their environments to supply them with resources so they can continue functioning. A closed system, then, would exhaust its resources and be unable to sustain itself. An organism without food would die; a business operating as a closed system would be trampled by its competitors. Imagine the numerous external resources a large organization such as Rona Home Renovations needs to interact with: customers and suppliers, staff recruitment, property contracts, government affairs, equipment, community relations, and competition from the U.S. The Home Depot is already established in the country; and Lowe's, another home-renovation giant from south of the border, is already building stores in Canada. For a business, all this information is essential for survival, especially in today's deregulated economies. A systems approach, then, shows us that an organization's effectiveness depends on the coordination of the entire enterprise. The interests of all stakeholders must be included in an organization's strategic plan to assure continued success. The strong emphasis on shareholder value in business today is an example of putting too much weight on one input at the expense of others. In a discussion of the greatest shortcomings of today's orgnizations, Henry Mintzberg, professor of Management at McGill University, states:

> [Shareholder value is] a philosophy of forgetting any other stakeholders, as if no one else exists other than the shareholders. I think that will have huge negative consequences for business.... The sooner we get rid of it—not the notion of fair return for shareholders, but the notion that there are shareholders and no one else—the sooner we'll be back on track.[6]

Origins of Systems Theory

A biologist, Ludwig Von Bertalanffy, is credited with the development of general systems theory, which applies the properties of living organisms to social phenomena. The term "general systems theory" describes the countless applications that can be encompassed by this model, from biology and chemistry, to economics and sociology, to engineering and physics, representing a single sets of concepts that can be applied across a variety of sciences. As Katz and Kahn state, "Methods of handling information overload, boundary crossing, subsystem coding, feedback, the transactions of input, throughput, and output, are proposed as characteristics of all 'living things.'"[7] Systems theory, then, sees organizations as social systems. Where classical and human relations approaches were seen as lacking because of their incomplete view of organizations, systems theory is capable of revealing the complex interconnected nature of the modern organization based on its communication patterns.

But an interesting thing occurs as we move from biology to human communication. Though human beings are highly social creatures, our social systems operate differently than biological systems. We continually share our views of the world, but no two people have identical ones. So, in the process of transferring information from person to person through the use of words, some ambiguity of meaning will always exist. As Eisenberg and Goodhall state, "the ambiguity of language makes the interdependencies between members of a social system . . . looser than those found in biology or those that connect a car."[8]

The process of communication, as stated in Chapter 2, involves the exchange of information that creates new realities between people. Open systems are called dynamic because, as new information constantly flows in, the system offers new ways of understanding the relationships within it and in the overall organization. As systems adapt to new information, old established ways of doing things are transformed into new ways of doing things. And thus, new information turns order into disorder, which through communication becomes a new order. Living systems have the potential for self-organization and self-renewal, and the disorder that is a natural part of the communication process is also an essential part of the renewal process. The particular advantage of living systems for self-renewal is that all parts of the system contain knowledge that contributes to its organizing activities—a concept known as distributed intelligence. The body's nervous system, for instance, is a network of information constantly adapting to changing conditions, both guiding an individual toward goal achievement and responding to new information along the way. If a person were built according to the classical structure, intelligence would be centralized in the brain, with very little information coming in to warn it of obstacles in its path. The experience would be similar to watching robots stumbling around and bumping into things, saying "I am not programmed for this." Distributed intelligence gives a person or an organization the ability to learn from its environment.

Jumping to a larger picture for a moment, we can look at distributed intelligence on a global scale. The concept that we are all connected by information is central to Marshall McLuhan's concept of the "global village." Instant electronic communication, especially in terms of the Internet, has expanded what once characterized social groups

An excellent example of turbulence in the marketplace is the world petroleum industry of the mid-2000s. As oil companies, producers, and countries scramble to maintain balance between supply and demand, new alliances and new ways of doing business are forming, and a new global business mindset is developing. Calgary-born David Lyons, chairman of Pan-Ocean Energy Corp and EastCoast Energy Inc., recently sold oil assets in Western Canada and began exploring in Gabon, Africa, and Tanzania. Pan-Ocean is based in London, England, and EastCoast, in Dar es Salaam. Both trade on the Toronto Stock Exchange. Why the move to London? For one thing they can tap into more globally minded energy investors. In fact, the Calgary-to-London bridge is quickly taking over Calgary's historic link with the U.S. oil capital, Houston. Mid-sized companies like Pan-Ocean and many others are joining the big players with U.K. operations such as Petro-Canada, Nexen Inc., and Talisman. According to David Lyons, Alberta's entrepreneurial culture helps them make it in on the world stage because it breeds "adventurous folks" who "want to be in the jungle going up the river with the wind in their hair. They want to see the crocodiles sloshing off the banks and the hippos in the next corner, and that gives them a charge." In terms of investment risk, U.S. oil companies are more insular, preferring big projects with quick payoffs within the North American region, while European investors are more patient and long-term focused. Many Canadian companies would not have found the same levels of financial support at home, with Canadian investors perhaps not comfortable with high-risk junior ventures. Says Robert Welty, CEO of Sterling, another Calgary oil venture with operations in the U.K., "One thing about Europeans is that they understand the world better than we do in Canada, and countries that we don't know about or are skeptical about, they deal with everyday." Three of the four super major oil companies are European based—BP PLC, Royal Dutch/Shell Group, and Total SA—while one is U.S. based—Exxon-Mobil Corp.

on a small, tribal scale to a global scale. The electronic communication networks that form a web around the earth can be seen as the nervous system of the planet. Time becomes instant, space is no longer a barrier, and cultural boundaries are diminished. In terms of ambiguity, the possibilities are endless, as we are dealing not only with the fuzziness of words but with many different languages. The enormous disorder created by this vast open system is a challenge for our electronic media agencies as they attempt to explain our world for us, and for us also as we develop new ways of understanding our roles within the numerous sub-systems of the "global information society." Economic globalization has put this information system to good use by allowing corporations, such as oil companies, to create knowledge networks that facilitate global business objectives.

Characteristics of Systems Theory

The following characteristics are common to all social systems. In this chapter, we are focusing more on open systems as opposed to closed ones, since openness is the desirable state for most business organizations. It is a premise of systems theory that organizations cannot function effectively without inputs from the environment.

Input–Throughput–Output
Open systems import information from their environment. A well-functioning organization depends on the continuous *input* of information from the external environment.

A social structure that is self-contained will deteriorate from lack of stimulation. In the *throughput* stage, open systems transform the energy or information they receive from the environment in ways that suit the purpose of the organization. Pulp and paper companies transform logs into newsprint. A musician transforms ideas, feelings, and experiences into music. A college or university transforms uneducated students into educated ones. *Outputs* represent a product or service that is exported back into the environment after being transformed by an open system. Skilled and knowledgeable students are the outputs of educational institutions.

Feedback, Entropy, and Balance

Inputs from the environment provide information, or feedback, about how the organization is performing. Based on these inputs, an organization can make adjustments to suit environmental conditions. For instance, if a company's sales go up, production will have to increase to meet demand. The increased demand is a message from the marketplace to increase production, and the sales people are the channels the messages travel along—they are the *boundary spanners*.

The concept of *entropy* describes the process of a system's energy running down and ceasing to exist—in other words, the system loses its *differentiation* from its environment. Take a hot bowl of soup, for example. If left sitting, the soup will eventually cool down to the match the temperature in the room. All systems naturally move toward *equilibrium*. It is the function of feedback to reverse the process of entropy by bringing new energy into the system. So, if the bowl of soup were heated up, it would regain its differentiation from its environment.

Through feedback, a balance of inputs and outputs is achieved, representing the ideal state of organizational performance. An excess of inputs would be unwieldy and confusing, while a shortage of inputs would lower production levels. To survive, then, open systems must have *negative entropy*—constant inputs from the environment that allow a system to adapt and energize itself.

Equivocality

Karl Weick, author of *Sensemaking in Organizations*, proposes that the main function of organizing is to reduce equivocality.[10] Inputs entering the organization are interpreted in different ways by people inside the organization, creating uncertainty and ambiguity. This process is common to all communication activity, since we all experience the world from our own unique perspectives. Organizations make sense of uncertainties and ambiguities in the same ways that individuals do—by communicating. So equivocality is reduced as people make sense of and establish common meanings for information coming in from the environment. Organizations that exist in highly complex environments, which is most organizations today, require equally complex sense-making systems in the throughput stage to process information efficiently enough to maintain an effective balance of inputs and outputs. As Gareth Morgan states, "the internal regulatory mechanisms of a system must be as diverse as the environment with which it is trying to deal."[11] This is called *requisite variety*. It proposes that simple answers are suitable only for simple problems. You wouldn't hold a meeting to decide which types of sandwiches to serve for lunch at a business meeting. For complex problems, such as dealing with budget cuts or planning product changes, a comprehensive analysis of all inputs would be necessary to make a good decision.

On an interpersonal level, relationships also exist on a continuum of simple and complex situations. To resolve problems, we often send flowers or a bottle of wine to a loved one. That's usually fine for a simple misunderstanding. If the problem is complex, the flowers need to be followed up with discussion. In this way a new shared understanding of the situation is created and the relationship experiences growth.

There is a parallel here to organizations. The tendency in business is often to avoid dwelling on problems. After a breakdown, we try to bury it and move on as quickly as possible. The discussion and reflection—the problem solving and learning part—is skipped over. So, organizations that do not support learning and growth make the same mistakes over and over. They are always treating complex situations with simplistic problem-solving methods.

Equifinality

There are many ways to achieve an ideal balance of inputs and outputs. If you are cold, you can have a warm drink, move closer to a source of heat, cover yourself with a blanket, or become physically active. In terms of the workplace, the principle of *equifinality* states that the same goals can be reached in a number of ways. A government's financial deficit, for instance, can be remedied in various ways: cutting spending, raising taxes, reducing the work force, selling assets, or simply borrowing more money. The measures an organization chooses to achieve its goals depends on the conditions it is operating in—economic, social, political, or technological. In today's political climate, cutting and reducing spending are popular measures at all levels of government for dealing with deficits.

Many companies give workers a high degree of latitude when it comes to accomplishing their tasks without interference from managers. At WestJet Airlines of Calgary, for instance, flight attendants are instructed to serve customers in a caring, positive, and cheerful manner. How they do that is left up to them, based on a philosophy of trust that runs throughout the company. As CEO Clive Beddoe says, "Workers have pride in what they do because they are the ones making the decisions about what they are doing and how they are doing it. They are no longer just functionaries. They actually take ownership of their jobs."[12]

Thus, the methods organizations decide to use are contingent, or dependent, on various factors in the environment. The implication for organizational communication is that an unpredictable and rapidly changing environment requires distributed styles of leadership, greater interpersonal communication, and a more integrated structure than stable and familiar environments. The highlighted article, "Oil Firms Tighten U.K. Ties," illustrates the diversity of environments and conditions across companies and geographic regions. By clarifying the importance of environmental inputs, equifinality offers a sharp contrast to the "one best way" principle of classical management, which proposed that ideal methods and strategies for accomplishing a work task can be developed without considering external conditions, or, in other words, within a closed system. While it is true that sports coaches teach the one best way to shoot a puck or catch a baseball, these methods apply only under fixed and known conditions. Talented players realize there are multiple methods for success.

Systems Theory and Organizational Communication

While classical management emphasized hierarchical structure and a machine-like style of work, and human relations addressed human needs and feelings, open systems theory focuses on the processes of communication in an organization. The potential of open systems lies in their ability to recognize the importance of inputs from the environment. But an open system must also be selective about the information it imports, since a totally open system would have no differentiation from its environment, and thus would cease to exist. An internal arrangement of systems must be developed for effective decision making about which inputs to focus on. In this way an organization can become knowledgeable about fluctuating business conditions.

The two main areas in which systems theory plays a role in organizational communication are the organization's internal communication systems and organizational–environmental interaction. Katz and Kahn break these activities down into five sub-systems.[13] The first three are generally inwardly directed and concerned with keeping the organization functioning normally. The fourth is externally directed and concerned with monitoring and forecasting. The fifth covers management activity.

1. *Production system*—the organization's main operation
2. *Supportive systems*—purchasing, marketing, sales
3. *Maintenance systems*—technical support, human resources
4. *Adaptive systems*—customer service, market research, corporate
5. *Managerial systems*—coordination and control of all sub-systems

The Impact of Systems Theory

Overall, systems theory sees communication as serving a central purpose in organizations, both in terms of internal communication systems and interaction with the environment. Let's turn now to the way systems theory can be applied to communication in organizations.

Purposes of Communication

- Systems theory emphasizes the flow of information and feedback from the environment into the organization. Communication is the activity by which this information is processed. A major purpose of organizational communication, then, is developing effective information-processing systems. A system operating at its optimum would have maximum output in return for minimum input.
- An efficiently running organization is able to deal with the uncertainties of a chaotic environment. Information load represents the amount of decision making required to process incoming information. A turbulent environment would increase an organization's information load. The communication goal of the organization would be to design information-processing systems that would not result in information overload.
- Communication is to accomplish goals in the five areas discussed above: production, support, maintenance, adaptation, and management.
- Boundary spanners are links between systems. They provide connections between internal systems and between the organization and its environment. Sales and customer service staff often perform this function.
- The context is especially important in systems theory, since it contains the unique and relevant information for the organization.

Types of Messages and Message Flow

- An organization is made up of systems of interdependent relationships. Messages flow along recurring patterns of interaction that connect the systems of the entire organization.
- An organization's structure is based on social relationships, since the processing of information requires recurring human interactions.
- These recurring human interactions represent the channels of communication in an organization.
- Systems theory does not focus on the content of messages or the mediums used to deliver them, such as face to face, memos and reports, electronic media, meetings, and so forth.

- Effective flow of messages between systems fulfills the need to integrate the activities of an organization—to create a recurring structure. Messages also serve the contrary function of differentiation—to create growth by enabling the organization to adapt to changes in the environment, thereby changing its structure.

Contingency Theory

Contingency theory proposes that the methods organizations decide to use to achieve their goals are contingent, or dependent, on various factors in the environment. It's a situational approach to management. Contingency theory includes numerous applications of systems concepts to organizations. In this section we will review some of the major concepts in this area.

Mechanistic and Organic Systems

Burns and Stalker, in their study of English industrial companies, identified two types of organizations: the *mechanistic* and the *organic*. They believed that the appropriate management style depends on factors in the company's environment. A stable, predictable environment with a slow rate of change is suited to a mechanistic style of management, much like the classical bureaucratic structure discussed earlier. A turbulent environment, having a rapid rate of change, is most suited to an organic system of management, featuring greater internal communication, more horizontal than vertical message flow, and a work style based on tasks and knowledge rather than rules and hierarchy.[14]

Centralized and Decentralized Structures

Lawrence and Lorsch proposed an information flow model based on stable and changing environments.[15] They focused on two concepts: integration and differentiation. Organizations can operate on a task-oriented basis using established rules and a chain-of-command structure when the environment is stable. This represents a centralized organizational structure that would have a high degree of *integration*—tasks are routine and repetitive. On the other hand, uncertain environments require greater information flow and more complex systems for dealing with them. A decentralized structure built on a high degree of differentiation increases interaction with the environment. In a complex environment, organizations have more *differentiation*—tasks are more specialized and non-routine. It requires a free-flowing communication style built on strong interpersonal relationships, flexible rules, and self-direction. These concepts are related to *loose coupling* (decentralized and differentiated structure) and *tight coupling* (centralized and integrated structure).

New Systems Approaches

Intriguing and comprehensive perspectives in systems theory have been developed recently that challenge our normal ways of experiencing and understanding not only organizations but the world itself. In this section we will review some of them, in particular the "new science" of Margaret Wheatley, Gareth Morgan's concept of autopoiesis, Karl Weick's sense-making model, and the learning organization of Peter Senge.

The New Science—Margaret Wheatley

> The science of self-organizing systems says that if you want order you need a free flow of information, because information is what living systems use to transform themselves.[16]

Margaret Wheatley applies concepts from quantum physics, self-organizing systems, and chaos theory to explain how systems adapt to change and transform themselves to create new internal and external relationships.[17] The quantum world-view proposes a relational universe—nothing material exists except in terms of its relationships with other people or things. And relationships are continually shifting, looping here and there. To survive in a quantum world, we will need to focus on process rather than task, build relationships, nurture growth, have excellent communication and listening skills, and be a team player rather than an individual. Systems theory and quantum perspectives have led to the view of organizations as webs of relationships.

Traditional systems theory helps us to understand how complex, interactive systems work, but what happens when things fall apart? According to Wheatley, the result is chaos. The role of chaos is twofold: it represents the final stage as a system moves away from order, and it is also the necessary transformation stage to the next system of order. Disorder becomes the source of new order. Chaos in this sense is not the opposite of order, only a different kind of order. Wheatley describes it this way:

> That's what I call chaos, when people move into such deep confusion that they let go of their present conceptions of how to solve a problem. When they move into that place of not knowing, and stay there for a while, what happens is that the process of "self-organization" kicks in.[18]

Interestingly enough, the above quote may describe the way students feel when they are preparing to write an essay. As you shuffle through the mess of notes, books, and Internet sites on your desk, you gradually, sometimes painfully, move through the place of "confusion and not knowing" toward a place where ideas start connecting—and a new system begins to take shape.

What makes a system constantly return to a state of order so that a new system can emerge? As everything is falling into confusion and disorder, a *strange attractor* comes into play. Wheatley says this happens as you watch the system develop over time and begin to notice the order that emerges out of the chaos. Some of life's more intense experiences, such as births and deaths in the family, marriages and divorces, or personal successes or failures, can cause extreme joy or grief, during which time a new way of seeing yourself develops. What causes it to happen? Numerous answers have been suggested: a need to create meaning of an event, to express a sense of purpose, to align self-perceptions with new realities. Workplaces with a strong sense of purpose possess a built-in capability to serve as a strange attractor and pull the system into a new form. These organizations have the following characteristics:[19]

- A climate of trust where employees can move and communicate freely
- Energy and creativity are encouraged
- Individuality is valued, promoting the concept of equifinality
- Employees develop fluid, complex networks of communication
- Organization takes place around relationships and mutually evolving identities, rather than policies and procedures

Chaos, then, according to Wheatley, is a positive, potentially generative, self-organizing force in an organization: "Self-organizing systems have the capacity to create for themselves the aspects of organization that we thought leaders had to provide. Self-organizing systems create structures and pathways, networks of communication, values and meaning."[20]

Our usual reactions to chaos depict it as unwanted. When it erupts, we try to shut it down and return to our former comfort level, instead of staying with the discomfort long enough to realize that the old model for organizing doesn't work any more and a new one is necessary. The result of this response is that information flow is shut down at a time when it is most critically needed. The idea of chaos generating order seems like a paradox. This is a product of old ways of thinking. New science proposes that you can have order without control and that a state of chaos does not mean lack of control. In fact, the whole notion of control becomes obsolete except as a facilitating function. Order arises through connections and communication; it is not imposed through direction and control.

An intriguing example of self-regulation is found on the streets of some European countries that have attempted to solve traffic problems with solutions bordering on sheer anarchy. Several German, Dutch, and Danish cities have created "naked streets" by removing traffic lights and stop signs and leaving drivers and pedestrians to coordinate their journeys by themselves.[21] Those who expected chaos and carnage were disappointed. Accidents and fatalities actually dropped. How did people's travelling behaviours change? Drivers and pedestrians began making eye contact to negotiate their way. They actively participated in the bump and flow of traffic activity. They adapted by matching the increased complexity in the environment with equally complex information-processing methods. People were forced to pay greater attention to their surroundings and to become responsible for their movements instead of simply obeying road signs. They became more open to new information and relationships, creating a stronger sense of community. A parallel experience would be a power blackout where the normal social controls systems are removed. During the great northeastern blackout in the summer of 2003, social self-regulation kicked in and took surprisingly good care of the situation.

Images of Organization—Gareth Morgan

In Chapter 3 we used Gareth Morgan's example of strategic termites from his book *Imaginization* to introduce the concept of organizational activity. To answer the question of how the termites direct and coordinate their architectural activity, he suggests that in the termite colony order emerges out of chaos through the process of self-organization. He states, "The 'masterpiece' evolves from random, chaotic activities guided by what seems to be an overall sense of purpose and direction, but in an open-ended manner."[22] This explanation is similar to Wheatley's ideas about order arising out of chaos, discussed above.

Gareth Morgan's influential book *Images of Organization* advances systems thinking by challenging the traditional notion that change originates in the environment. He abandons the simple and linear input-throughput-output process of an organization interacting with its environment in favour of a more fluid, ever-changing, and complex model. The difference is substantial—comparable to the difference between the mechanical sender–message–receiver communication model of Shannon and Weaver and the interactive, multidimensional model more common today, which shows communication to be a continuously evolving process of meaning construction, relationship building, and identity creation.

In place of the standard systems model, which states that an organization is constantly transforming inputs into outputs as a way of enabling its survival, Morgan offers the theory of *autopoiesis* (pronounced "auto-po-E-sis"). The term comes from two Greek words—*auto* meaning "self," and *poiesis* meaning "creation." The theory, credited to Chilean scientists Humberto Maturana and Francisco Varela, suggests that you cannot accurately describe how systems change if you draw distinctions between systems and their environments. Hence, all systems are closed. Yet, they are in constant, circular interaction with other systems. In fact, systems never end—they form a closed loop of interaction. Morgan uses the example of a beehive containing bees in constant interaction with the community of bees. In turn, the bee community interacts with other communities along the ecological chain. A change in one system will change the whole ecology. It's a matter of perspective—one system is another system's environment. In effect, there are no environments, just systems that are interconnected. What represents a person's or an organization's environment is simply numerous other systems. As Morgan states, "an understanding of the autopoietic nature of systems requires that we understand how each element simultaneously combines the maintenance of itself with the maintenance of others."[23]

Earlier in this chapter we were promoting the advantages of seeing organizations as open systems that have separate, though interdependent, environments. Autopoiesis proposes a shift in perspective. A system "interacts with its environment in a way that facilitates its own self-production, and in this sense we can see that its environment is really a part of itself."[24] What is it producing? It is producing itself, in a process of self-renewal. The theory of autopoiesis highlights the way the entire system of interactions continuously creates its own future. According to Morgan, the theory has several important implications for organizations:

1. Organizations are continually involved in the creation of self-identity in relation to the other systems in their environment.

2. Many problems organizations encounter with their environments are directly related to the identity they are trying to create and maintain.

3. The factors that shape an organization's self-identity must be examined to explain the changes occurring in the organization.

The Enacted Environment—Karl Weick

LIES THAT PREVIEW TRUTH—Why is it so hard to tell the truth? Because more often than not the truth is meagre and stale. By lying, we, as it were, reform the world—arrange things as we would like them to be. And often indeed the lie is a preview of a new truth.

—*Eric Hoffer*, Harper's[25]

Karl Weick takes the position that organizations are more proactive in creating their environments than reactive to them, as was the case with the earlier, more passive perspective of traditional open systems theory. For Weick, environments exist inside the individual minds of people in an organization. How do organizations deal with the resulting concoction of meanings? Through *equivocality reduction*. This involves using communication to make sense of the uncertainties and ambiguities in the environment.

Three parts—enactment, selection, and retention—make up Weick's model of organizing. *Enactment* is when people experience, interpret, and give meaning to their environments through subjective perceptions. Once an environment is enacted, the process of collective sense making, or *selection*, begins, as people determine which is the best meaning among numerous interpretations. In the *retention* stage, useful and effective collective meanings are preserved for future use. Weick says, "These organizing acts are acts of invention rather then acts of discovery, they involve a superimposed order, rather than underlying order, and they are based on the assumption that cognition follows the trail of action."[26]

Weick uses the example of playing charades to illustrate the process of enacting your environment. The person acting out the hidden words knows what he has enacted only after he hears the observer's guesses.

Does Winning Create Team Unity or Is Passionate Team Cohesion the Recipe for Success?[27]

Karl Weick describes organizational systems as loosely and tightly coupled.[28] Tightly coupled systems are mechanistic, linear, cohesive, and highly interdependent. Like a line of dominoes, if one falls, they all fall. Loosely coupled systems, on the other hand, are organic, non-linear, autonomous, and only partly interdependent. Put more simply, tightly coupled systems are centralized, while loosely coupled systems are decentralized. So, which type of system would form the best baseball team?

In 2006, a tightly coupled team, the Lethbridge Trailblazers, won the World Series of Fastball. They became known for energetic displays of team spirit that at times bordered on sheer idiocy, but nevertheless created a strong team cohesion that they were all proud of and that became the character of the team. You never knew what would happen next. Their sense of interdependence came from their shared ways of being goofy. And since they kept winning, they didn't bother adopting a more professional playing style. So it was surprising when Johnny Makluski, a team spark plug, was traded to their recent playoff rivals, the Thunder Bay Lakers, in the following off season. The Lakers, in contrast, have typically been a team of individuals, usually big name stars, which they have been able to afford because of their winning record. As a rule, they mind their own business, letting individual players take care of their own concerns. When it comes to mistakes, they are held personally accountable. They don't throw pies in each other's faces when being interviewed by the media like the Trailblazers do. Which team system is better?

Research shows that both types can achieve success in their own ways. A looser system like the Lakers' seems to have more advantages when it comes to winning: decentralized groups like the Lakers are more resilient to outside criticism and internal disagreements; and problems that arise in close-knit groups such as the Trailblazers have a stronger collective impact on the team.[29] A loose atmosphere is fun, but the strongest factor in creating team unity is a winning performance. Laker coach Joe Tortelli says, "Look, I was on teams in Winnipeg and Milwaukee, we would go out 10 or 12 of us at a time, but we finished third or fourth. We got along, we liked each other, all that stuff, but all that meant is you weren't alone a lot."

The concept of *retrospective sense making* illustrates one of Weick's many intriguing insights: the idea that sense follows action. You may notice that in Weick's three-part organizing model, people decide what an event means after it is completed. So, decision making is a retrospective process—people act first, then they interpret and give meaning to their actions.

The aspect of enactment that most closely applies to Wheatley's and Morgan's discussions, though, is the emphasis on coordinated system activity aimed at reducing equivocality. For Weick, this organic and continuous activity represents the heart of organizational life. As Gary Kreps says, "Weick contends that organizations do not exist but are in the process of existing through continual streams of organized human activities. Communication is the crucial process performed by organizational members to enable this ongoing organization to occur."[30] The focus is not on organizations as fixed, time-bound structures, but on the ongoing, interrelated interactions through time of members in an organization. Similarly, the environment is not a structure but an information environment. Organizational members *enact* their environment through perception and meaning creation.

The Learning Organization: Art and Practice—Peter Senge

In the spirit of systems theory, Peter Senge's *learning organization* proposes an increased emphasis on interconnections—both within and without the organization. The unique aspect of his approach is the focus on learning principles. A learning organization, according to Senge, is "an organization that is continually expanding its capacity to create its future."[31] With the publication of his book *The Fifth Discipline*, system applications in organizations gained widespread attention.

Though the learning organization places great importance on *adaptive learning*, which enables an organization to survive and maintain an effective balance of inputs and outputs, the true goal remains *generative learning*, which is learning that enhances our capacity to create. Adaptive learning is known as single loop learning. The organization copes with environmental uncertainty by relying on existing procedures and thinking processes. Generative learning is also called double loop learning. The potential for greater adaptability increases because new ways of thinking outside of normal practices are released. You move, as the saying goes, "outside of the box" (see Figure 6.1). A classic example of these two types of learning involves a furnace thermostat. In single loop, a thermostat set at 20 degrees starts the furnace whenever the temperature goes below 20. In double loop, the homeowner can question whether 20 degrees is the most effective setting and change it if needed.

Why do even professionals with such huge bodies of knowledge available to them have a difficult time with double loop learning? Often people take questions of and challenges to the status quo personally and become defensive. The focus shifts from the problem to the questioning behaviours. According to Chris Argyris, managers need to learn to change their defensive behaviours to open up the channels for organizational learning.[32] Single loop learning detects and corrects errors within an existing set of operating norms. Double loop learning has the ability to question operating norms and create new ones.

Through the process of generative learning we achieve deep human fulfillment. As the learning organization experiences self-renewal, the members engage in self-creation. Senge says, "People talk about being part of something larger than themselves, of being connected, of being generative. It became quite clear that, for many, their experiences as part of truly great teams stand out as singular periods of life lived to the fullest."[33] The learning organization brings out the ability of systems theory to comprehend the whole

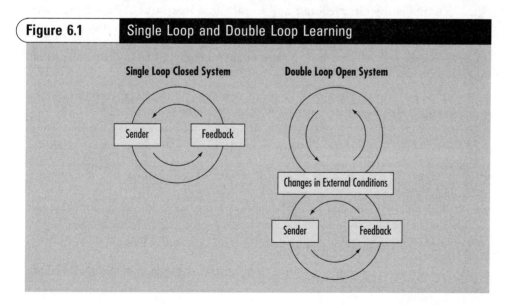

Figure 6.1 Single Loop and Double Loop Learning

picture, to examine the interrelationships of all parts, and to draw on the power of connection that integrated systems give to its members.

The practices of communication and teamwork are essential ingredients of the learning organization. Effective teamwork enables people not only to work together, but also to think together. Communication is the means through which team thinking, or dialogue, takes place. A member's sense of connection to the larger system overcomes one of the blocks to learning that Senge points out. We often apply systems wrongly in organizations because too many barriers remain that prevent members from experiencing a full connection with the whole. When the connection stops, so does learning. Organizations that focus on short-term instead of long-term strategies are characterized by these types of learning obstacles.

Revisiting Marshall McLuhan

All media are active metaphors in their power to translate experience into new forms. The spoken word was the first technology by which man was able to let go of his environment in order to grasp it in a new way.

—*Marshall McLuhan*, Understanding Media[34]

Does a parallel exist between McLuhan's discussions of "extensions" and the generative capabilities of new systems thinking? McLuhan proposed that human beings "extend" themselves by using mediums to help them experience and understand the world. We develop "extensions" through our senses. Radio is an extension of our ears, motorcycles are an extension of our legs, a telescope or the television extends our abilities to see. The McLuhan quote above expresses how technology enables us to create new realities. The Internet can be seen as an extension of our nervous system, providing us with information from a global arena where time and space are no longer barriers to communication. Information today connects us to a system at once both very small and very large, described in McLuhan's famous phrase as "the global village."

The concept of "extension," then, increases our capabilities for interacting with the world. Electronic media, of course, are dominant mediums used for extending ourselves. Through extending ourselves we are able to transform our ways of thinking. We are perpetually modified by our mediums and in turn find new ways of modifying them. As McLuhan states, people become "the sex organs of the machine world, enabling it to fecundate and to evolve into ever newer forms."[35]

Let's review a few ways in which extensions are similar to the concept of self-creation. Does McLuhan have a place in new systems thinking?

- Using new extensions gives us new ways of thinking and new ways of connecting to the world. Through extension, we develop new realities and new self-identities.
- Technology gives us access into systems we never would have reached before. The 500-channel television world offers great potential for connecting to faraway information sources.
- Using extensions represents the activity of processing information and of connecting to other realities.
- Extensions can be compared to information-carrying communication channels. According to the famous phrase "The medium is the message," channels not only alter messages but also furnish us with structures for thinking and making sense of our experiences.
- The "global village" is connected through information. Its sense of wholeness comes from a single consciousness.

This discussion is meant mainly as a thought-provoking exercise, and further research is required to draw conclusions. Today's abundance of communication technology has definitely generated interest in the influence of communication mediums on the messages they carry.

Systems Theory in Today's Organizations

Contemporary organizations have developed numerous ways for adjusting to changes in their environments. They have also designed more effective internal communication systems, usually interlocked with their external systems. As an example, the Wal-Mart empire has experienced some recent negative feedback. At their annual meeting, the message was that Wal-Mart needs to clean up its stores, reduce checkout lineups, treat employees better, and bring in some upscale goods to revive sagging profits. This recent news tops off years of bad publicity about its discrimination of women in pay and promotions, and clashes with union organizers in several stores that actually convinced Wal-Mart to close one of its Quebec operations.

Restoring and keeping organizational systems in balance is often difficult because of economic factors, and sharp rises in costs, services, or salaries can have unintended consequences. Recently, body shop garages across the country raised an uproar about the sharp decline in the amount of car repairs. In 2004, their sales dropped by about 50 percent across the industry, while customers paying out of their own pockets rose by 30 percent. The explanation is that drivers are afraid to make claims for damage under $1000 because of the price they will pay for increased insurance premiums. Most drivers can't afford to pay out of their own pockets, and don't want to go through their insurance company, so they don't fix their cars. They're scared to use a service that is set up to help them and for which they pay. Meanwhile, the profit of insurance companies rose 68 percent in 2004, representing $4.2 billion. What solutions have been proposed? Canada's auto insurers say they will reduce premiums by $1.4 billion, but this move took place only after some provinces announced they would investigate the recent sharp spike in profits and the 40 percent premium increase over the last three years. The Alberta government blames the insurance rate mess on provinces who allegedly helped fuel price gouging by establishing caps on injury settlements. Nova Scotia experienced an increase in work done by uncertified mechanics. Plus, claims stay on your record, and when they add up, long-term insurance costs could become unaffordable. Car rental companies are also crying for customers. They have lost 25 percent in revenue because customers no longer need rentals while their cars are being fixed. Rentals have suddenly become an unnecessary expense. It's easy to see the many interdependent systems at work in this one issue.

Many organizations have developed internal communication systems that reflect the complexity in the environment. Today, many corporate communication departments work closely with strategic planning in developing organizational goals. The squeeze for profits, though, can have an unbalancing effect and cause serious damage that could have been foreseen with effective information processing.

Systems theory, a perspective imported from the natural sciences, provides a framework for addressing the openness and complexity of social activity. A systems perspective is useful for revealing the interdependent connections among organizational members and with the environment at large.

Open systems are essential for organizations that exist in rapidly changing environments. An open perspective provides a way for organizations to recognize the importance of all factors, within and without the organization, playing a role in its success. Information is the source of self-renewal for individuals and organizations. Thus, open systems, which allow information flow, are better at adapting to changing conditions

In contrast to classical management, which uses a machine as a guiding metaphor, systems theory uses a living organism. A brain as a metaphor is also used to capture both the organism aspects of systems as well as their information-processing capabilities.

Recent developments have led to new systems approaches that combine the processes of community, self-identity, self-regulation, and self-creation as operating principles. Systems naturally move toward disorder or chaos, a state that represents the beginnings of a new order. Systems are constantly interlocked and engaged in self-renewal.

Systems theory relies on information processing in order to enable learning activity, a primary function of an open system. So the focus of an organization is not only on accomplishing tasks (as in the classical style) but on reflection on experiences, engagement in the people and cultures that make up the community, creating connections, and comprehensive problem analysis—all parts of the learning experience. Allowing employees flexibility in choosing how they will get their jobs done is also encouraged. Tight controls on employees tend to choke creativity.

360-Degree Feedback System at Paccar of Canada Ltd.[36]

As the builder of Kenworth and Peterbilt trucks since 1967, Paccar of Canada Limited, located in St. Therese, Quebec, is a model example of organizational restructuring. Most of the 800 employees are members of the Canadian Auto Workers union. It produces 120 trucks per three-shift day. The mission was to make the company "the best truck assembly plant in the industry."[37] A restructuring in 1999 trimmed the organization down to three production centres: the production team, the support team, and the management team. This flatter management structure improved client satisfaction by increasing model flexibility and held everyone more accountable.

To achieve excellence in innovation, quality, and efficiency, management adopted a 360-degree feedback system that emphasized communication, recognition, and employee development. These terms are important. At Paccar, *communication* means the raising of awareness, not performance appraisal; *recognition* refers to constructive, not disciplinary, feedback; *employee development* addresses training needs required for improvement. As an instrument, 360-degree feedback is a multi-rater system that offsets some of the problems with traditional employee feedback systems, such as the fear of retaliation for giving direct feedback, finding the right words for accurate feedback, worrying about damaging workplace harmony, and interpreting feedback effectively.

The Paccar 360 system involves numerous evaluators and is conducted by human resources. Employees are asked to rate managers against eight factors established through consultation with all employees: leadership, teamwork, personal efficiency, continuous improvement, client satisfaction, personal mobilization, personal development, and integrity. Consultants are brought in to help managers interpret the results and develop action plans. For instance, a development objective may be to be more proactive with clients. The system operates along a secure website to assure confidentiality. The role of consultants is to ensure that a custom-made program is developed. Off-the-shelf systems are usually not effective.

Because of the expense, Paccar uses this system only with senior managers (60 managers at $125 per report). A simplified 360 system is planned for the future for all employees. Assessment of plant employees is currently done on an informal basis, emphasizing regular, frequent, and immediate feedback to quickly address problems.

To help ensure success with both the formal and informal feedback systems, Paccar's 360-degree system was built on solid cultural values and principles; namely, a high priority on health and safety; a shared passion for quality; mutual respect; clear, open, and responsive communication; teamwork; continuous improvement; and customer satisfaction. All employees are considered to be ambassadors of these values. Through informal feedback, managers are able to reinforce these values with employees and facilitate career development. These are also opportunities for managers to provide recognition to subordinates, skills for which they are extensively trained.

Discussion Questions

1. Describe a 360-degree feedback system in terms of systems theory, in particular its open and closed features.

2. How does a 360 system improve customer satisfaction?

3. Discuss the importance of relationships and self-identity in a 360 system and how it helps to ensure not only order but self-renewal.

4. What types of organizational values and attitudes are essential for this feedback system to be effective?

Classroom Activity

Recall jobs or projects you have taken on in the past and take a few minutes to write down answers to the following questions:

- What was your actual goal (in five words or less)?
- What particular things did you have to do to accomplish it?
- Apply systems theory to the activities involved in accomplishing your task, focusing on what networks of people were involved, what technical systems or communication technologies assisted you and how they fit into your work systems.

- Seeing yourself as part of these systems, does the goal of your job (from question one) change at all? How important are relationships with internal and external people to getting your job done?

Form groups of three or four. Discuss and compare your experiences in terms of working within workplace systems.

Glossary

1. Eric Hoffer, "The True Believer" [1951], *Harper's*, July 2005, 74.

2. Margaret Wheatley, *Leadership and the New Science* (San Francisco, CA: Berret-Koehler Publishers, 1999).

3. William W. Neher, *Organizational Communication: Challenges of Change, Continuity, and Diversity* (Boston: Allyn and Bacon, 1997), 104.

4. Mitch Moxley, "'Adapt or Die' in Canadian Textile Sector," *National Post*, March 22, 2005, FP3.

5. Daniel Katz and Robert L. Kahn, *The Social Psychology of Organizations*, 2nd ed. (New York: John Wiley and Sons, 1978).

6. Stephen Bernhut, "Henry Mintzberg in Conversation," *Ivey Business Journal* (September/October 2000): 19–25

7. Katz and Kahn, *Social Psychology*.

8. Eric M. Eisenberg and H.L. Goodall, *Organizational Communication: Balancing Creativity and Restraint* (Boston: Bedford/St. Martin's, 2004), 96.

9. Claudia Cattaneo, "Oil Firms Tighten U.K. Ties," *National Post*, March 21, 2005, FP1.

10. Karl Weick, *Sense Making in Organizations* (Thousands Oaks, CA: Sage Publications, 1995).

11. Gareth Morgan, *Images of Organization* (Thousand Oaks, CA: Sage Publications, 1986), 47.

12. Peter Verburg, "Prepare for Takeoff," *Canadian Business*, December 25, 2000, http://www.canadianbusiness.com/article.jsp?content=14738 (accessed August 8, 2005).

13. Katz and Kahn, *Social Psychology*, 52–59.

14. T. Burns and G.M. Stalker, *The Management of Innovation* (London: Tavistock Publications, 1961).

15. P.R. Lawrence and J.W. Lorsch, *Organizational and Environment: Managing Differentiation and Integration* (Boston, Harvard University Press, 1967).

16. Margaret Wheatley, "The Power of Chaos," interview by Joe Flower, *The Healthcare Forum Journal* 36 (1993), www.learningtolearn.sa.edu.au/learning_workroom/files/links/Catalogue26July05.pdf (accessed July 10, 2005).

17. Ibid.

18. Ibid.

19. Ibid.

20. Margaret Wheatley, *Finding Our Way: Leadership for an Uncertain Time* (San Francisco, CA: Berret-Koehler, 2005).

21. Rick Salutin, "Hell is other people's cars," *The Globe and Mail*, April 1, 2005, A21.

22. Morgan, *Images of Organization*, 44.

23. Ibid., 237.

24. Ibid., 236.

25. Eric Hoffer, 1957, in "Sparks," *Harper's*, July 2005, 76.

26. Karl Weick, *Making Sense of the Organization* (Oxford, UK: Blackwell Publishers, 2001).

27. Benedict Carey, "Team Dynamics," New York Times News Service, *Hamilton Spectator*, March 8, 2005, SP4.

28. Karl Weick, "Educational Organizations as Loosely Coupled Systems," *Administrative Science Quarterly* 21 (1976): 1–19.

29. Carey, "Team Dynamics."

30. Gary L. Kreps, *Organizational Communication Theory and Practice* 2nd ed. (New York: Longman, 1990).

31. Peter Senge, *The Fifth Discipline: The Art and Practice of the Learning Organization* (New York: Doubleday, 1990), 14.

32. Chris Argyris, "Teaching Smart People How To Learn," *Harvard Business Review* (May–June 1991): 99–109.

33. Senge, *The Fifth Discipline*, 14.

34. Marshall McLuhan, *Understanding Media: The Extensions of Man* (New York and Scarborough: New American Library, 1964), 59.

35. Ibid.

36. Brigitte Banville and Sylvie St. Onge, "360-Degree Feedback at Paccar of Canada Ltd.," *Workplace Gazette* 7, no. 2 (Summer 2004): 63–68.

37. Ibid.

Chapter Seven

Organizations as Culture

Over the last 15 or 20 years, there's been such an emphasis on structural change in organizations that the soft part of change really gets left behind. Changing the lines in an organization chart really doesn't speak to how you improve performance. In order to do that, you have to dig down into the way that people work together. That's the culture.

—*Graham Lowe*, Communication Consultant[1]

Learning Objectives

- Examine the concept of organizational culture

- Analyze the characteristics and elements of culture in organizations

- Explore the importance of understanding organizational culture for organizations

- Look at how organizational culture is applied in today's organizations

- Identify the impact of organizational culture on communication

What Is Culture?

Like any country, Canada has its cultural elements. We have our founding fathers—John A. MacDonald, Lester Pearson, Tommy Douglas; our heroes—Terry Fox, Paul Henderson, Nancy Greene, Wayne Gretzky; our pastimes—hockey, curling, cottage life; our myths—the last railway spike, the great white north, the huge elephant south of the border; our storytellers—Gordon Lightfoot, Margaret Atwood, Pierre Berton; our cultural industries—daily newspapers, movies, television, radio; our social institutions—the CBC, bilingualism, universal medicare; our rituals, both common and quirky—swimming on New Year's Day, watching TV outside, barbecuing in the winter; our cultural symbols—the Rocky Mountains, the CN Tower, the Grey Cup, the RCMP, the wheat silo, the loon; our defining moments—the Canada–Russia Hockey series, the *Charter of Rights and Freedoms*.

Canadian culture is made up of the symbolic meanings in our environment, from the smallest subcultures—for instance, a pizza party in a hockey dressing room—to the most all-encompassing ones, such as Team Canada winning the men's 2002 Olympic gold medal in hockey in Salt Lake City, Utah. Our culture also contains our external geography—the meanings of our relationships with the United States, Europe, and the rest of the world. Finally, our culture is a fusion of events through time based on a collective interpretation of history. As a result of our cultural knowledge, we know who we are as a nation, a province, and a people, and as individuals.

The question for our purposes, though, is not about a country but an organization. Essentially, can we apply a cultural perspective to an organization the way we do to a country? In many ways we can, because, though the context is different, the processes are the same: by using communication, people organize, develop relationships, achieve goals, and establish identities for themselves and their organization. This knowledge then serves as a framework for understanding future experiences. So, a principal characteristic of culture is its double-action role: we use existing frameworks of meaning to interpret and explain things; at the same time, we are creating new frameworks of meaning to interpret and explain future events. As McLuhan Marshall said, "we shape our tools and thereafter they shape us." Let's begin our discussion by further examining the meaning of culture in organizations.

What Is Organizational Culture?

In Chapter 3, we introduced the metaphor of culture for an organization. It is different from the perspectives we've already discussed because it focuses on the shared meanings we create through social processes as well as the values, traditions, and practices we develop through social interaction. In contrast to the systems perspective, which sees organizations as organisms engaged in the life-sustaining activities of forming relationships and establishing patterns of communication, the cultural approach uncovers the meanings and identities created in organizational relationships. Using the culture metaphor, an organization is equated to a mini-society. As Clifford Geertz states, culture "denotes an historically transmitted pattern of meanings embodied in symbols, a system of inherited conceptions expressed in symbolic forms by means of which [people] communicate, perpetuate, and develop their knowledge about and attitudes toward life."[2]

Well-known cultural theorist Edgar Schein defines *organizational culture* in a more detailed way, with a definition that describes both the meaning-generating activities of cultural interaction as well as the functional purposes of those interactions; namely, coping with environmental uncertainty:

> Organizational culture is a pattern of basic assumptions, invented, discovered, or developed by a group, as it learns to cope with its problems of external adaptation

and internal integration, that has worked well enough to be considered valid, and therefore is to be taught to new members as the correct way to perceive, think, and feel in relation to those problems.[3]

A workplace culture is a very colourful mix of personalities. If you think workplaces portrayed on television or in movies serve up riveting moments with unique characters, they don't come close to the real-life drama and characters you find in most organizations. It is within this complex blend of eccentrics and absurdities that culture makes organizational life understandable to its members. We share language, nonverbal messages, styles of clothing, and ways of interacting that fall into taken-for-granted patterns of behaviour. These have been expressed by Deal and Kennedy in the down-to-earth expression that culture is "the way we do things around here."[4] These patterns serve as an operating system for conducting organizational activity and providing members with efficient ways of interacting.

An advantage of the cultural perspective is that it can make sense out of organizational activities that don't appear to be rational. In the early 1990s, for instance, IBM was going through a major cultural change. One new practice adopted was the wearing of casual clothes instead of the standard blue suit and tie. In the announcement, the business newspapers showed Bill Etherington, chairman of IBM Canada at the time, hustling to work in a plaid shirt, with sleeves rolled up, and khaki pants. It was meant to express to customers a new set of cultural values—IBM staff transformed from salespeople to working partners. What sense does it make to think that changing your clothing will change your work style? This example shows that style of clothing is a symbol for workers that may not be rational but is meaningful nevertheless.

Characteristics of Organizational Culture

Let's sum up our current section with a review of the common characteristics of organizational culture found in definitions from the field.

Shared Ideas

For a culture to exist, some shared or collective way of interpreting and understanding organizational activity is necessary. Establishing common meanings requires time; therefore, the activities must be ongoing. These meanings provide a framework for interpreting cultural activities. But they also allow individuals the freedom to think differently and form their own opinions. A strong culture contains a lot of different shared meanings that are constantly being negotiated. Cultures with a lot of diversity in the areas of gender, ethnicity, and age will have a larger amount of different meanings to share. To make full use of its diversity, an organization must encourage its members to discover new meanings. The differences that come out in day-to-day interactions are the necessary elements for a culture to evolve and remain dynamic (see Figure 7.1).

Many researchers on organizational culture, including some of the most influential, such as William Ouchi and Deal and Kennedy, describe culture as having a deeply

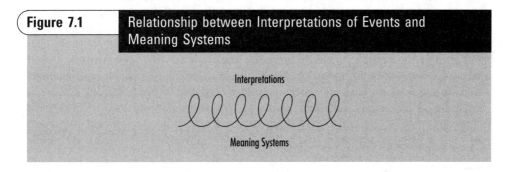

Figure 7.1   Relationship between Interpretations of Events and Meaning Systems

Interpretations

Meaning Systems

embedded nature that is resistant to change.[5] At the same time, however, researchers offer possibilities for changing culture. Mary Jo Hatch states that

> nearly all of this literature addresses the possibilities and benefits of intentionally altering organizational culture as a means of achieving greater managerial control or enhancing organizational performance. Thus, this literature pits the stability of organizational culture against managerial demands for organizational adaptability and change.[6]

Symbolic Expression

Culture exists in people's ideas and feelings, yet is expressed through objects and behaviours. The clothing style of an organization, as in the IBM example above, is a physical symbol of an internal value. Objects and activities in a organization must be rooted in a deeper, interconnected set of values, norms, and frameworks for creating meaning that are shared by all members.

For example, to boost civic spirit by creating a cultural identity, city planners have tried strategies such as installing banners on street poles reflecting the cultural highlights of different city regions. Often the deeper connection is not established because a change in surface elements is not the same as a change in culture. If a city region has not found shared values through the normal flow of life, it is a stretch to think that a banner might be the missing piece. Culture is far too complex and unpredictable to be created with such an easy strategy. Usually just adding one cultural symbol into the mix has little effect, as Trice and Beyer state:

> The question thus arises as to whether studying isolated cultural elements tends to produce distorted pictures and severely limited understanding of the cultures involved. If cultural elements interact closely, a more comprehensive approach to analyzing organizational cultures would yield better results.[7]

To reach deeper levels of meaning, companies can focus on rewarding behaviours, and not just performance. If you value teamwork, but reward employees with bonuses only for individual achievements, the message of the reward doesn't support the corporate value. At the eBay Canada office in Toronto, employees vote on the Hat Trick Award that is given to the best performance as it relates to integrity, excellence, and innovation. On a global level, the company presents the Out of this World award for overall performance based on some 90 criteria, none of which have to do with financial or business performance. According to eBay Canada's director, Jordan Banks, "There is no way at eBay that you can be a star performer unless you live the eBay behaviours and you care as much about how you're doing things as you do about what you're doing."[8]

Communication Activity

Through communication activity in organizations—such as meetings, presentations, written, electronic, and spoken messages, both work-related and personal—cultural values are expressed and established. Though we interpret organizational activities individually to begin with, subsequent stages of sense making involve a co-mingling of interpretations. The creation of culture is always embedded in social and organizational relationships. The desire to develop common values may be what pulls people together into groups, as we look for more substantial connections with people and our environments. In this way, differences between people are reduced. Viewing cultural activity as something people create together suggests that "organizational realities are not external to human consciousness, out there waiting to be recorded. Instead, the world as humans know it is constituted intersubjectively. The facts of this world ... are construed through a process of symbolic interaction."[8]

Historical Roots

We develop a sense of what it means to be Canadian by knowing our history. In the same way, an organization's culture grows out of its past. History provides a context for understanding current events. History also includes the element of time. As cultures develop, they explain and adapt to changes over time. The context provides a framework for interpreting experiences. An organization's history and past leadership can have a strong cultural influence.

Behavioural Guidelines

As a system of beliefs and values, culture prescribes guidelines for how things should be ordered and accomplished. Culture also helps workers make sense of experiences by giving them a framework with which to organize these experiences. Pacanowsky and O'Donnell-Trujillo have used a spider web as a metaphor for culture. Spider webs "limit a spider's range of movement to that particular slice of universe traversed by the web. At the same time, spider webs are the very things that make movement for the spider possible."[9] Organizations can learn why their members think and behave the way they do by understanding the cultural elements that guide and define them.

Personal Identification

Our personal identities emerge through dialogue with others. Effectively engaging with others can be an enriching experience because it brings differences together. A feeling of community in a workplace can help its members develop a sense of personal identification with the organization, leading to a strong organizational culture. An influential management approach based on identity and community in the workplace is found in William Ouchi's *Theory Z*.[10] Ouchi proposes a theory that combines the collective work style of Japanese companies with the individual-oriented North American style. It provides a strong sense of community to its members while also promoting individuality as a central cultural value. Though paradoxical on the surface, Ouchi believes that giving workers greater decision-making powers and leadership opportunities increases their participation in the workplace. They see themselves as bigger contributors to the achievement of organizational goals. For instance, when workers feel trusted by managers, they are more likely to exercise initiative. Through the development of organizational identity, a sense of symbolic boundary also emerges. Positive relationships and symbolic meaning systems among organizational members energize and increase commitment to a workplace. Organizational values develop that elevate a worker's role while creating an integrated sense of community.[11]

Elements of Organizational Culture

In the early 1980s, several books on organizational culture contributed to the popularity of the concept. A business bestseller, *In Search of Excellence*, by Thomas Peters and Robert Waterman, identified the following eight cultural properties of successful organizations:[12]

1. *A bias for action*—analysis combined with action
2. *Closeness to the customer*—customer satisfaction through service, quality, and innovative products leads to success
3. *Entrepreneurial work style*—self-initiative and risk taking are encouraged
4. *Employees regarded humanely*—a collective responsibility for productivity
5. *Value-driven culture*—company values, above all other resources, are at the heart of excellence
6. *Stick to the knitting*—a business prevails by doing what it does best
7. *Simple company structure*—a streamlined chain of command

"Rank and Yank" at Enron

When Jeffrey Skilling was CEO of Enron, performance rewards increasingly reflected individual instead of team results. In one review process, known as "rank and yank," employees ranked each other, and the lowest 15 percent each year were laid off. Says a former Enron employee of this system, "Because of that you never helped one another. Everyone was in it for themselves. People stabbed you in the back." The use of big performance bonuses also brought problems. Says another former employee, "It took everyone's eye off the big picture and made them focus on pushing deals through the system, even if the deal was a bad deal."[14]

8. *Loose–tight properties*—pairs of apparent contradictions based on the individual–organizational relationship: core cultural values are centralized and collectively held, while decision making is decentralized and entrepreneurship and individual achievement are encouraged

Another influential book was *Corporate Cultures: The Rites and Rituals of Corporate Life* by Terrence Deal and Allen Kennedy. This book identifies ways in which organizational culture is created through communication activity.[13]

1. *Language* is probably the most central element of organizational culture, including metaphors, symbols, and specialized vocabulary used by people in the organization. Through language, which represents a system of shared meanings, organizational members communicate all the other elements described below, as they navigate themselves through organizational activity.

2. *Values* are the collective beliefs of an organization. They serve as a guide for behaviour, sense making, achieving goals, and interpreting organizational life in general. Company slogans and websites illustrate corporate values; for example, "Think different" from Apple Computers or "Our product is steel. Our strength is people" from Dofasco or "Home of the handyman" from Home Hardware. Corporate mission statements serve the same purpose, though they normally have far less visibility than company slogans. In general, universities and colleges promote the value of cultural diversity as a learning advantage at their institutions, which is one reason North American schools attract so many foreign students.

3. *Heroes* are role models in the organization that best embody and demonstrate its most desirable values. Heroes are often founders of an organization. For example, Paul Demarais is chairman of Power Corporation of Montreal, whose assets have risen to over $100 billion despite the freefall of Montreal's economy since the election of Rene Levesque's separatists in 1976. His political convictions are described by Peter C. Newman in *Titans*: "Paul Demarais grew up to be not only the dean of Canada's establishment, but a bold advocate for federalism. Canada as Sudbury [his view of Canada reflected the cultural balance of the Sudbury, where Demarais was raised]. One nation, in which Quebec fought to speak French, surely, but not to secede."[15] Other legends in Canadian business are notorious for their penny pinching. Kenneth Thomson, once the richest man in Canada, bought hamburger buns on sale. Peter Pocklington, former owner of the Edmonton Oilers and arranger of the hockey trade of the century that sent Wayne Gretzky to Los Angeles, expressed his thriftiness this way: "[B]y doing what's best for me, I, in turn, look after and do what's best for everybody else around me. All this altruism has got to stop. I hate altruism. Hate it. It's destroying us."[16] Of course, heroes do not have to be presidents. We work side by side with many of our role models, people who demonstrate through concrete behaviour the intangible values of the organization.

4. *Rites and rituals* are behaviours that display an organization's values. Managers are responsible for spelling out the acceptable procedures for activities ranging from planning and budgeting to award presentations and social events. Strong cultures create corporate rites and rituals to serve as goals and guidelines for employee behaviour. To get to know employees better, for example, companies have started lunch programs where managers and workers can get to know what each other think. Rituals include routine activities such as where and when meetings are held, what communication channels are preferred, and how formally or informally people address each other. Rites include public events such as awards and ceremonies, and banquets and retirement dinners. They often originate by accident. A typical example is the "Golden Banana Award." As the story goes, an employee presented his boss with a great idea. The boss was impressed but had nothing handy to show his appreciation except for his lunch, so he took a banana out of the bag and gave it to the employee. The following year it became a ritual: a golden banana lapel pin for the best idea of the year.

5. *Stories, myths, sagas, and humour* convey important cultural information about an organization. Stories verbally recap people's experiences and allow them to be shared, forming a socially constructed view of organizational reality. Their purpose is threefold: they are entertaining; they provide a way to understand future scenarios by settings standards and boundaries for future behaviours; and they "weave an historical texture into the organization, a texture which members come to recognize and re-shape in their continual narration."[17] Stories are messages that have been passed from person to person and have changed over time. Their importance is not in how truthfully and accurately they describe an event in the past, but in how meaningful they are in explaining the present and navigating the future.

A key aspect of the corporate culture of WestJet Airlines Ltd. of Calgary is to maximize profit. To make this a universal desire of all employees, WestJet sells them shares in the company at half price. Profit-sharing cheques that range in the thousands of dollars are handed out twice a year. Many flight attendants have stocks valued in the hundreds of thousands. The company's success is evident is the financial numbers: it consistently ranks among the most profitable airlines in North America and is making loads of money in an industry where 90 percent of start-ups go under. So, it's understandable that all employees, from the boardroom on down, share in the responsibility to cut unnecessary expenses. Lavish living is not acceptable at company expense. One weekend, though, CEO Clive Beddoe threw a barbecue for senior managers at his private fishing lodge on the Bow River, close to Calgary. When Beddoe came in to work on Monday, news of the party had spread. A WestJet maintenance worker charged into his office and began pounding on his desk demanding to know why company profits, which he was entitled to, were being used for hamburgers and beer for executives. Beddoe told him not to worry. "I pointed out that I paid for the party out of my own pocket," he said with a grin. The employee was humbled, but Beddoe congratulated him on his attitude. "He's like a watchdog, and he hates inequities. That's the spirit of WestJet."[18]

Beddoe also takes prides in the fun WestJet employees have. Though mostly corny, flight attendants are often cracking jokes, holding contests, and playing games with passengers. The company's premium on fun is also evident in the signs on people's doors. The executive suite is mockingly labelled "Big Shots."

In organizations stories often fall into typical categories: rule-breaking stories about the consequences of not following company rules, career advancement stories about how and who will rise to the top, and stories about how bosses react to mistakes (Is the employee forgiven or punished?) and how the organization deals with obstacles. Common themes revolve around equality and inequality, security and insecurity, and power and powerlessness.

Interviewer: Toyota is one of the rare companies that has a coherent culture. The Toyota way is the same around the world. How do you manage to keep the consistency in the way the global business is run?

Kenji Tomikawa, CEO of Toyota Canada: Basically, that's Japanese culture. Let me give you an example: the growing of rice. Traditionally, in history, they grew rice on the mountainside where the water flowed from the top to the bottom.

All the owners of the fields are different but they got together periodically and they designed how to flow the water and do the work together. And when harvesting season came, they worked together, starting from the top field and working down. They helped each other. That's the basic culture in Japan. Not only for Toyota but other companies in Japan. And not only automotive, but other fields as well. It's a very cultural thing, an historical thing.[19]

6. *Objects, artifacts, space, and time* also carry cultural messages. Uniforms of police officers, nurses, judges, and teen groups such as "punks" or "gothics" indicate status, occupation, or cultural identity. Since status can be a barrier to communication, the use of uniforms or dress codes in the workplace has diminished. In schools, though, it's becoming more widespread for a number of reasons, among them that the use of fashion to express individuality was interfering with the collective effort to create an effective learning environment. Artifacts can be diplomas, wall decorations, or pictures. As an architectural feature, the use of space in office design often symbolizes prestige or power, such as in the lofty entrances of tall buildings. The former head office of Nortel in Brampton was designed to simulate the ambience of a cityscape, complete with parkettes, travel agencies, cafés, dry cleaners, and credit unions—all on one floor. Instead of control and hierarchy, an open workplace on a single floor promotes equality and teamwork. Chance meetings as people wander around the streets incorporate the element of coincidence into business days. Says Eugene Roman of Employee Services, "The city draws people out and creates interactions that wouldn't happen in other buildings. Those interactions unlock people's capabilities. I'm glad I'm not in the elevator business, because this city proves that vertical space simply isn't as good as horizontal space."[20]

The Impact of Organizational Culture on Communication

Communication and culture have a complimentary relationship—culture is created through communication, and communication is shaped by culture. This point is well illustrated in the transformation during the last 20 years that took place in many of North America's largest companies from a sales-oriented to a marketing-oriented culture. Facing increasing competition from nimble upstarts and new global players, companies soon realized the problem could not be solved by pushing sales people harder, the traditional whip-cracking approach, but by satisfying customer needs better. A sales culture fixes the sales people; a marketing culture achieves success by making a better product. So, an organizational culture shapes ways of thinking about solutions to problems. In this way, it excludes possibilities that could prove beneficial, which is a big reason for having a culture with open communication.

In times of rapid change in technology and economics, solutions to problems rarely come from practices already in place. The common approach is to name the problem and then get the tools out and start to solve it, based on the assumption that the solution is in the tool bag—or in the existing order of things. Cultural studies offer a

Saskatchewan Tickled "Pink" by Demand for Fertilizer[21]

After discovering a cultural secret and urging Chinese farmers to "think pink," Saskatchewan's potash industry has grown to a record $2.7 billion in 2005. The growing demand from China has the province's potash producers smiling, since they control more than 40 percent of the globe's supply. China's intense farming practices require a good fertilizer to put nutrients back into the soil, and the market shows signs of tripling in the coming years as China reaches its agricultural potential. To add to Saskatchewan's blessings, India and Brazil are also expected to increase potash consumption. But not long ago, China had no interest in the pink rock. What turned things around was part strategy, part marketing.

The strategy involved an education campaign that convinced farmers that potash was the way to go. The marketing campaign used infomercials that reached two-thirds of China's 800 million farmers on China's national television and took advantage of the discovery that pink is a lucky colour in China. Now, Saskatchewan potash is called Powerful Pink Potash and receives premium treatment in the market. The Saskatchewan company has since purchased 20 percent of one of its biggest customers, the Chinese fertilizer giant Sinofert. Fortunately, the province's potash reserves are expected to last hundreds of years. That's good news, especially for CEO William Doyle. He was seventh on the list of top executive compensation in the country in 2005, taking home over $22 million.[22]

different approach. Instead of solving problems based on past solutions, a problem is regarded as a mystery, as a state of disorder and ambiguity. The solution is a search for meaning and order, a process that involves thinking, dialogue, and questioning of existing orders of meaning. So, as mysteries are explained, new ones arise, in an ever evolving process of problem solving.[23] Communication activities, such as decision making, then, are obviously dependent on an organization's culture. The cultural perspective sees problems and solutions in terms of the ongoing creation of shared meanings. Geertz says, "The analysis of [culture is] therefore not an experimental science in search of law but an interpretive one in search of meaning."[24]

Cultural Context

All organizational cultures operate and interact within larger cultures. As Tomikawa expresses, the culture of Toyota comes from the overall culture of Japan and its history. Characteristics of national cultures influence the ways companies located within them work. Research has explored the effects that national cultures have on the behaviour of organizations and identified four characteristics of national influences.

1. *Power distance.* This is the degree to which people in a society accept differences in levels of power. Generally, in Western cultures, people believe in the principle of equality. They don't accept the notion that some people are entitled to greater power. In low-power distance cultures, power must be earned to be accepted. Monarchies and dictatorships are examples of cultures that have high power distance.[25]

2. *Uncertainty avoidance.* Some cultures are more comfortable living with uncertainty than others. Workplaces high in uncertainty avoidance value stability and are fearful of risk. Personal experiences, such as growing up in a time of war, as the generation that lived through World War II did, can create high uncertainty avoidance. Cultures with low uncertainty avoidance are more accepting of change and comfortable with conflict. The cultural characteristic is particularly relevant with the high degree of cultural diversity in today's workplaces. One of Canada's strengths is our cultural

tolerance—we are comfortable with cultural differences and, in fact, encourage cultures to celebrate their differences instead of suppressing them. Human nature in general, though, seems to prefer predictability over surprises. People stick with the same brand of toothpaste, beer, or political party as though trying something different is unpleasant. Upstart products trying to crack the market need to rely on thought-provoking questions to get people to consider other possibilities.[26]

3. *Individualism vs. collectivism.* Canada is a fairly individualistic culture. Our primary responsibility is to ourselves, though we also have some collectivistic qualities. This would make it easier for a company such as WestJet to adopt a team-oriented Japanese-style workplace culture. Members of collectivistic cultures feel stronger loyalties to the society they belong to. The United States is more individualistic than we are, whereas nations such as Japan, Germany, and Sweden have more socially oriented cultures, as is reflected in their political systems and organizations.[27]

4. *Short-term vs. long-term orientation.* Western cultures in general are interested in quick, short-term payoffs. Asian cultures, in contrast, are more patient and willing to put off instant gratification in return for long-term rewards.[28]

Corporations operating on a global scale find a challenge in maintaining cultural consistency. Generally, their human resources departments are distributed to the locations where variations in social, economic, and political circumstances may exist so that some degree of harmony between organizational and national cultures can be achieved. Creating a corporate culture in international locales is difficult because of the counter influence that local cultures may exert. It may also be egotistical to assume that the process of globalization will leave parent organizations unchanged. As a tool of economic expansion, globalization has changed the ways that we do business. It remains to be determined how cultures will be transformed as a result of globalized business operations.

Purpose of Communication

Earlier we discussed the functional and interpretive perspectives of communication. In organizational culture, the *functional perspective* is associated with messages intended to create values and attitudes in workers that will make the organization run better. So, awards, ceremonies, presentations, office design, barbecues, and volleyball tournaments all carry messages that attempt to change the culture of an organization to improve performance. It has become popular, for instance, to send groups of employees to weekend team-building retreats as a way of strengthening employee relationships and developing trust—qualities that are intended to help them perform their jobs better. The functional perspective looks at organizational culture as a set of variables that belong to the organization and can be manipulated to create a culture that best accomplishes the organization's goals.

The *interpretive perspective* is associated with understanding the ways in which employees make sense of organizational life in both work-related and personal ways. A culture is not a collection of things, as in the functional perspective. It is the process of creating meaning that members engage in through communication, and it exists not in outward symbols and activities but in human consciousness. Culture is not something an organization *has*, it is something an organization *is*. In fact, workplace activities often do not achieve any functional goal; they may simply reinforce the values and practices that have made the organization successful. Take a typical lunchtime meeting as an example. Everyone shows up with their lunches, sits in the same chairs, and follows the same rules of order that have been in place for years. Often, nothing much of substance happens, but the meetings provide a sense of identity and belonging—they are a celebration of a company that works. Deal and Kennedy state,

Meetings don't necessarily always have to be occasions where things get done. As rituals, they can provide opportunities for managers to stage events that dramatize cultural beliefs and values . . . good management rituals provide collective cohesion and solidarity.[29]

Types of Messages and Message Flow

The focus of the cultural approach is on the meanings of symbols and activities in organizations. In contrast to systems theory, which looks at how messages flow along networks of interaction, the cultural perspective is concerned with the meanings being created during those interactions. Other significant types of messages are stories and rituals.

Messages move among people in the organization through informal communication and through formal channels during established company events. The type of organization will determine the channel of preference. For convenience, sales people will communicate at a distance through electronic means, but when strategy needs to be developed, a personal meeting emphasizing consensus building would be more effective.

Organizational Culture and Communication Climate

These two metaphors for organizations overlap in certain areas. They both provide guidelines for behaviour. Take climate, for instance: if the mood in the room is "chilly," you may hold off on asking for the afternoon off. As for culture-guiding behaviour, if your boss invites you to his house for dinner, it could signify that your relationship has advanced to a more personal level, and you adjust your behaviour to become more friendly with him or her. There are also differences worth noting:

1. Climate focuses on an individual's psychological and emotional processes. Culture, on the other hand, describes the collective processes in organizations, such as people interacting and creating meaning.

2. Climate deals with an individual's perceptions about how it *feels* to work and communicate in an organization. In contrast, culture describes the shared perceptions of what things *mean* in an organization.

3. Climate, or the atmosphere in a workplace, is usually evaluated in positive or negative terms—warm or cold, friendly or hostile, trusting or suspicious. Cultures are often described as strong and integrated or weak and divided. We don't normally say "good" culture or "bad" belief, because a culture is regarded as value-neutral.

4. Climate is fairly easy to describe. Culture exists at a deeper level is and harder to conceptualize and put into words.

The use of climate and culture to explain people's experiences can also be combined. After the atmosphere is evaluated and labelled, cultural understandings can take over as guides for behaviour. In sum, the two concepts are closely related. Their main difference is that climate does not examine the production and maintenance of shared values.

Organizational Culture in Today's Organizations

Culture is not the kind of thing you can hang on a plaque and then keep. It's something you have to keep working at.

—*Rick George, CEO*, Suncor[32]

Practitioners of organizational change have been using strategies to promote cultural development since the 1980s, even though many theorists are hesitant to venture into

Breaking Down the Barriers at UPEI—Creating Cultures of Innovation

They're saying goodbye to the old ways of doing things at the University of Prince Edward Island (UPEI). Universities are traditionally a network of faculties that barricade themselves from each other and from the outside community. UPEI decided it was time to expand its small scope as a school whose main purpose was to give islanders a local education and look at the bigger picture in the community and beyond. The school has started collaboration programs linking research and commerce. Wade MacLaughlin, president of the university, has taken strategy planning not only out of the box but out of the boardroom. He often has planning meetings in his dining room or on the deck of his Covehead Bay home, where MacLaughlin drops his normal role and becomes the cook. According to *Atlantic Business* magazine, "It's about pushing boundaries and accepting risk, about encouraging freedom of expression and deconstructing inter-departmental barriers."

The rewards have started to come in. In five years, UPEI rose from 18th to 8th in *Maclean's* magazine 2005 annual rankings. Enrollments are up 40 percent since 1999, a $50-million fundraising program is halfway there, and new graduate programs are enticing local and international students. The open-minded approach to strategic planning has also brought in substantial investment—all based on a cooperative rather than competitive approach to doing business. Breaking down barriers can become contagious. The new spirit of cooperation helped overcome historical obstacles between the university and St. Dunstan's University. According to Richard Kurial, dean of Arts at UPEI, "Wade doesn't micromanage. The example he sets is an inspiration to us all and his faith in us instills in us a belief that we can do all that we do—and more."[30]

Similar centres of collaboration between universities and industry are occurring throughout the country. The University of Manitoba turned a sheep meadow on its campus into Smartpark, a $100 million research and office facility employing over 800 people and home to 20 private and public sector organizations in areas as diverse as telecommunications, pharmaceuticals, information systems, electronic payment systems, biodiagnostics, and nutraceuticals, a food research group bringing together scientists from agriculture, human ecology, medicine, and pharmacy. According to Larry Paskaruk, director of property management, "It's time to start connecting [the complex] with pathways and landscaping to create that community of innovators."[31] The concept of a university–industry research park has a proven track record at the University of Saskatchewan's Innovation Place, a research park with one million square feet and 2200 employees that opened in 1981. Paskaruk also had a hand in developing this project. Other educational centres across the country, including McMaster University in Hamilton, where a huge closed-down appliance factory once owned by Westinghouse is being turned into a bioengineering university–industry research facility, are also forging new links that will generate innovation. The image of the university as an "ivory tower," secluded from the messiness of the workplace, has evolved into an open, integrated environment where influences from all areas of life converge.

Discussion Questions

1. Discuss the benefits of using a more interactive organizational structure.

2. What effects could it have on organizational culture?

the area of cultural manipulation. Many training and human resources journals discuss specific communication tools that managers can use to build stronger corporate cultures, promote greater job satisfaction, and develop effective quality programs based on creating a sense of ownership in employees. Through these methods, individual and organizational goals and values are integrated, providing a potentially strong boost to the company's performance.

A simple place change specialists start is in internal communication. Newsletters are used to promote company values. Memos from superiors to subordinates also express cultural information. External messages create admirable impressions in the community about the organization. Awards carry generally positive messages of recognition. All these messages can be manipulated as variables to try to make the workplace function better. Companies who try, for instance, to change a sales culture into a service or marketing culture may find difficulty in turning a staff hired for their aggressive sales abilities into empathic customer service specialists. More drastic measures are also available, such as threats of layoffs or large-scale downsizing. Generally speaking, if newsletters and memos can change a culture, there probably was not that much wrong with it to begin with. And if there is a serious problem with an organizational culture, such as conflicting goals or lack of effort, a memo promoting a "new direction" may raise hopes in employees that things are changing for the better, but until concrete actions from management turn these hopes into realities, employees will not see any reason to change.

Though internal communication changes are easy to do, their outcomes are not easy to predict. Some of the difficulties in changing organizational culture include the following:

- Companies with dysfunctional cultures usually have poor communication. As a result, pinpointing the problem is the first challenge. Employees holding negative attitudes about bosses often are not usually forthcoming with information about operations. Superficial communication campaigns to bring about change may even harden their negative attitudes. To break through ingrained worker attitudes, practitioners have learned that groups are the building blocks of organizations, and that to create change, groups of employees, or teams, must be targeted.
- Reaching deeper levels of culture may not be practical or financially feasible on an organizational level. Many aspects of deeper culture are difficult to put into words.
- Organizations are actually made up of many cultures. Edgar Schein has categorized a typical organization as having three cultures: an operator culture, an engineering culture, and an executive culture, each with its own values, knowledge, and priorities.[33] Add to that the steadily greater mix of ethnic cultures in North American workplaces and the question of which culture is the one targeted for change becomes an issue. Maintaining an integrated, uniform culture is increasingly difficult in today's working environment.

Total Quality Management (TQM)

The drive for quality reminds me of my first job as a summer student at a car plant in Southern Ontario. I was in quality control. The rejected cars would pile up in the repair bay at the end of the line where I would mark them up with a purple pen, and the repair men would come and fix them, grumbling at me when I got too picky. There were a lot of rejects.

Total Quality Management (TQM) is a method of changing the way quality is achieved in the workplace. Instead of tacking it onto the end of the production process, it is built into every stage of the operation. It requires a cultural change that involves employees in a proactive and ongoing process of seeking out quality improvements and eliminating barriers to quality. Many companies have implemented TQM, usually large ones where cultures are not uniform such as Hydro-Quebec and Ontario Hydro. With thousands of employees, it can take considerable time. But TQM is a process, not a structure. The idea is that changing how work is done by putting people into teams will gradually change how workers interact with each other. Companies hope that workers will help each other change their work attitudes and behaviours by letting their actions lead the way and learning from each other.

A large part of the process of learning news ways of working, or cultural change, is unlearning the old ways and dropping the "old tools." The forces of resistance to change become powerful at this point in the process. Karl Weick has summed up reasons why workers resists change:[34]

1. *Lack of trust.* TQM is effective because direction comes from coworkers, where trust is usually high, instead of supervisors, where status may be a barrier to trust.
2. *Lack of control.* In the process of change, some degree of control is lost, which makes workers feel ineffective.
3. *Social dynamics.* As we saw in our section on human relations, work groups have a strong sense of self-preservation and will protect each other against threats from outside the group. This can be counterproductive if the group sees cultural change as a threat.
4. *Consequences.* People will resist change if they think it will not make much difference.
5. *Identity.* Tools and techniques are a worker's trademark, an "extension" of their identity, to use McLuhan's term. They define group membership, the way a firefighter's uniform designates that person as a professional. If you take them away, a worker may question, "Without my tools, who am I?" They represent meaningful artifacts that define the culture. As Weick says, "Tools and identities form a unity."

TQM efforts at Hydro-Quebec and Ontario Hydro have been in the works for years, but reaching quality goals has been a hit-and-miss affair. Fewer than half of organizations with quality initiatives have produced positive results. A common reason for failure is faulty and inconsistent implementation. Also, managers are uneasy about handing over authority to workers. The Hydro-Quebec effort was undermined by political pressures that squandered employee cooperation and overly simplistic management ideas about the scope of change. As a result, managers' abilities to facilitate the necessary change and coordinate the risks were impeded.[35]

Based on a study done in 2005 by Waterstone Human Capital Limited and *Canadian Business* magazine using in-depth interviews with senior executives at 107 Canadian companies, only 36 percent of companies are seen as having strong adaptive cultures.[36] The Ten Most Admired Cultures are:

1. WestJet Airlines
2. Tim Hortons
3. Royal Bank of Canada
4. Four Seasons Hotels
5. Suncor Energy Inc.
6. Starbucks (Canada)
7. Yellow Pages Group
8. Dell Inc.(Canada)
9. Canadian Tire Ltd.
10. Rothmans Inc.

The cultural practices these companies embody are the following:

- Don't fake it—corporate practices must reflect the organization's values
- Engage employees—encourage employees to bring their values to the surface—make values a topic of conversation
- Lead by example—top managers must "walk the talk"
- Hire for cultural fit—you can train skills, but it's much harder to teach values
- Reward behaviours—recognize how things get done, not just the final results
- Make values pay—make cultural behaviours a requirement for pay raises
- Perform checkups regularly—monitor cultural activity on an ongoing basis

While 82 percent of senior managers believed corporate culture has an impact on the ability to recruit and retain the best people as well as financial performance, an alarming 62 percent stated that they don't monitor the state of culture in their organizations. The study identified the characteristics of weak cultures as those companies managers described as "bureaucratic and top-down," "over-regulated and scared," having an "underlying fear of making a mistake," and demonstrating a "culture of complicity."[37] According to Don Bell, WestJet founder, "Culture is something that *is*. If you create the optimal environment, it's something that manifests itself."[38]

Our section on organizational culture began with a discussion of what organizational culture is: a set of assumptions about what a workplace is like that a group of people share and that determines their perceptions, interpretations, feelings, and behaviours. The culture of an organization embodies the values, beliefs, attitudes, and meaning systems of its members. Culture expresses itself in many forms, such as in objects, space, time, stories, heroes, practices, rites, and ceremonies. It also possesses certain characteristics: it is shared by its members, it is expressed through symbols, it has a historical context, it guides human behaviour, and it creates employee identity.

Researchers have identified cultural properties that are common in successful organizations, such as a collective work style and a shared sense of responsibility for productivity; an emphasis on customer service; a strong, shared set of values that reflect organizational goals; a streamlined chain of command; and a balance of stability and change where cultural strengths are collectively held and individual achievement is encouraged to allow a culture to grow. A relationship exists between national and organizational cultures according to several characteristics: power distance, uncertainty avoidance, individualism vs. collectivism, and short-term and long-term gains.

The differences between organizational culture and organizational climate are seen to have some overlap, though generally the differences are that climate is a more individual experience, dealing more with how things feel, rather than what things mean, and climate is easier to describe, whereas culture exists at deeper levels. The chapter also looked at the practice of cultural change in today's organizations. Though management is eager to use cultural change to boost performance, often the implementation is incomplete and the results are unsatisfying. Culture exists at a deep, interconnected level; the effort required to make real cultural change represents a cultural change in itself. Total Quality Management systems are programs designed to change the ways quality is achieved in the workplace. It is built into every step of the operation and requires employees to get involved proactively in the ongoing process of seeking quality improvements.

Case Study

B.C. Bio—Canada's Best Employer Three Years in a Row

This Vancouver-based company, with 650 employees (476 full-time), provides diagnostic testing services to hospitals in the Vancouver area. Ted Emond, a partner in the *Report On Business*'s Best Employers ranking, explains it in undramatic terms: "It sounds kind of corny, but there seems to be a real family feel in this company." According to Emond, the company is successful for the following reasons:

- Managers and employees share the same goals and compassionate attitudes toward customers.

- The organizational structure is horizontal. "Many employees receive no day-to-day supervision, and no one is more than two levels away from the CEO."

- Pay scales are similar throughout the ranks, even at entry-level positions, and are about the same as unionized labs. In addition, there are performance bonuses based on company results.

- Regular recognition of employee achievements is shown through awards and gifts certificates, though, as Karen Bernoe says, "it's the thought."

- A culture of trust and communication creates a workplace where everyone helps each other out.

- There are no special perks for head office. Employees in branch offices receive the same treatment as head office, creating feelings of equality. Regular picnics and volleyball tournaments help keep all employees informed about company news.

An example of the level of solidarity among employees is shown in the company's response to a 20 percent government cutback. Instead of layoffs, the company chose to reduce the hours and pay of 150 employees, a measure that confirms the company's belief in equal sharing of rewards and hardships.

Some highlights from the *Report on Business* Top 50 employers were:

- Microsoft Canada of Mississauga (741 employees) encourages employees to take 40 paid hours a year for volunteer work as a way of connecting with the community. Farm Credit Canada of Regina, in a similar effort, donates 1 percent of profits to community groups.

- National Bank of Canada in Montreal (8596 employees) and Bennett Jones LLP of Calgary (592 employees) both provide full benefits for part-timers.

- Scotiabank of Toronto (25 116 employees) uses frequent employee-organized breakfast, lunch, and educational gatherings.

- Husky Injection Molding Systems of Bolton, Ontario, provides extensive personal fitness services, including a doctor, nurse, naturopath, chiropractor, chiropodist, physiotherapist, and masseur.

What were the worst employers like? Here's some comments about dysfunctional organizational cultures from the 10 lowest-scoring employers:

- *Leadership.* Leaders develop plans for the future but they fail to build interest among employees and the plan is not implemented.

- *Business practices.* Managers don't deliver the goods, leaving plans unfinished and employees confused. Says one employee, "When my responsibilities and position were changed due to a change in business, I was not made aware of my new manager or my new title until I saw it on an organizational chart in a group meeting."

- *People-management practices.* Managers handle people poorly, leaving employees demotivated and directionless. Says one employee, "[We do] a good job of recruiting ... - with interviews, dinners with senior management, portraying a culture of fun and a career-oriented place; however, nothing could be further from the truth. I've worked with five people who have quit within the last ten months, one of them being my supervisor. I've worked for companies on your top-50 list and see the difference. It's like night and day."

- *Employee issues.* Hiring, promotion, and discipline are handled inconsistently, often with cronyism and discrimination. Says one employee, "[Politics] takes priority over actual work.... Career advancement is based on back-room meetings and more politics. You should be promoted based on intelligence, results, and ideas; promotion here comes from buddying up with senior management and creating a 'scene' of working hard. It's ridiculous."[39]

Discussion Questions

1. Discuss the corporate values that are communicated through the various programs offered by B.C. Bio and other companies from the top 50.

2. Outline in detail what kinds of communication activities and strategies could resolve the negative issues and practices of the worst companies.

How would these messages be initiated and implemented?

3. In groups, brainstorm and detail the cultural experiences you have had in organizations that made you enjoy being a part of them. Contrast these to negative cultural experiences you have had.

Classroom Activity

Creating Culture through Feedback

In Chapter 6, the case study discusses 360-degree feedback systems. One of the indirect strengths of this system is the opportunities it provides for communication between managers and subordinates. What managers say and do sets the tone for the entire workplace, and these messages are picked up and communicated rapidly along social networks. Discuss the cultural values that managers can create and reinforce as they give feedback to employees, particularly in terms of the following activities: showing sincerity, engaging employees, rewarding behaviours, realigning cultural activity, stressing the importance of both top-down and bottom-up communication flow, and stressing quality instead of quantity when it comes to communication.

Chapter 7 / Organization as Culture

Glossary

Organizational culture, p. 118
Theory Z, p. 121
Rites and rituals, p. 123
Power distance, p. 125
Uncertainty avoidance, p. 125

Individualism vs. collectivism, p. 126
Short-term vs. long-term orientation, p. 126
Functional perspective, p. 126
Interpretive perspective, p. 126
Total Quality Management (TQM), p. 129

Notes

1. Andrew Wahl, "Culture Shock," *Canadian Business*, October 10–23, 2005, 116.

2. Clifford Geertz, *The Interpretation of Cultures* (New York: Basic Books, 1973), 89.

3. Edgar H. Schein, "Organizational Culture," *American Psychologist* 45, no. 2 (1990): 109–19.

4. T.E. Deal and A.A. Kennedy, *Corporate Cultures: The Rites and Rituals of Corporate Life* (Harmondsworth: Penguin Books, 1982).

5. Mary Jo Hatch, "Dynamics in Organizational Culture," in *New Directions in the Study of Organizational Change and Innovation Processes*, eds. M.S. Poole and A. Van de Ven (New York: Oxford University Press, 2004), 657–93.

6. Ibid.

7. Harrison M. Trice and Janice M. Beyer, "Studying Organizational Cultures through Rites and Ceremonials," *Academy of Management Review* 9, no. 4 (1984): 653.

8. R.H. Brown, "Bureaucracy as Praxis: Toward a Political Phenomenology of Formal Organizations," *Administrative Science Quarterly* 23 (1978): 378.

9. Michael Pacanowsky and Nick O'Donnell-Trujillo, "Communication and Organizational Cultures," *Western Journal of Speech Communication* (Spring 1982): 115–30.

10. William G. Ouchi, *THEORY Z* (Reading, MA: Addison-Wesley, 1981).

11. Stan Klimowicz, "The Symbolic Territory of Organizational Boundaries" (paper presented at the Eastern Communication Association conference, Ocean City, MD, 1989).

12. Thomas Peters and Robert Waterman, *In Search of Excellence* (New York: Harper and Row, 1981).

13. Deal and Kennedy, *Corporate Cultures*.

14. G. Hassell, "Pressure Cooker Finally Exploded," *Houston Chronicle*, December 9, 2001, A1.

15. Peter C. Newman. *Titans*. (Toronto: Penguin Books, 1999).

16. Steve Brearton, "Hall of Fame," *Report on Business Magazine*, November 2003, 50 (quote from Peter Newman's *The Acquisitors*).

17. Pacanowsky and O'Donnell-Trujillo, "Communication and Organizational Cultures."

18. Peter Verburg, "Prepare for Takeoff," *Canadian Business*, December 25, 2000, 94.

19. Michael Vaughn, "It's a very cultural thing," *The Globe and Mail*, April 7, 2005, G2.

20. Lisa Chadderdon, "Nortel Switches Cities," *Fast Company* magazine, August 1998, 112–21.

21. Kelly Anne Riess, "China digs into Saskatchewan potash," *Business Edge*, March 16, 2006, Ontario Edition.

22. "Top Executive Compensation List," *The Globe and Mail*, May 9, 2006, B8.

23. Eric M. Eisenberg and H.L. Goodhall, Jr., *Organizational Communication: Balancing Creativity and Constraint* (Boston: Bedford/St. Martin's, 2004).

24. Geertz, *The Interpretation of Cultures*, 5.

25. Grete Hofstede, *Culture and Organizations: Software of the Mind* (New York: McGraw-Hill, 1997).

26. Ibid.

27. W.B. Gudykunst, S. Ting-Toomey, and T. Nishida, *Communication in Personal Relationships across Cultures* (Thousand Oaks, CA: Sage, 1996).

28. Ibid.

29. Deal and Kennedy, *Corporate Cultures*.

30. Ron Ryder, "The Collaborators," *Atlantic Business Magazine*, January 7, 2005, http://www.atlanticbusinessmagazine.com/more.php?id=A78_0_1_0_C - 40k (accessed November 25, 2005).

31. Bob Armstrong, "Investing in Big Thinkers: University of Manitoba's Smartpark," *Manitoba Business* magazine, July/August 2005.

32. Andrew Wahl, "Culture Shock," *Canadian Business*, October 10–23, 2005, 115.

33. Edgar Schein, "Three Cultures of Management: The Key to Organizational Learning," *Sloan Management Review* (Fall 1996): 9–20.

34. Karl Weick, "Dropping the Tools," *Administrative Science Quarterly* (June 1996): 301–13.

35. Taieb Hafsi, "Fundamental Dynamics in Complex Organizational Change: A Longitudinal Study into Hydro Quebec's Management," *Long Range Planning* 34, no. 5 (October 2001): 557–83.

36. Wahl, "Culture Shock," 115.

37. Ibid.

38. Ibid.

39. Jim Sutherland, "Unbeatable," *Report on Business Magazine*, January 2005, 46.

Chapter Eight

The Critical Theory Perspective

8

Organizations are not neutral sites of sense making; rather they are created in the context of competing interest groups and systems of representation.

—*Dennis Mumby*, Narrative and Social Control[1]

Learning Objectives

- Examine the concept of critical theory and its importance for understanding
  communication in organizations

- Explore sources of power in organizations

- Analyze the relationship between power and ideology

- Examine the concept of hegemony and its importance in today's organizations

- Review the impact of critical theory on communication

- Explore organizations today in terms of critical theory

What Is Critical Theory?

Our final perspective on organizations is critical theory. It views organizations as sites for the exercise of power, survival, and domination. An organization is "a battleground where rival forces (e.g., management and union) strive for the achievement of largely incompatible ends."[2] So, organizations can be seen as political systems.

Let's recap the other approaches for comparison. In the classical management and human relations perspectives, organizations had one common goal and one source of authority. Workers relinquished power to management for the good of the organization. Systems and cultural approaches further broadened the scope of organizational analysis. Organizations were made up of different groups with different interests that negotiated a balance of power through interaction. Management's job was to coordinate the creation of order out of diversity.

Critical theory takes a more radical view. Instead of having common goals, organizations are made up of opposing interests that reflect the deeper class differences in society at large. They are held together by various forms of coercion, much of it hidden, which serve to oppress workers' interests. Advancing the interests of workers requires radical changes in the structure of society and redistribution of power. By exposing imbalances of power, *critical theory* seeks to liberate workers from oppression. The roots of this line of thought are in Karl Marx and the Frankfurt School, who proposed that imbalances in the class structures of society would eventually lead workers to revolt against the capitalist system. Hence, by "criticizing" the system, oppressive conditions are uncovered.

Communication and Critical Theory

Communication scholars interested in critical theory have focused on the communication processes that create power imbalances in organizations. Of particular importance for understanding the essential processes that allow domination to be achieved are the communication practices that take place interpersonally and in groups through the organization. Remarkably enough, workers themselves contribute to their own oppression.

The formation of an imbalance of power is a two-stage process.[3] First, messages become distorted for various reasons: they may be untruthful, or incomprehensible, or insincere. This misinterpretation creates a disadvantage for one party, usually the weaker, that eventually creates an imbalance of power. Through repetition, this imbalance is reproduced until a set of meanings that give preference to the dominant group is established. These are eventually accepted as a natural part of work life and form the cultural values of an organization.

Sources of Power

Let's examine the concept of power, the central concept of critical theory, to explore how this process works. Organizations are typically categorized according to the ways they exercise political rules. To begin, let's look at the common political structures for organizations:

1. *Autocracy*—a dictatorship: power is held by an individual or small group.
2. *Bureaucracy*—power is exercised through written rules based on rational or legal authority.
3. *Technocracy*—power is held by a body of experts.
4. *Democracy*—power is held by elected officers.
5. *Cooperative*—power is shared equally by all members.

Examining an organization in terms of its political structure is another way of making sense of why people behave the ways they do. Let's take a closer look at where power is located in organizations to find out how the numerous organizational interests are accomplished.

Power involves the capability to force somebody to do something. Gareth Morgan has identified the following sources of power in organizations:[4]

1. *Formal authority*—the most common form of authority in bureaucratic organizations.

2. *Control of scarce resources*—the more someone is dependent on you, the more power you have.

3. *Organizational structure, rules, and regulations*—as well as being guidelines for achieving organizational goals, they can also be instruments for gaining political control by using them for your own advantage.

4. *Control of decision making*—the more you can influence the outcomes of decisions, the more power you have.

5. *Control of information*—the more information you have, the more you can influence and define organizational situations.

6. *Control of boundaries*—the effective management of boundaries between work groups or departments allows control of information and transactions that can be exploited to secure more control.

7. *Ability to cope with uncertainty*—operational uncertainties such as breakdowns offer opportunities for members to gain power by showing their ability to restore normal operations.

8. *Control of technology*—type of technology used influences the patterns of interdependence and the power relations in an organization; production-line factories give employees in one section power to halt all operations.

9. *Interpersonal alliances, networks, and control of "informal organization"*—participation in various networks gives the skilled "politico" information to influence business activity and deflect resistance to personal desires.

10. *Control of counter-organizations*—examples of counter-organizations are trade unions, consumer and environmental groups, and lobby groups; they aim to influence organizations to which they do not belong, such as a trade union in negotiation with a company.

11. *Symbolism and the management of meaning*—the tools discussed in organization culture—language, symbols, stories, rituals, objects, space—can be used to manage the creation of meanings and shape power relations; referring to problems as challenges, for instance, depicts opportunistic values.

12. *Management of gender relations*—gender-related values vary among organizations, often showing favour for one gender over another; a female in a male-dominated workplace may have to work harder to achieve goals than her male counterparts. So, the choice of gender management strategy can influence one's power and success (see Ped Box, Gender Representations, page 139).

13. *Deep power structures*—though individuals may carry substantial power, they are also limited by deeper forces posed by the environment, economics, and shareholder pressure—by power relations rooted in the overall structure of society.

14. *Power seeks to grow*—power leads to more power in three ways: a) coalition building, where, for instance, political parties join forces to topple or reinforce a minority government; b) favour gaining, where people lend support to those in power so they can cash in their favours in the future; and c) power empowering, or by energizing people who experience success to desire more of it.

The False Promise of Trickle-Down Economics

According to Jim Stanford, economist with the Canadian Auto Workers union, huge corporate profits since 2000 have contributed little to investment and capital spending. The gap between cash flow and investment has raised economist's eyebrows. As the Royal Bank's Derek Holt says, "Never before have companies experienced such cash surpluses."[5]

Since 2000, corporations have been piling up cash at a rate of almost $60 billion a year, fuelled by high export prices for energy and minerals, stagnant labour costs, and corporate tax cuts that saved companies $10 billion per year between 2001 and 2005. Where is the money going? Some goes to generous dividends for shareholders, some into overseas investing, but the lion's share just sits there doing nothing. Canadian businesses currently have $280 billion in cash and paper. Corporate tax cuts as an experiment in trickle-down economics failed because profits are not being re-circulated into the economy. Who's paying for the colossal cash surplus? A big part of it is being financed by Canadian taxpayers who were told it would benefit the economy with investments and new jobs, but so far it's just collecting interest.

Discussion Questions

1. If these corporations were individual people, how would you feel about them?

2. Do we have to apply different standards to corporations than to individuals in terms of wealth accumulation and sharing of wealth?

Let's now examine how these sources of power in organizations can be turned into forms of control.

Forms of Control

Power is the activity of getting a person to do something he or she does not want to do. The sources of power in organizations are established and maintained as forms of control in two ways:

1. through direct, visible means that aim to organize and gain compliance from employees, such as the scheduling of work tasks and the distribution of resources and paycheques; and
2. through indirect, hidden ways that generate attitudes and values in support of the interests of the dominant group.

The second type represents an extremely powerful form of control because people endorse a system of rules unknowingly. Let's look at a few examples.

- An example from society is consumerism. Television commercials for Canadian Tire tell us that we need more tools to give us more time to enjoy our lives. We're taught to deal with problem products by throwing them out and buying new ones instead of fixing them. We're constantly told, "Own one today!" The hidden message is that the more material possessions we have, the better our lives become.
- Another way hidden powers are exerted is through choices students make during their years in the classroom of what high-school stream to take: will it be university or college, technical or professional, sciences or arts? The pressure to choose an education that will provide a good "career" and prepare them with the job skills for a lifetime of work often devalues the pursuit of learning and knowledge not directly related to the

People achieve success by adapting effectively to different situations. When it comes to managing gender relations, the right choice can be important for success. Below are some common gender biases in organizations.[6]

Female Strategies

Queen Elizabeth I—rule with a firm hand, surround yourself with submissive men

The First Lady—exercise power behind the scenes

The Invisible Woman—adopt a low profile, blend in, and exercise influence whenever you can

The Great Mother—exercise power through caring and nurturing

The Liberationist—play rough and take a stand in favour of the role of women

The Amazon—exercise power by building coalitions of influential women

Delilah—use powers of seduction in male-dominated organizations

Joan of Arc—gain support by using the power of a shared cause to transcend the fact you are a woman

The Daughter—attach yourself to a "father figure" prepared to act as a mentor

Male Strategies

The Warrior—use the corporation as a battleground to attract submissive women

The Father—be a father figure for younger women in search of a mentor

King Henry VIII—achieve goals through the use of absolute power, using female supporters according to their usefulness

The Playboy—use of sex appeal to win favour from female colleagues

The Jock—use of public display of behaviours demonstrating corporate power intended to attract admiration and support from women

The Little Boy—use of childish techniques to get one's way, such as displays of anger, whining, or cuteness

The Good Friend—used to develop partnerships with female colleagues based on openness and sharing

The Chauvinist Pig—use of gender-degrading messages to undermine the status of women and their achievements

workplace. Again, we're translating intangibles such as quality of life and education into objects of mass consumption.

- Ontario's Progressive Conservative Party scored two huge majority wins starting in the mid-1990s on a platform attacking government employees as lazy and by praising private companies as hard-working. The widespread initiative to promote an increased workload as the key to a robust economy throughout Canada and the United States has made us the two hardest-working countries in the world in terms of hours worked per week. It's an achievement of sorts.

But the question from a critical theory viewpoint in terms of all three examples—consumerism, career-oriented education, and long work hours—is, Who benefits? It turns out the big beneficiaries are employers. They sell more products, are able to hire more specially trained workers, and get higher productivity. The important point about the exercise of indirect power is that it exists at a deeper level, and we are often not aware of it. Let's look more closely at the process by which people adopt the values of the dominant group as their own.

Power and Ideology

An *ideology* is a set of values that forms the basis of a world view. All three examples above, in which people endorse a system of rules unknowingly, illustrate assumptions we hold about how life works. As well as being a set of values, these assumptions have a strong influence on how we make sense of our experiences and interpret reality. Also, the assumptions underpinning an ideology are rarely questioned. In the workplace, for instance, a classical structure of management is often taken for granted as the proper form of organization. Deetz and Kersten state, "Most people assume that organizational hierarchy is a necessary and useful arrangement. When a person encounters superior–subordinate situations, he or she views them as normal, acceptable, and unproblematic."[7] We have seen, however, that other perspectives than this one can be effective. Finally, by giving meaning and structure to our experiences, an ideology can influence and be used to justify our behaviours, much the way that John Milton used Christian ideology to justify the ways of God to humanity in *Paradise Lost*.

Power and Hegemony

The process of *hegemony* (pronounced *he-je'-mo-nee*) occurs when a dominant group leads another group into accepting that subordination is normal.[8] The hidden mechanics of this process represent the source of the social damage caused by domination, and as a result are of special interest to critical theorists. Since the exercise of power requires stronger and weaker players, ideology is never neutral—it favours the dominant side's world view. It is not a direct form of domination, but "rather involves attempts by various groups to articulate meaning systems that are actively taken up by other groups."[9] The controlled group participates often unknowingly in the control process of its own domination.

Consider the 2004–05 National Hockey League lockout. If you go back to Gareth Morgan's list of sources of power in organizations, you can determine the strength and weakness of each side, the NHL and the NHL Players' Association. Who comes out appearing dominant? The NHL defined the lockout as a necessary measure to secure the future of hockey. What threatened hockey's future? Overpaid players. The majority of hockey fans accepted the argument because that was presented as the main angle on the story—even though opinions to the contrary were expressed by sports writers around the country. Time will tell if hockey's best interests were served or if owners succeeded in increasing their control of the league, but it would be a safe bet that one-sided information from the league will continue, and we'll never know whether the lockout really helped or not.

Power and media control often work together. The marriage of hockey and media serves mutual interests by generating profits (through game broadcasts, news, and advertising) and by decreasing expenses (through corporate ownership networks). The Toronto Blue Jays are an example—Rogers Communications owns the team, the stadium they play in, and the television network that broadcasts their games. This convergence of interests allows for greater control of the resources. Since most media channels today are owned by large, interlocked corporations, the picture of reality being presented will not be neutral. It will most likely reflect the interests of the dominant groups.

In addition, forms of media themselves, as we touched on earlier in our discussion of McLuhan, possess their own particular strengths and weaknesses for depicting reality. Television triumphs when it comes to action, spectacle, and emotion. Radio and print are leaders for ideas and debate. A television station that promises to be *the* authoritative source may still choose the blazing building over the story on student protest, choosing the story with visual rather than cerebral content. What we end up with, then, is a picture of reality that has been highly influenced by numerous factors to serve the interests of the content producers and channels of distribution.

The Impact of Critical Theory on Communication

Purpose of Communication

- The overwhelming purpose of communication for critical theorists is to free people from domination. To do this, communication scholars attempt to expose the communication practices of dominant groups that promote imbalances and abuses of power through the manipulation of messages, exclusion of voices, and control of communication channels. This is a functional approach. It views messages as having a direct influence on the attitudes that create acceptance of subordination. Exposure of oppressive communication messages will enable more participative practices.

- On the other hand, communication research over the years has equipped management with many techniques for abusing power. The purpose of communication for groups in power is to increase domination through the use of multiple meanings, ambiguity, and selective use of information. Management is able to frame organizational interests through expressions such as "downsizing," "rightsizing," and "re-engineering," which offer room for interpretations that ultimately serve the interests of managers and owners. Power relations as a result would be further unbalanced.

- Hidden imbalances of power create conflict between workers and owners. According to Marx, this conflict would eventually cause the working classes to revolt against the economic system. Since his declaration, numerous less dramatic measures have been taken by workers to express dissatisfaction, such as work-to-rule, slowdowns, sabotage, strikes, and information campaigns.

Types of Messages and Message Flow

- Messages become distorted when they are incomplete or untruthful. The result is that certain groups are excluded from the receiving and sending of messages, leaving one group at a disadvantage and causing an imbalance of power. According to critical theory, distortion of messages occurs at both a systemic and individual level. It originates with the dominant group and is repeated and duplicated by organizational members until power relations are re-established.

- Messages flow in a twofold way: from the dominant to the subordinate groups and then throughout the subordinate networks as meanings become interpreted and articulated.

- The issue of power is nowhere more unbalanced than in the workplace, where owners control the financial livelihoods of their employees. As a result, the acceptance of a subordinate role for workers is almost as natural as children toward parents. Though we live in a democratic society, workplaces were not founded on these principles. The greater the imbalance of power, the less opportunity subordinates have for feedback, for open communication, and for expressing the truth.

Communication and Critical Theory in Today's Organizations

As well as exposing abuses of power, critical theory attempts to show that an organization based on a balance of power can be a better workplace. Domination is not a necessary part of an organization. In our closing section we will look at three areas where critical theory can provide insight: globalization, feminist theory, and "whistle-blowing."

Globalization and Critical Theory

Since the early 1980s, the restructuring of the global economy known as globalization, aided greatly by reduced government regulations, has significantly shifted the balance of power in favour of owners. The result has been greater inequality in the sharing of wealth between workers and owners as corporations exploited cheaper labour in Third World countries. Where North American and European workers once had some control over working conditions and benefits, the gap has widened between the dominant and subordinate groups. For critical theorists, the situation has grown more urgent even at home, where average wages have not substantially risen for decades, while profits and executive salaries have climbed skyward.

Widening economic gaps between rich and poor are paralleled by greater imbalances of power, creating a situation that becomes increasingly characterized by one-way rather than two-way communication activity. Corporations that are spread across numerous countries often display highly centralized forms of control and close supervision. In contrast to the "invisible hand" that Adam Smith referred to as the guiding power of the free market, today we employ powerful and complex strategies for guiding market forces.[10] To better serve the interests of the economic elites, global corporations engage in vertical integration to acquire greater control of resources and raw materials and use their marketing clout to shape consumer preferences. To fend off negative feedback and create positive images, corporate communication departments are employed. And to make it socially and politically acceptable, the whole process comes across with an aura of virtue. As an ideology, globalization stands for freedom from regulation, international activity, efficiency, and productivity. It is promoted as a force that cannot be stopped. Corrupt practices, though, exist, usually behind the scenes. And the interests of a few take priority over the interest of the many.

Peter Newman in *Titans* describes the rules of international business: "It means having to compete, *really* compete, down and dirty, with rivals ten times your size, whose ethics hark back to the pirates who once swept the Caribbean, brooms tied to their masts and mayhem in their hearts."[11] As an example, Newman cites Victor Rice, CEO of Varity Corp., under whose watch Canada's renowned farm equipment manufacturer Massey Ferguson was dismantled and its pensioners abandoned. To rescue the dying company, he accepted $200 million in government money, and then skipped the country and set up shop in Buffalo.[12]

The size of global companies is difficult to grasp. According to Newman, Wal-Mart is bigger financially than the economy of Poland, General Motors is bigger than Denmark, and Toyota, bigger than Norway. Three Canadian corporations rank among the top 15 in the world: Thomson Corp., Seagram Inc., and BCE Inc. One way they grow so rich is by avoiding taxes. When New Brunswick oil baron K C. Irving died in 1992, he willed $7 billion to a Bermuda-based trust for his sons, with one catch—they had to become non-residents of Canada to cash it in, so Ottawa would not get a cent. Frank Stronach, founder of Magna Corp., has a Swiss address for tax purposes. A popular tax haven for Canadians is the Cayman Islands, a tiny country with no economy, but with 550 banks. It's the world's fifth-largest financial centre, after New York, London, Tokyo, and Hong Kong.[13]

As inequalities among employees, organizations, and countries grow, it becomes more important from a critical theory perspective to change the power relationships that devalue people. A key point to remember is that organizational effectiveness is measured by those who hold power in the organization.

Feminism and Critical Theory

Critical theory from a feminist perspective explores the gender-based power relationships that occur in a workplace. The traditional organization, according to feminist scholars, is patriarchal, highlighting masculine values such as competition, individualism, rationality, and results-oriented thinking. In contrast, female values include cooperation, emotion, supportiveness, and process-oriented thinking. As a result, women's voices are subordinated because they are not compatible with traditional workplace values.

You'll recall from our discussion of hegemony that it is a process where communication activity within the subordinate group reinforces and creates acceptance of a subordinate attitude. A hegemonic effect can be observed in the female workplace mindset that could maintain gender-related power imbalances.[14] A common finding of studies of sexual harassment in the workplace is that women use "framing devices" in communicating sexual harassment that trivialize the event. The expressions can either reinforce or challenge the dominant ideology. So, the way women talk about sexual harassment can make it sound "normal"—defining it as flirting, a harmless joke, or a simple misunderstanding.

The result is that sexual harassment is never openly discussed as an oppressive experience, and female subordination is maintained. A challenge to the dominant male ideology would place greater importance on the event. In addition, since workplaces are structured according to male values and generally downplay the importance of emotional experiences in favour of maintaining "professionalism," dealing with sexual harassment effectively from a feminist standpoint would require significant changes in the language and attitudes of the workplace.

Whistle-Blowing—"Get with the Program, or Else"

The concept of *whistle-blowing* refers to an employee exposing illegal or unethical practices in the workplace. On the floor of workplaces and in the pages of business publications, whistle-blowing has become a fairly common subject. It can be seen as a challenge to domination, and in this way is relevant to a critical theory perspective. Mark Hayes described whistle-blowing as "one of the many ways in which routinely dominated people seek to make sense of their dominated condition and deploy all sorts of ingenious tactics to carve out and protect their own liberated spaces, be they physical or mental, and resist their dominators."[15]

Whistle-blowing then represents the act of disconnecting yourself from the familiar set of meanings you have established with your coworkers that ensures your subordinate status and launching yourself into uncertainty and unrest. You leave behind the comfortable culture of self-preservation to liberate yourself from practices that you will no longer accept. But the path can be perilous. Most companies in Canada do not respond well to criticism from subordinates. Often, whistle-blowing will put your job at serious risk. Also, organizations typically lack procedures that will protect employees from retaliation. Both of these are strong reasons for not spilling the beans.

Employees are hesitant about whistle-blowing for two main reasons: they believe that no corrective action will be taken, and they are afraid that their concerns will not remain confidential. The Washington-based National Whistleblowers Association, set up to help employees disclose violations, found in a 2002 survey of 200 whistle-blowers that half had been fired after reporting wrongdoings by managers wanting to "get even" with the reporting employee by gradually building up a fabricated file of poor performance.[16] In another survey done by *Canadian Business* magazine, 18 of 25 companies had policies in effect that encouraged whistle-blowing, including Toronto-Dominion Bank, Shell Canada, and TransAlta. In fact, a recent piece of U.S. legislation has caused a surge in whistle-blowing policies. The new law allows whistle-blowers to sue for retaliation and provides prison penalties for those bosses who retaliate against informants. Corporations are now being advised by lawyers to create cultures that encourage employees to come forth with information. Such measures are not in place in this country yet.

Even with increased protections for whistle-blowers, the price an employee pays, whether through loss of work, isolation, miserable transfers, or court time, is still high. For example, there's the case of an employee of an electronics firm in Montreal who revealed that his company was buying back used equipment, using the parts, and selling the finished products as new equipment. He says, years after losing his job, that if he had to do it over again, he would have "stayed with the company. I would have done it for selfish reasons. I would have had that nice pay cheque. I did the right thing from a moral point of view, absolutely. But if you're morally right and broke, who gives a shit?"[17]

Probably the most famous whistle-blower of all time can teach us some lessons on protecting yourself when exposing wrongdoings. In June 2005, Mark Felt unmasked himself as Deep Throat, the unknown informant who opened the lid on the Watergate scandal for the *Washington Post* in the 1970s, eventually bringing about the resignation of President Nixon. How did he get away with it? For one thing, he remained anonymous, his identity cloaked behind his famous nickname. But here's the clincher: as director of the FBI, he was in charge of the hunt for Deep Throat. In addition to sending agents on wild goose chases, he protected his identity by criticizing news reports of the scandal as being fabricated and untrue. The lesson: if your workplace does not appreciate honesty and openness in employees, and does not have policies to protect whistle-blowers—in other words, if power and control are high priorities—send the message, but hide the messenger.

The critical theory perspective focuses on the element of power and how it affects relationships and communication. In organizations, the issue of power is especially important, since most organizations are not based on democratic principles, but on principles of hierarchy and control. Numerous sources of power are exercised in organizations. Power divides people into dominant and subordinate groups. Dominant groups are supported by ideologies, which are sets of assumptions used to make sense of organizational activities—in ways that favour the dominant group's interests. Hegemony is the process whereby subordinate groups accept their status as the norm and reinforce it through routine communication activity. It represents the hidden forces in play as domination is achieved.

Critical theory is especially useful for explaining globalization, which represents a new structure or power relations in the world economy. Feminist scholars also find critical theory useful for delineating the power imbalances of gender relations in the workplace. Finally, we looked at an example of speaking up and resisting domination in today's organizations in the form of whistle-blowing.

Rising above the Bunch

You always know you've met a player when someone tells you about an activity that's better than sex.

—Garret Keizer, Crap Shoot[18]

Our case deals with a cultural self-understanding at the centre of power relationships known as the "player." According to "player" culture, there are two kinds of people: those who play the game, and those who serve the players' needs. Society establishes this distinction from grade school on. In fact, the promise of education is to turn amateurs into professionals. Educators teach us how to "get in the game" and "grab a piece of the action." The result is two lifestyles: ordinary life, and the life of the "game."[19]

Players are motivated by the desire to transcend the boundaries of ordinary experience. They move faster, are quicker to make judgments, always say the right things, are never behind the times, are "successful" with the opposite sex, are always calm and playful (not needy and desperate) and, most importantly, follow a different set of rules than non-players. Samantha from *Sex in the City* comes to mind; in business, Conrad Black—characters who eat up life like Pac Man. In the world of Internet poker, players wait for "fish" to come by—usually on the weekends after they've cashed their paycheques. The world of Internet poker involves countless hours of sitting around not playing, waiting for the fish to show up.

A player's defining relationship with the world is escapist. To become exceptional, to conquer and rise above the ordinary life "here where we sit and hear each other groan," as Keats says, is achieved in numerous ways. Players embrace materialism by embodying the promises of TV commercials. Being the first one on your block to see a new movie entitles you to call it dated. Displaying name brands connects you to the desirable inner circle. Aspiring to be a gangster by joining a gang can make you special, as can retiring earlier than your peers. The idea of exclusion is part of what defines a player's self-concept. To have players, there have to be workers, just as to have fishermen there have to be fish. They define each other, but never will they join forces, since that would remove their reason for existence. The worker, in contrast, invites participation, the more the merrier.

When there are both players and workers, the player's interests normally prevail. Cheating for a player is defined by results rather than rules: if you have to break the rules to win, maybe the rules need to be changed. In politics, players choose the proprietary party—generally Liberals in Canada, sometimes Conservatives, usually Republicans in the U.S. The NDP or Green Party is for those who strive to create a better country. Work with us, they say, together we will prevail over the forces that oppress us. Liberals and Conservatives, on the other hand, give you the identity that comes from belonging to an exclusive club. Join us, we are the movers and shakers, we matter.

Various training programs are offered to help groups appeal to the powers that be; for instance, lobbying strategies to help non-profit organizations affect changes in government or corporate policy. In the North American power structure, players can be heard giving American culture and values a greater status than their Canadian counterparts, in music or movies, as though it connects them to those values. In the media, the *National Post* newspaper tries to become a player by overtly condemning Canadian ways of business in favour of U.S. ones.

Though the concept of being a player was popularized in the sports world, with metaphors such as "take it one day at a time," "our backs are up against the wall," and "batting a thousand," it is particularly relevant to the business world. In sports, players both make an impact and express victory with great emotion. The rebirth of Russian hockey, traditionally gloomy and studious, has been characterized by Alexander Ovechkin, who pumps his fists after scoring goals and watches his own replays on the scoreboard. He explains it by saying, "It's because we're happy. We're playing in the best league in the world and we feel it. Right now I live for this day. I try not to think about tomorrow...I just do it." His fellow patriot, Ilya Kovalchuk, confirms the idea: "It's an exciting sport. It's a show. It's a game."[20] Great athletes have historically been role models for players because of the ability to make spectacular plays that transcend those of ordinary mortals.

In business, the notion of the player can be defined by its opposite: the worker, just as the opposite of "play" is "work." "For the true worker, the pleasure is in the work. The pleasure of the 'player,' on the other hand, is in having it made."[21] Escaping ordinary life for the player, then, can be equated with escaping work, since players wouldn't be caught dead doing work. A player mingles in the restaurants, while a worker creates in the kitchen. For the worker, ordinary life is work, the rest is play. For the player, ordinary life is the "game," the rest—working at the gym or around the house—is something you do in your spare time. In the play *Death of a Salesman*, Willy Loman is a worker trying to be a player and never succeeding. His son, Happy, who succeeds without effort and breaks all the rules, such as taking bribes and sleeping with other people's fiancées, is a player.[22] To seriously work at improving yourself or your relationships would be far too earnest for a player.

The fact that players perceive workers as entertaining is maddening to workers. Environmentalists of the world, social justice seekers, fighters for human rights—all aspirers to power—find their causes trampled on. It's the nature of players to ignore the monotonies of survival, just as it's the nature of workers to fight. If it's a matter of nature, though, is it worth the fight? Is their hope for workers, or is it all about sustaining illusions?

Since open and effective communication reduces diversity among people and makes them inclusive, it is more naturally found among the workers in society. Through participation and the breaking down of individual differences, mutual goals are achieved, and relationships are formed. The player's communication style is highly customized to serve two objectives: to maintain exclusivity and to make it appear effortless while labouring in frenzy—skills that are very similar to those of effective public speaking. In fact, playing is a performance where the artificial is made to look natural. A player never forgets the audience.

By nature, players and workers are opposing forces. To bridge the gulf between them requires a special and drastically different definition of player. For instance, a training session in business development called *What Does it Take to Be a Player in the High-Tech Arena* defines players as managers of integration that create a unified, client-focused strategic plan.[23] This is a different view from the one we've discussed. These players work at an executive level, where they naturally want to be, yet their focus is organizational, not individual. The creator of the session describes players as rainmakers—they make things grow. The self-centred type of player does not qualify for this assignment.

Discussion Questions

1. Discuss how a person's approach to life, as a player or as a worker, affects communication in an intrapersonal, interpersonal, and organizational sense.

2. What are the costs and benefits of each approach? Is there one that is better than the other?

3. As a manager, how do you coordinate a staff that will probably be made up of players and workers?

4. As a nation, is Canada destined to take a worker approach to life because we are located beside the United States, or is there a player approach specifically for us? Should we be content with a worker approach?

Classroom Activity

Bring in newspaper clippings of articles that show a strong bias for one side of a story. The bias will usually reveal the newspaper's (or ownership's) side of an issue. For example, let's say a city politician was discovered collecting illegal campaign funds in an election. Which perspective does a major daily newspaper take in reporting the story? It might be for or against charges being laid. What would the vested interests of a newspaper be in deciding which side to take?

As a group, select one story from your group's clippings that expresses a bias. Analyze the story as a group, looking especially at the way issues are framed, at how quotations are expressed, at what information is included and not included, at whose point of view is primary. What concepts from our discussion of critical theory can be applied to the story?

Glossary

Critical theory, p. 136
Autocracy, p. 136
Bureaucracy, p. 136
Technocracy, p. 136
Democracy, p. 136

Cooperative, p. 136
Ideology, p. 139
Hegemony, p. 140
Whistle-blowing, p. 143

Notes

1. Dennis K. Mumby, *Narrative and Social Control* (Newbury Park, CA: Sage, 1993).
2. Gareth Morgan, *Images of Organization* (Thousand Oaks, CA: Sage, 1986), 188.
3. Dennis K. Mumby, *Communication and Power in Organizations: Discourse, Ideology, and Domination* (Norwood, NJ: Ablex Publishing Co., 1988).
4. Morgan, *Images of Organization*.
5. Jim Stanford, "Let's call it the 'corporate fiscal imbalance,'" *The Globe and Mail*, February 27, 2006, A15.
6. Morgan, *Images of Organization*.
7. Stanley Deetz and S. Kersten, "Critical Models of Interpretive Research," in *Communication and Organizations*, ed. Linda Putnam and Michael Pacanowsky (Beverly Hills, CA: Sage, 1983), 162.
8. S. Hall, "Signification, Representation, Ideology: Althusser and the Post-Structuralist Debates," *Critical Studies in Mass Communication* 2 (1985): 91–114.
9. Dennis Mumby, "Power and Politics," in *The New Handbook of Organizational Communication: Advances in Theory, Research, and Methods*, eds. F.M. Jablin and L.L. Putnam (Thousand Oaks, CA: Sage, 2001), 587.
10. Morgan, *Images of Organization*, 303.
11. Peter C. Newman, *Titans* (Toronto: Penguin Books, 1999).
12. Katharine Miller, *Organizational Communication, Approaches and Processes*, 3rd ed. (Belmont, CA: Thomson Wadsworth, 2003), 129.
13. Newman, *Titans*.
14. Miller, *Organizational Communication*, 129.
15. Mark Hayes, book review, "On Whistleblowing and why it's so hard to do," *Non-violence Today Journal* (Brisbane, Australia; April 24, 2004).
16. Matthew McClearn, "A Snitch in Time," *Canadian Business*, December 29, 2003.
17. McClearn, "A Snitch in Time."
18. Garret Keizer, "Crap Shoot," *Harper's*, February 2006, 31–38.
19. Ibid.
20. Steve Milton, "New breed have heart and soul," *Hamilton Spectator*, March 1, 2006, SP4.
21. Keizer, "Crap Shoot."
22. Ibid.
23. David Goehl, *Being a High-Tech Player*, Sugarcrest Development Group, dgoehl@sugarcrest.com (accessed February 28, 2006).

PART FIVE

Individuals and Groups in Organizations

Chapter Nine

Communication Networks

The crooked unimproved roads are the roads of genius.

—*William Blake*, "The Proverbs of Hell"[1]

Learning Objectives

- Describe the communicative organization—the importance of "walking the talk" in today's workplaces

- Identify formal and informal networks in organizations, including vertical, horizontal, and electronic communication networks

- Explain the importance of social networks and the "grapevine"

- Examine key techniques for managing the grapevine

- Identify communication roles in social groups

- Review techniques for effective collaboration and communication for excellence

Putting It All Together

Now that we have completed our discussion of perspectives of organizational communication, we can move on to more practical applications of what we've learned. First, though, let's put together some basic ideas of how these perspectives help us understand organizational life.

To begin with, organizations are complex creations. We've seen that though the classical approach is rational and functional—two kingpins of organizing—it leaves many questions unanswered, questions such as how to motivate workers and what explains different performance levels in employees. It also doesn't explain how communication connects the different parts of an organization the way systems theory does. Classical management also does not investigate the sources and dynamics of power in organizations the way critical theory does. Finally, cultural studies adds the perspective of meaning in an organization—what does an organization mean to its employees? What do employees mean to each other? How are meaning and values created in an organization?

Each perspective contributes to the whole picture. The weaknesses of one are compensated for by the strengths of the other. Where the functional approach to communication lacks depth because of its emphasis on the simple exchange of information, the cultural approach contributes by bringing in processes of storytelling and the negotiation of meaning. Where classical management sees only isolated individuals and disconnected organizations, the systems approach provides ways of looking at relationships between workers and between organizations and their environments. And where hierarchical organizations employ command and control methods to create participation in the workplace, contemporary views encourage participation through dialogue, the formation of networks and team-based structures, the reliance on horizontal rather than vertical coordination, and the development of personal identity through workplace activity.

Communication technologies have allowed numerous types of team structures that span across organizational boundaries, creating "virtual" team members. Team structures have also rearranged the traditional distinctions between superiors and subordinates in the sense that team leaders are facilitators who normally do not have formal authority over others on the team. Coaching, including not only task direction but personal and emotional development, has become a common activity for managers. Types of problems in the workplace have changed also. In the past, problems in the workplace related to equipment, materials, and methods—technical matters. Today's problems are often people issues—personality clashes, conflicts and misunderstandings, and different communication styles. The importance of collaboration stresses the practical nature of the ways organizations have been redesigned. Formal structures, representing authority and control, have become redundant, as companies strive to produce more with fewer staff and resources. The breaking down of barriers between departments and in some cases even between separate companies in order to allow easier collaboration shows the emphasis on interaction, autonomy, and results, and the decreasing importance of structure.

The Communicative Organization

Today's workplace has been described by Modaff and DeWine as a communicative organization.[2] This type of organization is concerned with uncovering misunderstandings in the workplace and using communication behaviours to resolve them. Traditional organizations believed that talking and working were different, and that work begins only after talk stops. This notion grew out of the one-way flow of information in classical management—managers talked, workers listened. The *communicative organization* is built on the principle that talk is action, and the two should not be considered as separate things. Talk in the workplace is related to action because it allows goal-setting discussions, task directions, and job appraisals; it provides frameworks for new employee orientation; and it generates metaphors, values, and guiding principles for all organizational members to follow. The talk-as-action model shows how closely the structure and tasks of an organization are related to the interaction of organizational members.

The communicative organization has the following characteristics:

- **Misunderstandings are considered to be normal.** No one is blamed for communication problems. Instead, misunderstandings are opportunities that can lead to new ways of completing tasks and new roles for interacting and dealing with issues that may once have been considered unresolvable. Misunderstandings are commonplace in the communication process because of the individual differences we all display. The activity of communication creates a sharing of meaning that reduces the differences and, as a result, resolves misunderstandings. Thus, communication is necessary for removing numerous problems involving technical and emotional issues, conflict, and differences in values, attitudes, and knowledge levels. It is particularly useful for turning cultural misunderstandings into positive learning experiences.

- **Effective social interaction is a highly valued activity.** It exhibits the following characteristics:
  a. Basic communication skills originating in a receiver-oriented perspective, including active listening skills that employ all the senses, effective use of verbal and nonverbal messages, and the use of confirming and disconfirming messages.
  b. Timely feedback, including identifying when feedback should be immediate or delayed and developing the ability to express complex and emotional topics and encourage feedback about them. These skills are especially important in teamwork.
  c. Awareness and analysis of communication situations and the tools available to achieve communication objectives, in particular the channels to be used and symbols to be used. This skill requires intense focus on the receiver's situation as well as the circumstances of the sender. Recognizing the unique features of each communication situation helps you to manage working relationships. Communication is a difficult activity because universal skills are not available. Competency in communication requires the ability to decide which behaviours and responses are most appropriate for a given situation.

- **Flexibility in relationships and ability to adapt to changes in context and patterns of interaction** are essential. For example, employees need to be able to cope when working relationships take on a social aspect as a result of a lot of personal interaction, which is what happens often in team-based structures. Organizations encourage social activity as a way of reducing differences and increasing the sharing of common meanings. Changes in job status such as a promotion require flexibility, since your communication patterns and relationships will change as a result. In fact, flexibility is a desirable quality for promotion candidates.

- **The human resources (HR) function has shifted to a company's centre stage.** A focus on bottom-line results is necessary, but organizations that excel also need high-quality mental and emotional activity from employees and productive engagement. Increasingly, the role of HR has shifted from administrative duties, such as compensation, benefits, and labour relations, to training and organizational performance. Key areas cited by the Conference Board of Canada include:
  a. *Dispersed leadership.* Leadership is a role, not a function. Employees must be called on to exercise leadership in their areas of influence.
  b. *Company branding.* A company's identity not only attracts the best employees, but also helps to align employee values with those of the organization.

c. *Employee engagement.* Most employees operate at 60 percent efficiency, despite a glut of reward programs. Effective motivational strategies aim at making a job meaningful to employees.

d. *Cultural diversity.* The rapid increase of females and visible minorities in the workplace—20 percent of all employees by 2016 will be visible minorities—offers new ways of maximizing talent.

e. *Effective communication.* It can make or break a workplace by turning unproductive employees into motivated ones.[3]

Communication Networks in Organizations

This section explores the communicative organization in terms of the formal and informal patterns of interaction normally found in organizations. Messages flow in upward, downward, horizontal, and diagonal directions. They flow along channels or networks, representing various linkages among organizational members. There are communication systems that contain internal networks, which carry messages within an organization, and external networks, which carry messages between the organization and its environment.

Formal Communication Networks

The basic communication system in an organization is the formal organizational structure represented by the chain of command and the lines of authority and responsibility from the top to the bottom of the hierarchy. Normally, it takes the shape of a pyramid. Tall organizational structures have many levels of authority. Flat structures, which are preferred today because of their efficiency, have eliminated all but a few levels (see Figure 9.1).

The *formal network* normally carries messages related to task accomplishment, specifically the following types:

- Job instructions for completing specific tasks
- Job rationale explaining how one job relates to another
- Procedures and practices related to organizational policies, practices, rules, regulations, standards, and goals
- Feedback and appraisal messages providing responses from superiors about job performance
- Mission statements related to overall organizational goals designed to align employee values toward a common purpose

Vertical and Horizontal Communication

In organizations, there are four directions, or channels, of information flow: downward, upward, horizontal, and diagonal. In this section we will examine these communication channels and the types of messages common to each.

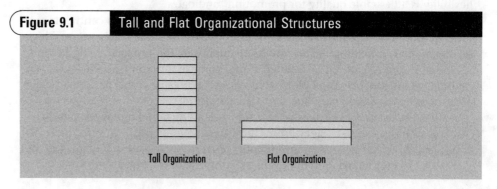

Figure 9.1   Tall and Flat Organizational Structures

Tall Organization   Flat Organization

Downward Communication

Downward messages usually follow the formal communication channels that make up the chain of command. Examples of downward messages are job assignments and directions, policy and procedure announcements, work schedules, performance appraisals, and the distribution of rewards and benefits. These functional types of messages are compatible with classical management theories. Going all the way back to Taylor's scientific management, which stressed the operational-level relationships between managers and workers, and Weber's bureaucracy, which provided an organization-wide framework based on different levels of authority, the emphasis has been on downward communication flow—messages originate with those in power.

The following are information channels used most often for downward communication:

1. Printed Messages
   - handbooks, instruction and reference manuals, job descriptions, work rules
   - newsletters, pay inserts, memos
   - advertising, bulletin boards, posters, brochures, company reports
2. Personal Meetings
   - interviews and evaluations
   - training and mentoring
3. Group Meetings
   - department and committee meetings
   - team meetings
4. Mediated Messages
   - e-mail and computer messages systems
   - video presentations and conferences
   - voice mail

The research generally shows widespread ineffectiveness with downward communication channels because they provide insufficient or incomplete information. Employees also feel that managers are not being honest with them and that more open communication would increase feelings of loyalty to the organization. In addition, managers are blamed for not being aware of problems that employees regard as serious.

Studies by the Canadian Policy Research Networks (CPRN) revealed the following information:[4]

a. Better communication is what most employees would like to see in their relationships with their employers.
b. Good communication was linked with three other dimensions of workplace relationships: trust, commitment, and employee influence.
c. Companies of over 500 employees are more likely to use formal channels to share information with employees. In small firms of 20 employees or less, the information sharing often occurs on an informal basis.

A common problem with downward channels is serial distortion. Messages travel down the ranks of hierarchy as though down a staircase, stopping briefly at each step as they move toward their destination. Message distortion happens for a number of reasons. Misunderstandings occur at each level, causing messages to be changed. People can add or remove pieces of information from the message. For example, a manager might say, "We need to service our customers more efficiently by returning voice mail messages the same day." A subordinate along the way might alter the message by saying, "We need to serve our customers better by answering their calls more promptly." Another manager might say, "We need to consider calling customers back more quickly in order to serve them better." Lower-level managers often add or remove information out of resistance to the message. Adding information may also make the message more exciting, and in this way give the sender a boost in importance. Removing information from an especially harsh message also serves the purpose of protecting your staff's feelings.

Upward Communication

The problem is when you look at the reporting structure of an organization, particularly the information that goes to the chief executive, it is always filtered. It may be unintentionally or it may be intentionally. The CEO is making decisions that are not necessarily based on reality.

—Ivan Kalley, Manager, Strategic Pathways[5]

Upward messages are required to provide feedback for downward communication. Recently, more companies are realizing the importance of creating a two-way loop where information flows both down and up along the lines of authority. Traditionally, though, it has not been the case. Decision makers in organizations have usually been isolated from employees. Problems of low morale or poor management have remained in the dark. A survey of 23 000 North American workers found that only 37 percent had a clear picture of what their company was trying to achieve and the rationale behind its goals. Only one in five employees was enthusiastic about company goals. And only 20 percent of employees fully trusted their company.[6] The importance of upward communication was highlighted by the human relations approaches, emphasizing the value of inviting employees to participate in the achievement of organizational goals. Feedback up the ranks gives employees greater involvement in the workplace and improves motivation. To put this lack of unity into perspective, consider how effective a hockey or football team would be operating with such a scattered focus.

The following are information channels used most often for upward communication:

1. Printed Messages
   - memos and reports
   - suggestion boxes
   - grievance procedures
   - surveys and evaluation systems

2. Personal Meetings
   - appraisal interviews
   - grievance hearings
   - conferences

3. Group Meetings
   - department meetings
   - project groups, team meetings
   - training sessions

4. Mediated Messages
   - e-mail and computer message systems
   - telephone
   - teleconferences

Studies by the Canadian Policy Research Networks (CPRN) showed the following results about using employee influence as a workplace strategy:[7]

a. Even though employee empowerment has been advocated by many management theorists as a strategy to bring out satisfaction, commitment, and performance in workers by giving them a greater say in workplace decisions, only 50 percent of workplaces in Canada say increasing employee participation is "important." Thirty per cent of workplaces view it as "very important," and 20 percent as "not important."
b. Large workplaces of 500 employees and more place greater emphasis on employee participation.

Studies by the CPRN also revealed interesting results on employee feedback:[8]

a. Two-thirds of employees in Canada say that their performance is measured against standard objectives.

Managing Your Manager[9]

Bad bosses are often just good people doing a bad job, many of them unaware of the hurt and stressed-out employees they've left along their path. Jim Clemmer offers some strategies for dealing with bosses that have become ineffective. There are several reasons why bosses go bad. The abundance of electronic communication devices has produced the notion that everything can be resolved by firing off another message. But e-mails and intranets can be barriers to understanding because of the incompleteness of electronic messages and lack of human contact. When things get bad or bosses want to show that they're in control, they often respond with closer supervision, or micro-management—a strategy suitable only for employees in training. Then again, maybe they had a bad boss for a role model, or just got promoted for the wrong reasons. And if they haven't received any feedback about their ineffectiveness, its possible they're not even aware of their flaws. So what do you do?

If your boss is simply a good person performing badly, it might be time for you to exercise some leadership skills. This strategy will not make your boss better, but it will allow you to take more control of your workplace responsibilities so your boss does not drag you down. Do some homework and find out what the key goals and priorities are. Connect with the networks that have power and influence so you can build support. Draw up a list of priorities and review them with your boss. Identify your boss's personal style—is it analytical, action-oriented, reflective, team-oriented—and approach him or her accordingly. Most important, don't let yourself become a victim. Build relationships you can lean on with peers and other managers.

Discussion Questions

1. As a manager, what are the advantages and disadvantages of electronic communication technologies?

2. Discuss the benefits and drawbacks of using a direct and indirect strategy for telling your boss about his or her flaws. Which would be best?

3. If you had a bad boss (or a bad teacher), how would you handle the situation?

b. Two-thirds of employees in Canada say that they receive formal feedback in the form of performance appraisals, typically once a year.

Horizontal Communication

The lateral exchange of messages between people at the same level of authority is called horizontal communication. These messages are usually work-related, so they perform a functional communication role. They are also useful for carrying social messages, and in this way would serve a human relations purpose. Usually the structure of a workplace prevents a lot of horizontal communication from occurring. Fayol's gangplank, that connects two coworkers along a short cut that cuts across the administrative hierarchy, is one example of horizontal communication. A lateral exchange of messages is useful for task accomplishment, information sharing, and increasing employee involvement in workplace activity.

Informal Communication Networks

The term *grapevine* originated from the military use of telegraph wires strung along trees during the American Civil War. The messages that travelled along the wires were often unclear and incomplete, and their sources were not always known, thus, the notion of rumour became attached to the grapevine. In organizations, messages that do not travel along the formal networks or the chain of command are described as informal. The well-known song *I Heard It Through the Grapevine*, by Marvin Gaye, describes someone finding out from a second-hand source that he has lost his girlfriend to another guy. It is an example of information travelling along informal networks.

The *informal networks* of an organization are established through social interaction and can take many forms as employees move around, are hired and retired, and develop new relationships. They are formed around coffee break groups or various social activities, such as sports teams, from outside the workplace. Grapevines can emerge through personal attractions, such as having things in common; by proximity, where people working side by side will develop a relationship; or by sheer accident—you take on a coworker's workload because of illness and discover a new group of acquaintances with whom you begin to share information.

Informal networks have proven to be surprisingly effective as communication channels for the following reasons:

- **Informal messages travel quickly.** After sharing a message, one group of six people will carry it to six new groups, and so on. So by the mid-morning coffee break, a piece of interesting news will have spread throughout the workplace. Of course, the bigger the news, the faster it moves. So, informal messages achieve quickness by travelling by clusters instead of in chain-link sequences (see Figure 9.2).
- **Informal messages are accurate.** Though we often regard unofficial information (messages not following the formal paths) as fabrication or rumour, in fact the opposite is true. The grapevine is accurate because the people along the networks know each other and personal credibility is at stake. False stories are quickly sorted out and dropped, and the sender of them may be left out of future message exchanges. So, the process is a self-monitoring one. In addition, the richness of face-to-face communication, with its numerous nonverbal cues, makes it more difficult to be deceitful.
- **Informal messages are sincere.** Since most informal networks involve workers on the same level of authority, a high degree of openness and trust exists. Many supervisors have no doubt overheard things about themselves or their staff that would never come out in formal communication channels. In this sense, the grapevine is a rich source of information.
- **Informal messages satisfy an information need.** The smart manager realizes that employees will get the story one way or another and it would raise the manager's profile in employees' eyes if it came from him or her. The presence of strong informal channels in a workplace usually indicates that the formal channels are withholding information. Organizations have learned that by presenting information openly, it can be framed in advantageous ways. When employees need to speculate on what's going on, the framing effect is far less positive and feelings of resentment and isolation can develop. So, informal channels serve the functional purpose of providing necessary information to organizational members. Since the grapevine is natural and inevitable, managers will never be able to eliminate it. It is far wiser to accept it and try to manage it. In fact, some managers have used informal networks as a way of communicating company messages.

Informal Networks of Organizations

Informal networks in organizations are invisible and dynamic structures connecting all parts of an organization. There are many eager contributors, and information flows at lightening speed. Like all dynamic, self-perpetuating systems, the grapevine can either work for an organization or against it. It can help managers get a sense of the morale of the organization and become aware of the anxieties and concerns of employees. It can also provide feedback about your formal communication networks, so you can

Figure 9.2 Messages Travelling along Informal Networks

see how well they are working. Managing the grapevine can be an important tool for organizations. Studies show that about 80 percent of the information that moves along the grapevine is work-related.[10]

Ignoring informal networks or trying to destroy them will usually lead to low workplace morale, a drop in productivity, and misunderstandings. If managers are incomplete with their messages, employees will fill in the gaps, either by fabricating information or explaining why certain details have been left out. Then the messages take on a life of their own, and the final story is out of the control of the manager. Employees learn where to find information in their workplace. If they don't get it from their supervisor, they go straight to the grapevine. Keeping a close watch of your company's informal networks lets a manager know if his or her messages are being received as they were intended.

Even so, many employee feelings are not articulated through formal channels. Employees often save sensitive subjects, such as job security, hiring activity, or unfair workplace practices, for personal audiences. Talking on the record to a manager about personal concerns could be too revealing. In the same way, challenging company policies might not be acceptable and could damage an employee's reputation. For certain subjects, you need to find people you can trust.

Misinformation or misunderstandings can flourish in online message boards or e-mail boxes because of the limited information in electronic messages. Compared to face-to-face communication, which is rich in verbal and nonverbal information and provides immediate context, e-mails are primarily verbal. As we said, where there are gaps in information, employees will fill them. The best grapevine sources in organizations, and often the first ones we turn to, are administrative assistants because they have open access to the entire organization.

Managing the Grapevine

It's essential to be open and honest with employees and coworkers. People want to know what's going on, and it's usually best to work with your employees than to leave them out of the process. When it comes to mean-spirited rumours, search out the instigators and find out what they really wanted to say. Perhaps their ill will was a response to a misunderstanding or a lack of information. The more information you provide, the fewer information gaps will have to be filled in by the grapevine. A manager runs the risk of losing touch with his or her staff if the grapevine is their main source of information.

Employee Networks and High-Performance Workplaces

A growing body of research has found that the network, or team, approach to the workplace has strong effects on productivity, quality, and profit. A survey of companies in the United States in 2000 finds that around 40 percent have self-directed work teams and nearly 60 percent use quality circles. Numerous studies have shown the importance of social networks in organizational learning, both internally among work groups and externally among colleagues from other companies. "By promoting social interaction, networks generate trust and norms of reciprocity—social capital—that are conducive to knowledge transfer. Reciprocity creates an incentive for information sharing, while trust enhances the quality of the information being shared."[11]

So why are more workplaces in Canada and the U.S. not adopting high-performance practices when empirical studies consistently demonstrate their benefits? One reason is financial. Unless a company is desperate and losing money, it will continue doing business as usual; also, smaller companies feel they do not have the resources to engage in networking activities. A second reason is that the intensity of workplace change and innovation does not reach all companies at the same time.[12] We might add that the personal investment required in creating a teamwork environment can be costly. Managers may feel disoriented and insecure in giving up the reigns of power to work groups. Half-hearted adoptions of team structures have failed because the engagement processes were not genuine.

Communication Roles in Networks

Each member of a communication network plays his or her unique role in the group. Below are examples of common network roles that individuals play. The roles we play in groups are situational, so we may play the role of isolate in one group and liaison

Expressways and Dirt Roads[13]

Formal and informal communication networks can be compared to expressways and dirt roads in some illuminating ways. Just as most of the world's roads are dirt, most communication channels in organizations are informal. They are social creations evolving from necessity and proximity, the driving forces behind community life. The dirt road was here first.

A dirt road fits its dimensions to its surroundings, just as informal communication suits its situations. It is interactive, responding to and reflecting its landscape, and providing clues about its users. An expressway, in contrast, disregards and flattens its landscape and takes the shape of the paving machines that created it.

A dirt road, on the other hand, is not a conquest, but a cohabitation.

While an expressway retains its rigid form indefinitely, like a chain of command, a dirt road is alive, changing from day to day and season to season, absorbing changes in climate instead of deflecting them. It needs to be navigated carefully, having its own built-in speed bumps, as do workplace conversations. To keep your car from falling apart, it enforces humility. It needs to be walked on, and to have things noticed, to make its traveller part of the countryside. An expressway, in contrast, has replaced the evidence of the journey with smooth, fast silence and a sense of urgency and purpose.

Once a road is paved, it prevents growth and change.

---

in another. They are also a product of many circumstances—knowledge, age, experience, position, group chemistry, and personal qualities[14]

Opinion leaders. Group members rely on opinion leaders to explain and interpret messages. Opinion leaders have more knowledge or are connected to more sources of information than other group members. They attain their status either through holding a formal status in the group or through expertise.

Gatekeepers. Gatekeepers are the link that controls which messages enter a network. Gatekeeping is performed regardless of status and can be done by both secretaries or presidents of companies. A substantial amount of power is derived from the gatekeeping function.

Boundary spanners. Group members who interact with people from outside the network are boundary spanners. Sales people often perform this function, carrying valuable information to and from the network. High-level managers are also boundary spanners in activities such as meetings and conferences.

Bridges. Members who connect two groups by being a member of both are bridges. Committee members and department heads are examples. This role is described as a "linking pin" by Likert.

Liaisons. These members, generally gregarious and social, make connections between groups by carrying messages back and forth. They often have more authority than other members and have considerable knowledge of the organization. Liaisons regard their integrative role as important.

Isolates. Isolates are characterized as being less interested in group interaction than other group members. Some workers, such as sales reps on the road by themselves or technical staff engaged in individual work, lend themselves to being this type of member. They tend to be uninvolved with the free flow of information, often because of lack of experience or authority.

Electronic Communication Networks

Though face-to-face messages from immediate managers are preferred by most employees, there are many advantages to electronic communication networks. Electronic newsletters, the intranet, and e-mail systems should be produced regularly or be accessible during regular times. They should have a defined purpose and format. Above all, electronic networks should not be downward only. To be useful, open, and inclusive of all employees' feelings, they need a two-way—downward and upward—flow of information.

The benefit of electronic networks is their efficiency. Larger numbers of employees can be reached more quickly than through personal meetings. Contract employees, shift workers, and at-home workers can be reached and can respond easily and with more flexibility of time. Detailed information can be sent more cheaply.

There are also disadvantages. Managers cannot guarantee that messages have been read and understood. Individual questions cannot be answered as effectively. Language differences in the workplace can decrease the fidelity of electronic messages. E-mail networks also pose the problem of accessibility to communication technology and technical skills of employees. Since two-way flow of messages is critical, it is important to assure employees that their views will be listened to and shared by others. The reach of e-mail networks is also an issue. Large external audiences can get to read about both good and bad business practices exercised in your company. E-mail dialogues containing messages of discontent can have an impact on the reputation of the organization. So, a manager's efforts to listen and respond to grapevine dialogue can improve employee satisfaction in the workplace.

In today's fast-changing work environments, upward communication channels that work particularly well are the following:

- Senior managers "walking the job" to find out what employees want and what they like and dislike
- Listening to employee committees or trade union representatives to establish a partnership approach to achieving goals and relationships of trust, especially during major changes
- Using team briefings and feedback forums
- Conducting employee surveys
- Having intranet discussion formats
- Establishing project teams

Communicating for Excellence

Communication is a social process that engages employees in the activities of an organization. Engagement refers to employees becoming personally implicated in the performance of their own team. The term "personally implicated" means that the conditions are created where people choose to *volunteer* themselves to participate in a personal journey that connects the organization's goals, their own work, and the attitudes and values they possess that will contribute to the new environment.[15] The concept of engagement specifies that the communication activities required for organizational change are built into the change process—that's the essential ingredient for success. This allows employees to see that their involvement is making a difference to them and to the organization.

Unsuccessful communication strategies leave employees feeling like spectators in the process. Instead of feeling like they are making valuable contributions, they feel like the

To overcome the barriers to upward communication, such as lack of trust, fear of punishment, or a history of disinterest, Strategic Pathways, a communication consulting company, has opened up a call centre. Its client base is made up of all sorts of companies in the area. The Calgary-based office takes in calls from workers who want to pass information directly to their company president, whether it's complaints or new ideas, but don't want to do it directly or in their own workplace. The information remains unfiltered and anonymous, providing executives with information they normally wouldn't get. And employees don't have to worry about any harmful effects of being connected to the message. In the six weeks after it opened, the centre received 4000 calls from employees.[16]

change is being done to them, despite the promises of listening and involvement that managers offer. In the end they feel disengaged from the process.

Here are some keys steps for successful engagement:

1. Begin with authentic agreement from all members of the change team so that the value each member will be contributing is understood.
2. Clearly express how engagement will be achieved and how it will add value to the project.
3. Engage change advocates who will create positive momentum early in the process as an example for others.
4. Select a leader with a management style that is compatible with a participatory process.
5. Get team members to discuss what styles of engagement are suitable to their organization.[17]

Examples of Communication Engagement

Reinventing Canada Post

Effective communication in a company requires a combination of both vertical and horizontal channels—and some reinventing to get rid of old communication barriers. Canada Post has been bragging lately about its successful journey to excellence. The 150-year-old company restructured itself into work teams that create greater interaction among employees and participation in the work process. It has been profitable eight years in a row (from 1995 to 2003) and has generated $274 million for its shareholder, the federal government. The reinventing was accomplished through a change in its leadership culture. Over 3600 employees, including senior management, received leadership training on change readiness and managing work teams—the new structure of the huge organization. Chairman André Ouellet states:

> The concept of value streams has been introduced at Canada Post, with leaders focused on improving the end-to-end processes. Employees work in small work groups, and rotate through different jobs within the value stream. This makes for more interesting work, teamwork and relationship building, and better ergonomics. Employees also see how value flows, better appreciate internal customer/supplier requirements, and get a real sense of where they fit in the overall system. This leads to employee satisfaction.[18]

A *value stream* brings together two ideas: the *stream* refers to the process of work; *value* represents the degree of quality built into each stage of the work process by an organization's employees. By allowing greater participation, teamwork puts more emphasis on each employee's contribution along the value stream.

Payoffs of Participation at Purolator

Organizations have realized the financial benefits of a culture of involvement and commitment. Purolater Courier, a branch of Canada Post, considers quality not only the route to customer satisfaction and competitiveness but also to better health and safety in the workplace. Since joining Alberta's Partners in Injury Reduction program, the company has earned more than $600 000 in Workers Compensation Board premium rebates.

Employee Communication in the Caterpillar "Piazza"

Caterpillar, a global manufacturer of large construction machines, employs people from many cultural backgrounds. At its European headquarters in Geneva, the challenge was how to make members of this diverse and dynamic population think of themselves as a team. Communication manager Gottardo Bontagnali thought about the role played by the "piazza" in European villages—a place where people go to shop, exchange news, and spend time socializing. He saw it as an efficient communication tool, so he created a "piazza" at Caterpillar's Geneva office.

Walls were painted with village scenes featuring Cat machines. The villagers portrayed were Cat employees. The atmosphere, with the help of a little imagination, was that of a European market square.

Employees were encouraged to use the piazza for casual meetings, coffee get-togethers, and regular social exchanges. As well as becoming an important means of sharing information among employees, it allowed a team spirit and a common sense of purpose to develop in the organization.[19]

Collaborating in the Workplace

The three examples above illustrate what can happen when the potential within an organization's pool of human capital is released. Engaging employees' creativity and energy by allowing them to collaborate will repay the company's investment with interest. If managers devalue workers, they should not expect high performance. If they treat people like subordinates, they will never have a chance to grow. If managers treat them like partners, employees will participate like owners. As far as two-way communication goes, the principle is simple: when downward communication is insufficient, rumours and misinformation will fill the gaps; where upward communication is constricted, employees will be alienated, morale will suffer, and performance will drop. In unionized workplaces, strikes or lockouts could result.

Traditionally, business plans and change programs in organizations were kept secret. Company insiders and expensive consultants designed strategies and selected messages that would have the intended impact on the workforce. Employees were regarded as passive and compliant receivers of information. The thinking was similar to early media effects theories that saw messages as magic bullets or hypodermic needles. Today's organizations have realized that business strategies are greatly enhanced by engaging those who will implement them. As well as increasing employee acceptance for the change, engagement taps into the collective intelligence of the workers. But there's still a long way to go. A survey by the Right Management Consultants in conjunction with the International Association of Business Communicators Research Foundation found that "just one in three companies have employees who understand and live up to the corporate business strategy." About 100 Canadian companies were among those surveyed. According to Janice McNally, vice president of marketing for the Toronto chapter of the IABC Research Foundation, "many managers, including senior level leaders, lack the necessary skills to effectively engage employees."[20]

We began this chapter by describing the communicative organization. This type of organization integrates communication into its operational activity—also known as "walking the talk." In traditional organizations, communication was something that was done by managers and employees to achieve organizational objectives. The communicative organization realizes that talk is action. In fact, most organizational objectives are achieved through talk. An organization's structure and tasks are more closely related to employee interaction than was ever before realized.

Employee interaction takes place along formal and informal networks. The formal networks are rigid and follow the structure of the chain of command, while informal networks are based on social and personal activities and are constantly changing. Information in organizations usually flows down and up the formal structure and horizontally across the informal networks. Many organizations today have flattened their structures by eliminating vertical levels of authority, thus creating the need for more horizontal communication. These structures are usually based on groups or teamwork.

Social networks in organizations are important because most of the information travelling through them is work-related, so a lot of an organization's knowledge exists along its social networks. Managers who discourage social interaction will often lower worker morale and in turn productivity. Maintaining good relations with social networks can connect a manager to a valuable source of information.

Employees have communication roles in their social groups, such as gatekeepers, liaisons, opinion leaders, bridges, and isolates.

Organizations can cultivate their social groups, and in this way expand their organizational knowledge, by providing opportunities for interaction. This is one way of bringing out the hidden potential in workplace groups.

Case Study

TELUS Enhances Corporate Dialogue[21]

When Darren Entwistle became CEO of TELUS in 2000, a company formed by combining Alberta Government Telephones and BCTel, his aim was to transform a telephone company based in Western Canada into a national telecommunications powerhouse. He did it by opening a mailbox—a weekly electronic letter to employees, along with a mailbox for employees to respond to him. This communication strategy would eventually transform the traditional entitlement culture of the monopoly-era telephone business into a competitive, high-performance organization with informed employees who are engaged in the success of the business.

Strategic objective. The goal was to develop an internal communication system based on regular monitoring of employee issues as expressed to the CEO mailbox. A communication audit done in 2001 found that only 70 percent of TELUS employees had online access. The others shared a computer or had no access to the mailbox. The questions asked by the auditors were:

- Would employee use of e-mail change as a result of the CEO mailbox?

- Would dialogue begin to reflect the cultural shift in the corporate agenda?

- Would concerns, questions, and stories that employees shared in the CEO mailbox illustrate the cultural shift at TELUS?

Methodology and challenges. The communication team aimed to develop a tracking system to summarize shifts in tone, level of employee engagement, and subject matter of issues discussed in the mailbox. For consistency of tracking, a decision-making tool was designed to standardize interpretations of employee messages. Another challenge involved submissions in English and French, since the mailbox is available in both official languages. TELUS also faced organizational and business challenges, such as merger issues, budget target reductions, rapid growth in employees, geographic expansion, and a changing union environment. Cultural differences such as communication styles, meeting styles, changes in leadership, and historical tradition were major issues.

Results. The CEO mailbox is a strategic communication management system at TELUS. It enables management to communicate the corporate agenda, transformation efforts, and organizational values to members. Employee correspondence provides feedback on how much employees are adopting corporate policies, allowing managers to make policy adjustments as needed. In 2002, the mailbox received 1541 letters, up 17 percent from 2001. About 25 percent of letters came from customers and 75 percent from employees. TELUS achieved its goal of providing e-mail access to 100 percent of employees by the end of 2002. TELUS also received numerous awards recognizing achievements in corporate culture, change mastery, work–life balance programs, leadership, and communications.

Epilogue. In 2002 TELUS underwent a major operational efficiency program, resulting in significant office closures and staff reductions of 6000—25 percent of the work force. This was followed by labour negotiations with its workers that went on for four-and-a-half years, as each decision by the Canada Labour Relations Board was appealed by the company. On July 21, 2005, thousands of employees walked off the job, a day before TELUS was scheduled to unilaterally impose a new labour contract. According to one disgruntled employee, whose comments probably never made it into the CEO mailbox,

> I used to really like working for TELUS....Now I hide my [identification] badges and never wear a TELUS logo for fear of repercussions from angry customers....My manager hides (nay, cowers in fear) in a cubicle and doesn't manage his team properly. He's completely lost control....TELUS has completely lost touch with both the customer and the workforce....You want a quality work force? Treat them with respect and dignity. Eliminate panoptical management. Eliminate pulse check surveys. Eliminate spying....Get rid of meritocratic programs like Team Machine and variable pay and give us true rewards: job security, wages and benefits.[22]

TELUS had argued that it required greater flexibility in staffing, especially the ability to outsource jobs. The union was concerned that the language in the new contract would let TELUS contract out any position in the company.

The new contract merges six collective agreements and covers about 14 000 employees.

For discussion, try to answer the questions asked originally by the TELUS communication team when the CEO mailbox began:

1. Would employee use of e-mail change as a result of the CEO mailbox?

2. Would dialogue begin to reflect the cultural shift in the corporate agenda?

3. Would concerns, questions, stories that employees shared in the CEO mailbox illustrate the cultural shift at TELUS?

   Let's also consider these questions:

Discussion Questions

4. In view of the major layoffs and labour problems, how open and "real" was the dialogue created by the CEO mailbox?

5. Did the feedback received by the mailbox reflect the corporate agenda?

6. How could TELUS have improved employee communication in its CEO mailbox program?

7. What other obstacles to success existed for the TELUS change effort?

Classroom Activity

Pulling Together

Think of a group, team, or organization you've belonged to, such as a sports team, school or volunteer group, or workplace group. Form class groups and discuss your individual group experience with the others in your class group. What were some of the obstacles you faced in achieving the group's goals? How did they make you feel? How did you overcome them? Did you feel like an important part of the group? Why? Share your experiences with other group members and develop a list of common obstacles and techniques of overcoming them. Share them with the class.

Glossary

Communicative organization, p. 152
Dispersed leadership, p. 153

Company branding, p. 153
Employee engagement, p. 154

Notes

1. William Blake, "The Proverbs of Hell," *The Marriage of Innocence and Experience* (London: Dover Publications, 1994).

2. Daniel Modaff and Sue DeWine, *Organizational Communication* (Los Angeles, CA: Roxbury Publishing, 2002).

3. Prem Benimadhu, "HR chief moves to centre stage at companies," *National Post*, February 1, 2006, WK6.

4. Canadian Policy Research Networks, "Information Sharing" (2004), http://JobQuality.ca/indicator_e/com003.stm (accessed October 5, 2005).

5. Gillian Shaw, "Pulling Together," *National Post*, February 8, 2006, WK6.

6. Ibid.

7. Canadian Policy Research Networks, "Information Sharing" (2004), http://JobQuality.ca/indicator_e/com002.stm (accessed October 5, 2005).

8. Canadian Policy Research Networks, "Information Sharing" (2004), http://JobQuality.ca/indicator_e/com004.stm (accessed October 5, 2005).

9. Jim Clemmer, "Bad Boss? Learn How to Manage your Manager," *The Globe and Mail*, August 5, 2005, C1.

10. "Did You Hear It Through the Grapevine?" *Training and Development Journal* 48, no. 10 (1994): 20.

11. Christopher L. Erickson and Sanford M. Jacoby, "The Effect of Employer Networks on Workplace Innovation and Training," *Industrial and Labour Relations Review* (April 2002): 6.

12. Ibid.

13. Tim Brookes, "The Driveway Diaries: A Dirt Road Almanac," *Harper's*, November 2005, 29–30.

14. Everett M. Rogers and Rekha Agarwala-Rogers, *Communication in Organizations* (London: The Free Press, 1976).

15. John Smythe, "The Democratization of Strategy and Change: Headlines from a Recent Study into Employee Engagement," *Communication World*, March/April 2005.

16. Shaw, "Pulling Together."

17. Ibid.

18. Andre Ouellet, *Canada Post's Excellence Journey*, National Quality Institute, Roadmap to Excellence (1-800-263-9648 x221).

19. Carol Kinsey Goman, "Unleashing the Power of Creative Collaboration: A Look at Three World Stories about Human Potential," *Communication World*, November/December 2004.

20. "Firms lag in relaying strategy to employees," *The Globe and Mail*, October 14, 2004, C2.

21. Mary Pat Barry, director, Corporate Communications, TELUS Inc., Burnaby, B.C., from "Canadian Telephone Company Enhances Corporate Dialogue with CEO Mailbox," *Communication World*, July/August 2004.

22. LaborNet: Online Communications for a Democratic Labor Movement, "Another employee's feelings . . . Pulsecheck comments from a disgruntled employee about the TELUS workplace," http://labornet.org/news/0604/pulse.htm (accessed October 13, 2005).

Chapter Ten

Interpersonal Communication

All the world's a stage, and all the men and women merely players.

—William Shakespeare, As You Like It

Learning Objectives

- Explore the nature and functions of intrapersonal and interpersonal communication

- Examine intrapersonal communication processes, including self-identity, perception, and emotions, and their theoretical foundations

- Examine interpersonal communication processes, including relationship formation, maintenance, and change, and their theoretical foundations

- Identify skills for managing intrapersonal communication related to self-concept, perceptual processes, and communication and emotions

- Identify skills for managing and increasing effectiveness in interpersonal relationships

- Explore the concept and practice of emotional intelligence

- Review techniques for effective superior–subordinate communication

Communication

In previous chapters, we have discussed perspectives for understanding organizational communication, contexts of communication in the workplace, and formal and informal communication networks. In the remaining chapters we will examine the communication skills, structures, and processes essential for success in contemporary organizations.

We will look at the individual communication processes involved in human perception, the formation of self-identity, and communication and emotions. This will be followed by a discussion on the formation and maintenance of interpersonal relationships, group communication in the workplace, and the skills involved in emotional intelligence. We will look at the communication activities necessary for effective leadership, employee motivation, and learning skills. Conflict-management skills will also be covered. Finally, internal and external communication systems, commonly known as corporate communication and public relations, will be discussed.

The Nature of Interpersonal Communication

Interpersonal communication is unique compared to other forms of communication. It involves few participants, usually taking place between two people. So few participants allows for close proximity, with most interpersonal exchanges occurring at arm's length. Interpersonal communication has been described as being very "rich" in information because it uses many sensory channels. This physical closeness allows all of our senses, including smell and touch, to be engaged. Also, feedback is almost always immediate.

The central distinguishing factor, though, is that in interpersonal communication a relationship exists between the participants. So, we are not simply acting out social situations, but we see each other and ourselves as unique individuals. We change our behaviours from situation to situation, from our conversations with store clerks to those with friends and with bosses, to reflect the differences in our relationships. In turn, each relationship contributes meaning about ourselves through the feedback that we receive and forms part of our self-identity.

Functions of Interpersonal Communication

One reason for engaging in interpersonal communication is to gain information about other people. Getting to know people better allows us to interact with them more effectively. It also gives us the ability to predict how they will think, feel, and act in certain situations. This information is gained through normal communication behaviours, such as observing people, talking about them with others, and having conversations with them directly. The concept of self-disclosure, where we reveal personal information, is often used to increase closeness in relationships because people will usually reveal their own personal information in response.

We also use interpersonal communication to build a context of understanding. We understand better people with whom we have close relationships. Just as human communication has verbal and nonverbal elements, interpersonal messages have two parts. Words can have a *content meaning*, which refers to their literal meaning, such as the words "I love you." Words also have a *relational meaning*, which refers to how the message is said. A parent can say "I love you" to a child matter-of-factly or emotionally. Often in romantic relationships, it's not what you say but how you say it that is important, because the method of expression describes the relationship. You will recognize people engaged in conflict by the way they talk to each other. Interpersonal communication helps us understand each other better.

Interpersonal communication is also essential for *personal identity*. The feedback we receive in social communication gives us information about ourselves, which, over time, becomes our self-concept. Awareness of ourselves allows us to understand who we are and helps us deal with internal problems, such as low self-esteem, conflict, and emotional experiences.

Finally, interpersonal communication allows us to satisfy our needs. In terms of relationships and interpersonal communication, research on satisfying human needs is vast. Normally, satisfaction of needs falls into three areas: inclusion, control, and affection.[1]

- *Inclusion.* Communicating with people provides a sense of belonging. We all need to feel included by other people, whether it's family, friends, or coworkers. If we communicate effectively, we will form relationships, and our social need of inclusion will be met.
- *Control.* People also have a desire to influence others. The closer your relationship with someone, the more influence you have *over each other.* Say you need to move your refrigerator out of the basement. How many people (other than family) could you ask for help and expect a "yes" answer? In close friendships, you can usually make a request and expect compliance by virtue of your relationship. And the important point here is that's it's reciprocal—your partner expects the same from you. This is not control as domination, which normally destroys relationships. This is control as mutual influence.

  The issue of control in relationships is often discussed in terms of symmetrical and complimentary exchanges.[2] In symmetrical relationships, people communicate as equals, the way personal friends or coworkers of the same status in the workplace would. Complimentary relationships involve dominant and submissive partners, where one partner's plans are normally accepted and not the other's. This type of personal relationship is not healthy and usually will not last long, though in the workplace most superior–subordinate relationships follow this pattern. The issue is also important in gender communication, traditionally a complimentary-style relationship dominated by the male, but changing rapidly as greater equality is achieved in male–female relationships.
- *Affection.* The third social need that interpersonal communication satisfies is the need to be liked, respected, and important to others. We favour people who respect us over those who don't. Lack of respect can decrease our level of self-esteem, since our self-esteem is created by the value others place on us. Those who demonstrate respect for us will usually satisfy this social need through communication.

What is the importance of these three needs in terms of communication and relationships? They provide a method of defining an *interpersonal relationship*. It's an association in which people meet each other's social needs. And they allow us to judge whether a relationship is good or bad. The more a relationship satisfies the needs of inclusion, control, and affection, the better it is. We can look at relationships on a continuum. At one end there are impersonal relationships, people we communicate with but don't know personally, such as store clerks. These satisfy very few social needs. At the other end are interpersonal ones, people with whom we have close friendships. These satisfy many of our social needs. In the middle are casual relationships—with coworkers, neighbours, acquaintances. These satisfy our social needs in varying degrees, but because most of our social time is spent maintaining our close friendships, our casual acquaintances are less important for meeting our social needs. By balancing the needs of each partner, relationships maintain equilibrium and are able to carry on (see Figure 10.1).

Figure 10.1 | Continuum of Interpersonal Relationships

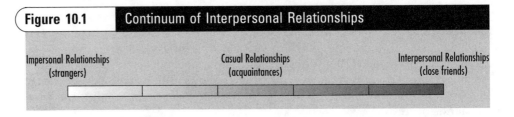

Impersonal Relationships
(strangers)

Casual Relationships
(acquaintances)

Interpersonal Relationships
(close friends)

Interpersonal Communication in the Workplace

Interpersonal communication is essential for organizations because it is through this type of communication that social relationships are established. The ability to communicate interpersonally also enables people to coordinate their activities for the achievement of common goals, which places it at the centre of the organizing process.

As individuals, we bring to the workplace a unique and complex set of values, attitudes, feelings, backgrounds, cultural differences, skills, and knowledge. We have developed these personal characteristics throughout our lifetime through an internal type of communication called *intrapersonal communication*—the process of thinking, or communicating,

| Mini-Case | Creating an Enthusiastic Workplace[3] |

The three interpersonal needs discussed on page 171 easily translate into superior–subordinate relationships in the workplace. Inclusion becomes achievement: having a sense of pride in your work and your company. Affection becomes camaraderie: having productive and positive relationships in the workplace. Control becomes equity: feeling you're treated fairly in terms of wages, benefits, and job security. Workplaces having these three characteristics will have enthusiastic and motivated employees. Despite declarations by companies such as "employees are our greatest asset," when the bottom line is the issue most companies treat employees as faceless, disposable objects.

What are the benefits of an enthusiastic workplace? Stock prices of companies with enthusiastic employees outperform those with unenthusiastic employees. They also receive fewer customer complaints, have better quality products and services, and less employee turnover.

So, why is an enthusiastic work force not that common? For one thing, many managers hang on to the old myth that workers will never be happy with their pay. In fact, only 23 percent of workers surveyed by Sirota Survey Intelligence rated their pay as poor. Another myth, reminiscent of Theory X, is that

workers don't want to work. The survey shows that 76 percent of workers like their jobs. Many managers miss out on the fact that just about all workers want to be proud of their work, want to have constructive relationships, and want to experience being part of the success of their employer. Too often, company policies and managers' styles focus on the 5 percent of workers described as "allergic to work" who should never have been hired in the first place. As a result, the energy is sapped from the overwhelming majority of enthusiastic employees.

Enthusiastic workplaces rely on collaborative structures such as work teams, often self-managed ones. They exploit their employee's talents and celebrate success. They achieve goals through cooperation.

Discussion Questions

1. Think about your own interpersonal relationships. How many of them would fit on the interpersonal end of the continuum in Figure 10.1?

2. How does the workplace affect interpersonal relationships?

3. How can managers use interpersonal communication to better satisfy people's needs and create better relationships with employees?

with ourselves. When we interact socially, we become engaged in *interpersonal communication*, the external process of sharing our personal characteristics with others. In this way, we develop relationships and social networks. Interpersonal communication refers to the process of individuals relating to others. Both intrapersonal and interpersonal communication take place within the overall context of the organization—the collective identity of the organization, representing the entire body of self-perceptions and relationships throughout the organization, as well as the goals, values, policies, and practices of the organization. So it is within this diverse mixture of people, groups, meanings, and relationships that the study of interpersonal communication takes place.

It is important to remember that although we participate in organizational life collectively, we experience it individually on an intrapersonal level. The meanings that we create are personal, subjective, and internal. An understanding of how the internal sense-making processes work inside people's minds will help us explain the workplace realities created through social interaction. Since we spend so much time at our jobs, our workplace experiences contribute significantly to not only how we see and evaluate ourselves as employees but as people in general. An employee's relationship with a supervisor, for instance, has a big impact on how the employee perceives the organization. A positive relationship with a supervisor often leads to good feelings about the company, and vice versa. Having many good relationships in your workplace generally leads to feelings of satisfaction, comfort, trust, and openness of communication. In the same way, working at a particular company can be a source of pride or disappointment outside of work. So, by understanding our individual and interpersonal experiences, we can develop communication skills that will increase our job satisfaction and help to achieve organizational goals more effectively.

Here we will examine individual experiences in organizations, our personal characteristics that influence how we define and make sense of our organization, and the relationships that grow out of them, and explore the skills and strategies useful for increasing interpersonal communication competencies. Let's get a feel for interpersonal communication by briefly exploring some established theories about it.

Theoretical Perspectives

Symbolic Interactionism

This milestone theory by Herbert Blumer embodies the core process of communication: we interact through the use of symbols.[4] In this process, meaning is created and shared, self-identities are generated, and social activity becomes possible. Our common use of symbols, especially language, binds us together as people. As a result of common understandings, we are able to form satisfying relationships and positive impressions of ourselves. The process of role taking is important for relationship building because it allows a person to see things from the other person's point of view.

Symbolic interactionism separates a person into the "I" (the active part of a person), the "me" (the public person providing social control and reflection), and the "self" (the combination of both and the part that is at the centre of the self-concept). The various thinking processes we become involved in, such as self-observation, evaluation of options, and directions for action, represent the I, me, and self negotiating social realities, similar to the discussion of the Coordinated Management of Meaning theory discussed on page 178.

Uncertainty Reduction Theory

Information can be useful for reducing uncertainty about other people we have relationships with.[5] High levels of uncertainty make interpersonal communication more difficult. We like to have control and predictability in our lives, and this sense of security becomes threatened when interacting with strangers whose behaviour we can't predict. To reduce the anxiety caused by uncertainty, we seek information, which can be used to predict another person's behaviour. In the workplace, reducing uncertainty about others becomes important for two reasons: we generally establish frequent interaction with our coworkers, so continuing uncertainty would be undesirable; and many interactions can potentially provide significant advantages or disadvantages. Effective work relationships are characterized by communication.

The stronger the desire that exists between two people to form a relationship, the more information-reducing communication will be used. We use three methods to find out information about the other person:

- *Passive strategies*—we observe the person.
- *Active strategies*—we ask others about the person.
- *Interactive strategies*—we communicate directly with the person.[6]

As cultural diversity increases in today's organizations, cultural factors, such as different values, expectations, and behaviours, add to the amount of uncertainty in relationships. We can begin to explain cultural differences in relationships with the concept of high-context and low-context cultures.[7] In high-context cultures, people derive the meaning of a message from nonverbal cues and the situation in which the communication is taking place. To reduce uncertainty, Asian cultures, such as the Japanese and Chinese, pay particular attention to people's behaviours or to objects, such as office size, for signs of professional status, social position, and personal qualities. Background information is important. On the other hand, low-context cultures, such as Western cultures, are more verbally oriented, preferring to rely on the spoken word to bring out meaning. Canadian culture would be categorized as Western, though we are probably a little more context-oriented than our American neighbours. An example of extreme low-context business culture in Canada would probably be the oil explorer from Alberta, ignoring alligators, elephant stampedes, and hostile natives in the unstoppable quest for new oil wells.

Another useful concept to help us explain how we reduce uncertainty in culturally diverse relationships is individualism—collectivism, previously touched on in the section on organizational culture.[8] In individualistic cultures, typically Western cultures, people see themselves as responsible for taking care of themselves, they value independence over community, and they are more loosely knit socially. In collectivist cultures, typically Asian and to some degree European, people strive for the good of the community over the individual, they expect more support from others, and they show more loyalty to the community. Team structures in the workplace tend to work better in collectivistic cultures, where the emphasis is on "we" instead of "I."

Self-Disclosure Models—Social Penetration Theory and the Johari Window

Social penetration theory describes how close relationships are formed, as people's private selves are disclosed through interpersonal communication to reveal their core personality or inner self.[9] The decision to disclose is based on the rewards a person expects to gain by disclosing information. If it is perceived that the costs of disclosing will be greater than the rewards, no information will be disclosed. Disclosing normally begins with superficial information, because the risks are minimal. The deeper people penetrate socially, the more personal the discussion becomes.

The self-disclosure process usually involves three stages.

1. When meeting people for the first time, we rely on cultural information, based on understandings shared by a society of people. If we run into a Canadian on the streets of Paris or Chicago, we feel a cultural connection even before getting to know the person. The common practices of Canadian culture will guide us through our

communication activity. The person is defined in terms of the culture he or she belongs to.

2. In the next stage, we begin to use social information. We learn about the person's occupation, education, leisure activities, family life, and economic background. We develop a profile of the person based on this information from our own knowledge of social categories. The person is defined as a member of his or her social groups.

3. The third stage involves psychological information about the individual characteristics of the other person, apart from his or her cultural or social connections. In this stage people often defy our social expectations. We are surprised to discover that Mary in Shipping and Receiving plays in a string quartet, or that Joe in I.T. writes detective novels.

As relationships develop, they go through cycles of dialectic tensions. They do not continuously get better day after day the more information that gets shared. Meanings are not always shared and understood. Instead, relationships ebb and flow, as partners work through contrary opinions and try to balance their needs for privacy and closeness.

The *Johari Window* is also used for modelling degrees of self-disclosure from relationship to relationship.[10] The Johari Window has four "windows," each representing a type of knowledge about the relationship (see Figure 10.2). This knowledge often focuses on people's personalities. Interesting insights can be discovered if you apply the model to your relationship, say, with your supervisor. Your boss may see you in a very different way than you see yourself.

The Johari Window breaks down communication between two people into simple terms and displays it graphically. To use the model, first think of a relationship you have with someone, such as a friend or a boss. The first pane, the Arena, contains things that you know about yourself and that your friend also knows. It's open and public knowledge. For instance, you might be a very honest person, and this is known by both partners. The second pane, the Blind Spot, contains information that you do not know about yourself but that your friend or boss does know about you. We communicate lots of messages to people without being aware of it. For example, you may be outspoken and boisterous with people because you think you're popular, but others may see you as a bully.

The third pane, the Façade, contains things that you know about yourself but of which your boss is unaware. An interesting example occurred in the hockey world. Long-time NHL coach Jacques Demers, who had stints with the Montreal Canadiens,

| Figure 10.2 | Johari Window[11] |

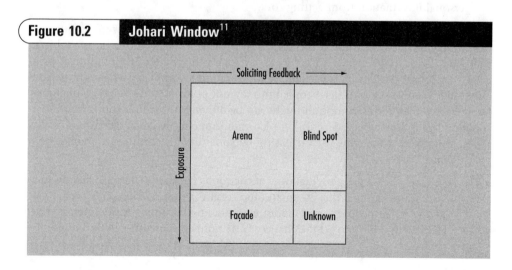

St. Louis Blues, and Detroit Red Wings, shocked sports fans and personal friends when he revealed in a biography in 2005 that he could barely read or write. Those who are illiterate learn to bob and weave to avoid being discovered, or to keep up the façade. When Demers coached in St. Louis and Detroit, for example, he would push away paperwork, saying to other staffers that his English was not that good. When at the helm in Montreal in 1992, he played the opposite card with paperwork: my French has become too rusty. And the façade worked so well no one ever caught on.[12]

The fourth pane, the Unknown, contains information that neither you nor your boss knows about you. Examples are memories from childhood, undeveloped abilities, or information in the unconscious that is inaccessible. Knowing all about oneself or knowing all about someone else is an impossible state to attain.

The Johari Window works according the dynamics of exposure and soliciting feedback. The exposure process reveals information about yourself. By exposing your feelings and opinions about things, your boss or friend does not need to guess what your behaviour means. So, your arena expands and your façade gets smaller as you reveal information about yourself to others. The more you self-disclose, the farther the horizontal line in the Johari Window diagram will go down. You may also want to move the vertical line to the right to decrease your blind spot. Since this area contains information that you are unaware of, the easy way to increase your awareness is to get feedback from your boss or friend. You can solicit information by encouraging others to provide feedback about you.

Below are four different combinations of exposure and soliciting feedback (see Figure 10.3):

1. *The Close Friend.* This combination is characterized by a large Arena, suggesting open and shared communication and very little guesswork for interpreting behaviour. Norms have been developed in this relationships to facilitate open communication.
2. *The Interviewer.* The Façade window is very large, suggesting a communication style where one person asks a lot of questions but does not expose much about him or herself—high on soliciting feedback, low on exposure.
3. *The Bull-in-a-China-Shop.* The Blind Spot is very large, suggesting a person who self-discloses a lot but receives very little feedback—high on exposure, low on soliciting feedback.
4. *The Turtle.* This mystery person neither discloses nor solicits feedback. As a result, the Unknown window is very large. The "shell" prevents people from coming "in" and personal information from getting "out."

The goal of communication according to the Johari Window is to move information from the façade and the blind spot into the arena where it can be available to everyone. This allows people to get to know each other better and relationships to grow. The Johari Window is especially important in the workplace, where our personality traits are obvious to other people but may not be seen by ourselves. Sometimes, being passed over for a promotion might not be a matter of qualifications but of personality. The following is a description of common ineffective managerial personality types, along with some tips for increasing personability, according to management coach Diane Davies:[13]

- *The Taskmaster.* These people plug away at their jobs constantly because talking to people is a waste of time. But life in an office is also about relationships.
  What to do: Get people to care about you more by becoming more interested in them. Help them out if you get the chance. And eat lunch sometimes in the employees' lunch room.

Figure 10.3 Common Johari Window Combinations

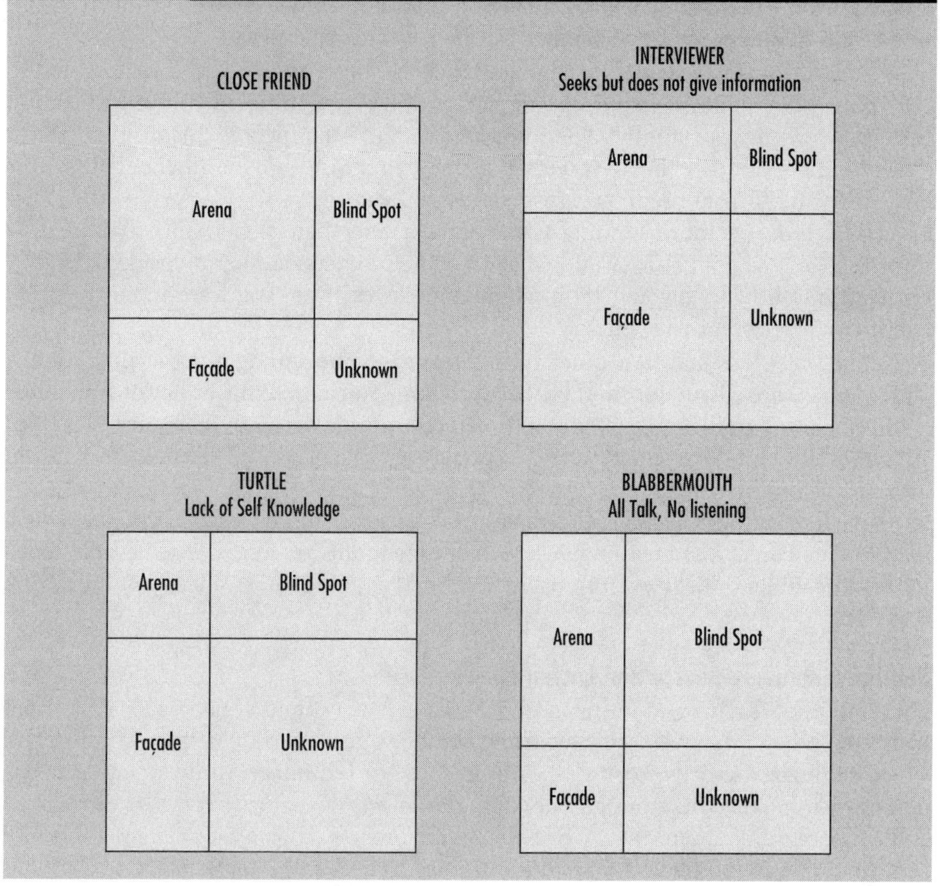

CLOSE FRIEND

Arena	Blind Spot
Façade	Unknown

INTERVIEWER
Seeks but does not give information

Arena	Blind Spot
Façade	Unknown

TURTLE
Lack of Self Knowledge

Arena	Blind Spot
Façade	Unknown

BLABBERMOUTH
All Talk, No listening

Arena	Blind Spot
Façade	Unknown

- *The Trust Buster.* Nobody trusts these people because they have failed on numerous occasions to be a team player, deciding instead to focus on self-serving, ego-building activities. They crush those who get in their way.

     What to do: Try to identify your miserly behaviours and whom you inflicted them on so you can make amends. Join in a project with people whose trust you've broken, and to rebuild damaged relationships.

- *Mr. Articulate.* These people use complex language as a cover for their lack of knowledge. They're quick with answers, but not often correct. The performance may be amazing, but it's all an illusion.

     What to do: Engage others in dialogue by letting them discuss problems openly with you. Admit it when you lack knowledge instead of hiding it. Try to recognize the signs that Mr. Articulate is coming to take over and change your behaviour to fight off his arrival.

- *The Politician.* A consummate brown-noser, this person seeks out and plays up to the seat of power, ignoring the underlings. Nobody trusts your flattering ways, and all your apple-polishing is probably beginning to bother your boss. Credibility is lost among colleagues who see through this person.

     What to do: Ask questions that address the root cause of problems to speak honestly and avoid pandering. Learn to do something for the sake of the task, not the political payoff.

- *The Victim.* When things go wrong, this person blames anyone but him or herself. So much time and energy is spent plotting how to lay blame that very little else gets done. People who do not take responsibility for their actions lose respect.

What to do: Learn to become aware of how the blame process operates inside you. An occasion to lay blame could actually be an opportunity to solve a problem. Don't be afraid to take some risks. Failures can be learning experiences.

- *The Expert.* This know-it-all has all the answers, so he or she doesn't have to listen to anyone else. You are always dropping names and expounding on your own experiences, which in your mind have more validity than other people's. Unfortunately everyone stopped listening to you long ago, and your disregard for other people's ideas has cut you off from useful expertise discussed by coworkers.

   What to do: Do more listening. Give people quieter than you a chance to share their knowledge. Use your conversational skills to help others develop their ideas. Pay attention to how long you're dominating the conversation, and learn to rein yourself in if you go beyond your quota.

- *The Bulldozer.* This person is quiet and patient at the beginning of a meeting, then blows up, stops discussion, and pushes through a solution of his or her own making. You're a bomb waiting to explode, and everyone around you lives in a state of fear. But it's all a façade. You're actually afraid of being seen as ineffective. This insecurity causes you to be domineering.

   What to do: Be open to the feedback of others so you know when you've intimidated them. Set a reasonable length of time for discussions and achievable goals. Find a healthier outlet for your frustrations, such as going for a walk or getting a drink of water.

Self-Presentation—Saving and Losing Face

The concept of "saving and losing face" is based on the claim that people are concerned with how others perceive them. We try to project a positive public image of ourselves when we interact socially. Losing face diminishes our self-image, while saving or maintaining face enhances it. Through our conscious efforts to shape what others think of us and what we think of ourselves, we engage in the process of *impression management*—the behaviours we use to create a desired social image. The "face" represents the social identity we want to present to others. The following are a few principles to remember in presenting yourself to others:

- We have many complex aspects of ourselves. The self you present to your parents or your boss will probably be different than the one you use with your friends. People's emotional, romantic, adventurous, and responsible sides all take prominence according to the situation.
- We vary our self-presentations with different receivers or audiences. Our behaviour may be more formal, as in a job interview, or casual, as when watching a sporting event with friends.
- Our motives in self-presentation may be strategic, as when we try to gain influence, sympathy, or approval; or they may be self-verifying, where we try let others see us openly, the way that we see ourselves, so that the public impression is in agreement with the private self.

Coordinated Management of Meaning

Communication is a process that allows us to create and manage social reality. To make sense of the complex assortment of personalities and activities in an organization, theorists have developed the Coordinated Management of Meaning theory.[14] We make sense of our world by creating meanings that explain it. Meanings exist on a seven-level hierarchy, based on the following sources:

1. *Raw sensory data*—stimuli from our environment that will be received through the senses

Signs, Signifiers, and Signified

Let's very briefly touch on semiotics, the study of words and meanings, to highlight where meanings come from. Signs are made up of a signifier and a signified. Let's use a tree as an example. The image of a tree is the signifier. The idea of a tree in an observer's mind is the signified. The actual tree is the sign. So, a sign is an object that combines the signifier and the signified. This meaning-creating process highlights the interplay of internal and external worlds through language.

2. *Content*—stimuli after it has been interpreted
3. *Speech acts*—content takes on additional meaning when it is connected to a speaker with whom there is a relationship
4. *Episodes*—the context of the conversation provides further meaning
5. *Master contracts*—the relationships define what each can expect of the other in a specific episode
6. *Life scripts*—a set of episodes a person expects to participate in
7. *Cultural patterns*—culturally based sets of rules that define what normal communication is in a given episode

We follow rules to help us navigate the various levels of meaning and to stay within the boundaries of normal communication. The process starts at the micro level with basic perceptual activity, proceeds through increasingly complex social situations, and ends with all-encompassing cultural patterns. As we go from level to level, we use various language devices to reduce ambiguity and help each other understand what we mean. For example:

- *Definitions*—we tell each other what we mean by a certain word
- *Metaphors*—these allow us to talk about something unfamiliar in terms of something familiar—for example, "my workplace is a circus"
- *Feedforward*—we provide feedback to ourselves before we speak to choose the best way to communicate
- *Simple English*—we use a small vocabulary (probably not more than 1000 words) in most normal communication

The Communicative Relationship

We like to think of relationships as fixed instead of constantly evolving. The labels we give relationships show this, as in being married, going steady, "seeing" someone, and being a best friend. But relationships are more about process than product if we apply Weick's theory of organizing.[15] They require constant sense making and the reducing of equivocality, or multiple meanings, and they are always changing. In fact, they are the sum total of their communication activity.

Weick developed the concept of the double interact as the basic model for sense making. An act occurs, such as asking a question ("How about getting a coffee after class?"); an interact occurs when you respond ("I just had one, but I could join you anyway."); a double interact is the second response ("Okay, that sound good."). Reducing equivocality involves receiving ambiguous information, responding to it to increase clarity, and creating new, shared information. In this way, relationships are constantly being defined. Double interacts are also convenient for re-establishing normal patterns in relationships after a misunderstanding. If you have an argument with your coworker, you might initiate a double interact to smooth things over by asking if he still needs a ride home from work.

Ten Principles of Interpersonal Communication

Interpersonal communication has a dyadic nature, meaning that two people are interacting directly and immediately. Let's sum up our discussion of this section by looking at some principles of interpersonal communication:

1. **Communication can be intentional or unintentional.** You plan some of your messages, the rest you make up spontaneously. Most verbal messages are intentional, as are some nonverbal ones, such as gestures or facial expressions. Other messages are communicated unintentionally by your tone of voice or your mannerisms. They are all, nevertheless, received.

2. **It's impossible not to communicate.** We can stop talking, but we cannot stop communicating. The act of stopping communicating with your partner is a message in itself that says you don't want to communicate any more. And even after we stop talking, our nonverbal messages would continue communicating.

3. **Communication is irreversible.** You cannot "unsend" a message or wipe it from the receiver's memory. The most you can do is correct a message. The irreversibility of communication is evident for anyone who has ever unintentionally hit the send button on an e-mail message that was not ready for sending. The only thing you can do is send another one to finish the message.

4. **Communication is unrepeatable.** The element of time in the communication process constantly changes the situation, so it's impossible to repeat the same message to the same person because conditions have changed. The fact that you are saying it again makes it different than the first time around. Of course, if the audience changes, it will be the first time again.

5. **Meanings are not in words, they are in people.** A dictionary definition of the word "home" or "kangaroo" is good for reference, but can be far from the meanings we hold for these words. Each of us has a personal mental image of the word "home," and those who have seen a real kangaroo will form a different image than those relying on photographs or definitions. The meanings we have for words come from the ways we have experienced what the word represents. In relationships, the differences in personal meanings can be both an obstacle to understanding and an incentive for conversation.

6. **Communication is not a natural ability.** Communication skills can be learned. Though communication does come naturally for us, most of us communicate at a level of effectiveness far below our potential.

7. **There is no ideal or universal communication style.** Because we will interact with numerous people in the workplace, a variety of communication styles is effective. What works with one individual may not with another. There are no simple rules that will guarantee success.

8. **Effective communication is situational.** Competence in communication is not something you either have or don't have. Everyone has areas of competence. It's wrong to say "I'm a terrible communicator," when what is more accurate is "I didn't communicate very well in that situation." Learning new communication skills expands our areas of competence.

9. **Delivering an effective message requires skills.** Once you have decided on an appropriate message for a situation, you must deliver it. Competent communicators know what the skills are as well as how to use them.

10. **Effective communication requires effort.** Interpreting symbols and understanding ideas and feelings is not always easy. External obstacles, such as noise or distractions, can become barriers to communication. So also can internal problems, such as stress, conflict, or anticipation. Suitable effort is often

required to navigate your attention past the numerous communication barriers we encounter.

The Individual in the Organization

Intrapersonal communication takes place in three areas related to the individual: the self-concept, the process of perception, and emotions.

Self-Concept—The Intrapersonal Experience

The self-concept is a collection of perceptions of our experiences over our lifetimes. It evolves through time and changes slowly as new experiences become part of our self-identity. Major experiences, such as graduation or marriage, have more impact on shaping our self-concept than routine events. The process of defining who we are is called intrapersonal communication—or communication within ourselves. Since everyone's experiences are different, the intrapersonal experience differs from person to person. To have effective and satisfying relationships in the workplace, it is essential to build skills in discovering, understanding, and appreciating each other's intrapersonal differences.

Development of the Self-Concept

Take a minute to list five things you think of when you ask yourself who you are. You might include "adventurous" (from experiences travelling), "independent" (from the way you work or socialize), "practical" (from your interests in mechanics or money), "competitive" (from how frequently you have won races or contests), or numerous other descriptions. It is evident from your descriptions that your self-concept comes from your experiences. And as our experiences change, so does our *self-concept*. Because of the constant change in our lives, we represent many different selves as our lives progress. We are a different person today than we were yesterday because our experiences have changed us, and we are also the same person because the basic template of our character was laid down early in our lives.

The self-concept develops mainly through the feedback we receive from others through social interaction. So, communication is an essential process in the formation of people's identities. This looking-glass process is called reflected appraisal.

> The self is essentially a social product arising our of experience with people. . . . We learn the most significant and fundamental facts about ourselves from . . . "reflected appraisals," inferences about ourselves made as a consequence of the ways we perceive others behaving toward us.[16]

When people give us feedback, they mirror our behaviours. Through this appraisal, we develop a self-concept that matches the way we believe others see us. If people are friendly to us, we feel sociable. If they shun us, we feel negative. People's evaluations of us are like mirrors. Verbal and nonverbal messages, such as tone of voice, mannerisms, time, posture, and facial expressions, contribute to the way we see ourselves right from infancy. Some people's evaluations, though, are more important than other's. The feedback from these "significant others," such as close friends, family, and bosses, usually has a stronger influence than those with whom we have less significant relationships. A classic example of the power of reflected appraisal is the *Pygmalian effect*, a story of a poor, homeless woman who is turned into a Broadway celebrity by an agent who coaches her into believing that she is beautiful. All the positive attention she receives leads her to change her behaviour and her self-concept. So, how we see ourselves is greatly influenced by how others see us.

Self-Esteem and Beauty

One of the Canadian commercials in the 2006 Super Bowl was for Dove soap's "Campaign for Real Beauty." In the 45-second ad, we see one dark-haired girl who wishes she were blonde, another girl who thinks she's ugly, and a red-haired girl who hates her freckles. "Let's change their minds," the ad declares. In a daring about-turn for advertising, Dove goes beneath skin-deep to promote naturalness and authenticity as a definition of beauty.[18]

We also use social comparison to evaluate ourselves, as a form of personal appraisal. "Social comparison is gauging your own attitudes, emotions, attributes, and abilities by comparing them to those of other people."[17] Our social interactions create a frame of reference that situates us along continuums of differences, such as tall or short, rich or poor, funny or serious. So, we define ourselves by how we measure up with others. These descriptions also establish our level of self-esteem—how superior or inferior we feel to others.

Self-Concept and Communication

Most people demonstrate some consistency in their behaviour. This is commonly called our personality. But though people do possess some innate personality traits, the term "personality" may be inaccurate because much of our behaviour is not consistent. It varies from one situation to another, and is often determined more by the situation than by an inherent personality trait. A child, for instance, might be reserved with strangers, yet outgoing with family and friends. Would it be accurate to label the child as shy? Our tendency to label our personalities overlooks the strong influence of situational factors on behaviour.

In fact, people are capable of behaving in many different ways than their personalities would indicate. This is important for effective communication, because having a wide range of behaviours at our disposal provides a lot of options when it comes to choosing appropriate responses to communication situations. A consistent personality may be a drawback in this way because it brings inflexibility to our social interactions. For example, consider the awkwardness Superman's rigid personality brought to his romantic encounters with Lois Lane. Often, heroes are portrayed with strong personalities and single causes to make them stand out from the complexity and diversity of real life.

Self-Concept and Change

The self-concept develops along a series of stages that form a circular process (see Figure 10.4).

The left and right circles represent two different self-concepts. The one on the left is afraid of public speaking, and the one on the right is comfortable with public speaking. The circular nature of the process is based on behaviour being repeated and channelled back into an existing self-concept, thus reinforcing it. So the X self-concept remains the same. What one thing could we change in the X self-concept to create the Y self-concept on the right? The Behaviour stage is critical for changing the rest of the process. If we substitute the Behaviour from the X self-concept with the one from the Y side, the effect will change the rest of the process. "Other's responses" will become like the Y side's, as will "Perceptions of Events." As a result, positive feedback will flow into the X self-concept, combating the existing self-concept. If enough positive feedback is experienced, the self-concept will gradually change to reflect the new types of feedback and become more like Y.

Figure 10.4 | **Relationship between Self-Concept and Behaviour**[19]

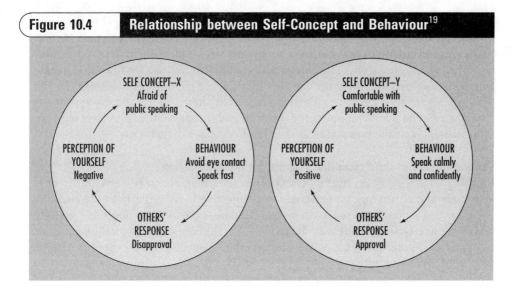

Our self-concept influences our behaviour as well as that of others through a process called the self-fulfilling prophecy. A self-fulfilling prophecy occurs "when a person's expectation of an outcome makes the outcome more likely to occur than would otherwise have been true."[20] For instance, if you are about to meet someone, and your friend previews the introduction with a negative statement about the person, there is a good chance you will find something negative because of your friend's prediction.

You can substitute many management skills that rely on social feedback into this process, such as leadership, decision making, conflict resolution, and negotiation skills. By learning and adopting behaviours that influence others' feedback to be more positive, you will begin to see yourself in ways that reflect their positive responses.

Perception and Communication

Perception is the process by which we use our senses to experience objects, events, and people. It accomplishes two things: it makes us aware of our surroundings, and it gives us information with which to make meaning out of our surroundings.

Being aware of our surroundings has obvious practical benefits. It allows us to function safely and effectively as we negotiate our way through life's activities. Most things that we perceive we pay very little attention to, such as other people we pass on the sidewalk or other cars on the road as we are driving along. We observe things, and then keep going without thinking about them again.

Creating meaning about our surroundings is more complex. Perception is a process that brings together our objective and subjective worlds. Meanings we generate are a function of both worlds interacting—the external world of objects, and our internal

Ped Box | **Enhancing Self-Esteem**

Teens Strap on Snow Boards to Boost Self-Image

To help troubled inner-city teens, the B.C. government will teach snowboarding to 100 youths from across the Lower Mainland. In a program called "Chill," disadvantaged youths will attempt to boost their self-image by learning the value of sport and team participation. The program, one of many, is funded by a non-profit agency aiming to develop positive and sustainable legacies for B.C. from the Vancouver Olympic Games in 2010.[21]

world of experiences, needs, values, biases, personality, and everything else that makes up an individual. Take the classic example of the instructor delivering a lecture. He notices that some students in the class look sleepy, and begins thinking that his lecture must be boring. As the class shows more signs of sleepiness, his feelings become more intense, and the lecture becomes more boring. Finally, a student raises a hand and asks if a window could be opened because it is very hot and stuffy in the room, and it is making the class drowsy. The instructor opens the window, and the class's attention level improves immediately—and the instructor's anxiety level decreases dramatically.

The Importance of the Perception Process for Communication

Knowing what's going on in the perception process helps us to perceive things more accurately and communicate messages more effectively, particularly in the encoding and decoding stages. In these critical stages, ideas are turned into symbols by the sender and then turned back into ideas by the receiver. But the idea sent is never the same as the one received. Receivers filter messages through their own values and experiences. In the process of perceiving a message, the receiver will be rejecting, accepting, or ignoring different parts of it. Our emotions also affect how we perceive and respond to messages, especially with intense interaction, such as conflict or major differences of opinion. The following are some principles of perception that have important implications for communication:[22]

- **Perception is a selective process.** Since it's impossible to be aware of everything, we use our needs, desires, and motivations to select what is meaningful and disregard the rest. Your motivations, such as a conflict with a boss, could distract you from focusing on the message and audience.

- **Message selection can be influenced by attention-grabbing techniques.** Certain messages stand out more than others, such as those that are louder, larger, or brighter than their surroundings. This is a common advertising technique. And fans at sporting events know that a bizarre costume will get them on camera. Anything that breaks an established pattern stands out, such as choruses in songs. Repetition is another attention-grabbing technique. Think of the how the repetition of the last line of Robert Frost's poem *Stopping By Woods On A Snowy Evening* takes the meaning of the words to another level:[23]

    The woods are lovely, dark, and deep
    But I have promises to keep,
    And miles to go before I sleep
    And miles to go before I sleep.

- **Objects are not perceived in isolation, but as parts of a larger assembly.** Numerous organizing methods are used when people put together bits and pieces of information into meaningful wholes. If two people are standing together, we tend to see them as a group and assume that they know each other. Also, relationships are influenced by the proximity of the partners. Simply being located closer to someone, such as a classmate or coworker, will increase the amount of communication between them, resulting in a social relationship. We often organize things or people according to their similarities, such as age, level of education, culture, occupation, and so on.

- **We make sense of incomplete information by putting it into perceptual sets.** We take the available information and find the appropriate category or perceptual set for it. In this way, we translate partial information into a meaningful whole. Once we have categorized a person, we often grant him or her characteristics for which we have no evidence. So perceptual sets also determine which characteristics of people we put together. For instance, complete the following sets: Bill is energetic, assertive, and ... intelligent or stupid? Susan is loud, argumentative, and ... sensitive or selfish? The

Halo Effect functions in a similar way. If a person has some positive qualities, you assume he or she has other ones too. Or, if you socialize with a certain group, you are given the attributes of that group. The process is also similar to stereotyping.

- **Our assumptions about human behaviour influence our perceptions.** Our interpretations of events are shaped by our experiences, and we form basic assumptions from them, such as government is incompetent, corporations are corrupt, and people are basically lazy. Theory X and Theory Y styles of management discussed by Douglas McGregor are relevant here in terms of assumptions that shape managerial styles.

- **Your expectation of an event can help make it happen.** We use perceptual sets to understand people's actions similar to the ways we use them to describe people. Because we expect people to be consistent, they should fit in with our perceptual sets. So, we are surprised when people act against accepted codes of behaviour or ethics, such as when a serious, responsible working person quits his or her job and travels around the world, or when people we trust such as politicians or corporate leaders break the law. In all these cases, it's not people acting out of character, it's simply people who violate our conceptions of who they are. Our social roles create powerful expectations of us, based on what our role stands for in society.

- **Cultural differences are a strong influence on perception.** They work in two ways. First, they provide people with unique assumptions and perspectives on life, so we all see things differently. This is commonly referred to as cultural diversity. Second, our experiences with people from different cultures can lead to stereotyping, a process in which we attribute the qualities of a group to an individual in that group. Stereotyping makes life more predictable and easier to explain, but it also creates inaccuracies and can devalue an individual.

Attribution Theory—Attaching Causes to Actions

One way of making sense of a person's behaviour is by determining what caused it. When we attach a cause to someone's behaviour, we must determine if it's internally caused (due to some personality trait) or externally caused (due to situational factors). We evaluate people based on what motivates their behaviour. If a stranger is being friendly to us, and we decide it is because of a friendly personality—an internal cause—we evaluate the person positively. However, if the person is being friendly and we discover it's because he or she wants to ask a favour—an external cause—we will form a negative evaluation. If we incorrectly attribute the cause of someone's behaviour, we are committing an attribution error, which leads to incorrect perceptions.

A well-documented phenomenon, the *fundamental attribution error*, explains that when making attributions about other's behaviours we often put too much weight on personality traits, or internal causes, and not enough on situational factors, or external causes.[24] Why? There are two main reasons.

The first is that it's the far easier path to take when explaining why things happen. It's much easier, for instance, to attribute a student's low grades or an employee's poor performance to lack of effort, laziness, or bad attitude than to consider other explanations, such as an ineffective teacher or boss, personal problems, an excessive workload, or unfair policies. Uncovering situational explanations is a more complex process. For instance, on what do you blame the homelessness of people who live on the street? An internal cause could point to laziness or drug addiction, whereas an external cause could be systemic—a lack of financial or educational opportunities; political or economic conditions, such as cutbacks in funding for the poor; or mental illness. Think back to the homelessness of the Great Depression of the 1930s to get an idea of the numerous and complex issues that form the picture of homelessness in society.

The second reason deals with the *self-serving bias*, a tendency to a shift the blame away from ourselves.[25] This self-serving explanation for behaviour proposes that if you are the actor, you blame it on the situation, and if you're the observer, you blame it on the person. Let's say you're a car driver who failed to make a complete stop at a stop sign. You rationalize it by saying there were no cars coming, or maybe that the stop sign isn't even needed there. An observer standing on the street, however, might see you as a careless driver who breaks the rules of the road. The self-serving bias occurs because we like to think of ourselves as good and law-abiding citizens, and something minor such as not making a complete stop will not change our self-serving point of view. Another reason why it occurs is based on the amount of information each person has to work with. As actors, we have much more information about the causes of our own behaviours, and, as a result, can rationalize them very effectively. An outside observer has far less knowledge about reasons for our behaviours. When it comes to observing ourselves in action, obviously we have more information about the causes of our own behaviours.

On a societal level, the issue of the self-serving bias was addressed in a recent film by Michael Moore called *Bowling for Columbine*. It explores the reasons behind the multiple shootings of high-school students in Columbine, Colorado, but could refer to numerous acts of violence anywhere, including the shootings of female engineering students at the University of Montreal in 1989. It is convenient to conclude that the killers were extremists or lunatics. But the Moore film uncovers other explanations, such as the availability of guns in American culture (the students bought bullets over-the-counter at Wal-Mart, and Moore received a free rifle for opening a bank account). Social conditions and violence in the media could also play a role. The Montreal shootings raise the additional issues of feminism and the increasing presence of women in traditionally male programs such as engineering. The more difficult answer lies in considering the complex social, psychological, and cultural factors at work in the situation.

Using Perception Checking to Improve Perception

We've discussed many ways in which our perceptions can lead to misunderstandings. Let's finish off our discussion of perception and communication by learning an effective method for preventing misunderstandings between people. Sometimes we observe a person's behaviour and we don't know how to interpret it. The *Perception check* helps us make accurate perceptions by doing the following things:

1. It keeps us from jumping to conclusions about the reasons for people's behaviours.
2. It focuses on the interpretation aspect of the perception process—we interact with people to create meaning instead of passively accepting our interpretations of their actions as facts.

Perception checking involves two steps:

1. Describe the behaviour you observed that you are not sure how to interpret.
    Example: "I noticed you slammed the door on your way out of the office."
2. Suggest two interpretations for the behaviour and request clarification about which interpretation is correct.
    Example: "Was it an accident or were you angry?"

Through the simple use of perception checking, many common misunderstandings can be prevented.

Communication and Emotion

Emotions in the workplace have both an intrapersonal and interpersonal function in the communication process. Daniel Goleman, author of *Emotional Intelligence*, has written extensively on the roles of emotions in communication.[26] Intrapersonal communication focuses on areas of personal emotional competence, such as:

- Self-awareness of one's internal states, such as recognizing emotions and their effects, having an ability to accurately assess yourself, having a sense of your levels of self-confidence and capabilities
- Self-regulation of one's internal states, such as managing emotions, maintaining standards of honesty and integrity, taking responsibility for personal performance, flexibility in handling change, and being comfortable with and open to novelty
- Self-direction for goal achievement, such as striving to reach standards of excellence, committing to group goals, showing initiative to act on opportunities, and having persistence in pursuing goals despite setbacks

Interpersonal communication, on the other hand, focuses on areas of social emotional competence or how you handle social interaction and relationships, such as:

- Empathy skills or awareness of others' needs and feelings, such as understanding the other person's point of view; anticipating, recognizing, and meeting the other person's needs; sensing what others need to develop; cultivating opportunities through workplace diversity; and reading a group's emotional energy and power relationships
- Social skills or bringing out desirable responses in others, such as using effective persuasive strategies, sending clear and convincing messages, guiding groups of people, negotiating and resolving disagreements, nurturing relationships, and collaborating and cooperating to achieve shared goals

Having the ability to manage our emotions in the above ways can contribute strongly to a person's professional success. According to Goleman, success in the workplace is 80 percent dependent on emotional intelligence, or EI, and 20 percent dependent on IQ. Let's examine how emotions work and where they come from so we can gain a better understanding of this quality called emotional intelligence.

Emotions and Cognitive Labelling
There is nothing good or bad, but thinking makes it so.

—William Shakespeare, Hamlet

Emotions generally come from three sources:[27]

1. Physical changes cause emotions, such as the experience of nervousness and fear before delivering an oral presentation, accompanied by an increase in heartbeat or blood pressure, tension in the muscles, and perspiration. The physical experiences of nervousness or surprise create the accompanying feelings in us.
2. Observing our body language can provide an indication of what feelings are being experienced. The spontaneity and honesty of nonverbal messages reveal information about ourselves that we may not be aware of. Being dishonest, for example, can make our voices rise in pitch. Observing this in ourselves may bring about feelings of anxiety.
3. Cognitive labelling of events includes the perception process in identifying the sources of emotions. The emotion we experience is a result of how we label our perceptions. Physical symptoms such as nervousness and fear are the same as those that accompany feelings of joy and excitement. The perception process is important for understanding emotional experiences because we need to accurately interpret the context of the event to know how we are feeling about it. The way we interpret a situation can have a big influence on how we feel about it.

The *cognitive labelling theory of emotions* combines emotional and mental activity in the experience of feelings.[28] As an example, let's say your friend ignores you when you

Emotions and Senses

"Seventy-five per cent of the emotions we generate on a daily basis are affected by smell."—Martin Lindstrom[29]

pass by in the cafeteria. What you feel as a result depends on the meaning you give to the event, taking into account the context. You might feel compassion, thinking that your friend may have been distressed about a failed course he told you about, or anger, if your friend purposely chose to ignore you, or dejection, possibly thinking that your friend no longer wants a relationship with you. To accurately interpret the situation, you need more information. How you feel at the time also adds to the meaning you give to the event. If you feel good, having just received a high grade on a term paper, you might not think twice about your friend passing you by. If you feel bad, it may affect you negatively because you define the situation in terms of your current level of self-esteem.

In fact, the labels we give to our own behaviours can affect our self-concept. For instance, we all exhibit behaviours of shyness at some point in our lives. Some people, though, regard themselves as having shy personalities, whereas others say they behave shyly only in certain situations. The big difference is what you attribute your shyness to. For the first person, it's a personality assessment ("I'm a shy person."). This label would make the person uncomfortable in similar future situations because it's part of his or her self-concept. For the second person, it's a one-shot occurrence ("I was shy in there, but that happens.").

Managing Difficult Emotions

Keeping in mind the important role of interpretation in experiencing and identifying our emotions can help us to manage and overcome difficult emotions. Emotions have been described as *facilitative*, which means they are positive and make us function effectively and feel good about ourselves, and *debilitative*, which means they prevent us from feeling good about ourselves and functioning effectively.[30]

Two characteristics distinguish facilitative from debilitative emotions. The first is intensity. An emotion such as anger can be a constructive force because it can motivate you to improve unsatisfactory conditions. Too much anger, though, can make things worse. The same is true for nervousness. A little bit of it before making a speech is necessary to give you a lively, spontaneous speaking style. Too much nervousness, though, can produce fear, or even terror, and can incapacitate you from performing well. So, an emotion with too much intensity can have debilitative effects.

The second characteristic is duration. Feeling sad or depressed at times, say after a death in the family, is natural and allows people the time to appreciate their experiences and provide closure to events in their lives. But spending years grieving over your loss would accomplish nothing. In the same way, staying angry with someone for something that happened a long time ago becomes a punishment to both you and the other person. To be facilitative, feelings should be attached to specific events, and should pass after those events are no longer relevant.

The approach to handling unproductive emotions developed by psychologist Albert Ellis aims to get rid of debilitative feelings by making a rational choice to confront them directly.[31] This opens up the way for facilitative feelings. The key to changing unproductive feelings is to change incorrect thinking. It is not events that give people negative feelings, it is the beliefs people hold about those events. So, changing our interpretations of events will change the emotions we experience from them.

Let's use the following example to illustrate this point. You are walking by your friend's house. He sticks his head out the window and calls you a string of obscene names. What do you feel? The cognitive labelling theory of emotions states that the emotional experience would occur in the following sequence: you would first experience the event; then you would respond physiologically by shedding tears, feeling sickness, getting a rush of adrenaline, or gasping with joy; next, you would interpret this arousal and decide which emotion you were experiencing; finally, you would experience the emotion. The key stage is the third, where you interpret and decide your emotion.

The answer to the question of where emotions come from, according to this theory, is that you consciously and purposefully select your emotions. Thus, seeing your friend shout names at you would under normal circumstances make you feel hurt or upset, perhaps even angry. Now imagine that instead of passing by your friend's house you were walking down the street and you notice your friend asking strangers for spare change and looking intoxicated. When he sees you he starts yelling obscene names at you. In this situation, your feelings would likely be different. Perhaps you'd feel sadness or pity.

The activating agent in both cases, being called names, was the same, yet the emotional result was different. The reason according to the cognitive labelling theory is that our feelings are caused by our thoughts. In each case your thinking was different. In the first case you would probably think that your friend is angry with you, perhaps for something you had done, so you would feel hurt. In the second case, you would probably assume that your friend is angry for a different reason, so you might feel concern or sympathy. It is the interpretations people make of events, through the process of self-talk or intrapersonal communication, that determine their feelings. We start with an event, develop a thought about it, then decide on the appropriate feeling. Our feelings come from ourselves. This may be a little difficult to accept, since in normal practice we often blame others for how we feel. We say things such as "You make me angry when you leave a mess in the kitchen," or "You made me feel guilty when you said I wasn't taking good care of grandma," or "You made me love you." Simply put, you can't make anyone feel any particular feeling unless they decide to feel it. The most you can do to make someone love you is set up the romantic conditions that are favourable for feelings of love to happen. In fact, blaming your feelings on other people can often bring about defensive responses and lead to argument.

Irrational Thoughts, Illogical Conclusion, Negative Feelings

Focusing on the thinking process going on while we experience events is the key to understanding and managing debilitative feelings. Many negative feelings come from accepting irrational thoughts, which ultimately lead to illogical conclusions and bad feelings. Below is a list of common irrational thoughts people hold about themselves that can lead to negative feelings:[32]

- **Striving for perfection.** People who strive for perfection think that a good communicator should handle every situation with competence and success. If you are imperfect, people won't appreciate you, and you will feel bad about it. A more sensible approach is to accept like everyone else that you make mistakes, and there is no reason to hide this fact of life.

- **Requiring constant and unanimous approval.** This mistaken belief states that it is essential to gain the approval and acceptance of every person. It implies that others will like and respect you more the more that you go out of your way to please them, even to the point of sacrificing your own principles and happiness. One ridiculous situation this can lead to is feeling apologetic just to please people when others are clearly at fault. When you must abandon your own needs and principles to satisfy the needs of others, the price is too high.

- **Wishing for what should be instead of what is.** It is unreasonable to believe you live in an ideal world and to feel deprived when things aren't ideal. The stronger your belief is in an ideal world, the more negative feelings can result. It can lead to unnecessary disappointment. Communication behaviours can become complaining and nagging.
- **Overgeneralizing.** There are two types of overgeneralization. One is when we base a belief on a limited amount of evidence, as in the statement "I'm so stupid, I can't even figure out my microwave oven." It's unfair to focus on one shortcoming as if it represented everything about us. The second type occurs when we exaggerate shortcomings, as in the statement "You never pay attention to me," or "You're always late." Replace overgeneralizations with accurate messages to reduce debilitative feelings.
- **Blaming others for your feelings.** We have suggested that emotions are determined by our interpretations of events, so to say that somebody caused you to feel a certain way would be an irrational thought. In the same way, it's inaccurate to say that you caused a certain emotion in someone else. People respond to your actions with feelings of their own. Consider the issue of motivation in the workplace. You can't motivate your workers any more than you can make someone fall in love with you. What you can do is act in certain ways so that workers will motivate themselves. A person's emotional response involves his or her own thoughts and decisions.

  Blaming others for your feelings can cause numerous problems. You might become overcautious about communicating for fear of hurting someone's feelings. Or, you might keep silent when another person's behaviour is bothering you. In either case, your own communication needs are not being met. You might even begin resenting the person you find bothersome, which is unfair because you have not voiced your feelings. Then when people discover that you hold things in, it will be more difficult for others to read when you are really upset. Realizing that it's thinking, not the actions of others, that determines how you feel is an important step in achieving emotional intelligence.
- **Feeling helpless.** The feeling of helplessness is based on the idea that your happiness is determined by forces beyond your control. Examples of helpless comments are, "I'm too small to do that," or "There's no way that somebody like me can get ahead in this society," or "I'm a shy person, and there's nothing I can do to become a good communicator." Helplessness often comes from turning "won't" statements into "can't" statements. They are rationalizations for giving up. Once you've convinced yourself that there's no hope, it's easy to give up trying. Conversely, acknowledging that there is a possibility of change puts the responsibility on your shoulders and gives you the will to take action.
- **Waiting for a catastrophe.** This irrational thinking is based on the idea that if something bad can happen, it will. Typical catastrophic comments are, "If I try to do something about this problem, it will just make them more angry," or "If I apply for the job I want, I probably won't get hired." One way to avoid the problems of catastrophic thinking is to imagine the consequences of a catastrophe happening. What's the worst that could happen if they get angry or if you don't get hired for the job, or if people laugh at you? Usually the consequences are not that serious. It's naive to think you'll be successful at everything you attempt.

Overcoming Irrational Thinking

Developing the following skills can help reduce self-defeated thinking:

- **Be aware of your feelings.** One way to notice your feelings is to observe your physiological behaviour. Is your jaw tense? Is there a frown on your face? We often suffer from negative feelings for some time before noticing them.

- **Note what triggered the experience.** Sometimes the activating event is obvious, which makes it easier to deal with. It could, however, be something that happened yesterday that you've been carrying around with you. It could also be a series of small events that piled up into one big one. Try to notice a negative feeling as soon as it happens so you will be close to its source.
- **Analyze your thoughts.** To get rid of negative feelings, analyze the thinking process that took place when these feelings first developed. This is called self-talk. It's an internal monologue that can take place quickly and automatically to uncover the thinking process that formed your irrational thoughts. Recognize these, and correct them before they produce an inaccurate idea.
- **Dispute your mistaken thinking.** This step is critical for correcting irrational thinking. First, decide whether your thought is rational or not. Second, explain why the thought process does or doesn't make sense. Last, if the thought is irrational, replace it with a more sensible thought that leaves you feeling better.

This rational–emotive approach allows us to talk ourselves out of feeling bad. After all, since we talked ourselves into feeling negative in the first place, what's wrong with talking ourselves out of it? This technique will help you manage your emotions intelligently.

Emotional Intelligence in the Workplace

Watch your thoughts; they become words. Watch your words; they become actions. Watch your actions; they become habits. Watch your habits; they become character. Watch your character; it becomes your destiny.

—Frank Outlaw[33]

Evidence is accumulating that shows a relationship between emotional intelligence and improved workplace performance. A study at American Express Financial Services showed an average 25 percent increase in productivity for management and sales staff who were trained in emotional competence. In addition, stress levels of the participants decreased 29 percent, while positive emotional states were up 24 percent. Quality of life, occurrences of anger, and physical vitality all demonstrated statistically significant positive change.[34] Effective leadership has also been found to rely on emotional competence,[35] and well-functioning teams have been shown to require emotional literacy.[36]

Emotional intelligence can also be beneficial for continuous learning programs at work. The process of learning involves dealing with new information and experiences that don't easily fit into our existing frameworks of meaning. New information introduces change into our meaning systems, throwing them into disorder and causing uncertainty. We are taken out of our comfort zones, where we are used to experiencing positive emotions that confirm the existing order of things. The discomfort we feel is a negative emotion associated with change and disorder. Dealing with new information forces us to develop new frameworks of meaning that will return us to our comfort zones. Effective learning strategies teach workers how to become comfortable with constant change, uncertainty, and disorder.

Let's look at overcoming fear of public speaking as an example of a learning experience that creates new comfort zones. Most of us are comfortable speaking to people during normal conversations. Stepping in front of an audience, though, takes us out of our common framework of meanings, or our comfort zone, because we are not used to speaking in public. In your discomfort zone, you feel uncertainty, anxiety, and nervousness that may show in your presentation. The benefit of communication training for public speaking is that it allows us to create new comfort zones, reducing the anxiety and nervousness and making us better public speakers. Emotional intelligence makes us better communicators by expanding our comfort zones and helps us to feel more comfortable around uncertainty, change, and disorder. Continuous learning in the workplace means workers are facing disorder and adapting to change on a constant basis. So the real lesson of continuous learning is not all the new information we are taking in, it is that we're continually learning how to be comfortable with uncertainty. Using emotions effectively helps us use communication to reduce the uncertainty in our workplaces.

The trend in today's workplaces is to embrace the entire person, according to Louise LeBrun and Dawn Rae Downton in an article in the *Ivey Business Quarterly*.[37] Traditionally, workers were asked to bring their intellect to work and leave the rest at home. Organizations wanted only your "professional" self. Our feelings, fears, passions, and intuitions didn't get past the security desk. What remains of the person is sterile and alienated—virtually an empty shell of a human being that managers expect to be creative. The standards of professionalism dictate that we suppress feelings and conversations that are inappropriate or unproductive, including those involving social and emotional needs. But it is precisely these skills that are important in workplaces that emphasize communication and relationship building.

LeBrun and Downton say that there are only two activities at the heart of organizational life, and both are conversations. There is self-talk, or the conversations we have with ourselves, and there are the conversations we have with coworkers. Everything, from sales reports to marketing strategies to company policies, is produced from these two communication activities. If we improve the quality of our conversations, we increase company performance. But getting better at talking requires first that we change the conversations we have with ourselves and realize the huge creative power of emotions. Instead of holding them in, they need to be unleashed. Bringing our emotions to work takes courage, but the results can be impressive.

This chapter discussed interpersonal communication, a big topic with many parts. We looked at interpersonal communication theories, specifically focusing on how meaning is created between people and how relationships develop and are maintained. We also looked at ways of defining relationships, such as the Johari Window. We then applied some of these ideas to interpersonal communication in the workplace, pointing out specific factors in organizations that make workplace relationships unique.

Next, we discussed intrapersonal communication, the process of talking to yourself, or thinking, as it's commonly called. Both intrapersonal and interpersonal communication activities combine to create the self-concept, a fairly stable set of perceptions we have about ourselves. We use the processes of reflected appraisal and social comparison to develop our self-concept.

The process of perception is important for good communication. Understanding the perception process helps us to perceive things more accurately and communicate messages more effectively. People are actively engaged in the perception process. Our motives, experiences, feelings, and attitudes all play a role in how we understand our perceptions. Often, our judgments are biased in our own favour, as in the self-serving bias, and can lead to attribution errors.

Finally, we discussed emotions and communication. Emotions have a strong influence on many aspects of our lives, such as self-esteem, and can affect our performance and relationships in the workplace. Facilitative emotions make us feel good and work effectively. Debilitative emotions cause us to be preoccupied with unresolved feelings and can make us unproductive in the workplace. Often irrational thinking leads to debilitative emotions, so the way to get rid of them is to retrace the thoughts that produced them. Emotional intelligence in the workplace allows us to expand our comfort zones and become better performers. It also contributes to our learning abilities.

Case Study

Maintaining Relationships in a Culture of Self-Interest

When I was young I used to be very tolerant of smoke. I did masses of passive smoking and that's the price you paid for going out. We must have always had the same physical reaction, but we just ignored it. When I was growing up there was much more noise and nobody from next door ever complained. What we define as rudeness now was, in the past, just people having to get along with each other. Increased sensitivity is definitely part of the issue. Self-interest is not something now that you are ashamed of having. It used to be.

—Lynn Truss[38]

As a professor, Albert was an expert in his subject matter and well-known in the field. Yet students constantly complained about his classes. They never said anything directly to Albert, though. The grumbling took place only within student circles. Albert had a strict "no food or drink" policy in his classes, though he regularly had coffee and sandwiches during his lessons. If assignments were poorly done, he would belittle people by naming them as examples in front of the class. He often made promises, such as bringing in additional handouts, that he didn't keep. Yet when students missed deadlines even by a few minutes, he penalized them without considering explanations. Students had even talked about him lying to colleagues, having overheard him boasting about doing classroom group activities that never took place. Albert's rigid teaching style left little room for class discussion, which he regarded as an interruption to his lecture, and he expressed this indirectly through his condescending attitude toward students' questions. It didn't take long for students to stop asking questions all together. Despite Albert's exaggerated self-image and highly inconsiderate attitudes, his success had allowed him to get away with being rude to people and to remain clueless about the feelings of others.

Traditionally, good interpersonal relationships are characterized by reciprocal behaviours. If someone is kind to us, we make a point of showing kindness to them. In the same way, disrespectful behaviours are returned to the sender.

1. Identify the issues from an interpersonal communication point of view. Discuss the communication barriers and their effects on relationships in the classroom.

2. Describe the classroom morale. Is learning a collective or individual effort? Is attendance affected? How might relationships between students be affected?

3. How would the learning atmosphere be affected? Would the free flow of information and ideas be helped or hindered? What effect does too much emphasis on status differences have on forming effective relationships?

4. Should the students address the disrespectful actions of their professor or disregard the issue and keep it a secret? What steps could the students take to address the issue? Should they use a direct approach or report it the department chair?

5. If the professor is unresponsive, what payoffs could be discussed to motivate him to change?

6. How are issues of emotional intelligence relevant to Albert's situation?

Classroom Activities

Best Relationships

As a class, break into two equal groups. Students in Group One will take a few minutes to list the behaviours—their own and the other person's—that created a special relationship with a friend. Students in Group Two will take a few minutes to list the behaviours—their own and their boss's—that created a special relationship with a boss. Students from Group One will share their lists in small groups and develop a group list, as will the students in Group Two. When the lists are complete, write them on the board and discuss them. Compare the behaviours between best relationships with friends, and best relationships with bosses. What are the similarities? What are the differences? Account for the differences.

Self-Concept and the Self-Fulfilling Prophecy

Think of situations you have experienced in which a self-fulfilling prophecsy was at work. How did it affect the outcome? If you didn't use self-fulfilling prophecies, would you communicate differently? How would it affect your self-concept?

Perception and Cultural Values

As a class, examine several pictures of pieces of art from different historical periods—for instance, one from the Orient from 3000 B.C., from ancient Greece or the Roman Empire, from the Renaissance in Europe, from the nineteenth-century Impressionists, from modern abstract art, and so forth. Look closely at what the artist was trying to focus on, as these elements reveal the values of the historical period. The pictures might emphasize spiritual qualities, physical power, beauty, peace or war, social and economic status, technology and humanity, and so on. How does each different piece of art express that artist's unique perception of life and human values? Discuss some factors that could explain the differences in perception. Can we relate these factors to our own differences in perception?

Popularity and Personal Success

During the trial of Martha Stewart in 2004, her former staff testified against her, saying that she was "mean-spirited, prone to tantrums, hypocritical, and overly demanding."[39] Her negative treatment of employees finally caught up with her when times got tough. She not only went to jail, but lost a lot of sympathy with her fans. At a press conference after her release, she admitted the lesson she'd learned: people need the support of other people to remain successful. "I really like people a tremendous amount and I like talking to them."[40]

Popular employees are friendly, open, and enjoy communicating with others. They are perceived as honest, trustworthy, and generous. They are high on the likeability scale. Those with low likeability are unfriendly, quick to anger, selfish, and hold grudges. As with many interpersonal skills, no matter how popular you are there's always room for improvement. The following are some communication behaviours for making yourself more likeable:

- Be aware of how people react to you and what you can do to make people warm up to you.

- Make an effort to express friendliness by returning smiles and showing good listening skills by being sensitive to the feelings of others.

- Become relevant to people by learning about their interests.

- Be empathetic and nonjudgmental to encourage people to open up to you.

Take a few minutes individually to think of a few communication behaviours you regularly display that may be unlikeable. Break up into groups and share them with others. Come up with ways that you can change them to increase your likeability.

Glossary

Content meaning, p. 170
Relational meaning, p. 170
Personal identity, p. 171
Inclusion, p. 171
Control, p. 171.
Affection, p. 171
Interpersonal relationship, p. 171
Intrapersonal communication, p. 172
Interpersonal communication, p. 173
Social penetration theory, p. 174

Johari Window, p. 175
Impression management , p. 178
Self-concept, p. 181
Pygmalian effect, p. 181
Fundamental attribution error, p. 185
Self-serving bias, p. 186
Perception check, p. 186
Cognitive labelling theory of emotions, p. 187
Facilitative emotions, p. 188
Debilitative emotions, p. 188

Notes

1. W.C. Shutz, *FIRO: A Three-Dimension Theory of Interpersonal Behaviour* (New York: Holt, Rinehart, and Winston, 1958).

2. Mark L. Knapp & Anita L. Vangelisti, *Interpersonal Communication and Human Relationships* (Boston: Allyn & Bacon, 2000).

3. David Sirota, Louis A. Mischkind, and Michael Irwin Meltzer, "Nothing beats an enthusiastic employee," *The Globe and Mail*, July 29, 2005, C1.

4. H. Blumer, *Symbolic Interactionism: Perspective and Method* (Englewood Cliffs, NJ: Prentice-Hall, 1969).

5. C.R. Berger and J.J. Bradac, *Language and Social Knowledge: Uncertainty in Interpersonal Relations* (London: Arnold, 1982).

6. Ibid.

7. E.T. Hall, *Beyond Culture* (New York: Doubleday, 1976).

8. W.B. Gudykunst, S. Ting-Toomey, and T. Nishida, *Communication in Personal Relationships across Cultures* (Thousand Oaks, CA: Sage, 1996).

9. I. Altman and D. Taylor, "Communication in Interpersonal Relationships: Social Penetration Theory," in *Interpersonal Processes: New Directions in Communication Research*, eds. M.E. Roloff and G.R. Miller (Thousand Oaks, CA: Sage, 1987), 257–77.

10. Ibid.

11. J. Luft, *Group Processes: An Introduction to Group Dynamics* (Palo Alto, CA: Mayfield, 1970).

12. Mario LeClerc, "I've Lied All My Life," *National Post*, November 18, 2005, A23.

13. Diane Davies, "Meet the Seven Deadly Executive Types," *The Globe and Mail*, November 4, 2005, C1.

14. V. Cronen and W.B. Pearce, "The Coordinated Management of Meaning: A Theory of Communication," in *Human Communication Theory*, ed. F.E.X. Dance (New York: Harper & Row, 1982), 61–89.

15. K. Weick, *Sensemaking in Organizations* (Newbury Park, CA: Sage, 1996).

16. Arthur W. Coombs and Donald Snygg, *Individual Behaviour* (New York: Harper and Row, 1959), 134.

17. David W. Johnson, *Reaching Out, Interpersonal Effectiveness and Self-Actualization* (Boston: Allyn & Bacon, 2003).

18. Keith McCarthur, "Hard Sell Goes to the Super Bowl," *The Globe and Mail*, February 7, 2006, B3.

19. Figure adapted from Ronald B. Adler and George Rodman, *Understanding Human Communication* (New York: Oxford University Press, 2003), 53.

20. Ibid.

21. "B.C. puts teens on snowboards to boost their self-image," CanWest News Service, *National Post*, February 12, 2005, A8.

22. D. Hamachek, *Encounters with the Self*, 3rd ed. (Fort Worth, TX: Harcourt, Brace, Jovanovich, 1992).

23. Robert Frost, *Collected Poems* (New York: Holt, Rinehart & Winston, 1966), 86.

24. F.D. Fincham, S.R. Beach, and D.H. Baucom, "Attribution Processes in Distressed and Nondistressed Couples," *Journal of Personality and Social Psychology* 52 (1987): 739–48.

25. C. Sedikides, W.K. Campbell, G.D. Reeder, and A.J. Elliot, "The Self-Serving Bias in Relational Context," *Journal of Personality and Social Psychology* 74 (1998): 378–86.

26. Daniel Goleman, *Emotional Intelligence* (New York: Bantam Books, 1995); Jennifer - Salopek, "Working with Emotional Intelligence," *T&D Journal* (October 1998): 26.

27. Joseph A. DeVito, Rena Shimoni, and Dawne Clark, *Messages: Building Interpersonal Communication Skills* (Toronto: Addison Wesley Longman, 2001).

28. Stanley Schachter, "The Interaction of Cogntive and Physiological Determinants of Emotional State," in *Advances in Experimental Social Psychology*, vol. 1, ed. Leonard - Berkowitz (New York: Academic Press, 1964), 379–99.

29. Martin Lidstrom, "Brand Sense, Build Powerful Brands through Touch, Taste, Smell, Sight and Sound," in Michael Kesterton, "Social Studies," *The Globe and Mail*, August 4, 2005, A18.

30. Ron Adler, *Looking In, Looking Out* (Toronto: Holt, Rinehart, and Winston, 1990).

31. Albert Ellis, *How to Stubbornly Refuse to Make Yourself Miserable about Anything, Yes Anything* (Secaucus, NJ: Lyle Stuart, 1988).

32. Ibid.

33. Frank Outlaw, "Frank Outlaw Quotes," http//en.thinkexist.com/quotation/watch_your_thoughts_they_become_your_words-watch/13673.html (accessed November 17, 2005).

34. Fred Luskin, Rick Aberman, and Arthur DeLorenzo, Jr., "The Training of Emotional Competence in Financial Advisors," www.eiconsortium.org/research/training_of_emotional_competence-in_financial_advisors (accessed October 18, 2005).

35. Steven Perkel, "Primal Leadership: Realizing the Power of Emotional Intelligence," *Consulting to Management* 15 (September 2004): 56.

36. Jim Welch, "The Best Teams Are Emotionally Literate," *Industrial and Commercial Training* 35 (2003): 168.

37. Louise LeBrun and Dawn Rae Downton, "Unleash the Hidden Powers of Emotion," *Ivey Business Quarterly* (Winter 1997): 35.

38. Heather Mallick, "Rude," *The Globe and Mail*, November 12, 2005, R1, quote from Lynn Truss, author of *Talk to the Hand: The Utter Bloody Rudeness of the World Today*.

39. Wallace Immen, "You like me, you really like me," *The Globe and Mail*, June 1, 2005, C1.

40. Ibid.

Chapter Eleven

Communication in Groups and Teams

In a few hundred years, when the history of our time will be written from a long term perspective, I think it is very probable that the most important event these historians will see is not technology, it is not the Internet, it is not e-commerce. It is unprecedented change in the human condition. For the first time . . . substantial and rapidly growing numbers of people have choices. For the first time, they will have to manage themselves. And let me say, we are totally unprepared for it.

—Peter Drucker, "Managing Oneself"[1]

Learning Objectives

- Examine types of social groups and their characteristics

- Identify group roles and their importance for communication

- Discuss methods for conducting effective meetings

- Examine the roles of teams in the workplace

- Explore the importance of communication for effective teamwork

The Teamwork Trend

A common theme throughout this book has been the steadily increasing reliance on groups to accomplish organizational goals. Human relations shows us that people satisfy needs and receive enjoyment through social interaction. Systems theory focuses on the multitude of relationships and networks that organizational members are engaged in. Cultural studies points out how meaning is accomplished through communication. In today's organizations, the nature of work has changed, and modern workplaces have undergone a dramatic transformation to better utilize human potential through collective rather than individual effort.

Even production-line work, the monster created by classical management, has been restructured to introduce a team element. At the Toyota assembly plant in Cambridge, Ontario, workers sharpen their skills so that everything is done the same way every time. You pick up a bolt with your left hand, drill it in with the right, then do it again the same way. This highly developed routine allows problems to be found quickly. The team element is introduced to reduce the monotony of line work. Each worker spends two hours at one job, then transfers to another within the six-member team. As well as providing a degree of variety, the rotation fosters a collective feeling and affords flexibility when employees are away. North American auto makers, in contrast, stick to traditional-style line work, arguing that workers who do the same task repeatedly are more specialized. Who's right? Toyota made $16 billion in 2004—more than Ford, GM, and Daimler/Chrysler combined.[2]

What's GM doing to fight back? Mike Quinton, plant manager at GM in Oshawa, Ontario, keeps a baseball bat in the boardroom. Carved into the barrel of it are two words that express the company's priorities: "Beat Toyota."[3] The Oshawa GM operations are consistently rated at the top in quality of GM's plants and have drawn considerable attention. Manufacturing efficiency has come a long way since the plant's opening in the 1950s when workers would build half the car on one floor then ship it on elevators to another floor for final assembly. Such a waste of time today would be laughable. An engine today is installed with hydraulic hoists and robotic arms in less than 90 seconds. Efficiency in the overall industry is measured by how long it takes to build a car. North America's most productive plant, the Oshawa, Ontario, operation, does it in 15.85 hours. Second place goes to a Nissan plant in Tennessee that comes in 15 minutes later. In all, the difference among the top 10 North American plants is fewer than four hours.

The trend has also reached academic training grounds. At York University's Schulich School of Business, M.B.A. students are immediately put into teams who will share notes, do presentations, and write projects as a group for the whole semester. To make it realistic, students cannot change teams, since in a workplace you rarely get to choose whom you will be working with. They fail or succeed by making the best of what they have to work with. The first few days of the program are spent on exercises emphasizing cooperation, communication, and, of course, success. Teams of five balance on a tiny block of wood, and then each member swings on a rope attached to a tree to reach another block a few feet away. If someone touches the ground, the team starts over. Another exercise is building a bridge out of a hodgepodge of pipe cleaners, sticks, elastic bands, and paper clips that will support a six-pack of bottled water.[4] The exercises teach members to trust each other to make important decisions, to overcome obstacles effectively, and to critique each other without attaching blame—essentially to eliminate the barriers to social interaction.

These are some examples of team processes. Industry as a whole is embracing teamwork enthusiastically for numerous reasons: the promise of increased productivity, better problem solving, more creativity and innovation, and a stronger sense of connection with the organization. In the rest of this chapter we will examine the different ways employees work in groups, beginning with a discussion of the nature of groups, then moving on to conducting effective meetings, and, finally, working effectively in teams.

Characteristics of Groups

The members of a group must have a common goal and must work together to achieve it. The goal creates a sense of attachment among group members that holds them together through times of disagreement and conflict. A group has more than three and less than twelve members. If there are more than twelve members, it becomes too difficult for members to communicate with everyone else in the group. When group members communicate openly and easily with all other members, a group identity is created, which brings us to our first characteristic of groups—cohesiveness.

Cohesiveness

Cohesiveness is a force that bonds group members together. According to Fisher and Ellis, cohesiveness is "the ability of group members to get along, the feeling of loyalty, pride, and commitment of members toward a group."[5] Cohesiveness is a highly positive characteristic of a group that creates strong group harmony and rewarding personal relationships, and makes it desirable to remain a part of the group. As we saw in the example of M.B.A. teams at York University, highly cohesive groups allow members to develop trust in each other and to deal openly and quickly with conflict, leading to effective decision making. Companies and sports teams have applied principles of cohesiveness by holding special activities, such as pep rallies or barbecues, to create a team spirit and energize its members.

Group cohesiveness is promoted when certain conditions exist in the group. Below are six strategies for increasing cohesiveness in groups.[6]

1. **Establish interdependent goals.** Common goals increase group members' reliance on each other, which increases the need for cohesiveness.
2. **Develop relationships and shared norms.** When group members like each other, the group will be more cohesive. Mutually accepted and understood norms of behaviour make it easier to cooperate and coordinate goal achievement.
3. **Create history.** Retelling stories helps to create a group's history. Special events can be held to develop common historical experiences.
4. **Encourage external threats.** Group members become unified when they perceive a threat to their existence.
5. **Accomplish something.** Set short-term goals so the team notices progress quickly and experiences a sense of accomplishment.
6. **Promote acceptance for group members.** Participation increases when members are accepted and not threatened by the group.

Groupthink

When a group has too much cohesiveness, the result is "groupthink," a concept developed by Irving Janis. He defined it as "a mode of thinking that people engage in when they are deeply involved in a cohesive in-group, when the members' strivings for unanimity override their motivation to realistically appraise alternative courses of action."[7] It describes the process of how groups can lose sight of their goals in order to preserve positive feelings and group harmony. The outcome is faulty decision making. A big indicator of groupthink is the absence of conflict. Gareth Morgan states:

> The existence of rival points of view and of different aims and objectives can do much to improve the quality of decision making. Conflict can also serve as an

important release valve that gets rid of pent-up pressures. It facilitates processes of mutual accommodation through exploration and resolution of differences.[8]

Other symptoms of groupthink include:

- not examining each other's ideas critically
- considering few alternatives
- exercising pressure on others to "get with the program"
- not seeking outside opinions
- relinquishing responsibility for the group's security to other members
- maintaining an illusion of unanimous agreement
- censoring your feelings and ideas so as to not impede the reaching of agreement

A common pitfall of workplace meetings is the assumption that the purpose of a meeting is to reach agreement. This mindset creates a concurrence-seeking pattern in discussions around the table—members are driving toward agreement instead of communicating, critically appraising alternatives, and developing plans. If the above symptoms are present when a decision is reached, it may need to be re-examined.

The ability of a group to handle conflict and diversity shows that it is open to criticism, change, and new alternatives, and it is one of the most important ingredients of effective decision making. There are measures to prevent the symptoms of groupthink from arising. One of them is to bring in critical appraisers from outside the group if there is a concern about the ability of the group to critique itself openly. External focus groups are often used for objective feedback. This would provide honest feedback for those managers who may be interested only in getting compliance from group members. Another strategy is to let group members have a discuss on their own, without the manager present. This injects openness into the discussions. Also, individual members can fortify themselves to resist pressures to conform to the opinions of the group. This can be a difficult process if a high degree of loyalty exists among group members. The key is to focus on the decision and maintain critical thinking.

The increasing levels of diversity in the workplace, in the form of more females and more people from different cultures, will challenge our abilities to create cohesive groups. The differences to overcome among members will be greater. At the same time, however, workplace diversity may help fight off groupthink, since it will be more difficult to achieve a high level of conformity, and differences of opinion will be more commonplace. As Canadians, our long-held policy on multiculturalism and bilingualism may give us an advantage, since we have become used to accepting differences as a way of life. Our major cities are among the most multicultural in the world. Multicultural teams have great potential for success given the unique contributions each member can bring. The critical point remains at how effectively an intercultural group can deal with differences. Modaff and DeWine state, "It is critical to examine conflicting values and attitudes directly and openly in the group, or the advantage of having a variety of points of view will be diminished by the conflict they caused."[9]

Norms

Norms are a group's rules for behaviour, established to guide the actions of its members. They may be explicit, such as procedures for meetings, or implicit, such as bringing a coffee for everyone at a meeting if you are bringing one for yourself. Implicit norms change over time as members' behaviours change. Norms become a part of the group's culture, including its shared values, rituals, beliefs, and stories, that provides a framework for understanding patterns of interaction. Members bring in values from their communities, from society at large, and from their cultural backgrounds.

Group norms develop though communication. But as well as giving us things to share, communication also brings out our differences and causes disagreement.

Reducing tension from disagreements is a major reason for establishing group norms. We seek opinions and information that reduce group differences and establish a consensus. We act in ways that allow people to predict our behaviour, such as sitting in the same seats in the classroom. In this way, as we develop a sense of our group, our individual norms and attitudes are transformed into a single group-held norm.

Group Communication Roles

The roles that we play in groups are a set of communication behaviours performed in response to the expectations of other members of the group. Generally, we behave consistently and in this way we fulfill the expectations of others. At times, though, we may behave inconsistently, or "out of character." Roles are created informally over time as the group itself develops. The amount of positive or negative feedback group members receive for certain behaviours determines whether those behaviours will be retained for future use or be rejected. Behaviours that receive positive reinforcement from group members will eventually accumulate and a person's role will emerge.

Group members develop expectations of each other in the workplace based on individual personalities, occupations, and social roles. People develop personal styles. For instance, you might be known in your group as an analyzer or a mediator, and people will learn to expect those behaviours from you. Similarly, a person occupying the position of manager has certain role obligations based on what his or her staff expects from a manager. Simply appointing a leader in a group of students working on a class project will usually trigger that person to display what he or she considers to be the tasks of the leadership role, such as organizing the discussion or scheduling tasks. Group members develop a set of expectations about each member's role retrospectively. After the behaviours have been performed, each member becomes identifiable and develops a unique and distinct role within the group. So, exhibiting leadership behaviours can make group members think you have leadership abilities, and their expectations of your role will expand to include those activities.

Let's look at examples of different roles people can play in groups. They are categorized according to three types: group task roles, group-building and maintenance roles, and individual roles.[10]

Task Roles
These roles involve performing tasks and making progress toward achieving the group's goal.

- *Initiator*—presents new ideas, develops new directions
- *Information Seeker*—seeks clarification, evidence for verifying ideas
- *Opinion Seeker*—checks on opinions and levels of agreement and disagreement of other group members
- *Elaborator*—explains and clarifies ideas of others
- *Coordinator*—shows relationships between ideas, compares
- *Orienter*—keeps the group on subject and moving toward goal
- *Evaluator–Summarizer*—applies critical standards to group's ideas
- *Procedural Technician*—deals with procedural details, such as room booking
- *Recorder*—keeps group's records

Group-Building and Maintenance Roles
These roles focus on interpersonal relations and the social and emotional atmosphere in the group.

- *Encourager*—accepts and reinforces ideas of others
- *Harmonizer*—resolves tensions, often through humour or sarcasm

- *Compromiser*—offers solutions that try to satisfy everyone
- *Gatekeeper and Expediter*—encourages even participation, asks for opinions
- *Observer*—makes general comments about the progress of the group
- *Follower*—goes along with the group, supports group decisions
- *Leader*—determines agenda, takes responsibility for the group
- *Energizer*—stimulates the group into action

Individual Roles

These roles satisfy personal needs rather than group goals. They are self-centred and counterproductive, but most of us engage in them from time to time, often without realizing it.

- *Aggressor*—seeks to enhance personal status by expressing disapproval and attacking status of other group members
- *Blocker*—responds negatively to most ideas, does not cooperate, and opposes much of what the group tries to do
- *Recognition Seeker*—dwells on personal past accomplishments to enhance personal status
- *Clown*—uses humour and jokes excessively, refuses to take ideas seriously
- *Dominator*—monopolizes discussion by talking too long and interrupting
- *Help Seeker*—constantly asking for help, expresses insecurity a lot
- *Private Agenda Promoter*—steers discussion toward a personal agenda rather than contributing to group's goal

The roles just described are not a complete list by any means. Your own group experiences, whether from the classroom or the workplace, could no doubt add to them. In general, task roles and group maintenance roles lead to effective group interaction. Self-centred individual roles are obstacles to the achievement of group goals. Good communication skills in group settings involve identifying which roles will be effective in a given situation based on the needs of the group. A major advantage to developing clear task and maintenance roles and to sticking to them closely is that they don't give self-centred roles a chance to develop. Any teacher or manager knows that a lack of structure in your classroom or workplace creates a breeding ground for self-serving behaviours.

Holding Effective Meetings

Meetings can be an effective problem-solving and decision-making tool if they are planned and conducted properly. In this section we will discuss the causes of unproductive meetings, examine strategies for removing group communication problems, and review a checklist for planning and conducting effective meetings.

As mentioned above, groups function best when members make the needs and goals of the group their primary focus. Small issues such as poor punctuality and straying off topic can add to the frustration people experience in meetings. If people are late for a meeting, those present begin unrelated discussions about sports, current events, or personal issues to pass the time. If the family photos start being passed around, you know you're going to end up seriously behind schedule. Negative feelings may develop about members who are late, which can affect interaction once the meeting begins. Or meetings can be cancelled at the last minute, causing resentment. They can also run right through lunch time because the agenda wasn't followed and discussions wandered off track.

Another pitfall is social loafing, which occurs when there are too many people in a group. The result is a lack of structure and focus. "Social loafing occurs because participants perceive that their individual efforts cannot be identified or evaluated."[11] With too many people, the normal anxiety that accompanies communication activity is reduced, as our performance becomes anonymous and free from evaluation. We goof off in meetings because nobody's watching. So, an appropriate amount of performance anxiety, or attention from others, gives our contributions a sharper focus. Research has shown that as the group grows larger than five members, it becomes more difficult to achieve consensus,[12] so groups of five would be most efficient for problem solving.

Causes of Social Tension in Meetings

Meetings are essentially communication activities involving group interaction, strategic thinking, and goal achievement. A natural part of group interaction is social tension. It occurs in varying degrees in all communication activities, from answering the telephone, to attending a party, to going to a job interview, or, the most dreaded, public speaking. Fisher and Ellis outline some examples of social tension group members experience as they are getting to know each other in the early stages of a group, much of it arising out of performance anxiety, or stage fright, as they call it:[13]

- People are unsure how to behave, and their spoken comments are quiet and tentative with long pauses in between.
- Interruptions are rare, and if they occur, excessive apologizing reveals the presence of tension.

  Zaremba specifies additional common causes of social tension in meetings:[14]

- Members at a meeting may feel nervous about communicating and not confident about their abilities to do so effectively.
- The topic itself may make them uneasy, such as changes to staffing or budgets, or redistribution of work resulting in increased or decreased workload.
- Members may be unprepared.
- They may have had negative experiences working in groups or may not get along with certain members.
- They are too busy with urgent projects to have time for the meeting.
- Personal issues may be making group work difficult to focus on.

  The following sources of tension can decrease meeting effectiveness after the meeting gets going:

- Procedural tensions are triggered by an agenda that is either unclear, is not being followed, or is nonexistent.
- Equity tensions are caused by feelings of unfairness arising from unequal distribution of work (the presence of social loafers) or being ignored by other group members, usually those of higher status, leaving people to question why they are at the meeting in the first place.
- Affective tensions arise through personal dislike, causing a range of communication barriers involving ineffective listening, suspicion of hidden agendas, and unnecessary argument.
- Substantive tensions are caused by differences of opinion about the legitimate issues on the meeting's agenda. These need not be negative, since conflict can have positive outcomes if handled properly, as we will see in our section on conflict management.

Managing Social Tensions in Meetings

Social tension is a problem only when it exceeds a tolerance threshold. If it is below it, it is considered a form of positive energy commonly experienced by professionals in business, sports, theatre, social and family gatherings—anywhere that performance anxiety happens. A tolerant amount of social tension stimulates people and focuses their concentration, bringing the energy of the group into focus. Too much of it will bring out the priorities of individuals and reduce group feeling.

Some problem-solving groups in business require a greater tolerance threshold than others in order to be successful, depending on the levels of uncertainty and turbulence in their organizational environment. High-technology companies, with their strong task orientation, high levels of competition, and rapid change, need to be able to function in a tense social and emotional atmosphere. More maintenance-oriented groups, such as financial or government agencies, generally have rules that prescribe acceptable levels of tension. The challenge for a workplace group is to identify the level of social tension appropriate for dealing with the levels of uncertainty and turbulence in the environment of the organization.

Building the Emotional Intelligence of Groups

In the previous chapter we discussed emotional intelligence as it applies to intrapersonal communication. But emotional intelligence is just as important at the group level, perhaps even more so, since so much work is done in teams in today's workplace.

Traditionally, work-group training focused on task processes such as cooperation, coordination, participation, and commitment. Emotional intelligence takes this training to a higher level by focusing on the process of wholehearted engagement. As Druskat and Wolff state:

> Three conditions are essential for a group's effectiveness: trust among members, a sense of group identity, and a sense of group efficacy. When these conditions are absent, going through the motions of cooperating and participating is still possible. But the team will not be as effective as it could be, because members will choose to hold back rather than fully engage. To be most effective, the team needs to create emotionally intelligent norms—the attitudes and behaviours that eventually become habits—that support building trust, group identity, and group efficacy.[15]

The differences between intrapersonal and interpersonal communication also apply to emotional intelligence. Personal competence comes from being aware of managing your own emotions. Social competence is the ability to be aware of and regulate other people's emotions.[16] A team with emotionally intelligent individuals needs to become aware of its own character to develop relationships and a team atmosphere based on norms that promote emotional capability: the ability to respond constructively in emotionally uncomfortable situations and influence, as team members, the emotions of others in constructive ways.

Group emotional intelligence is not about catching and disposing of emotions, as though they were obstacles to effective group performance. It's about incorporating emotions into group activity, bringing them to the surface and understanding how they affect the group's work. It's also about building relationships that promote the growth of individual identity. The dynamic benefit of an emotionally intelligent group is its ability to use creative friction to achieve the best results. Its chief strength is its ability to let members be totally themselves, emotions, humanness, and all.

Various techniques have been used to develop group emotional intelligence. Perspective taking is one method that can build trust among members. It involves more than simply collecting and combining perspectives in a mechanical way. Effective perspective taking allows team members to observe each other grappling to understand each other's points of view. Interpersonal understanding is another trust-building technique. It must be established as a group norm to be effective. It grows out of a group's realization that workplace morale can be improved when workers put effort into hearing and understanding each other accurately.

Strategies for Effective Meetings

Perhaps the lowly meeting has taken on a new cultural importance—one that allows us to actually get work done.

—John E. Tropman, From Doodling to Daydreaming[17]

The word "meeting" in the workplace can conjure up images of colossal wastes of time, as you envision your coworkers practising their doodling skills, meditating on the clouds passing outside the window, or, if they're bold enough, practising their skills at catching grapes in their mouths. For others, portable communication devices, such as Blackberrys, do fine for passing the time. Meetings have become so predictable that they are now called by different names, such as briefings, seminars, presentations, and videoconferences. According to Tropman, the author quoted above, hundreds of billions of dollars are wasted each year on pointless meetings. You would think we could fix them, but Bernie DeKoven, director of the Institute for Better Meetings, was forced to close his business because he couldn't get any clients.[18] He realized there was a cultural resistance to improving meetings. According to DeKoven, meetings are ceremonies to reinforce the hierarchy, to remind people who's boss, and to praise or chastise anyone who isn't. He says that if people would just accept the fact that that is their purpose, meetings would be shorter and cheaper. But we cloud the issue by trying to get something done. This idea recalls the description of meetings by Deal and Kennedy in our chapter on organizational culture: meetings are simply exercises that reinforce structures of authority and maintain established ways of doing things.

Fortunately, there are better ways for conducting meetings. Adler and Elmhorst have outlined strategies for conducting a successful meeting.[19] Many of these are designed to avoid the problematic group issues described above and to incorporate practices that can develop group emotional intelligence.

Planning a Meeting

The most important step, as with most communication activities in the workplace, is planning. Many managers report in surveys that 25 percent of their meetings could have been replaced with an e-mail message and that about half of them are unproductive, or not worth the time and expense required to assemble a number of people in a room for a given time period. The first question, then, is whether to hold a meeting at all. Meetings are not an appropriate tool when the subject matter can be dealt with over the phone, e-mail, or in a memo, or when the issues are routine and don't require group consensus, or when sufficient time and key people are not available. Meetings should be called only when the following questions can be answered with a yes:

- *Is the issue beyond the capacity of one person?* A decision-making problem may require more information than any single person has, so other people's expertise is required. Also, a job may require more time than one person has, so others are brought in to share the workload.
- *Are people's tasks interdependent?* People often use meetings to get together to coordinate their functions and then work independently, without input from others, such as a student group preparing a panel presentation. Once the individual topics are decided, each person completes his or her part. If each person is responsible for a different function, meetings become little more than information-sharing sessions. Progress

reports can be exchanged more easily by e-mail. Meetings made up of people with similar functions, such as a group of decision makers steering a fundraising drive, may improve individual performance in meetings by playing complementary roles made up of the group roles mentioned above—contributing information, providing critical commentary, showing empathy, or reinforcing ideas of others.

- *Is there more than one solution?* Questions that have one right answer and that can be resolved by presenting the appropriate facts or figures, such as whether the budget will allow payment of overtime to complete a job, do not require a meeting. Problems that require discussion focus on finding the best answer, rather than the right or wrong one, such as what a company can do to improve health and safety.

- *Are misunderstandings or reservations likely?* When compliance to a controversial issue is important, meetings are necessary to clearly present both sides of an issue and to prevent unpopular issues from causing grumbling and resistance among the members. By letting members in on the discussion, they will more willingly accept changes. The interpersonal communication element of meetings enables a sharing and acceptance of ideas to occur much more than e-mails or written messages.

Setting an agenda is also an essential step for effective meetings. An agenda is a list of topics that will be discussed in a meeting. Without an agenda, meetings do not have an objective and leave people without a sense of purpose. A good agenda contains several pieces of basic information and is easy to write.

- *Time, length, and location.* These details should be clearly stated on the agenda to avoid confusion about starting times, to let people schedule enough time in their day for the meeting so that other appointments don't get in the way, and to avoid people wandering in late after not being able to find the meeting room.

- *Participants.* Problem-solving groups rely on considerable participation from all members, so it's best to keep the number small to avoid the likelihood of some members falling silent. If the meeting is mainly informational in nature, a larger group would work, since a lower level of group interaction would be required. The agenda should clearly identify who will be attending, so members know who to expect.

- *Background information.* Emphasize the relevance of the meeting, new developments on the issue, or details that people need to remember in a short background statement.

- *Items and objectives.* List topics of discussion along with objectives to make the meeting outcome-driven. The more specifically stated the objective, the better chance there is of achieving it. A poorly worded objective, such as "Let's discuss ways to improve things at in our organization," should be specified to say, "We will discuss ways we can improve communication among departments in our organization." The agenda is also a good place to tell people what they need to do to prepare for the meeting, such as bringing financial reports or making copies. The Bell-Shaped Agenda Structure by Tropman (see Figure 11.1) structures a meeting around the group's energy and attention levels. The first few easy items help get the members working efficiently as a group before tackling more difficult items in the second half.

Conducting the Meeting

Well-run meetings don't happen by accident. They are the result of good use of time, proper preparation, and important communication techniques. Let's look at the parts of an effective meeting.

Beginning the meeting. State what will be accomplished, how the group will do this, and encourage a team spirit to get good results.

- *Identify the goals of the meeting.* Though they appear on the agenda, stating them helps focus the discussion.

Figure 11.1   The Bell-Shaped Agenda Structure[20]

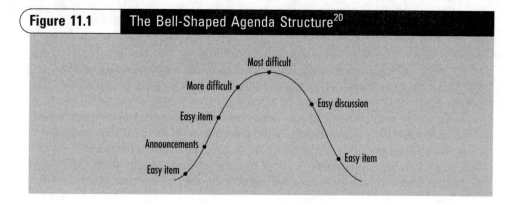

- *Provide background information.* Explain the context of the issues to bring out their relevance and give everyone the same frame of reference.
- *Identify key contributors.* Detail the contributions that members will make, whether specific persons or the group in general.
- *Preview the agenda.* State the order of issues to be covered.
- *Identify time constraints.* Give people a sense of how much time they have to spend on the topics.

Conducting the meeting. The following techniques will help a discussion leader achieve his or her main objective: to bring out the unique talents of all members and to do it in a specified time.

- *Encouraging participation.* Below are several ways to encourage participation at meetings:
  - Individual differences, such as gender, status, culture, or age, may give some members advantages when speaking up and prevent other voices from being heard, thus making participation uneven. The Nominal Group Technique reduces the effects of individual differences. The meeting leader invites each member to write ideas down, then posts them up for everyone to see. The ideas remain anonymous. Each member ranks the ideas, and those with the most votes are discussed critically, after which a decision can be made. The process ensures equal participation while sidestepping potential conflicts.
  - Encourage turn taking. Though cumbersome, this method is useful at the beginning of a meeting to start people talking, or if a few people are dominating the discussion. Ask questions to the group as a whole or at certain people who are being quiet.
- *Staying on track.* When there is too much discussion, time may be wasted. Use the following techniques to stick to your agenda.
  - Remind people of the time. Cut into the discussion at an opportune time, saying something like, "Hiring a consultant sounds good, but for now let's focus on using our own marketing department because we have to be out of here by 10 a.m."
  - Summarize. When the discussion stays off topic long after it's done, use a summarizing technique to bring it around. Recap what has been decided and introduce the next topic.
  - Challenge the relevance of discussions. Ask a group member to explain how the discussion applies to the subject at hand. This will either return the group to the discussion or clarify a potentially valuable point of view.
- *Keeping a positive atmosphere.* Keeping a tone of goodwill and sincerity is important for showing respect for fellow group members. If, as a group leader you, for instance, tell a group member to save an idea for later in the meeting, make a point of

returning to it to maintain your credibility in the eyes of group members. Try to prevent defensive responses by criticizing in a constructive manner. Ask for clarification of what on the surface sound like stupid ideas. You can also paraphrase a group member to get more information. This provides a way of verifying your interpretation of someone's comments and gives the other person a chance to add details.

- Build on the comments of others. Always probe for merit in ideas by working with them, even if they sound useless. If there is no hidden merit, at least you have acknowledged the value of the idea, and shown appreciation for them.
- Consider cultural differences. Ways of conducting business vary from culture to culture. Learn to watch for different rules for conducting effective meetings. For example, an uninhibited expression of emotion in some cultures is normal; in others, emotions are more restrained.

Concluding the meeting. The following steps will help you to bring the meeting to a successful close.

- *Close the meeting on schedule.* Attention can drift if a meeting goes overtime as people think about other commitments. Continue only if members agree to keep working.
- *Close the meeting when the agenda is finished.* In most workplaces, if you finish early, it doesn't mean extra socializing time. The group leader is responsible for summarizing the meeting's accomplishments, reviewing future actions, and closing the meeting by thanking members for their participation.

Following up on the meeting. After the meeting, follow up on agreed-upon outcomes with members in informal ways, such as personal remarks or friendly phone calls, so as not to appear snoopy. This gives continuing importance to the initiatives taken in the meeting.

The above strategies provide you with a blueprint for one of the most common group activities in the workplace—holding effective meetings. Another frequently used group process is teamwork. Let's turn to that one now.

Teamwork in Organizations

Teamwork is one of today's most widely adopted ways of changing an organization to achieve greater productivity. The purpose of teamwork, or self-directed work groups, is to elicit greater effort from workers. Teamwork practices are implemented in conjunction with flexible job design and greater emphasis on training, because employees who work in teams use a larger variety of skills than those in traditional work environments. Teamwork is usually accompanied by alternative compensation packages that reward greater productivity, such as profit sharing, merit bonuses, and skill-based pay. Formal training on various group processes, such as decision making, problem solving, leadership, and communication enables team members to successfully perform their tasks in the new environment.

Teamwork in organizations has two aspects.[21] A company that structures itself to use teams to accomplish tasks is known as a *team-based organization*. The change involves replacing a vertical hierarchy with a horizontal, "flat" structure, allowing significant cost savings and downsizing of staffing levels. The need for supervisors is eliminated, as teams are responsible for managing themselves and assume many of the supervisory activities that used to be done by managers. Work teams are involved in job scheduling, training, problem solving, and individual and group evaluation. The second aspect is the concept of *teamwork*, which refers to the social and emotional skills individuals need to collaborate effectively in order to accomplish tasks. So, the first involves organizational structure, the second group, processes.

The benefits of teamwork include increased efficiency and innovation, error reduction, quality improvement, greater ability to adapt to changes, better customer service, and increased job satisfaction. Teams are effective for both

> achieving change as well as accomplishing work in changing environments. Because of their integrative structure . . . teams are more flexible, innovative, permeable, responsive, and adaptive than hierarchies. Teams also engender greater commitment from members who develop a sense of purpose and ownership by having a voice in what does and doesn't get done.[22]

About 75 percent of major corporations today employ team structures in parts of their operations. In a national sample of Canadian companies, team-based organizations were found to have significantly lower employee turnover rates than those without them, particularly in higher-skill workplaces.[23] In addition to outperforming hierarchical structures, teams have fewer accidents, less absenteeism, and more effective problem solving. To reduce the high cost of employee turnover, including hard costs, such as severance packages and recruitment fees; and soft costs, such as the loss of corporate knowledge, broken relationships with coworkers, customers, and suppliers, and the time it takes for new employees to get up to speed; organizations have begun developing more cooperative structures in the workplace such as teamwork. Team-based workplaces do much more than work in teams. They embody a work style that gives employees an opportunity to become more involved in many aspects of the organization, well beyond their immediate jobs. This gives individuals a sense of personal identity in relation to the organization, and creates a sense of connection with their coworkers, the organization, and the community at large. Among Canada's top 100 employers, *Maclean's* lists the following companies and details the cooperative strategies they use to create a spirit of teamwork:[24]

- The Hamilton-based steel maker Dofasco, a pioneer in teamwork structures, spends $15 million a year on employee training to keep its 7600 workers from leaving. Its profit sharing in 2004 amounted to $9000 per employee, not to mention the annual Christmas party for 30 000 that it holds at Copps Coliseum.
- The University of Toronto appeals to the loyalty of 7592 employees by offering free tuition and on-site daycare.
- New Flyer Industries of Winnipeg (1081 employees) offers year-end bonuses of up to $20 000.
- The fuel-producer North Atlantic Refining Company of Come By Chance, Newfoundland, provides its 596 employees discounts on fuel and heating equipment.
- Sasktel Communication of Regina enriches the work experience of its 3800 employees with large-scale volunteer work—75 000 hours logged in 2004, almost $3 million donated to non-profit organizations. Spreading the wealth can become a cultural value that extends into the workplace and brings benefits back around to employees in the form of feelings of accomplishment and spiritual well-being.
- To celebrate the end of the workweek, Hill and Knowlton Public Relations of Toronto wheels around a beer cart Friday afternoons for its 154 staff members.
- To stem the overuse of contract workers, Hewlett Packard Canada of Mississauga with 4260 employees limits the length of part-time work contracts to two years. At that point, a manager should know if the work is a core function and if the person should become permanent. According to CEO Paul Tsaparis, "By committing to full-time employees, you absolutely get back commitment from them."

- At Ottawa-based defence contractor General Dynamics Canada Ltd., everybody's "draftable"—to one of the company's six in-house hockey teams. This plan, among others such as discounted tickets for the Ottawa Senators, helped put this company on the Top 100 employers in Canada list for 2003 compiled by Mediacorp Canada Inc.

Though these rewards are largely tangible, their meaning goes beyond material value. In a survey asking Canadians what they want in a job, the highest rating (74 percent) said they wanted to be treated with respect, followed by interesting work (72 percent), a feeling of accomplishment (71 percent), and good communication with coworkers (70 percent). Job security and good pay came in at 62 percent and 60 percent.[25] One area where teamwork has proven to be a bonus is that of trust. Normally the workers' level of trust in their supervisor will range across the spectrum—some will have no trust, some a lot, and many will be in the middle. Because of the greater emphasis on relationship building and interdependence in teams, trust is an essential ingredient. Trust exists when team members show a strong belief in sticking to their commitments, are honest, and don't take advantage of one another. It allows a person the freedom to take a risk. The face-to-face context of teamwork allows people to employ verbal and nonverbal communication clues to interpret each other's intentions. Coupled with frequent and meaningful interaction, the communication activity in successful teams allows for deep relationships to develop.[26]

The concept of equity is highlighted in team structures that give employees genuine involvement in decision-making processes. Equity involves the process of turning employees into owners, not by handing over the company, but by distributing enough of a stake to make their contributions feel valued. A recent book called *Equity: Why Employee Ownership Is Good for Business* discusses the benefits of employee ownership programs in the form of giving employees stock options. Cisco Systems CEO John Chambers states, "There's not been a single successful company in high-tech in the last two decades that has done that without broad-based stock option plans.... [I]t is a very effective way to align interests."[27]

But stock giveaways are not the whole picture. The authors of *Equity* say that an organization must develop a "culture of ownership," characterized by a flatter structure, information and responsibility sharing, and effective listening skills, especially on the part of managers. A small business success story the book offers is that of Jackson's Hardware, a 100 percent employee-owned company. When giant Home Depot came to town, common sense dictated that Jackson's would close. Instead, business increased. The staff cared about making a sale because it would profit them personally, so they developed a competitive edge; friendly and knowledgeable service. An example on a larger scale is that of Algoma Steel of Sault Ste. Marie, a troubled major steel producer for many years. On the verge of bankruptcy, an employee ownership system was developed that has kept the company going for a couple of decades, even though some bumps were encountered.

Despite the many rewards of teamwork, creating successful teams often involves difficult and complex changes to work systems. The concept of teamwork can be defined by the degree of self-direction a team possesses. Organizations that become team-based, or truly horizontal structures, allow greater self-management than organizations that create work teams yet retain their hierarchical structure. In the hierarchical case, teamwork would be limited to group maintenance issues, such as increased emphasis on communication, relationship building, and conflict management—skills for keeping the group working together effectively. Authority and decision making remain in the hands of the bosses. Team-based organizations, on the other hand, involve goal setting, problem analysis, decision making, and solution identification and implementation—task roles that give teams the authority and responsibility for achieving organizational goals.

Characteristics of Effective Teamwork

Let's examine some characteristics necessary for effective teamwork, keeping in mind that teamwork in its most effective and dynamic form is an organic and evolving process.[28]

1. Involve employees at every stage of the process. Managers can implement team structures, but if workers have not been consulted they will feel coerced and their level of participation will decrease. The message to employees is that their input is not needed, and their ideas are not important. Managers should show value for employee input at every stage of the participation process, even during design.

2. Commitment often includes conflict. Establishing a commitment to a participative workplace means being prepared to accept conflicting and diverse points of view. So, commitment is not about agreeing with managers, and disagreement does not equal deviance. Companies need to recognize that alternative positions can represent an even stronger demonstration of commitment than agreement.

3. Leadership is about results, not status. Teamwork strives to give employees a greater voice, in this sense giving them leadership capacity. But workers should continue thinking like workers, where their skills and knowledge reside, instead of identifying with management concerns. Teams are given task-related authority.

4. Reward participative, not individual, achievements. Old ways of appraising and recognizing employee performance must be changed with team structures to provide incentive for cooperation. If collaboration is the goal, compensation systems must reinforce communication activities that demonstrate effective participation.

5. Identify norms and cultures that may be barriers. Employees cultivated on playing subordinate roles, as in the classical management style, may be uncomfortable or incapable of engaging in regular feedback, especially with superiors. Implementing teamwork in traditional organizations or ones with labour unions may require a deeper cultural change to be successful.

6. Don't forget about individual needs. Though the team approach offers certain freedoms, such as increased decision making and goal setting, tighter controls and group pressures are also evident. Workers in a team are responsible not only to their manager, but to coworkers. Since each group member is a leader for the others, actions are more closely monitored by more people than in the traditional work structure where a worker has one boss. Individual concerns can easily be buried under the driving force of a group, but they need to be addressed before they have a negative impact.

7. Balance individual and group recognition. Teams bring together diverse talents. Should they swallow up the strong and weak members without recognizing individual contributions? Some team members, usually the strong ones, like to see a direct link between their work and the outcome, while others don't mind blending their efforts into an undifferentiated whole. Coordinating rewards and recognition in teams remains a challenge. Raising the issue of individual recognition in our collectively minded workplaces, though, can hang the career-threatening label of "not-a-team-player" on you. The issue has the potential to sap motivation and must be dealt with. Try openly telling your group the way you operate the best and work it out. This type of problem, though, is best dealt with during the team-forming stage where the team's individual–collective chemistry is decided. The following questions should be answered before a team gets off the ground:
    - *What are our team's objectives?* State the desired outcome in specific language. To "perform well" is an activity, not an outcome. To improve on-time deliveries by 30 percent is a clear, measurable outcome.

- *What are the team's ground rules?* Establish procedures for how the team will do its work by writing them down. Our memories are limited. By doing this work up front, problems will be avoided down the road.
- *What leadership model will we use?* Teams that determine their own leadership style are far more successful than teams with appointed leaders or managers who supervise but do not participate in the process. Three models are usually used. The choice of model establishes the team's personality, its focal point, and the team climate:
  - Leader-led teams are based on a command model. Leaders are responsible for all decisions and outcomes.
  - Consensus-led teams are the most flexible. Members develop a shared understanding of their task and devise specific strategies for achieving agreement. Problems with power and status differences are eliminated with the consensus approach.
  - Managed teams combine people with specific areas of expertise—for example, legal or technical experts—and these become their independent responsibilities, while at the same time maintaining interdependence with other team members.
- *What strategies will we need for this effort?* Teams need to clearly outline what communication processes will be used and what roles members are responsible for to establish a dynamic climate for accomplishing tasks. How will the team deal with conflict, for example? Effective teams do not suppress conflict. Team performance is improved when members are allowed to express negative feelings and confront others on issues. Risk taking is another example. Mistakes should be treated as a learning experience rather than as warranting punishment.
- *What evaluation measures will we use?* Set evaluation methods for individuals and for the team at the beginning. Often these will be consistent with previously established evaluation methods. Formal evaluation measures and forms allow members to communicate frequently and openly according to set standards.

Refining Team Communication Skills

What are the essential communication skills for effective teams? Once the core skills discussed above are in place, team members can fine-tune their communication skills in a number of areas.

Effective listening involves being tuned into your environment and is difficult because we've spent all of our lives tuning our environment out. Gordon Hempton, an acoustical ecologist from Washington State, teaches a course called "The Joy of Listening."[29] One of his suggestions is to wear earplugs for half an hour, then take them out. You'll immediately experience enriched sound. Another is taking a walk with a child. Before children are sent to school and taught to pay attention by filtering out every sound except the teacher's voice, they are naturally attuned to their surroundings. In addition to removing selective listening barriers, put value on every word you hear. Listen with intent. Also, be conscious of your nonverbal messages, since they make up the majority of the meaning in a message, especially in work teams where relationships are so important.

Teams need to define their values and priorities frequently. This helps to separate the problem from the person, so that interpersonal conflict can be held to a minimum. Specific procedures can be established for depersonalizing discussions to focus on the issue and not on the person. This helps control aggression or prevents feelings of superiority from developing on the team.

Clearly defined procedures set a positive emotional tone for the group, so that cynics or naysayers can be quickly dealt with. An effective technique is addressing problems in

Whipping up Team Spirit in France[31]

True to their culture, the French have bypassed the more traditional team-building activities, such as bungee jumping and karaoke competitions, for a more civilized one—getting teams of employees to whip up a cheese soufflé or a *confit de canard*. When executives use cooking courses to develop team spirit, they quickly learn that they must get along with their team members or go hungry. The courses are so popular that they make up a quarter of the cooking courses offered by one of France's leading chefs, Alain Ducasse. According to his colleague, Emmanuel Perrier, "The difference between this and bungee jumping is that it introduces the notion of pleasure to something which, up until now, has been mostly about fear and competition. Making a good meal is a great incentive for motivating people to work together." Cooking allows managers to rediscover the basic business principles of discipline, a respect for time, emotion, and creativity.

analytical fashion: first, brainstorm the issues, then organize them into issues the team directly controls, has some influence over, and can't control at all. Then prioritize and make plans for action. As management author Jim Clemmer states, "Effective teams navigate their way through setbacks, misdirection, and negativity that cloud most organizations in mediocrity and low morale. They refuse to be victims of weak senior leadership, cynical colleagues, flawed organizational processes, demanding customers, or poor suppliers."[30]

In communication, the feedback process is essential. Feedback should produce learning, validate effort, and create a sense of accomplishment. Effective teams engage in self-monitoring and self-correcting throughout the problem-solving process, not just at the end. These can be a combination of formal and informal methods. The results of formal methods should be discussed as a group. Feedback should be freely given as a form of support and evaluation and received constructively. Conflict is not suppressed, but welcomed. Confrontation among team members is a natural part of open group activity. It is essential that team members develop communication skills that focus on work tasks and avoid personalizing team activity so that conflict can become a progressive group experience instead of a dispute over petty individual differences. To foster risk taking and creativity, treat mistakes or failures as learning experiences instead of using punishment to deal with them. This way, team members develop confidence and learn not to be afraid of trying different strategies to solve problems.

Using a proactive rather than a reactive approach to accomplishing team goals sums up the above team skills. Members' attitudes and resources must be aligned with the team's overall goal. This is done by established a clearly defined, mutually agreed-upon purpose. By detailing the ground rules, members adopt a positive attitude toward change and realize that patience is required. By taking a participative approach, members are empowered and have a strong sense of control. Using effective communication skills, members are able to openly express support for each other's efforts and minimize negative comments that tear the team down and are personal attacks.

Creating a Culture of Teamwork

Traditional business culture has engrained in us the value of individual effort and rewards based on individual accomplishments. In fact, this is a norm in society in general. This attitude can leave team members disconnected from the group's collective effort. Team building means creating a culture that values collaboration and group accomplishments. The team skills described above operate much more effectively in an environment that supports and reinforces them.

The Culture of Yes, No, and Maybe

I won't take yes for an answer.

—*Groucho Marx*

Effective teams need to deal with dissent and disagreement constructively. Often this necessary disagreement is restrained and concealed behind agreeable head-nodding around the table at meetings, only to be released after people retreat to their workplaces. This is the type of yes that means nothing will be moving forward. It represents a false consensus. The dynamics of the *culture of yes* dictates that people don't tell the truth during meetings. We say yes, but mean no. Instead of objecting to an idea in a meeting, people become quiet, then begin voicing objections informally after they leave the room to undercut the consensus that appeared to have emerged. In contrast, effective teams have an atmosphere that invites disagreement. When people are uncomfortable expressing disagreement, they suppress the honest and creative ideas essential for participation of all team members and good decision making.

One way of creating an open climate for discussion to determine if people really agree with a decision that has been made is for team leaders to actively seek out disagreement—in short to establish dissent as a cultural value in the group. As Michael Roberto, author of *Why Great Leaders Don't Take Yes for an Answer*, states, "leaders cannot wait for dissent to come to them; they must actively go seek it out. [T]he mere existence of passive leadership constitutes a substantial barrier to candid dialogue and debate within organizations."[32]

The *culture of no*, on the other hand, represents barriers to progress deriving from power and status. This organization's purpose is to control dissenting voices by stifling dialogue and alternative thinking, often to satisfy the goals of particular members or divisions of the organization. Members expressing disagreement are censored rather than given the opportunity to defend their views logically and show how their views are consistent with what's best overall for the organization. A culture of no gives greatest voice to those with greatest power.

An example of the culture of no is IBM in the early 1990s. In addition to exhibiting all the above cultural traits, IBM gave dissenters veto power in decision making, giving everyone with power the authority to close off avenues of inquiry. Initiatives would be scrapped if a member involved in the decision "failed to concur." The emphasis was not on flexible and progressive thinking, but on ensuring that new ideas would not upset the status quo. In contrast, the slogan at Apple Computers at the time was "Think Different," an attitude that was reflected in the user-friendly operating systems they designed. IBM's management style has since then abandoned many of its crippling rigid structures.

The *culture of maybe* describes organizations that are highly analytical. It emphasizes the gathering of all relevant facts before a decision can be made, earning itself the nickname "paralysis by analysis." To deal with the uncertainties of decision making, this organization tries to find certainty by turning every option into a yes or no answer by gathering more and more data. This pursuit can be costly and time-consuming. Insufficient data represents an impasse for the culture of maybe that could be addressed with more task-oriented discussion to get the team moving forward. A positive quality of this type of culture is its ability to be comfortable dealing with the long periods of ambiguity before decisions are made. At least the decisions will not be rash.

Managing Virtual Teams[33]

Virtual teams are formed of people who rarely meet physically. There are many benefits: employees get out of the office and closer to customers, they have more flexibility in their schedules, and time and travel costs are lowered—ideal characteristics for sales representatives. The rise of virtual teams has been fuelled by an increasingly global economy and the availability of communication technology. Today, about one-third of employees participate on virtual teams.

Running a virtual team requires using electronic communication to accomplish all the things done interpersonally on a traditional, co-located team. Ground rules and expectations need to be emphasized because of the absence of physical meetings and chance run-ins. For example, how quickly should e-mails be answered? Or, if you communicate with a client, should you send the answer to everyone so another member doesn't ask the same question? Generally, because of the reliance on mediated communication, extra effort is required for effective sharing of information and to maintain an interdependent spirit.

To make up for the lack of introductions and "face" time, members are encouraged to share photographs, short biographies, and locations, so that everyone can put a name to a face, a set of skills, and a place. Common courtesies, such as recognizing birthdays, also help far-flung teams maintain a sense of belonging.

Communication is a challenge because of the limitations of the written word. Managers have to be more supportive because verbal messages are harsher than spoken words. A smiley face can't replace an affectionate response or a pat on the back. Much of our communication is nonverbal, and if we become undisciplined in our meetings we can always run into each other later and make up for it. The lack of face-to-face interaction can create obstacles to promotion since there are fewer opportunities for networking.

Managers of virtual teams need to emulate the attributes of traditional teams, such as allowing time for small talk and socializing, to reduce the feeling of isolation and build team rapport. Communication plays a big role in establishing trust among team members. It's a manager's responsibility to set the tone with the first few messages for how the team will interact.

Discussion Questions

1. List some of the advantages and drawbacks of using communication technology in teams.

2. What techniques could virtual groups use to develop trust among members?

3. What personal experiences have you had in virtual groups? How satisfying have they been?

Problems with Teamwork

Though teamwork has been the buzzword in business, the results have been somewhat disappointing. The reason, according to Peter Drucker, is that there are three kinds of teams. They each have different structures, strengths, and capabilities.[34]

The Baseball Team

Instead of playing *as* a team, these players play *on* the team. They have fixed positions. Examples of this type of team are operating teams in hospitals and Henry Ford–style automakers. Second basemen never help pitchers, doctors never consult with nurses, and auto design teams do their work and pass it on in sequence to manufacturing and then to marketing.

The Football Team

Emergency units in hospitals that rally around a patient play like a football team. Though the players have fixed positions, they play as a team. Japanese automakers that employ design, manufacturing, and marketing teams in parallel or concurrently operate like a football team.

The Jazz Combo

Product development or problem-solving teams have primary rather than fixed positions, allowing them to multitask. They cover for their team members and adjust to each other's strengths and weaknesses and to changes in the performance. An experiment in this type of team took place at General Motor's Saturn Division.

Pros and Cons

The baseball team represents classical structure. Each member can be evaluated and held accountable separately, and can be trained for a specific position. Traditional mass production methods of automakers that required long runs and minimum changes relied successfully on this team structure for decades. New designs depreciated the value of used cars (a big factor for new car buyers), so they were stretched to every five years. In fact, new car designs often caused dips in sales and market share.

Japanese auto makers are modelled after the football team, which allows new car models to be introduced in parallel with older ones. North American auto makers dumped the baseball team when they realized the football team provides the flexibility they needed to compete in today's market. The difference for operations is in the precision of specifications, in terms of style, technology, performance, weight, price, and so on, and the strictness with which they are followed. Whereas baseball allows players individual flexibility to do things their own way, football teams are not as permissive. There are no individual stars, as members subordinate themselves to the goals of the team.

The jazz combo is usually a small team of from five to seven members. Members are trained together and need practice before they can fully function. One clear overall goal exists for the team, though considerable flexibility is allowed to each individual in terms of his or her performance. In a jazz combo, the team "performs," and individuals "contribute."

So why do some teams work and others don't? According to Drucker, gradual change cannot work. Team structures require a total break with the past, a daunting task for the highly traditional and unionized auto industry. Workers report to the team leader instead of the old supervisor. Compensation systems are tied to performance. Partial implementation of teamwork also does not work. GM's Saturn kept authority in the hands of supervisors and shop stewards instead of handing it over to team leaders. So it was like playing in a jazz combo using baseball structure. The result is frustration and nonperformance.

Teamwork and Accountability

One common criticism of teamwork, especially in circumstances that benefit from a high degree of structure, is lack of accountability. Accountability deals with being able to recognize the contributions of individuals in the collective effort, and either assigning the blame or giving the credit for the results. In this way, problems can be corrected and improvements made. Though team members are supposed to become motivated and committed to participate in the team's success, not all members contribute equally. Measures to ensure accountability try to identify clear lines of responsibility for tasks. These vary from team to team, depending on situational factors. Some general guidelines are the following:[35]

1. Team leaders should be chosen by the manager.
2. Resources should be arranged with the help of the manager.

3. Avoid co-leadership—it obscures responsibility.
4. Establish clear timelines and deadlines.

Wherever people work together, they do so as a team. The degree of integration on that team depends on the unique factors of each situation—in other words, a contingency approach. Amanda Sinclair says, "Contingency models match the appropriate structure to the context—the technology, the environment and level of turbulence, the managerial style, and the degree of differentiation within the organization."[36] The challenge for managers is deciding which type of team to use for their organization and to realize that teamwork is not a magic path to higher performance. The use of teams just because they are popular will be neither rewarding nor effective.

Chapter Summary

Our chapter on groups and teams began by recognizing the magnitude of the changes happening in workplaces as a result of using teamwork. Many foreign companies, such as Asian car makers, have become successful because of team-based structures.

We then examined the characteristics of groups, such as cohesiveness, a force that bonds group members together, and groupthink, a process where groups lose sight of their goals to preserve group harmony, and the outcome is faulty problem solving. Through communication, groups establish norms, which represent a group's rules for behaviour. In groups, members play certain roles, which develop according to the expectations others have of us based on our personalities, occupations, and social roles. Group roles are categorized according to task roles, maintenance roles, and individual roles.

Meetings are one of the most common workplace activities, yet many of them turn out to be not very effective. Social tension is one cause of poor participation in meetings. Directors can reduce social tension by having a clear agenda and creating an atmosphere of equality. Emotional intelligence is a valuable skill for group members so that groups can function effectively. It focuses on developing trust and a sense of group identity and group efficacy in group members. Group competence starts with personal competence. We also discussed strategies for holding effective meetings.

Our final topic was teamwork. Team-based structures in workplaces embody a work style that gives employees an opportunity to become more involved in many aspects of the organization, creating a sense of personal identity in relation to the organization, and a sense of connection with coworkers, the organization, and the community at large. Benefits of teamwork are increased efficiency and innovation, error reduction, quality improvement, and greater ability to adapt to changes. One of the problems with teamwork is accountability, or being able to recognize the contributions of individuals in the collective effort. Measures to ensure accountability vary from team to team, depending on situational factors.

Case Study

Accountability in Teams

There's much evidence showing that the collective effort of teams can accomplish far more than individuals working by themselves. But a team's potential can also be wasted if its activity is not structured effectively and if people are not held accountable. Accountability answers a simple question: who gets the blame or credit for team results? The picture of accountability becomes hazy in team-based workplaces because of their complexity. Self-managed teams, cross-functional teams, interlocking teams, all blur the lines showing who is responsible for what. Consider the case of Marion's department.

Marion's company embraced teamwork with great enthusiasm. Employees were excited about their newfound freedom from the old management hierarchy. In fact, one of the teams Marion was in charge of was made up of volunteers from her unit. To take advantage of new ideas, the team had picked a couple of new employees as team coordinators, hoping this new responsibility, with the team's help, would quickly bring them up to speed. But it didn't take long for some common problems to arise. The team requested an extension on their deadline. They told Marion they were having problems with scheduling and couldn't obtain the resources they needed. Though Marion sensed some troubles earlier on, she didn't want to interfere with the new team spirit by monitoring it too closely.

The team's final report was inconsistent. Some ideas were good, some were awful, and some necessary parts, particularly the financial sections, were missing. Part of the problem, Marion learned later, was that the finance department had little interest in the project, partly because of not having been involved in the planning stages. It would take Marion a lot of work to correct and complete the report for presentation to the management committee, or she would be held responsible for the failure. But who was accountable to Marion? Who deserved credit for good work, and who deserved blame for not coming through?

Discussion Questions

1. Apply the four principles of accountability discussed at the end of the chapter to the case to determine what went wrong and how it could have been done better. Who should be held accountable?

2. Discuss the importance of accountability for effective teamwork. Could better team communication skills have been used to avoid the problem? Which ones in particular?

What Will the Meeting Be About?

As an exercise you can have a little fun with, break up into groups of from five to seven members. You will be conducting a meeting about what to have a meeting about. Two of your group members will be observers who will not participate in the meeting. Take a minute to individually decide what your suggestion for the meeting's topic will be. Select a Chair, and let the Chair begin the meeting with a clear statement of purpose and procedure. Go around and hear everyone's ideas. Make a group decision on the best suggestion. After the decision is made and presented to the class with justification, the observers will comment on the effectiveness of the meeting, including clear goals, efficient process, fairness, and participation.

Classroom Activities

Teams in the Classroom

Form groups and share experiences you have had working on group projects in the classroom. What were your positive and negative experiences? Make a group list of techniques for effective group projects in the classroom based on your own experiences and the ideas in this chapter. Share the list with the class to compare the ideas of different groups.

Glossary

Norms, p. 200
Team-based organization, p. 208
Teamwork, p. 208

Culture of yes, p. 214
Culture of no, p. 214
Culture of maybe, p. 214

Notes

1. Peter F. Drucker, "Managing Oneself" (paper presented at the Drucker Foundation Leadership and Management Conference, New York, November 9, 1999).

2. Grant Robertson, "Everybody wants it, Toyota's got it," *The Globe and Mail*, September 15, 2005, B19.

3. Grant Robertson, "In the Boardroom at the General Motors Oshawa plant is a baseball bat," *The Globe and Mail*, September 15, 2005, B16.

4. Richard Bloom, "Life Lesson: teamwork really means pulling together," *The Globe and Mail*, September 16, 2005, C1.

5. B. Aubrey Fisher and Donald G. Ellis, *Small Group Decision Making, Communication and Group Process* (New York: McGraw Hill, 1990), 34.

6. Ibid.

7. Irving Janus, *Victims of Groupthink: A Psychological Study of Foreign Policy Decisions and Fiascoes* (Boston: Houghton Mifflin, 1972).

8. Gareth Morgan, *Images of Organization* (Beverly Hills, CA: Sage, 1986), 191.

9. Daniel Modaff and Sue DeWine, *Organizational Communication* (Los Angeles: Roxbury Publishing, 2002).

10. Kenneth T. Benne and Paul Sheats, "Functional Roles of Group Members," *Journal of Social Sciences* 4 (1948): 41–49.

11. Stewart L. Tubbs, *A Systems Approach to Small Group Interaction* (Boston: McGraw Hill, 2001), 163.

12. William Barnard, "Group Influence and the Likelihood of a Unanimous Majority," *Journal of Social Psychology* 131 (1991): 607–13.

13. Fisher and Ellis, *Small Group Decision Making*, 34.

14. Alan Jay Zaremba, *Organizational Communication: Foundations for Business Collaboration* (Mason, OH: Thomson-South Western, 2006).

15. Vanessa U. Druskat and Steven B. Wolff, "Building Emotional Intelligence of Groups," *Harvard Business Review* (March 2001): 80.

16. Daniel Goleman, *Emotional Intelligence* (New York: Bantam Books, 1995).

17. John E. Tropman, in Jared Sandberg, "From Doodling to Daydreaming: An Office Meeting Survival guide," *The Wall Street Journal Online*, http://www.careerjournal.com/columnists/cubiclecture/20040521-cubicle.html (accessed November 10, 2005).

18. Ibid.

19. Ronald B Adler and Jeanne Marquardt Elmhorst, *Communicating at Work*, 6th ed. (New York: McGraw Hill, 1999), 266–82.

20. John E. Tropman, *Making Meetings Work: Achieving High Quality Group Decisions* (Thousand Oaks, CA: Sage, 1996), 33.

21. P. Shockley-Zalabak, *Fundamentals of Organizational Communication* (Boston: Pearson, 2002).

22. Christopher M. Avery, "How Teamwork Can Be Developed as an Individual Skill," *Journal for Quality and Participation* (Fall 2000): 5–13.

23. Statistics Canada and Human Resources Development Canada, *Innovative Work Practices and Labour Turnover in Canada*, The Evolving Workplace Series, Catalogue No. 71-584-MIE, August 27, 2003.

24. Katherine Macklem, "Showing the Love," *Maclean's*, October 24, 2005, 26.

25. Canadian Policy Research Networks, "Work Teams," http://www.jobquality.ca/indicator_e/des002.stm (accessed November 26, 2005).

26. Society for the Advancement of Education, "The Paradoxes of teamwork in the workplace," *USA Today*, April 1996, quotations from Cynthia Stohl, http://www.findarticles.com/p/articles/mi_m1272/is_n2611_v124-20k (accessed November 5, 2005).

27. Corey Rosen, John Case, and Martin Staubus, *Equity: Why Employee Ownership Is Good for Business* (Boston: Harvard Business School Press, 2005); quote from John Simpson, "Equity Stock Options Make for Better Employees," *Financial Post*, book report, October 26, 2005, WK2.

28. Bonnie T. Yarbrough, *Leading Groups and Teams* (Mason, OH: Thomson-SouthWestern, 2003).

29. M. Kesterton, "How To Listen," Social Studies, *The Globe and Mail*, November 22, 2005, A24.

30. Jim Clemmer, "A coach's playbook for workplace teams," *The Globe and Mail*, October 28, 2005, C1.

31. Kim Willsher, "French Whip up Team Spirit," Guardian News Service, *The Globe and Mail*, June 22, 2005, C5.

32. Michael Roberto, "Don't Listen to 'Yes,'" *HBS Working Knowledge*, interview with Martha Lagace, senior editor, http://hbswk.hbs.edu/item.jhtml?id=4833&t=leadership (accessed July 14, 2006).

33. Carla Johnson, "Managing Virtual Teams," *HR Magazine*, June 2002.

34. Peter Drucker, "There's Three Kinds of Teams," in *Managing in a Time of Great Change* (New York: Penguin Books USA, 1995), http://www.leadertoleader.org (accessed October 21, 2005).

35. Ibid.

36. Amanda Sinclair, "The Ideology of Teamwork," *Organization Studies* 13, no. 4 (1992): 611–26.

12

Chapter Twelve

Decision Making, Conflict Resolution, and Leadership

However good our future research may be, we shall never be able to escape from the ultimate dilemma that all our knowledge is about the past, and all our decisions are about the future.

—*John S. Ratcliffe, "Scenario Building"*[1]

Learning Objectives

- Examine the role of communication in decision making

- Identify types of decisions in organizations

- Review techniques for effective decision making

- Explore the nature of conflict in the workplace

- Discuss conflict resolution techniques

- Examine the concept of leadership and the role of communication in effective leadership

- Identify effective leadership styles

Introduction—Making Effective Decisions

Communication skills are essential for sound decision making in the workplace because good decisions require effective information processing, including analyzing the problem carefully, considering all alternatives, and collecting all relevant data. And, since decisions are often made in groups, these activities normally involve a lot of social interaction. Yet despite the sophisticated information-processing systems we have developed, many decisions still involve a significant amount of risk. In this chapter we examine some of the barriers to good decision making, the role of communication in decision making, and traditional and contemporary methods for making effective decisions. We will also examine the nature of conflict and methods of conflict resolution. Finally, we will explore probably the most complex role in an organization, that of leadership.

Communication and Decision Making

Rational Decision Making

Decision making is often described from the classical management point of view, based on the traditional view of communication as a rational and logical method for reducing uncertainty and eliminating unknowns. Typical *rational decision making* models in organizations include the following steps:

1. Managers analyze and define the problem by gathering information from operators.
2. They develop ways of dealing with the problem.
3. They determine the pros and cons of alternatives, perhaps by testing them or getting more feedback from operators.
4. They do a final analysis of the information and determine the costs and benefits of each alternative.
5. Managers decide on the best alternative.
6. They implement the decision.[2]

This model may work well for simple decisions, such as selecting a restaurant for dinner, but organizations start to have problems even before they get past step one. Defining the problem is not easy for a complex place such as an organization because of the many different points of view involved. An educational institution, for example, may provide conflicting viewpoints about an issue. Teachers may emphasize learning, while administrators will focus on funding and expenses. Unions and professional associations may further splinter the organization's goal. One of the reasons why decisions are difficult to make is our desire to satisfy multiple goals. Even a fairly simple task of buying a used car for getting to school and work can become complicated. You start with your need for transportation, then you throw in fuel economy as an additional goal after looking at several options, and then quality, and then appearance—and before long you have multiple goals and a difficult decision.

Another difficulty with the model is collecting information. Not enough information can result in a poor decision, and, in fact, important information may not always be available. Too much information can be too time-consuming to deal with, especially with the time constraints imposed by organizational schedules. The virtually endless media and Internet sources of information available to managers today can cause information overload very quickly. It is no wonder that many organizations have established positions specifically for knowledge and data management.

Alternatives to Rational Decision Making

So, I mustn't move the knight. Try the rook move again.... At this point you glance at the clock. "My goodness! Already 30 minutes gone on thinking about whether to move the rook or the knight. If it goes on like this you'll really be in trouble." And then suddenly you are struck by the happy idea why move rook or knight? What about B–QN1? And without any more ado, without analysis at all, you move the bishop. Just like that.

—Alexander Kotov, chess master[3]

Making the best possible decision often requires looking at all possible options—a very time-consuming task—and then picking the best one. To shorten this painstaking process, decision theorist Herbert Simon developed an approach to decision making called *satisficing*.[4] Instead of selecting the best solution out of all possible options, he suggests picking a solution that will work well enough to accomplish the task. Let's say you're shopping for a car. It would be incredibly difficult to research every car on the market to arrive at the best possible deal. Simon's approach, on the other hand, sets out the criteria that the solution must satisfy first and searches for a solution that meets them. This approach takes into account the drawbacks of rational decision-making models. For example, people are not always perfectly logical. We insert feelings into our decisions, evaluating factors such as colour, comfort, and status. Also, workplaces impose restrictions on time and resources. Often, to save time in making a decision, we will count on the opinions of experts to suggest workable, if not optimal, solutions to problems.

A shortage of time often forces managers to make quick decisions, employing largely non-logical thinking processes based on intuition and experience. These processes rely on the manager's network of knowledge, much of it implicit and unspoken, so that relevant pieces of information can be accessed and applied to the current problem. A good athlete uses similar processes in the rapid action of moving a puck down the ice or dodging tackles down the field. A study of intuitive decision making supports these approaches.[5] The majority of managers in the study stated that they used intuition in decision making. Intuitive methods not only speeded up the process of decision making, they improved the quality of the decision, promoted greater staff involvement, and produced decisions in keeping with the cultural practices of the organization. Recent research has discovered the numerous irrational processes at play in decision making in the workplace, some going so far as to describe the decision-making process as a lucky coincidence of problems, choices, and people. This notion is supported by the sense-making process of Karl Weick discussed in our chapter on organizational culture, which maintains that the decision-making process is constructed retroactively—only after the decision has been made do managers realize how they arrived at it.

Ped Box	Thinking Skills

"According to cognitive neuro-scientists, we are conscious of only about 5 per cent of our cognitive activity, so most of our decisions, actions, emotions, and behaviour depends on the 95 per cent of brain activity that goes beyond our conscious awareness. The adaptive unconscious makes it possible for us to, say, turn a corner in our car without having to go through elaborate calculations to determine the precise angle of the turn, the velocity of the automobile, the steering radius of the car."

—Michael Kesterton[6]

Power and politics in organizations can harm optimal decision making by introducing further irrational elements into the mix. These often serve personal or group interests rather than being best for the organization as a whole. Often solutions to problems are seen as favouring one group over another, thus leading to battles over turf. Alternatives can be supported or rejected not on their merits but simply because they favour a rival group. Multiple interests are common in large organizations, and the relationships of power and influence they generate must often be considered as factors in decision making, even though they do not contribute to the effectiveness of the decision. In this perspective, decisions are the outcome of the interplay of competing interests in the organization.

Which Strategy to Use—Rational or Intuitive?

Reason only discovers the shortest way; it does not discover the destination.

—George Bernard Shaw[7]

Let's look at some of the alternatives to the rational decision making models to see where they could be used effectively. Recent research by Frances Wesley and Henry Mintzberg has focused on intuitive and action-oriented strategies for decision making.[8] These models have been referred to as "thinking first," "seeing first," and "doing first."

A rational, or "thinking first," model of decision making uses the step-by-step strategy outlined at the beginning of this section: define the problem, analyze causes, design solutions, decide on the best one, and implement the decision. In reality, though, the steps of a decision process are usually not this clear and sequential. They are interrupted by new events, cycle back, and circle around and around until finally a solution emerges—much like the way a thesis finally takes shape as additional research and new perspectives are introduced when writing a term paper, or the way the chess master in the quote at the beginning of this section decided which move to make. Sudden insights follow periods of groping in the dark. Despite the systematic approaches we have designed to apply to decision making, the real-life messiness of the process may be beyond description using rational methods.

The "seeing first" model relies on visual and conceptual insights that produce a picture of the whole problem in a single glance—a flash of illumination. Consider the story of the paint salesman starting his career after World War Two trying to sell paint to a commissioner from the Department of Transportation.[9] The commissioner turns down the offer, saying she doesn't need any paint, she needs safety because of the high number of highway accidents. Driving home down a paved, undivided highway, a light bulb goes off in the salesperson's head. Why not paint lines down the middle of the road so cars stay on their own sides to increase highway safety? The commissioner buys the idea and the paint. Strategic insights require the imagination to see what others do not.

The "doing first" model is useful when the sequential process and the seeing process isn't working. If all else fails, jump in with both feet and experiment. It's difficult to adequately assess the pros and cons of a business strategy when you are entering uncharted territory, such as overseas expansion or new technology. The approach has been proposed in Karl Weick's enactment model. As Mintzberg and Wesley say, it

> means doing various things, finding out which among them works, making sense of that and repeating the successful behaviours while discarding the rest. Successful people know that when they are stuck, they must experiment. Thinking may drive doing, but doing just as surely drives thinking. We don't just think in order to act, we act in order to think.[10]

These three approaches to decision making—thinking, seeing, and doing—correlate closely with preferences people have for either facts, ideas, and experiences, respectively.

Problem-solving workshops conducted in the three approaches revealed interesting characteristics. The "thinking first" workshops quickly converged on analytical frameworks such as cause and effect, problem and solution, costs and benefits, and so on, using linear and categorical arguments. To achieve efficiency, depth of analysis was sacrificed. The "seeing first" workshops achieved a greater integration of ideas because members had to reach consensus on the essence of an issue. People asked more questions and were more playful and creative. This developed closer collaboration and invited more interpretation of the problem. Pictures have a way of connecting people. Whereas the "thinking first" workshop focused on problems, the "seeing first" workshop focused on solutions. The "doing first" workshop generated more spontaneity, a group characteristic that teaches members to remain open to messages from others. This finely developed skill is evident in groups of jazz musicians: "Organizations that recognize opportunities for innovation—and hone the skills required—increase their capacity for learning. In improvisation, people have to respond with a speed that eliminates many inhibitions."[11]

Researchers are not suggesting that managers abandon planning and programming as a decision-making system, merely that they should open the doors more widely to include intuition, visioning, and venturing. Below is a summary of when each approach is most effective.

Use "thinking first" when:

- the issue is clear
- the data are reliable
- the context is structured, such as an established production process
- thoughts can be clearly expressed

Use "seeing first" when:

- many elements have to be combined in the solution
- an original solution is required
- commitment to the solution is essential
- communication across boundaries is required, such as in new-product development

Use "doing first" when:

- the problem is unique and confusing
- detailed data can get in the way
- solving some relationship issues by establishing some simple rules can help people move forward, such as in the implementation of new technology

Avoiding Mental Decision-Making Traps

Imagine you have to visit London, Ontario, Dallas, Chicago, and Saskatoon in a week. What is the optimal route? Most people will use sequential thinking. They will pick the route of the closest cities. They may save money on their first choice, but by the last destination it might cost a huge amount. Simultaneous thinking looks at the whole route at the same time. It looks at all combinations and possible solutions and finds the best one. Humans don't handle simultaneous problems well; computers do. We tend to pick the low hanging fruit first, but often that leaves some real uglies at the end.

—Peter Bell, Ivey Business School[12]

Where do bad decisions come from? The way decisions are made is often the cause. Alternatives may not be clearly defined, the data may be incorrect, or the costs and benefits may have been inaccurately considered. Sometimes, however, the fault lies in the way the brain of the decision maker works. The routines that our minds use to cope with complex situations are known as *heuristics*. They are mental short cuts that help us make the numerous judgments required to get through a normal day. For example, we equate size with proximity, so the bigger something is, the closer we think it is. Anyone who has ever walked toward downtown thinking it's not far because the tall buildings could be easily seen knows that they are farther away than they look. It's the buildings' size that makes them appear closer. A number of similar flaws in thinking have been identified by researchers. Heuristics can be caused by misperceptions, biases, or all sorts of irrational mental processes.

Below are some psychological traps that can derail business decisions along with methods for guarding against them, from the book *Smart Choices: A Practical Guide to Making Better Decisions.*[13]

The Anchoring Trap

Our mind gives greater importance to the first information it receives, which serves as an anchor for subsequent information. For example, last year's sales volumes can be used as a predictions for this year's. This approach may turn out accurate, but it puts too much weight on past events and does not consider other factors. In rapidly changing markets, historical anchors can lead to misguided decisions. Negotiators use this technique when they start with high demands to influence the counteroffer from the other side.

Use the following techniques to reduce the dangers of anchors:

1. View a problem from different starting points to get a clearer value of your position.
2. Consider the problem on your own before consulting others.
3. Be careful not to anchor your advisors by being too specific with your own ideas.
4. In negotiations, submit your offer first if you want to create an anchor.

The Status Quo Trap

Decision makers show a definite preference for alternatives that preserve the status quo. For example, when new products are developed, they are described by what preceded them. The first automobile was the "horseless carriage." Marshall McLuhan described this tendency as the "rear view mirror" way of seeing the present. Sticking with the status quo puts us at less psychological risk and avoids the effort of dealing with the unknown. In business the status quo is especially attractive because making a bad decision is far worse than making no decision. The fear of "rocking the boat" deprives managers of the chance to take appropriate actions.

Use the following techniques to reduce the false comfort of the status quo:

1. Reconsider you objectives regularly and ensure that they serve the status quo.
2. Look for other alternatives than the status quo for comparison.
3. Avoid exaggerating the effort it would take to switch to a new path.
4. Don't stick with the status quo just because the decisions for change are too complex.

The Sunk-Cost Trap

Our past decisions are what economists call sunk costs—old and unrecoverable investments of time and money. Sometimes we make decisions to justify our past decisions, especially if they were poor ones. Usually it's because we are unwilling to admit we made a mistake, expressed in the popular saying "throwing good money after bad." Professionally, it can seriously harm your business reputation. A workplace culture that harshly punishes people's mistakes can influence workers to let failed projects drag on endlessly instead of admitting to them and cutting their losses. In politics, where credibility is especially critical, admitting to bad decisions is a rare event, since it can lead to an election loss.

Use the following techniques to avoid the sunk-cost trap:

1. Listen carefully to the views of people who were not involved in the original decision and therefore will be less committed to it.
2. Examine why it upsets you to admit to a mistake. If it is a blow to your ego, deal with the thought processes rationally to dig yourself out of the hole.
3. Cultivate a culture that does not fear failure.

The Confirming Evidence Trap

Managers often seek advice from other managers in a similar situation. Let's say your company is planning to expand to Alberta because of the energy boom. Before making your final decision, you call up a manager at a company that has recently opened an office in the province to get her viewpoint. You receive a strong endorsement for the expansion plan. What else did you expect from someone who has just made the same decision? The confirming evidence trap is a bias that reflects the sources of information we use. We usually seek supporting information to confirm our existing plan and avoid seeking conflicting information that contradicts it. A psychological process at work here is our tendency to decide subconsciously what we want to do before figuring out why we want to do it. The decision process, then, involves merely choosing the reasons that fit. And once we figure out what we want, we naturally favour information that supports it.

Use the following techniques to avoid the confirming evidence trap:

1. Always put your choices through a rigorous test and don't accept confirming evidence without questioning it.
2. Build counterarguments to test your choice with an open mind.
3. In seeking out advice, ask open-ended questions so as not to lead the answer.
4. Don't surround yourself with "yes" people. Encourage your managers to think critically.

Numerous other mental traps exist that sabotage our decisions without us even knowing it. We can be overconfident about our accuracy when it comes to estimating and forecasting business outcomes. Or we include adjustments in our decisions "just to be on the safe side." Because we predict future events based on memory of past events, we often give too much significance to events that make a strong impression on us. If someone we know wins a lottery, for example, we think the chances of us winning also have increased. One experiment showed lists of famous men and women to different groups. Though each list had an equal amount of men and women on it, on some lists the men were more famous than the women and on others it was vice versa. After subjects studied the lists they were asked to estimate the percentages of men and women on each list. Those who had lists with more famous men thought there were more men on the list, while those who had lists with more famous women thought there were more women. In this case, the different degrees of fame of each of the famous people on each list distorted people's ability to estimate objectively the number of men and women. To avoid this trap, carefully examine your assumptions to ensure they are not being overly influenced by a single dramatic factor. The best protection against psychological traps in decision making is awareness. Build tests into your decision-making methods to catch errors before they happen. In business decisions, there's no such thing as a "no-brainer."

Decision Making and Organizational Communication Perspectives

Decision making is one of the most frequent activities in the workplace. It relies heavily on information gathering, interpretation, and group communication processes. The

Who Will Ride?

You are driving down the road in your car on a wild, stormy night, when you pass by a bus stop and you see three people waiting for the bus:

1. An old lady who looks as if she is about to die.
2. A close friend who once saved your life.
3. The perfect partner you have been dreaming about.

Which one would you choose to offer a ride to, knowing that there could only be one passenger in your car?

Think of your answer before you continue reading. This is a moral and/or ethical dilemma that was once actually used as part of a job application. You could pick up the old lady, because she is going to die, and thus you should save her first. Or you could take the old friend because he once saved your life, and this would be the perfect chance to pay him back. However, you may never be able to find your perfect mate again. So, who will ride?

The answer is at the end of the chapter.

various styles of decision making discussed in this section have been summarized by Miller[14] and Mintzberg[15] in terms of the organizational perspectives described in the opening chapters of this book.

Decision Making and Classical Management

- Decision making is a rational, step-by-step, problem-focused process.
- The highly analytical approach generalizes the problem and removes it from its practical context.
- Emphasis is on finding the optimal solution using established procedures.
- Decision making is a managerial responsibility.

Decision Making and Human Relations

- Decision making is a rational, analytical process,
- Participation of non-managers in the decision-making process is a source of satisfaction for workers and a valuable source of knowledge for the organization.
- Participation in decision making is motivating and leads to greater productivity.

Decision Making and Systems Theory

- Decision making is a complex process that takes place among interconnected parts of an organization.
- The heightened sense of context places greater emphasis on practical and analytical factors in decision making.
- A greater emphasis on relationships, both within and outside the organization, creates a collaborative mindset.

Decision Making and Organizational Culture

- Decision-making styles reflect an organization's cultural values and practices.
- Aligning individual and organizational values to create a single purpose can improve the quality of decisions.
- A culture that emphasizes action, risk taking, and reflection helps workers connect analytical and practical issues in decision making and fosters collaboration and personal growth.

Decision Making and Critical Studies

- Decision making is a process through which managers control subordinates.
- When workers engage in participative decision making, such as TQM, it represents their acceptance of this control, contributing to hegemonic relationships in the workplace.

What we have in organizations today is a variety of decision-making models from which to choose. Intuitive and non-rational decision-making models have been used where their particular strengths would be appropriate. In some situations, however, a strict rational model is still effective. The management style of a workplace also influences the ways decisions are made. When non-rational styles are used, the potential for disagreement and possibly conflict becomes much greater because there is usually more discussion and more diversity of opinions. In the next section, we will explore the nature of conflict and the role it plays in decision making and communication.

Conflict and Communication in Organizations

The Nature of Conflict

Conflict can be generally described as any opposition to the achievement of goals. Joyce Frost and William Wilmot define conflict as an "expressed struggle between at least two interdependent parties who perceive incompatible goals, scarce rewards, and interference from the other parties in achieving their goals."[16] On an interpersonal level, conflict occurs when there is a difference in how each person perceives an issue. Work teams, with their diverse collections of talents and perspectives, frequently experience conflict. Larger groups, such as departments or organizations, can experience the same types of frustrating obstacles. In organizations, the presence of power and politics can be an additional cause of conflict, since it adds more factors to consider when striving to achieve organizational goals. Conflict can also occur on an intrapersonal level, as when someone is under emotional stress.

Conflict is made up of three critical ingredients: incompatible goals, interdependence, and communication.[17] Incompatible goals in the workplace are numerous, often arising from opposing ideas about the distribution of resources. For example, for several years in the mid-2000s, Stelco went through desperate negotiations between management and union about ways to preserve the workers' pension plan while paying off creditors and making the company profitable again. On a smaller scale, a manager who disapproves of informal communication in the workplace may have a difficult time with his or her subordinates when the employee "grapevine" becomes established. Interdependence also characterizes the Stelco situation. Both management and union, representing integral parts of the same organization, are joined together in whatever outcome they will produce. The notion of togetherness that interdependence brings can be an important first step in resolving conflict if both sides can agree on a common obstacle and join forces to defeat it. Scarce rewards represent a common objective that is of limited quantity.

The third ingredient, communication, is significant because it enables both the expression and resolution of conflict. Communication makes possible

> the setting and reframing of goals; the defining and narrowing of conflict issues; the developing of relationships between disputants and constituents; the selecting and implementing of strategies and tactics; the generating, attacking, and defending of alternative solutions; and the reaching and confirming of agreements.[18]

Even in the best of circumstances, conflict is a natural phenomenon that is unavoidable. We are all different, and when you put a lot of people with different backgrounds, values, and expectations together under one roof and subject them to tight schedules and challenging situations disagreements will happen. Dissonance is far more common than harmony, except that it often hides behind a hear-no-evil-see-no-evil mask to make it appear that everything is fine. For many years, going back to classical management days, managers viewed conflict as a negative event. More and more, though, organizations are viewing conflict not only as an inevitable part of the workplace, but as a source of renewal and positive energy—only, however, if people learn how to handle conflict effectively.

The key is to deal with conflict proactively by building conflict-resolution mechanisms into day-to-day decision-making activity. This way all workers are in command of communication tools that address sources of conflict before they cause bad feelings. At National Bank of Canada, all employees have access to formal help for solving interpersonal conflicts, all managers are trained in alternative dispute resolution methods, and trained mediators are sprinkled throughout the company to help employees identify their conflict management weaknesses.[19] Let's look at some common causes of conflict, and then at some strategies for handling them.

Causes of Conflict in Organizations

Individual differences are the starting point of many workplace disagreements because of the highly psychological and personal nature of conflict. As Charles Conrad states, "perhaps more than any other factor, employees' perceptions influence what happens during conflicts and what effects conflicts have on organizations."[20] We use our conceptual filters to make messages meaningful to us. We communicate using verbal and nonverbal messages that express dominance, such as raising our voices, gesturing aggressively, or questioning comments with unnecessary detail. The communication styles we use to handle conflict can be sources of conflict themselves. If we feel threatened, conflict will escalate as our defensive messages increase in strength. So conflict strategies that often start with cooperative styles escalate to become competing ones because of the tendency toward reciprocal behaviour. If one side starts shouting, the other side responds in kind.

Pondy describes conflict in terms of five stages.[21] Let's examine these stages and the communication activities that might accompany them. The first stage is latent conflict, in which the possibility of an incompatible goal arises. Next is the stage of perceived conflict. Both parties perceive the issue only from their own perspective and begin fortifying their position to win the argument. This stage can demonstrate an increasing investment of ego—one person is right and the other is wrong. Let's say you're deciding on where to locate the water cooler and one person wants it in the lunchroom and the other in the office area. Once the ego is invested, it becomes a case of complete victory for one side and defeat for the other, with nothing in between.

This stage is followed by felt conflict, in which the parties begin to personalize the issues. The focus begins to emphasize the conflict, not the conflict resolution. Communication could be characterized by heightened hostility, such as name-calling and personal attacks. The result is a deepening mistrust, accompanied by suspicion of hidden agendas, as the conflict moves into its fourth stage, manifest conflict. Perhaps the person preferring the lunchroom wants the water cooler away from the work area for an unstated reason, such as a suspicion that it may prove to distract people from their work. Or the discussion could expand to include unrelated issues and past events. One party might complain that he always gets what he wants, so it's time she got her choice. Ultimately, the conflict could threaten each side's sense of relational power, an escalation that can seriously destroy a relationship. In our discussion on interpersonal communication in Chapter 10, we found that one of three building blocks on which relationships are formed is a sense of equal control over each other. A win–lose outcome imbalances that control, creating a dominant–submissive relationship, which people generally do not stay in for the simple fact that their need for a sense of control is not satisfied. Effective conflict resolution involves peeling back these layers of obstacles to return to the real issue, a difficult process once mistrust and power imbalances set in.

The above example demonstrates a competitive conflict. Conflicts may also originate in procedural differences, such as how a group will structure its work, a common experience when organizing group projects in class. How to deal with people who do not "carry their weight" can become an especially sensitive topic. Groups members may join together to apply pressure on the slacker, or a teacher may be called in as an outside party to use authority to resolve the problem. As described above, the conflict can escalate to include previous experiences, maybe with these same people, suggesting ongoing problems in the relationships. Establishing clear ground rules for group work is essential to avoid counterproductive behaviours.

Conflicts also arise in institutional differences. Each organizational level, from operators to executives, has different interests. Operators are concerned with work processes, job security, wages, and benefits; administrators with cost management; executives with shareholder profit. Contract staff has different interests than permanent staff. Recently, workplaces have been troubled with moral issues involving questions of ethical and unethical behaviour. These issues include a wide range of subjects, from allowing cigarette companies to sponsor events, to exploiting cheap labour in Third World countries, to accounting scandals and executive fraud, to environmental and ecological issues.

Communication Styles for Expressing Conflict

Communication researchers have identified five communication styles people use to respond to conflict: non-assertive, directly aggressive, passive aggressive, indirect, and assertive.[22]

The *non-assertive style* is used by a person who is unable or unwilling to engage in a conflict. A child, for example, may choose to avoid responding to conflict because he or she doesn't know what to say. Accepting the status quo is easier than facing the problem. People may choose to accommodate someone in a conflict, as parents might in arguments with children, as a way of putting the children's needs ahead of their own. An employee might be wise to choose an accommodating response with a boss if it poses a risk to job security.

The *directly aggressive style* attacks conflict head on, leaving the other person feeling hurt or humiliated. It often includes verbal personal attacks that discount the other person's intelligence or dignity, such as "Be serious, will you?" or "You don't know what you're talking about." This style can also be expressed nonverbally with facial expressions, groans, waves of the hand, or simply ignoring someone's comment. Success in business comes from overpowering opponents. Revenge is the most common response to direct aggression. Workplaces that exhibit the aggression–revenge cycle pay a high price tag. It kills feedback, especially of ideas, and reduces productivity. Organizations also bruise employees' dignity with policies that exclude certain employees from benefits and privileges.

The *passive aggressive* response is a subtle form of aggression where the attack is concealed behind false cooperation. Hostility and revenge are expressed in indirect ways. For example, people will do small things to annoy you instead of confronting the

Fridge Rage—"Your mother doesn't work here, so clean up!"

Move over, road rage. Fridge rage is taking over. In a work climate steeped in downsizing, frozen wages, and morally questionable practices, it doesn't take much to push someone over the edge. In this case, it's a three-week-old egg salad sandwich. Office culture experts say dealing with fridge rage has become a pervasive issue in today's workplace. "We're very territorial creatures," says Judith Glaser, author of *Creating WE: Change I-Thinking to We-Thinking.* "We're given our cubicles, but this is shared space and, in many companies, people don't work out the rules for shared space until it gets to the level of rage." In a 2005 poll by the *Globe and Mail,* 27 percent said they were sickened by mouldy, smelly food in the workplace fridge, and 8 percent admitted to being the causes of fridge rage, while only 10 percent of workplaces had established a strict fridge policy.[23]

After many futile fridge-cleaning measures, such as putting up signs saying "Your mother doesn't work here, so you're expected to clean up after yourself," workplaces have taken to putting names on lunches, and after a week they get trashed. But nothing has worked. Workers just can't take the issue seriously enough to pitch in. Says Glaser, "If you're in an environment that has a lot of rage in it anyway—factions, people that aren't getting along—if your office has people that love to tell stories about other people, then why would they want to fix the problem? The refrigerator just adds another wonderful story in the process of gossiping, and also creates more opportunities for people to be attacked or picked on or create blame around." Fortunately, no incidents of fridge rage have been lethal yet.[24]

problem, or people will agree with you while never intending to comply with the agreement. Success in business comes through manipulation.

The *indirect style* attempts to communicate an unsatisfactory situation without being blunt and hurting someone's feelings. For example, instead of directly rejecting someone's invitation to dinner by claiming, "I'm not interested in spending time with you," an indirect response would save face by saying, "I'm busy." Of course, the intention is for the real message to get through. For these reasons, indirect messages are also the most common way people make requests. Success in business comes from strategically gaining compliance from others.

The *assertive style* handles conflicts skillfully by stating thoughts and feelings directly, yet respectfully. Problems are discussed openly and without judgment, with the focus remaining on the issue, not on the people. A certain level of communication competence and courage is required to work through the discomfort and tension of problem solving. An assertive approach takes the point of view that "I'm okay, you're okay." Success in business comes through designing win–win solutions. Those not accustomed to assertive communication styles may feel exposed until they develop the appropriate skills.

Though the assertive style is most effective from a communication and a problem-solving standpoint, context must be considered as always when selecting the best communication style. Different workplace cultures value certain conflict communication styles over others. So it helps to know the cultural practices of a workplace before a suitable communication style is selected.

Strategies for Conflict Resolution

Let's now look at conflict-resolution strategies, in particular how we can use verbal and nonverbal communication for handling conflict constructively. The above conflict styles roughly relate to the five conflict orientations described by Kenneth Thomas[26] on the Conflict Grid (see Figure 12.1). Thomas supports the idea that people prefer one conflict style over another. The Conflict Grid locates five conflict styles on continuums between satisfying individual needs and satisfying the needs of the other person in the conflict. The five styles are avoidance, competition, accommodation, compromise, and collaboration.

People with an *avoidance* orientation find conflict uncomfortable. Avoiders may flee when conflict arises or when they are forced to see themselves as part of the problem. This style of expressing conflict is similar to the non-assertive style described above. On the grid they are located low on both scales, showing neglect for both their own concerns and those of others. The approach reflects a lose–lose strategy.

The *competitive* orientation shows a high concern for satisfying personal needs without considering the needs of others. The conflict is depicted as a win–lose strategy, which is also known as a zero-sum game where gains and losses cancel out, since what one wins, the other loses. In the workplace, a *competitive* approach can be positive or negative depending on the situation. It can decrease participation and two-way communication flow. However, it can show leadership when a situation is in need of direction and people's feelings must be put aside.

The *accommodating* approach is used by people who want to be liked and will give in to the other side instead of engaging in conflict. It is a lose–win strategy focused on maintaining peace. As an organizational strategy, it may be effective if maintaining relationships does not interfere with the quality of the work. It has also been used with the expectation that the other side will accommodate in future negotiations.

A *compromising* approach, though showing a balance between personal concern and concern for other, is a lose–lose approach where each side gives something up to reach agreement. It minimizes losses while achieving some gains. People settle for this approach when partial satisfaction is acceptable. The hidden drawback with compromises is that they resolve the conflict without resolving the problem, so it is important with this approach to emphasize problem solving and not just a convenient way out of a conflict.

A *collaborative* approach is a win–win strategy that attempts to satisfy the needs of both parties in the conflict by working together and examining issues completely and supporting each other's needs. This process is called integrative bargaining. It assumes a non-zero-sum game where parties expand alternatives by seeking solutions beyond the immediate issues on the table. In contrast, the competitive style uses distributive bargaining, which restricts the discussion to a fixed prize.

Figure 12.1	The Conflict Grid[25]

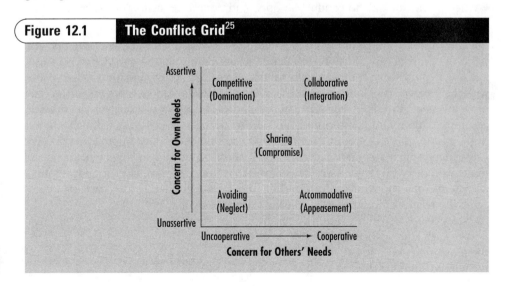

Chapter 12 / Decision Making, Conflict Resolution, and Leadership

The following list, adapted from Putnam and Poole, summarizes the factors that are most relevant for choosing a particular conflict style.[27] Though people naturally have preferred styles based on our personalities—some of us are by nature peacemakers or fighters—the appropriate conflict style is generally determined by factors in the situation.

Use the avoiding approach:

• To avoid engaging in conflict for which you may not be prepared.
• To avoid the winner and loser labels normally attached to conflict.

Use the competing approach:

• When the issue is important.
• When the other party will take advantage of you by playing hardball.
• When parties recognize and accept power differences, such as between superiors and subordinates.
• When shortage of time is a factor.
• When the interpersonal relationship between parties is of low priority.
• When the issue is not negotiable.

Use the accommodating approach:

• When you discover you are wrong.
• When the other side is too powerful or of higher rank.
• To let others learn by making their own mistakes.
• When the long-term cost to a relationship may not be worth the short-terms gains of winning an argument.
• To smooth things over.

Use the compromising approach:

• When there is not enough time or desire to achieve a win–win outcome.
• When the issue is not important enough to debate at length.
• To minimize tense communication.

Use the collaborative approach:

• When the issue is too important to compromise.
• When a long-term relationship between both parties is important.
• When communication breakdowns are common, as in management–labour negotiations.
• When parties are able to conduct an open and honest discussion of issues.
• When parties share the same goals.

The approach that employees decide to use depends on a number of factors. The position or title of each party will influence their communication styles. Supervisors usually use a competitive approach with subordinates, and accommodation or avoidance with their superiors. Assertive approaches, such as collaboration and competition, are more stressful, so employees may choose the less assertive approaches—avoidance, accommodation, and compromise—to minimize communication tension. The level of friendship of each party in a conflict will also influence which approach is chosen. Close friends often accommodate each other. Thus, establishing interpersonal networks in the workplace can be an career advantage. The bonds between close friends, though, are often strong enough to permit truthful and competitive styles without risk of damaging the relationship. Approaches may also change as the conflict progresses because each side learns new information about the other's point of view. Though the effectiveness of each strategy depends on the situation, the collaborative approach is generally the most preferred because of the quality of the solution and the positive impact on the relationship of the parties.

Creating Positive Climates for Conflict Resolution

Since communication styles are often mirrored in conflict discussions, a useful strategy for resolving disputes is to create a positive communication climate. Messages that confirm the other party's viewpoints, either verbally or nonverbally, are more effective for reaching agreement than messages that disconfirm the other party. Confirming messages create a climate in which people see themselves as valued and important.[28] Confirming messages have three elements:

1. They recognize the other person through any number of ways: returning messages, eye contact, being courteous—not recognizing someone is a disconfirming act.
2. They acknowledge someone by listening, asking questions, paraphrasing, or other supportive means.
3. They endorse the other party by agreeing with them—not on everything, but on points such as praising someone for an achievement or empathizing with someone's feelings.

Disconfirming responses impoverish a communication climate by creating a tone of indifference and inequality. For example, messages that begin with statements like "I don't want to insult your intelligence, but . . ." or "Get your facts straight" show a disregard for the other person. Disconfirming communication leads to defensive behaviours. Theorist Jack Gibb outlines defensive and supportive behaviours.[29] Using supportive communication will create a positive climate for conflict resolution.

1. Describe instead of evaluating. Judgments often start with the word "you," as in "You're lazy," and can provoke defensive responses because the focus is on the person rather than his or her behaviour. Descriptive statements, in contrast, highlight the effect of the behaviour, such as, "It puts me behind schedule when you don't get your work done." Descriptions focus on facts, judgments on opinions.
2. Use a problem orientation instead of a controlling one. Focusing on the problem establishes a collaborative spirit, as opposed to controlling the situation by issuing directives. Managers gain commitment from workers and save time by inviting them to participate in the problem-solving process. Use questions such as, "Tammy, what is your view on how to handle this problem?" instead of statements like, "Tammy, this would be a good project for you. Why don't you work on it and report on it at our next meeting?" Disregarding someone's contributions builds barriers and makes him or her feel worthless. A problem orientation makes everyone feel like a winner.
3. Be spontaneous instead of strategic. Working from a strategy implies manipulation. People become defensive because they feel someone is taking advantage of them. Asking openly for what you want suggests honesty and creates an atmosphere of trust. You don't have to blurt out the first thing that comes to your mind to be spontaneous; being sincere is enough to create a good communication climate. Trust is an issue managers must deal with when conducting feedback forums with employees to get ideas for improvement. Employees may sense that the discussions are a waste of time because the decision has already been made, and their participation is simply a masquerade.
4. Use empathic instead of neutral attitudes. Positive climates are produced when people accept and relate to each other's ideas. A neutral attitude expresses indifference, which shows lack of concern for others. We are more likely to express disagreement if we feel secure that others will consider it thoughtfully. The act of discounting, in which we discredit another person's ideas with rash statements like "That's ridiculous," shows lack of empathy. Nonverbal messages are particularly effective for expressing empathy.

5. Show equality instead of superiority. Acting superior to someone when there is no plain reason for it generally brings out defensive responses and damages communication. A common response is an aggressive counterattack. Supportive groups focus on things they have in common rather than on building differences. Even higher ranking managers can create bad feelings by flaunting their authority. As the saying goes, "It takes effort to be humble."

6. Instead of certainty, use a provisional approach. People who act like know-it-alls exclude others from the problem-solving process. Being over-certain about solutions often suggests a lack of analysis. A provisional approach, on the other hand, may propose solutions strongly, but will also entertain other possibilities, opening the discussion up to explore many alternatives.

Formal Conflict-Resolution Methods

Some conflicts need help from a third party. Labour negotiations or athletes in salary disputes with owners call on mediators; personal claims can be filed with government agencies, such as the Ministry of Labour or workers compensation boards; and the courts can intervene to help solve problems. All of these groups are involved in some form of structured conflict resolution. The following methods are the most commonly used to help groups in the workplace reach agreement.

- **Negotiation** is an open process that allows two parties to meet and discuss issues to achieve an agreement. Often, the two sides compromise on some middle point. A common example is a labour negotiation in the workplace.

- **Bargaining** is a form of negotiation with more structure, common in labour–management negotiations where established groups such as unions or associations are involved.

- **Mediation** involves a neutral third party who guides people to reach agreement. Parties in mediation create their own solutions. The mediator does not have any decision-making power over the outcome.

- **Arbitration** involves a neutral third party who listens to arguments and has the authority to make a binding decision to settle the case. Athletes often end up in front of arbitrators arguing over salaries. The arbitrator's decision is final.

Conflict and Collaboration

So far, we have focused on conflict resolution as an individual and team skill. These methods have generally viewed conflict from a human communication standpoint as a nuisance that should be cast out. We have suggested methods for eliminating conflict by using appropriate communication strategies so that workplaces can get true value out of collaboration and teamwork. In spite of the time and effort spent on training programs to improve collaboration, to restructure organizations, and to improve business processes, many companies are not happy with the results. What's the problem? According to Jeff Weiss and Jonathan Hughes,

> most companies respond to the challenge of improving collaboration in entirely the wrong way. They focus on the symptoms ("Sales and delivery do not work together as closely as they should") rather than on the root causes of failures in cooperation: conflict. The fact is, you can't improve collaboration until you've addressed the issue of conflict.[30]

Some organizations, according to Weiss and Hughes, have changed their thinking about conflict. Instead of looking at conflict as a nuisance that must be eliminated, they have accepted conflict as not only a natural but a necessary part of doing business. "Instead of trying simply to reduce disagreements, senior executives need to embrace conflict and, just as important, institutionalize mechanisms for managing it."[31] One strategy for turning conflict into a positive force is devising a common method for resolving conflict. Usually managers and employees engage in conflict resolution as if they were reinventing the wheel, leaving employees to find their own ways of fixing problems. Establishing a company-wide process for working out conflicts provides the following benefits:

- It will speed up conflict resolution and avoid bad feelings.
- If used properly, it will also produce innovative results, capitalizing on the multiple perspectives employees bring to the discussion.
- It will add consistency to conflict outcomes. If managers tell employees to stop squabbling and put the company's interests first, it's not clear whose interests will take priority—the company's, a team's, or an individual's.
- It curtails the "hot potato" game, where employees not willing to resolve a dispute toss it up the management chain until it ends up on a senior manager's desk—the person least knowledgeable about the issue.

But the resolution process must be built into the normal business routines of the workplace. Canadian telecommunications company TELUS, after a merger that created a much larger organization, found itself paralyzed by "hot potatoes"—unresolved conflicts bumped up the management hierarchy. These ate up huge amounts of senior managers' time. To resolve conflicts at their source, the company announced that all problems would be jointly presented by both bickering parties to their managers, where questions would be answered and a solution hammered out. With the help of a system for documenting and presenting the conflict, the problem was often resolved on the spot without having to be flipped upstairs.

New Frontiers in Conflict Management—Beyond Collaboration

Traditional views of conflict saw it as a negative force that was the enemy of the scientifically managed workplace. Contemporary views of conflict have not only abandoned this negative connotation, they have begun encouraging organizations to embrace conflict as a source of transformation. In open and dynamic systems such as workplaces, conflict creates the disorder necessary to take "the system to higher levels of complex functioning through a process of self-organization."[32]

The organization of the twenty-first century is distinguished by change. Scientific theories such as chaos theory and quantum mechanics have brought new ways of understanding organizations—a dramatic departure from classical views. New theories describe the universe as dynamic and random rather than as fixed and predictable. Furthermore,

> these new science theories demonstrate that change, even in nonbiological systems, typically involves conflict. For example, the very existence of matter is a result of subatomic particles colliding together. Out of these collisions, matter is birthed. This is a wonderful metaphor for looking at conflict from a new perspective. From this vantage point, conflict is not only essential, it gives all involved an opportunity to integrate their beliefs with others who have very different ones and out of these collisions, a higher level of personal and organizational functioning emerges.[33]

The new sciences provide management with a new set of skills to manage conflict: Quantum Skills (summarized from Charlotte Shelton and John Darling).[34]

- **Quantum Seeing**. The first skill is based on the idea that reality is subjective: what we see is a function of our expectations and beliefs. Quantum seeing enables managers to break out of their thinking patterns to see conflict as an underlying set of assumptions about the situation. Managers would develop skills in stating observations as subjective perceptions instead of proven facts. The skill is different from traditional tactical approaches such as collaboration because it centres on new ways of looking at conflict.

- **Quantum Thinking.** Quantum phenomena operate according to paradoxical principles. Matter, for instance, is composed of invisible energy that can be both here and there simultaneously and makes unpredictable leaps through barriers. Conflict resolution is also a paradoxical process, especially when one party's position is opposite to the other's. Win–win outcomes are difficult to achieve using traditional linear thinking. We need to kick-start the right side of our brains, which thinks in images instead of words.

- **Quantum Feeling.** This skill focuses on feeling the power of life. Our bodies are composed of the same quantum energy as the universe. Our heart, for example, generates an electromagnetic signal that is a function of thoughts and emotions. Negative emotions, such as stress and fear, decrease the signal, causing the mind–body system to lose energy. Positive emotions increase energy. Managers using the skill of quantum feeling "recognize that energy is never depleted by other people or events but rather by perceptual choices."[35]

- **Quantum Knowing.** Knowing is an intuitive skill existing in a climate of mindfulness—an environment where we are attentive to both the outside world and our internal intuitions. Normal decision making leads to a state of certainty or mindlessness, where we cease to pay attention. Instead of endlessly gathering information, we should be staying aware. It is an alternative to information gathering as a decision-making or conflict-resolution process.

- **Quantum Acting.** Systems, once connected, remain connected across great distances of time and space. A change in the state of one component creates a change to all components in the system. Distant or local events can transform organizations. As human consciousness interacts with the energy around it, spontaneous changes can occur. There is no such thing as coincidence. A manager who adopts new ways of thinking about conflict can transform the surrounding energy field. Each choice affects everyone. Thus, acts of integrity or understanding increase the probability that others will choose to act accordingly.

- **Quantum Trusting.** Derived from chaos theory, this skill is the ability to trust the organizing processes of life without trying to control and direct them, to let the "strange attractor" create order out of chaos. It allows self-organization to take place. Managers support those in conflict by encouraging them to use their inner resources to discover win–win solutions. Nonjudgmental feedback encourages the parties in conflict to experience the perceptual transformation necessary to see the solution.

- **Quantum Being.** This skill recognizes the relational nature of the universe. People come into being through relationships with other people; in this way, a group becomes greater than the sum of its parts. In a quantum relationship, people begin to see the world through each other's eyes—a necessity for win–win solutions. Negative emotions vanish. Having emotional intelligence helps people get through the direct and open discussion so that negative emotions are eliminated. Over time, the parties in conflict realize they are there for a reason: to learn from each other.

Communication and Leadership

... the person who influences me most is not he who does great deeds, but he who makes me feel I can do great deeds.

—Mary Parker Follett, "Leading Us On"[36]

Creating a Respectful Workplace at the City of Saskatoon

Personal harassment is a common cause of conflict in the workplace. At the City of Saskatoon, personal harassment issues were reaching crisis levels before they were resolved. By this time, high levels of management were required, and the result was growing resentment as a result of witnesses being put into difficult social positions, an increased use of sick leave and work site transfers, and unions sometimes having to defend members on opposing sides of a complaint. The solution: the Respectful Workplace Policy. A committee with representatives from all unions and associations developed a new policy. Conflict-management training would be given to all managers, supervisors, and union executives. A communication plan was designed to deliver the message to all employees. In less than a year, more than 300 employees had taken the training. Course objectives included:

- The management of conflict constructively to support a respectful workplace.
- The development of essential skills for managing conflict constructively.
- Awareness of the dynamics that affect conflict situations.
- An assessment to determine personal conflict-handling preferences.

The techniques learned were applied in re-framing conflict issues to uncover opposing interests, dealing with angry people, learning how not to let small problems escalate, and finding the courage to confront issues rather than avoiding them. Employees also learned to appreciate the effects of what they say to others, to use non-defensive behaviours in conflict situations, and to notice the early warning signs of conflict.

The City of Saskatoon plans to offer the training sessions annually to train new employees and has designed a streamlined course for front-line staff on diffusing anger. Employee communication was pegged as a critical ingredient from the start because of the number of stakeholders in the project (transit, administration, fire and police, parks, sanitation, etc.) and the explosive nature of the problem. The message emphasized that it was a joint project and everyone had the same concerns and goals. Involving everyone takes longer, but it ensures greater success.

Discussion Questions

1. Discuss the elements of a respectful workplace in terms of conflict management.

2. What role did communication play in promoting the project to employees and ensuring its success? What messages could be included? Discuss a marketing graphic that would characterize the respectful workplace campaign.

3. What are some of the communication strategies suggested in the case that relate to conflict-resolution strategies discussed in this chapter?

Organizations are about getting work done, and no one is more responsible for this than a manager. To do this, managers must practice effective leadership—bringing people together, processing information, making decisions, and providing direction to accomplish tasks. Communication is essential for effective leadership because it is the primary means through which leaders exert influence to achieve organizational goals. Today's workplace poses the additional challenge of ongoing change. People are no longer in the same jobs for a long time. Good managers continually tweak and redefine employees' roles to capitalize on developing talents and ambitions. In this section we will examine the nature of leadership, what good leaders do, and the importance of communication for leadership.

The Nature of Leadership

Workplaces often have designated leaders—usually called managers, supervisors, or bosses—that establish goals, organize resources, and direct people to accomplish tasks. When you start a new job, the boss is usually the first person you meet. After a few days on the job, you notice that others are also showing initiative and making decisions that move the job forward. Some workers provide technical expertise, some organize meetings and schedule events, others replenish supplies, and others simply mingle around inspiring greater activity and cohesiveness. Each person, from the manager to the janitor, plays a role in influencing the desired outcome. Leadership behaviour, then, can come from anyone in the organization. The relationships between power, leadership, and management are complex and interwoven. Let's define the types of influence organizational members have, in particular the concepts of power, management, and leadership, to further explore the nature of leadership.

Definitions of Management, Leadership, and Power

The basics of managing involve the principles established by Henry Fayol, the activities of directing and controlling the operation of a business. Leadership is generally defined as a process of influence that advances the goal of a group. Definitions of leadership consistently reveal three underlying themes: relationships, context, and outcomes.[37] Leaders and followers have a relationship in which the leader has a greater degree of influence, and this imbalance is acceptable to the follower. Leadership takes place in a context that is meaningful and familiar to leaders and followers and that provides rules for engagement, such as a formal or informal context. The relationship produces a variety of outcomes—for example, task accomplishment, customer satisfaction, admiration, or friendship. A solid grasp of the concept of leadership requires an understanding of how leaders and followers get along, where it takes place, and the results of leadership activity.

The observations in a study of what top-level managers actually do at work concluded that their daily activities revolve around creating and maintaining relationships, sending and receiving information, and decision making.[38] Top-level managers exhibit leadership by being a figurehead at ceremonial occasions, guiding and motivating employees, and playing the liaison role by establishing interpersonal networks with peers and external groups. They also serve an informational role by monitoring internal operations and external activities. This information is dispersed internally to subordinates, while information related to external interests, such as suppliers, shareholders, and government, is sent out into the organization's environment. The decision-making roles a manager plays involve initiating change, such as exploiting new markets, and handling disturbances, such as workplace conflicts or operational disruptions.

Power is commonly defined as the ability to persuade or force others to act in a desired way. French and Raven in a pioneering study identified five types of power in an organization.[39] The study shows that power extends far beyond the formal chain of command. Though only managers hold positional power, all subordinates possess some degree of power. The following are the five types of power described by French and Raven:

1. **Legitimate power** is structured according to the positions on the formal hierarchy of the organization. Subordinates accept the power of their superiors as legitimate. Even though the ability of legitimate leaders can be questioned, the boss is still the boss until that position is taken away.
2. **Coercive power** is the capacity to give out punishment. It is issued from a superior to a subordinate, since positional power is required. In the workplace, coercive power must also be legitimate power because a manager must have the authority to administer punishment.

3. **Reward power** is based on the authority to distribute pay, benefits, and intangibles, such as praise and recognition.

4. **Referent power** is based on how attractive a role model a manager is to employees. People with referent power make us want to be like them. This type of power can be held by either managers or employees. Famous people exercise referent power in advertising. In organizations, referent power is established through behaviours such as handling difficult situations well, using humour effectively, being helpful and understanding, showing integrity, or simply being "cool." Because referent power is assigned by other employees, it is a substantial social force in organizations.

5. **Expert power or knowledge power** resides in technical expertise or special knowledge that a person has. Jobs in engineering, law, accounting, medicine, or the technical trades are given considerable power, possibly overriding position power in a crisis situation. In organizations where innovation and creativity are valued, this type of power is conspicuous.

The first three types of power—legitimate, coercive, and reward—come from the person's position in the bureaucracy. The other two, referent and expert, are known as personal power, based on an individual's interpersonal skills, personality, knowledge, popularity, social connections, and so on. The job of leadership is challenging because it involves focusing the complex distribution of positional and personal power in an organization onto a single purpose. Research generally shows that effective leaders are motivated by power. In addition to desiring power, leaders have the ability to operate independently, because they do not have strong social needs, and to restrain the use of their power, so they do not appear impulsive or forceful.

Differences between Managing and Leading

The practice of managing has changed considerably over the years as managers have taken on more and more leadership functions. This trend reflects the shift in management from classical management to human relations, or from Theory X to Theory Y. Traditional managers focused on directing and controlling subordinates, while new managers use a style based on guiding and facilitating. Traditional managers viewed workers as interchangeable, mechanical parts, whereas new managers treat workers as unique human beings. While old managers stressed conformity and imitation, new managers encourage initiative and risk taking.

These differences also correlate to Weber's three styles of management: autocratic, laissez faire, and democratic. The autocratic manager dominates employees with continual pressure and unilateral decision making to achieve a predetermined objective. This style works best when the situation calls for urgent action or in low-skilled workplaces where subordinates may prefer clear direction. The laissez-faire style lets workers figure out their roles and responsibilities on their own. This approach is effective when employees are highly skilled and motivated. The manager delegates power and responsibility by handing over ownership of the work task. If employees lack skill and motivation, strong direction is required, so this approach would be counterproductive. In the democratic approach, a manager makes decisions by consulting with his employees, allowing the team to participate in planning and organizing the work, yet still retains control of them. Democratic managers empower employees by letting them direct themselves. But the responsibility of leadership lies in the hands of the manager. A democratic manager who relies on employees for all decisions is demonstrating a lack of leadership. The advantages of a democratic style are the following:

1. greater job satisfaction and cooperation among employees;
2. better quality of work;
3. greater self-responsibility to continue working when the manager is away.

| **Figure 12.2** | **Managing and Leading**[40] |

Managers achieve results through others by:	Leaders achieve results through others by:
1. Coping with complexity and producing consistency	1. Coping with change and creating new direction
2. Preserving value	2. Creating value
3. Planning and budgeting	3. Establishing direction through vision and strategy
4. Organizing and staffing	4. Aligning people and gaining commitment
5. Controlling and problem solving	5. Motivating and inspiring
6. Making the organization run efficiently	6. Making the organization grow, evolve, and adapt
7. Emphasizing transactional processes, such as shared goals, team work	7. Emphasizing transformational processes such as empowerment

It is evident that the traditional roles of managers as planners and controllers have expanded to include some degree of leadership activities based on influencing and relationship building. Though basic responsibilities of managers and leaders may not have changed drastically, the ways they achieve results through others have expanded. Figure 12.2 gives a summary of the differences between managers and leaders.

A major difference between managers and leaders hinges on their responsibilities. Managers achieve goals. They organize resources and establish concrete and measurable goals, procedures, and systems for accomplishing tasks. For example, a manager will say, "We need to boost production by 10 percent." With the help of logic and technical expertise, they ensure business goals are achieved with efficiency. Leaders, on the other hand, are seers. They mobilize resources and set courses of direction to influence and inspire workers to higher levels of achievement. They communicate a vision to the organization by appealing to people's spiritual and emotional values and sense of commitment to a common goal. For example, a leader might say "We want to help people experience pride in their work." This message gets people excited by suggesting a destination but does not provide tangible targets. But is the work of leadership exclusive to leaders, or can managers or even operations-level staff engage in leadership activity?

What Makes an Effective Manager?

Today's managers have a mix of both management and leadership responsibility. Our fast-paced, technology-driven workplaces have downloaded many leadership responsibilities to managers and even subordinates. Teamwork is a common method by which leadership is practised at lower levels of authority, since "the information society requires leadership from diverse organizational positions."[41] As leadership skills have been folded into the manager's portfolio, researchers have identified a new set of skills that outlines what good managers do, as opposed to poor managers. According to Marcus Buckingham, there is one quality that truly lets good managers stand out from the rest: they find out what is unique about each employee and make the most of it. In this way the diversity in today's organizations is turned into a strength.

Buckingham illustrates the difference through the metaphor of playing checkers and chess:

> Average managers play checkers, while great managers play chess. The difference? In checkers, all the pieces are uniform and move in the same direction; they are interchangeable. You need to plan and coordinate their movements, certainly, but they all move at the same pace, on parallel paths. In chess, each type of piece moves in a different way, and you can't play if you don't know how each piece moves. More important, you won't win if you don't think carefully about how you move the pieces. Great managers know and value the unique abilities and even the eccentricities of their employees, and they learn how best to integrate them into a coordinated plan of attack.[42]

One way of exploiting workers' unique abilities is to tailor the task to the employee's learning style. A few of the main learning types are analyzing, doing, and watching. Employees who learn through analyzing understand a job by breaking it down and examining the parts that make it up and then rebuilding it. Their thirst for information is unquenchable, their struggle for perfection is endless. Mistakes are not tolerated. Training an analyzer requires lots of preparation time so that all the details can be considered. The logical, linear, objective-based style of analyzers makes them suitable to be managers or supervisors. The next type, learning by doing, relies on trial and error. These learners consider preparation boring. In training a doer, start with simple tasks and directions and let him or her go to it. Mistakes are the means by which doers learn. Many leadership training programs are based on a trial-and-error approach, incorporating a person's work experience with the ability to learn on the job. The last one is watching. These types need to assemble the whole picture of a task, how everything fits in with everything else, before anything makes sense. To train a watcher, let him or her tag along with an accomplished employee to watch the action.

The skills of a manager are particular. Each employee represents a specific resource. Organizing this collection of talents so they can move freely, individually, and effectively is the challenge. For leaders, the challenge is the opposite. Leaders seek universal goals that bind differences between race, gender, age, occupation, and personality. Instead of using a manager's tools of analysis, a leader inspires by celebrating achievements and evoking values that all workers share.

Leadership Theories

Personal Trait Theories

Great leaders we have all heard about, such as Alexander the Great, Mhatma Ghandi, and Nelson Mandela, seem to possess extraordinary personal characteristics. They demonstrate high levels of vision, strategy, ambition, and persistence that appear to come from personal traits such as intelligence, self-confidence, persuasive abilities, and a dominating personality, or even physical factors, such as strength and height. Selecting the best leaders, then, involves simply identifying these traits and finding people who possess them.

Yet the personal traits approach has shown weakness in explaining the nature of leadership. The trait of intelligence, for example, has proven to be an inconsistent ingredient in the leadership mix. As Peggy Byers explains, a low level of intelligence will not be effective because of the challenges of leadership, but neither will a high one. Leaders who are too intelligent will have difficulty communicating with followers. "The most effective leaders are those with a moderate amount of intelligence, seemingly because they will be able to communicate most effectively with their subordinates."[43]

Recent research, though, has shown a return to interest in the traits theory, in particular personal traits such as

- *Drive*—high ambition and energy
- *Desire*—motivation to lead
- *Honesty and integrity*—sticking to commitments
- *Strategic thinking*—good judgment
- *Emotional intelligence*—energizing and enabling others[44]

Task and Maintenance Leadership Theories

You are actually striving for two things at the same time: an organization where people understand the importance of their jobs and are committed to living within the confines of those jobs and to taking direction; and an organization where people feel creative and adaptive and are willing to change their minds without feeling threatened. It's a tough combination to achieve. But it's the ultimate in management.

—Bill Walsh, football coach, San Francisco 49ers[45]

Two major research streams, at Ohio State University and the University of Michigan, under pioneers Robert Kahn and Daniel Katz, contributed to the development of theories based on leadership behaviour. The studies focused on two aspects of leadership: a task focus, concerned with production, and a maintenance focus, concerned with employee well-being. A strong task focus was related to an autocratic style of leadership, whereas a strong employee focus was related to a democratic one.

The theories were later developed by Robert Blake and Jane Mouton into the Managerial Grid, a graph showing various leadership styles based on different levels of task and maintenance functions (see Figure 12.3).[46]

The theory describes different management styles. A 1,9 style is aptly called Country Club Management. The emphasis is on satisfying employee needs and creating friendly relationships to produce a comfortable atmosphere. Whether any work gets done is beside the point. The opposite, 9,1, eliminates human factors to focus on efficiency using an autocratic, classical style manager. The most effective style is 9,9, a team approach emphasizing commitment, interdependence, and a sense of ownership built on trusting relationships. But was this approach best in all situations? Though the management styles theories described leader behaviours clearly, they did not take into account differences in circumstances. That's where situational theories enter the picture.

Figure 12.3 — Managerial Grid[47]

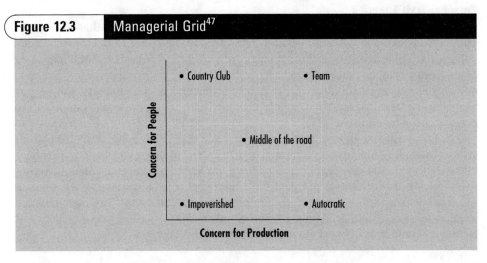

Situational Leadership Theories

Paul Hersey and Kenneth Blanchard expanded the management styles theories to include situational factors.[49] They proposed that an effective leadership style could be determined only by how suitable the style would be in a certain situation. An effective leadership style must suit the maturity level of the follower, determined by such factors as technical ability, emotional maturity, motivation, and self-confidence. When the follower's maturity level was pinpointed on a graph, indicating his or her readiness to perform, a leader could select corresponding style from four choices: telling (a directive style), selling (persuasive), participating (consultative), or delegating (self-direction) (see Figure 12.4).

Bill Walsh, former football coach of the San Francisco 49ers, shows this concept in action when he describes the different coaching styles he used for each player.[50] In contrast to traditional coaches, who simply discarded players who did not fit the mould, Walsh introduced an analytical style that focused on recognizing and developing each player's unique strengths. Team solidarity grew out of a clear appreciation of the role each athlete plays on the team. To develop skills, Walsh designed extremely precise drills and highly structured practices. For example, before the ball is snapped, an offensive lineman has three or four seconds to decide what kind of blocking technique to use on his opponent. He selects the best one out of four or five blocking techniques he learned in practice based on situational factors, such as the way the man is positioned, the situation in the game, or his knowledge of the opponent. It's the thinking and decision-making part of a highly physical game, and it can make the winning difference. Commitment to the team is another essential ingredient for a winning team. Walsh's team tried to create a balance between a very structured system of football and a game that allowed players to be instinctive and spontaneous when responding to change. To create commitment, Walsh dropped the ego barrier so people could communicate without fear.

> I try to remove the fear factor from people's minds so they can feel comfortable opening their mouths....They have to be comfortable [knowing] that they will not be ridiculed if they turn out to be mistaken or if their ideas are not directly in line with their superior's. That is where the breakthrough comes....The goal is to create a communication channel that allows important information to get from the bottom to the top.[51]

Figure 12.4	Situational Leadership—Hersey and Blanchard[48]

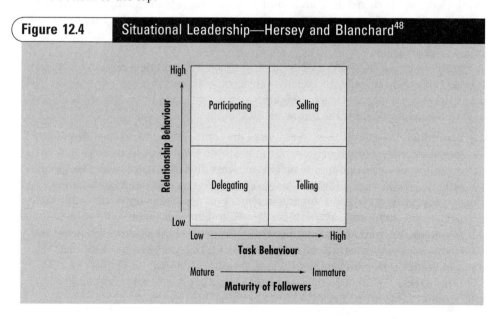

To nurture the instincts and talents of players, Walsh designed personalized training techniques for each player. Quarterback Joe Montana, for example, had a high level of both technical skill and self-confidence. On Hersey and Blanchard's Situational Leadership Grid, the management style suitable for his needs would fall into quadrant 4, "delegating." Montana's practices and game preparation emphasized repetitive drills to maintain top physical shape. Walsh nurtured Montana's greatness by not criticizing him when he used his creative abilities. This allowed him to break out of pattern occasionally and rely on his instincts.

A wide receiver, John Taylor, needed a different approach. He came to the team with tremendous physical talent but no professional experience. As a result, he didn't adapt to a sophisticated game quickly enough, became frustrated, and lost his enthusiasm. On the grid, he found himself in quadrant 1: high task ability, but low emotional readiness to play at a high level. Walsh took a patient approach and gave him another year to mature and grow into the role he was capable of, and he eventually became an all-pro. But miscalculations also happen. When Walsh obtained Thomas "Hollywood" Henderson, a bright and charming person with an uncontrollable drug habit, from Dallas, he thought he could influence him to become a great linebacker once again. He realized finally that it would not work and acknowledged his mistake. Walsh removed Henderson from the team to send the message that drug abuse would not be tolerated and that he was still in control.

Transformational Leadership

The leadership approaches we have discussed so far focus on two areas: leadership qualities possessed by individuals, as in the trait theories, and communication exchanges between leaders and followers. For example, managers train in return for performance, and subordinates work in return for rewards, transactions done by both parties to achieve goals. The exchange of rewards and punishments between leaders and followers has been called *transactional leadership*. Both superiors and subordinates, through the process of exchange, affect each other in reciprocal ways in leadership activity. Though they can be very effective, such approaches are limited. Their focus is narrow, being concerned only with changing the task and the situation. Also, a subordinate is viewed as being fixed in his or her role and routine. And they appeal mainly to lower-level needs and desires. The *transformational approach*, on the other hand, creates opportunities for leadership for all organizational members and at greater individual and organizational achievement.

Transformational leadership goes beyond normal exchanges between leaders and followers. It has the capability to literally transform situations or people by empowering and inspiring workers to achieve higher levels of satisfaction and motivation. This type of leadership displays the following five abilities:[52]

1. **Visioning.** A leadership vision describes the ultimate goal of an organization. It must be communicated persuasively to motivate employees to embrace it as their own. It is also essential that managers reinforce the vision as it relates to specific projects. Visioning is a form of energy everyone must experience and share. A corporate vision such as a mission statement on a wall display is inert without the powerful communication activities required to launch a vision.

2. **Inspiring.** In communicating their vision, leaders use a high level of energy and passion that builds self-confidence in followers. Leaders must "walk the talk" by setting themselves as examples, "doing" instead of "telling."

3. **Stimulating.** The transformational leader encourages new ways of thinking and questioning of old ways of doing things. Some effective methods are encouraging

people to make mistakes, since that is how innovation happens, allowing independence of thought, having brainstorming sessions, and thinking about possibilities. Motivational techniques should reinforce the transformational behaviours managers are aiming to create.

4. **Coaching.** The leader uses coaching methods—listening, encouraging, supporting, showing confidence in employees—to improve performance. Employees are empowered to work on their own tasks. Each employee's role is appreciated as a critical part of the whole organization.

5. **Team Building.** Building effective teams through information sharing and positive feedback increases trust and self-confidence. Many decisions normally done by managers are shared among team members.

Transformational Leadership and Empowerment

The concept of empowerment is central to understanding transformational leadership. It has been defined this way:

> Empowerment is not simply the giving or sharing or organizational power. Empowering others involves helping them to find their own power, to realize their own potential, and to gain the sense of confidence and autonomy necessary to make choices. The truly empowered individual, just like the truly empowered team, no longer depends on others for validation, but draws that from within.[53]

Numerous challenges await the transformational leader. To help employees grow and find their own power, the transformational leader must engage in continuous communication with them. This degree of communication activity may be a new experience for many managers. Employees, though, may not always develop in ways the manager expects, since at the heart of empowerment lies the freedom for employees to grow in their own way, according to their natural abilities. Leaders will need to work through employees' growing stages much the same way parents nurture young adults.[54] The frequency of communication between leaders and followers in an empowered workplace brings many personal issues, such as feelings and relationship boundaries, to the surface. Thus, it may become necessary for leaders to empower themselves: to find their own power, to develop confidence in their subordinates, and to use communication as a tool to monitor progress. Often, personal tragedies, such as deaths of loved ones or illnesses, have a sharpening and strengthening influence on a person's sense of self. A study of 150 Canadian senior male executives shows that empowerment in the workplace is strongly correlated with high levels of self-disclosure between leaders and followers.[55] Businesses where self-disclosure was not common were described by respondents as politicized, closed, autocratic, and alienating. One of the leader's main jobs is getting people to be enthusiastic about achieving great goals and adapting to change, and this challenge is ultimately dependent on the quality of personal relationships involved. People respond positively if they trust and respect the managers in charge.

Persuasive Skills for Transformational Leaders

The watershed capacity in leadership is unquestionably communication. Through it, people are informed, convinced, united, motivated, and directed— things that are critical to group enterprise from the inside and to buy-in from the outside. The powers to inform and persuade win the battles for hearts and minds.

—*Mark Sarner*[56]

Appealing to Higher Goals

Well-known management author Warren Bennis tells a story of the role of altruism, or self-sacrifice for a greater cause, in leadership. When Steve Jobs was recruiting John Sculley, then head of PepsiCo, for Apple Computer, he appealed not only to Sculley's ambition but to a desire to leave a legacy beyond just boosting profit margins. The issue came out when Jobs asked the man who was to become Apple's next president how many more years he wanted to spend making flavoured water.

Energetic displays of leadership originate in two different types of power. There is personalized power, which seeks influence for personal gain, or socialized power, which enhances the success of a group with shared objectives. Even model capitalists such as Alfred Sloan, legendary CEO of General Motors, are said to have had a desire to serve the nation while making money for the auto giant. In today's CEO world, cluttered with casualties of unethical practices and boundless salary raises, it appears more difficult to find evidence of socialized power.

To find out which type you have, ask yourself why you are trying to exercise influence. Those who are driven by socialized power tend to make the most effective leaders. But though many have the knowledge to be leaders, few possess the voice and eloquence to communicate a common dream. The following are specific techniques for effective leadership, employing skills from the art of persuasion:

- **Connect emotionally.** Communicate your passion to your commitment to others using a combination of reason and emotion. Be sensitive to your employees' feelings and use emotional intelligence. Leadership and empowerment start inside the leader, so develop strengths in self-awareness by taking time to think and reflect. Remember that many decisions involve emotional factors.

- **Find common ground.** Use framing skills to present your position in ways that are relevant and significant to employees. Get feedback to discover what people are concerned about. Follow the strategy of Shakespeare's Henry V. To get ready for battle, he dressed up as a foot soldier, wandered around to campfires, and prepared his speech from what he heard. Gandhi practised similar deep listening skills when he travelled around India learning what was in the heart of his people.

- **Develop communication skills.** Inject dramatic effect into your conversations by using vivid language and compelling evidence. Factual answers do not excite people. Employ nonverbal messages, such as gestures, tone of voice, and facial expressions to support your ideas.

- **Tell stories.** One colourful and persuasive strategy for leaders is telling stories. Stories are effective not just because people learn through them, but because they relate it to a story of their own and personalize the meaning. Stories are a memorable way to communicate values and priorities. The richest source of stories is your experience. Because these are so close to you, they can be told with passion and authenticity. After their meaning is internalized, they are easily retold and shared with others in the workplace.

- **Build credibility.** The cornerstones of credibility are technical expertise and relationships based on trust. Put simply, leaders who lack them are not believed by followers. Building trust starts with telling the truth. Your actions demonstrate credibility when you stick to commitments. Trusting relationships are also built on caring, which is demonstrated effectively with a coaching style of leadership.

- **Build effective teams.** A leader's job in a group setting is to ensure that people feel inspired, involved, and committed to something important. Also, learn to manage conflict effectively. In close relationships, differences are accented. Effective conflict-resolution skills calm everybody down when emotions are aroused.

- **Don't be afraid to make a fool of yourself.** Though radical, it can be effective. This strategy was recommended to Virgin Group chairman Sir Richard Branson by Freddie Laker, the swashbuckling head of Laker Airways. Branson took it to heart. He dressed up in an astronaut's suit and descended from the skies to launch a new airline service. The stunt created buzz and excitement—exactly the result that was intended. It also demonstrated Branson's courage to reveal the playful side of his personality. Pierre Trudeau endeared himself to the hearts of Canadians by showing his personal feelings. One memorable incident was his famous pirouette at a royal function behind Queen Elizabeth II's back.

Leadership Skills for Supervisors—Motivating the Troops

Supervisors can employ the influence strategies of leaders to increase motivation and performance in their staff. Instead of using a "do-it-my-way" style that relies on control and rarely inspires excellence, supervisors can tap into the diverse motivational needs of their employees by increasing their participation in the workplace. A number of factors have been identified that influence employees to give a greater effort.[57]

One of them is flexibility. Too much "red tape" and too many procedures are irritating and hinder innovation. Explaining why certain rules exist helps people accept them. It's also good to encourage employees to explore alternatives and to reward good ideas.

Delegating responsibility gives employees a sense of ownership of their work. Protect people from the negative outcomes of risk taking to show your support for their efforts. Ensure that people are held accountable for their work outcomes. Set standards high, but be realistic, so employees get regular feedback on their performance instead of just at appraisal time. Ensure that performance standards are applied fairly to all workers.

Invite employees to participate in setting goals so they understand the rationale behind them. In addition, help employees understand the big picture about the company's strategy by expressing clear goals. Invite questions about how things are organized and how they could be improved.

Employing these strategies helps supervisors use their personal power to influence how the work is done. Establishing clear goals is probably the best place to begin. When employees understand the big picture the same way top managers do, they accept the reasons for why things are being done a certain way. They will be able to align their own decisions with the overall rationale of the organization's goals. And when people feel appreciated for their unique role in the big picture, they tend to make their best contribution. If workers become the owners of their jobs, a supervisor can spend more time coaching from the sidelines.

Leadership—Concluding Thoughts

Leadership has been analyzed in a number of ways. It is something that is done by managers, yet is in many ways the opposite of what managers usually do, which is controlling and directing. It is a function all organizational members can participate in, yet it is mostly reserved for top managers. Let's summarize our section on leadership by taking a look at the whole picture of leadership through its four guiding principles:[58]

1. **Leaders are people who know what to do with themselves.** A leader operates by example, by modelling a leadership style that reveals an inner personal mastery. In this way they constantly communicate and live shared values.
2. **Leaders are people who know what to do with their people.** If people feel cared for and safe, if they feel passion about their job and the values of the workplace, they

will perform at high levels. Leaders empower people by bringing out the best in them. In this sense, the leader works for his or her subordinates. The people are responsible, the leader is responsive. One practical technique for accomplishing this is to ask questions instead of giving answers.

3. **Leaders are people who know how to communicate.** Leaders are able to unclog communication channels by removing barriers to communication. Open communication systems allow everyone to frame problems in common ways. Leaders should concentrate on facilitating dialogue by listening and learning, instead of passing judgment. Leaders operate in the arena of action, while at the same time keenly observing group dynamics, so as to constantly be in the "present"—watching and encountering people's needs and ideas.

4. **Leaders can see the big picture.** Seeing an organization as a whole helps the leader address the root causes of problems at the system level and what things need to be changed to overcome challenges. Once a leader sees the big picture, he or she can help the workers realize the essential roles they play in the system. A shared understanding of organizational goals comes from knowing how everyone contributes to the outcome.

This chapter began with a discussion of decision making, looking particularly at rational decision-making methods that followed a logical, sequential style, and non-rational and intuitive methods that use non-logical thinking processes. Both are effective, depending on the problem. A more detailed set of decision-making strategies was described with the "thinking first," "seeing first," or "doing first" approaches to decision making. Many barriers to effective decision making originate in our mental processes. We also summarized decision-making processes in terms of the various organization perspectives discussed earlier in the book.

The next section covered conflict in the workplace. Though conflict can be a negative experience and can damage relationships, it is a natural and inevitable part of organizational life, and if dealt with effectively it can provide learning and growth. Dealing with conflict effectively requires communication skills. An assertive communication style focuses on the problem instead of on the person and treats people respectfully, leading to a mutually satisfying resolution. Strategies for resolving conflict are described in terms of conflict orientations. A collaborative approach, which shows a concern for the interests of both sides of a conflict, leads to a win–win solution. All conflict orientations, though, can be effective in certain circumstances. Finally, we looked at new frontiers in conflict management that have emerged out of recent perspectives on the dynamics of conflict. Quantum skills provide employees with a new set of skills to manage conflict. The skill set is based on certain principles: reality is a subjective experience; many conflict situations are not resolvable using rational methods; a faith in the organizing aspects of life; and an acceptance of life as a set of interconnected, relational forces.

Leadership and communication were the final topics. Recent developments in management studies have pointed out the differences between managing and leading. Traditional managers focused on directing and controlling while leaders use a style based on guiding and facilitating. We examined leadership theories, specifically trait theory, situational theory, and transformational leadership, a challenging leadership approach that focuses more than the others on empowerment and communication.

Case Study

Leadership for High Performance

At times, leaders are faced with tough issues, and effective mobilization of everyone's skills and talents is essential. Leaders face two types of problems: technical challenges, which may be difficult, but with the proper knowledge and techniques can be overcome; and adaptive challenges, which require new ways of thinking, learning, and problem solving. The first problem requires transactional leadership skills. The second one requires transformational leadership skills. Consider the case of Eric, a supervisor newly assigned to a work team. His boss decided to start him off with a difficult task. The team had worked for several years with Paul as their supervisor, a respected and knowledgeable boss, but Paul had not been comfortable with change or challenges to his managing style.

When Eric explained the task to his team, they became dejected—it was too far out of their reach. The meeting produced some bad feelings. Then Eric tried a different tactic. He said, "I know it's a big job, but let's see what we can do. You guys are the experts. What would you do? And what can I do to help?" The mood in the room changed instantly. One worker, who hadn't bothered giving ideas to Paul because the former supervisor hadn't listened, laid out some ideas, others pitched in with ideas, and soon a plan of action started to develop. Eric took responsibility to see that the team members had the necessary resources to accomplish the task. Over the next few weeks, Eric recognized the team's progress with little things, such as pizza lunches and donuts and coffees, and results were posted in the company newsletter. New ideas continued to be developed. Employees monitored their progress at the end of each shift. When they reached the goal, there was great celebration. After, they continued to improve operations and production levels.

Discussion Questions

1. Discuss the transformational leadership techniques Eric used, paying attention to vision, motivation, communication, coaching, sharing responsibility, team building, and recognition.

2. Discuss the reasons why these techniques were effective.

Rational Decision Making—Left-Brain Thinking

Form into groups of three or four. Each group will be responsible for making a decision for one of the following situations:

1. Choosing a location for a vegetarian restaurant.
2. Spending $1 billion.
3. Purchasing a car.
4. Choosing a costume for a Halloween party on campus that will win the $1000 first prize.

Use a rational approach to decision making to come up with a group decision for your group's situation. Follow these steps: define the problem, analyze it and gather information, establish decision criteria, discuss possible solutions, and choose the best one. Assign one member of your group to be an observer to record the processes and strategies you use to make a unanimous group decision and to move the group along toward agreement. After the group presents its decision and the rationale for it, the observer will comment on his or her group's decision-making activity, looking at attitudes of members, knowledge levels, thinking and speaking abilities of members, keeping on track, levels of participation of members, and summarizing at the end.

Creative Decision Making—Right-Brain Thinking

For some types of problems, rational decision-making methods put limits on our thinking that block our problem-solving abilities. Creative problem-solving techniques offer another way of generating solutions. Creative thinking is often described as "thinking outside the box."

The process usually begins with group members brainstorming the problem to produce numerous ideas. Often, group members prompt each other to continue their train of thought by asking "Why" once, or even several times, after a suggestion. In this way, normal thought patterns are bypassed for original, many times irrational, ideas. Worthy ideas are critiqued and developed by group members in a cumulative effort. This method is often used in product-development efforts to overcome the problems in envisioning products that do not yet exist. The two exercises below can be solved with creative thinking processes. The first one is easier. The second one will take some brainstorming, but makes ingenious sense once it's figured out. Remember, don't let predictable thinking patterns block you from creative solutions. When you get the answer, you will know it.

Porthole Rising Frank was sleeping in an anchored ocean liner. At noon, the water was six meters below the porthole and was rising one meter per hour. Assuming that this rate doubles every hour, when will the water reach the porthole? Answer is on page 253.

Evil Moneylender An evil moneylender offered to settle a debt with a young woman if she would agree to a simple wager. She was to reach into a bag and draw out one of two pebbles. If the pebble was white, the debt would be forgotten. If it was black, she would have to marry the moneylender. The young woman noticed, however, that the moneylender put two black pebbles into the bag. What did she do? Answer is on page 253.

What Would You Do? A leadership expert stands in front of a room of students with varying degrees of work experience. He observes the class silently, making eye contact with the students. Then he throws the students for a loop with his first words by asking them what they would do if they were in his position. To learn about leadership, the students are going to have to tell him what he should do to lead them.

Take a few minutes to write down some ideas about what the leadership expert should do. When you are finished share them with the class.

Learning from Your Own Experiences Learning from your own successes and failures can be a lesson that sticks with you much more than learning from other's experiences. Think of a personal example where you failed in your own leadership. What did you do wrong? What could have been done differently? What was effective? How was your behaviour different from successful leadership experiences you have had? Prepare a short discussion for the class to share what you learned.

Personal Experiences of Conflict Think of two experiences of conflict you have had and which conflict solving method you used—win–lose, lose–lose, lose–win, or win–win. Try to include one that shows a win–win approach. Form groups and share your experiences with the others in your group. What can you learn from looking at conflict in terms of these approaches?

Rational decision making, p. 222
Satisficing, p. 223
Heuristics, p. 226
Non-assertive style, p. 231
Directly aggressive style, p. 231
Passive aggressive style, p. 231
Indirect style, p. 232
Assertive style, p. 232

Avoidance approach, p. 233
Competitive approach, p. 233
Accommodating approach, p. 233
Compromising approach, p. 233
Collaborative approach, p. 233
Transactional leadership, p. 246
Transformational approach, p. 246
Transformational leadership, p. 246

Answers to Questions on Page 252

Who Will Ride?

Give the car keys to your old friend and let him take the lady to the hospital. You stay behind and wait for the bus with the partner of your dreams. Sometimes, we gain more if we are able to give up our stubborn thought limitations. Never forget to think outside of the box.

Porthole Rising

The water level will never reach the porthole because the ship will keep rising with the water.

Evil Moneylender

The woman quickly reached into the bag, pulled out the pebble and nervously dropped it before anyone had a chance to see its colour. The pebble was hopelessly lost among the other pebbles on the ground. After a moment, she reached into the bag again and removed the remaining pebble. Since it was black, the first one must have been white. By turning the trick against the moneylender, the young woman was free.

Notes

1. John S. Ratcliffe, "Scenario Building: A Suitable Method for Construction Industry Planning?" Dublin Institute of Technology, Ireland, http://www.buildnet.csir.co.za/cdcproc/docs/1st/ratcliffe_js_pdf (accessed July 29, 2006).

2. P.H. Hill et al., *Making Decisions: A Multidisciplinary Approach* (Reading, MA: Addison Wesley, 1979), 22.

3. Alexander Kotov, describing a sudden game decision after lengthy analysis, in Henry Mintzberg and Frances Wesley, "Decision Making: It's Not What You Think," *MIT Sloan Management Review* (Cambridge) 4, no. 3 (Spring 2001): 89.

4. Herbert Simon, *Administrative Behaviour*, 2nd ed. (New York: MacMillan, 1957).

5. Mintzberg and Wesley, "Decision Making," 89.

6. Michael Kesterton, Social Studies, *The Globe and Mail*, March 7, 2005, from U.S. News and World Report.

7. George Bernard Shaw, in Michael Kesterton, Social Studies, *The Globe and Mail*, December 19, 2005, A18.

8. Mintzberg and Wesley, "Decision Making," 89.

9. *Salesmanship on the Line*, video with Don and Dirk Beveridge (Chicago, IL: Dartnall Corp., distribuited in Canada by ITF, 1987).

10. John S. Hammond, Ralph L. Keeney, and Howard Raiffa, "The Hidden Traps in Decision Making," *Harvard Business Review* (January 2006): 47.

11. Mintzberg and Wesley, "Decision Making," 89.

12. Natalie Southworth, "Math + Plus Decisions = Management Science," *The Globe and Mail*, July 5, 1999, quoting Peter Bell, Management Science Professor, Ivey Business School, University of Western Ontario.

13. Hammond, Keeney, and Raiffa, "The Hidden Traps," 47.

14. Katherine Miller, *Organizational Communication Approaches and Processes*, 3rd ed. (Belmont, CA: Thomson Wadsworth, 2003).

15. Henry Mintzberg, "Third Generation Management Development: The International Master's Program in Practicing Management at McGill University," *T + D* (March 2004): 62–67.

16. Joyce Frost and William Wilmot, *Interpersonal Conflict,* 5th ed. (New York, McGraw Hill, 1997), 32.

17. Linda L. Putnam and Scott M. Poole, (1987), "Conflict and Negotiation," in *Handbook of Organizational Communication: An Interdisciplinary Perspective,* eds. F.M. Jablin, L.L. Putnam, K.H. Roberts, and L.W. Porter (Newbury Park, CA: Sage, 1987), 549.

18. Ibid.

19. Susan Pinker, "The brass tacks of handling the brass," *The Globe and Mail,* March 9, 2005, C5.

20. Charles Conrad, *Strategic Organizational Communication,* 3rd ed. (Fort Worth, TX: Harcourt Brace College Publishers, 1994), 344.

21. L.R. Pondy, "Organizational Conflict: Concepts and Models," *Administrative Science Quarterly* 12 (1967), 296–320.

22. L.A. Baxter, W.W. Wilmot, C.A. Simmons and A. Schartz, "Ways of Doing Conflict: A Folk Taxonomy of Conflict Events in Personal Relationships," in *Interpersonal Communication: Evolving Interpersonal Relationships,* ed. P. J. Kalbfleisch (Hillside, NJ: Erlbaum, 1993), 89–108.

23. Weekly Poll, *The Globe and Mail,* April 22, 2005, C1.

24. Heather Svokos, "Fridge Rage: Frosty feelings hit the office," New York Times Service, *The Globe and Mail,* April 13, 2005, P3.

25. Ibid., 434.

26. Kenneth Thomas, "The Conflict Handling Modes: Toward More Precise Theory," *Management Communication Quarterly* 1 no. 3 (1988), 430–36.

27. Putnam and Poole, "Conflict and Negotiation," 549.

28. Ronald B. Adler and George Rodman, *Understanding Human Communication* (New York: Oxford University Press, 2003).

29. Jack Gibb, "Defensive Communication," in *Bridges Not Walls,* ed. J. Stewart, (New York: Random House, 1982), 235–40.

30. Jeff Weiss and Jonathan Hughes, "Want Collaboration?" *Harvard Business Review* 83, no. 3 (March 2005): 93–101.48–49

31. Ibid.

32. Charlotte D. Shelton and John R. Darling, "From Chaos to Order: Exploring New Frontiers in Conflict Management," *Organization Development Journal* 22, no. 3 (Fall 2004): 22.

33. Ibid.

34. Ibid.

35. Ibid.

36. Vivian Smith, "Leading Us On," *Report on Business Magazine,* April 1999, 91.48–49.

37. John Kotter, "What Leaders Really Do," *Harvard Business Review* 79, no. 11 (2001): 85.

38. James Bowditch and Anthony F. Buono, *A Primer on Organizational Behaviour,* 6th ed. (Hoboken, NJ: John Wiley & Sons, Inc., 2005).

39. John R. P. French and Bertram Raven, "The Bases of Social Power," in *Studies in Social Power,* ed. D. Cartwright (Ann Arbour: University of Michigan, 1959).

40. Robert Blake and Jane Mouton, *The Managerial Grid: The Key to Leadership Excellence* (Houston TX, Gulf Publishing Company, 1985), 12.

41. Pamela Shockley-Zalabak, *Fundamentals of Organizational Communication,* (Boston: Allyn & Bacon, 2002).

42. Marcus Buckingham, "What Great Managers DO," *Harvard Business Review* 83, no. 3 (March 2005): 70.

43. Shockley-Zalabak, *Fundamentals of Organizational Communication.*

44. P. Hersey and K. Blanchard, *Management of Organizational Behaviour,* 3rd ed. (Englewood Cliffs, NJ: Prentice-Hall, 1977).

45. Richard Rappaport, "To Build a Winning Team: An Interview with Head Coach Bill Walsh," *Harvard Business Review* 22, no. 1 (Jan./Feb. 1993): 111.

46. Robert Blake and Anne Adams McCanse, *Leadership Dilemmas—Grid Solutions,* formerly the *Managerial Grid: The Key to Leadership Excellence* by Robert R. Blake and Jane S. Mouton (Houston, TX: Gulf Publishing Company, 1985).

47. Ibid., 29.

48. Ibid.

49. P. Hersey and K.H. Blanchard, *Management of Organizational Behaviour,* 5th ed. (Englewood Cliffs, NJ: Prentice Hall, 1988).

50. Blake and McCanse, *Leadership Dilemmas.*

51. Richard Hossack, "A New Style of Leadership," *Canadian Business Review* (Ottawa) 20, no. 3 (Autumn 1993): 30.

52. Mark Sarner, "Can Leadership Be Learned?" *Fast Company* magazine, February 2001, http://www.fastcompany.com/articles/archive/msarner.html (accessed July 29, 2006).

53. Warren Bennis, "The Leader as Storyteller," *Harvard Business Review* 74, no. 1 (Jan./Feb. 1996): 154–61.

54. Ibid.

55. Ibid.

56. Sarner, "Can Leadership Be Learned?"

57. Susan H. Surplus, "Motivating the Troops: Moving from the Power of 'Me' to the Power of 'We,'" *Supervision* (Burlington) 65, no. 4 (April 2004): 9.

58. Xin-An Lu, "Surveying the Topic of 'Effective Leadership,'" *Journal of American Academy of Business* (Cambridge) 5 no. 1–2 (September 2004): 125.

PART SIX

Professional Applications

Chapter Thirteen

Contemporary Issues

It is not the strongest of the species that survive, nor the most intelligent, but the ones most responsive to change.

—*Charles Darwin*, Origin of the Species

Learning Objectives

- Examine the concept of knowledge management and its importance in today's workplaces

- Identify techniques for effective knowledge management

- Examine the concepts and practices of workplace diversity in today's organizations

- Explore the concept of ethics and its importance in today's organizations

- Define and analyze corporate social responsibility and how it is practised in Canadian organizations

- Explore the concept of work–life balance and the elements of a healthy workplace

Introduction—Contemporary Issues

In this chapter we will look at communication issues that are receiving a lot of attention in today's organizations. Some of them tie in with the areas of concern we started with in our first chapter. *Knowledge management* is important today for several reasons. Our jobs are more complicated, and workers need more knowledge today than formerly to do their jobs effectively. We've gained more knowledge because our efforts today are more collaborative than individual. More communication has resulted in more information exchange. And workers are no longer simply replaceable parts in an organizational machine. They are a company's knowledge assets, and, in many ways, a company's major competitive advantage. Knowledge management officers strive to extract and harness the knowledge that gets built into organizations, through day-to-day operations over the years, so that it can continue to be shared and used by the organization.

Cultural and workplace diversity is an area of particular significance to Canadians. Our major cities from coast to coast are prime examples of cultural coexistence. Our universities and colleges are proud of their multicultural traditions. Though cultural diversity is a world phenomenon, our practices, built on tolerance and openness, seem especially workable. Differences will exist, as will unfair judgments. Communication is critical because it has a big impact on relationships. But diversity also goes beyond culture. The Canadian workplace for several decades grew comfortable with the baby boomers. Today, younger generations are pouring into the workplace and the number of females in the work force is rapidly growing, bringing diverse outlooks and new ways of working. At the same time, Canadian companies are extending their reach around the globe. Diversity is a two-way flow.

As competition continually gears up, the pressure to increase profits also increases, bringing with it some perilous practices. The issue of ethics has never been more important in organizations than it is today, judging by the numerous cases of illegal business practices coming to light from around the world. Ethics in business covers many areas, from employee theft and fraud, to ethically responsible business practices involving the environment, competition with the business community, employee health and safety, fair wages and benefits, and honesty to consumers—areas normally described under the term "social responsibility."

Our final section deals with the growing interest among working people to achieve a balance between workplace obligations and personal responsibilities, known as work–life balance. Let's begin our discussion with the section on knowledge management.

Knowledge Management

In firms of all sizes there is a sense of concern over knowledge loss, especially the loss of tacit knowledge that can so easily walk out the door.

—Louise Ear[1]

Workplaces are sites of social activity. As employees accomplish tasks, they share information, experiences, and feelings. In the process they learn from each other, and their knowledge becomes a storehouse of knowledge belonging to the organization. By creating networks that enable employees to communicate, organizations can facilitate the flow and buildup of knowledge. According to Julien Birkenshaw, effective knowledge management has two requirements: "First, the firm should encourage individuals to interact—to work together on projects or share their ideas informally. Second, systems are needed to codify the knowledge of individuals so that others can have access to it."[2] Other authors have referred to this knowledge as "social capital."[3] If workers don't share what they know, their knowledge will never belong to the organization.

Closely related to knowledge management is the concept of the learning organization—a forerunner of the knowledge management field. Learning, and hence knowledge, takes place when "continuous information gathering, boundary spanning initiatives and active internal debate stimulate the cross-pollination of ideas throughout the firm."[4] In a turbulent business world, success comes to the company that is better at learning. These concepts relate to organizations as "open, adaptive systems that naturally gravitate to the borders of chaos, but in doing so also naturally create the conditions for self-selecting strategies designed to meet the challenges facing the organization and keep it moving forward."[5]

Another related field is called intellectual capital, defined as a combination of competence and commitment "embedded in how each employee thinks about and does work and in how the organization creates policies and systems to get work done."[6] A company's intellectual capital is identified and measured by breaking down its intangible assets—employees' knowledge, its best practices, its internal relationships and those with customers—so that they can be evaluated and developed just like financial or operational resources.

Management of Knowledge

Building the Knowledge Organization at CIBC

The CIBC started a knowledge management program in 1996 that focuses on four key elements. The goal was not to gain knowledge for its own sake, but to raise performance by improving output for the customer.

1. **Individual learning.** Each position's knowledge requirements—theoretical understanding, skills, and experience—were mapped out. Extensive training programs were provided for learning these requirements.
2. **Team learning.** Employee groups were encouraged to take responsibility for their own learning. To facilitate this goal, management styles changed from command and control to coaching and advising.
3. **Organization learning.** Team knowledge and achievements are shared with other teams through learning networks.
4. **Customer learning.** Employees provide custom-made solutions to customer's problems by developing an understanding of their industry and concerns, rather than selling them previously defined products and services. Customers are also informed about the CIBC's services through workshops, websites, and meetings.

Various tools are used for managing knowledge. Information technology *systems* are stockpiles of codified knowledge that can be accessed quickly and easily. Informal workplace designs, such as open-concept office areas, can promote social interaction. Best practices transfer is a method of transplanting effective work practices to other locations. Centres of excellence perform similar functions, as recognized role models of expertise. Communities of practice, which originated in the "learning organization" movement, demonstrate that knowledge is created by and belongs to communities. "Communities of practice are groups of people who share a passion for something that they know how to do, and who interact regularly in order to learn how to do it better."[7] The most effective communities of practice emerge informally and naturally, based on common interests and goals, though many organizations have tried to formalize these groups. So, we manage knowledge through social interaction, but what exactly is this thing called knowledge that we are managing?

What Is Knowledge?

It is helpful to distinguish between *data, information,* and *knowledge.*

> Data is a collection of facts, measurements and statistics, whereas information is defined as organized or processed data that is timely (i.e. inferences from the data are drawn within the time frame of applicability) and accurate (with reference to original data). Knowledge is information that is contextual, relevant, and actionable.[8]

Knowledge gives us meaning based on experience and reflection that is useful for solving problems. Information by itself is not as valuable because it does not focus on what is important. Also, the value of information diminishes over time, whereas knowledge is historically relevant. As information accumulates, we can experience information overload, whereas knowledge evolves and perpetually keeps itself relevant.

An organization contains many types of knowledge that can be categorized under two main headings: *explicit knowledge* and *tacit knowledge.* Tacit knowledge represents deep thinking structures embedded in the brain that cannot be expressed easily. Explicit knowledge can be easily expressed.[9] For example, let's say after you graduate your friend asks you what you learned in school. It would be difficult to answer easily. However, if a classmate asked you what you learned in class yesterday, it would be fairly easy to answer. In the workplace, explicit knowledge relates to performing the basic operations, such as knowing what things need to be done, how to do them, and why they need to be done. Tacit knowledge relates to methods of communicating with each other, interpreting people and events, and learning new methods of solving problems. Codified databases in companies are mainly collections of explicit knowledge that apply universally to all employees. Personalized approaches bring out more tacit knowledge, as they require direct interaction between people.

> In a very real sense, management is about life itself. When managers face problems, they face life in its complexity, not compartmentalized packages of life. Managers need specialized knowledge, to be sure, but more importantly, they need wisdom, which is the ability to weave knowledge together and make use of it. Management is rooted in tacit knowledge at least as much as explicit knowledge, which means that much of it cannot be codified and taught formally.[10]

The Goal of Knowledge Management

Knowledge management combines both explicit and tacit forms of knowledge. Explicit knowledge is collected as an end in itself, whereas the goal of tacit knowledge is to provide a means with which to improve continuously the organization's ability to execute its tasks. The value of explicit knowledge is limited. For instance, knowing that sales figures last year rose 15 percent says nothing about what this year's sales figures will be. To estimate the coming year's sales figures, you would need information about markets, competition, customers, production, and shipping, among other things. After careful analysis of all these factors, some knowledge would emerge on which to base a sales forecast. The goal of knowledge management can best be described in a definition by Gupta:

> Knowledge management is a process that helps organizations identify, select, organize, disseminate and transfer important information and expertise that are a part of the organizational memory that typically resides within an organization in an unstructured manner. This enables effective and efficient problem solving, dynamic learning, strategic planning and decision making. Knowledge management focuses on identifying knowledge, explicating it in a way so that it can be shared in a formal manner, and thus reusing it.[11]

The Chief Knowledge Officer

A job title that is appearing more and more in career ads and company directories is that of *Chief Knowledge Officer* (CKO). Effective use of knowledge management principles can reduce duplication, streamline information flow, and save a lot of money. Consider the following facts:[12]

- Ninety-one percent of Canadian business leaders polled by Ipsos-Reid in 2001 believed that knowledge management practices improve organizational effectiveness.
- The Canadian Centre for Management Development in 2001 launched a knowledge management training program for senior federal government officials.
- Health Canada conducted a knowledge management diagnostic in 2001 to identify its knowledge flow bottlenecks.
- Eighty percent of Fortune 500 companies in 2002 had knowledge management staff and 25 percent had CKOs.
- From 1997 to 2000 the Ford Motor Company saved over a billion dollars as a result of knowledge management programs.

Interviews conducted by Nick Bontis of McMaster University in 2002 showed two principle areas of expertise required by CKOs. An information systems background gives CKOs technical skills in collecting, storing, and sharing codified forms of knowledge. A background in human resources and communication provides CKOs with an understanding of social networking behaviour so that knowledge-sharing activities can be developed. The key to effective knowledge management, though, hinges on this critical point: you can't do knowledge management.

> Unless you are able to involve practitioners directly in the process, your ability to truly manage knowledge assets is going to remain seriously limited. It is their knowledge. They know what needs to be documented and what should be left as a tacit understanding. Practitioners...are in the best position to manage this knowledge.[13]

CKOs and their bosses must remember that knowledge resides in the person and not in the collection of facts—a common cause of failure for knowledge management programs. Many organizations define knowledge management in terms of inputs of data, information technology, and best practices without considering the influence of personal employee factors, such as motivation, creativity, and commitment.[14] This would indicate a failure to coordinate the efforts of information technology and human resources.

Workplace Diversity

Managing diversity is "a comprehensive managerial process for developing an environment that works for all employees."

—*R. Roosevelt Thomas*, Beyond Race and Gender[15]

If we look at workplaces or campuses today, we will notice that the number of differences among people—meaning the level of diversity—is higher than ever before. These differences involve gender, cultural backgrounds, age, education levels, values, attitudes, and sexual orientation. As Canadians, we may have a head start in handling the challenges of a diverse workplace because we have traditionally seen diversity as a cultural strength and as part of our national experience. And the trend is growing. In 2001, Canada, at 18 percent, was second only to Australia at 22 percent in its percentage of foreign-born population. In contrast, 11 percent of the population in the United States in 2000 was born outside the country. In Vancouver and Toronto, nearly 4 in 10 residents belong to a visible minority group.[16] China and India currently provide the greatest number of immigrants. Our three largest cities, Vancouver, Toronto, and Montreal, absorb 58 percent of new immigrants. In terms of provinces, Ontario's share in 2003 was 55 percent, Quebec received 19 percent, British Columbia, 15 percent, Alberta, 7 percent, and Manitoba, 3 percent. Immigrants are increasingly well educated. Among those arriving in the 1990s, 41 percent had university degrees, 13 percent had college diplomas, and 8 percent had certificates in skilled trades.[17]

The issue of workplace diversity breaks down into two areas: 1) initiatives for promoting *equal opportunity*, and 2) programs for *managing workplace diversity*. The equal opportunity area has to a large degree been written into law. Hiring, promotions, and other equality and human rights issues involving employees are followed by employers as a form of legal compliance. Provinces, for instance, have established laws that require companies to remove barriers for disabled workers. Media organizations are also affected. The Canadian Radio-television and Telecommunications Commission monitors cultural representation of visible minorities and Aboriginal people on television to examine whether they are fairly represented in programming. These initiatives aim to equalize the personal, social, and economic opportunities of all diverse groups.

Traditional diversity programs emphasized sensitivity training, which taught skills in discovering each other's identities and avoiding delicate areas. Today, the challenge of diversity training has evolved into a larger goal that directly relates to the financial bottom line: the process of building company capability by tapping into the many talents that a mixture of backgrounds, perspectives, and abilities bring to the workplace. Instead of dodging the sensitive spots, diversity training engages people in the bump and grind of energetic workplace activity—so long as a climate of openness, trust, and respect has been established.

> You have to create enough safety in the group so that people feel comfortable talking about what's on their minds ... and that means avoiding political correctness.[18]

The traditional approach to diversity was the practice of being blind to differences; managing diversity calls attention to them. From a business point of view, then, let's explore what a company can gain from managing diversity and how diversity programs can be used as a competitive advantage.

The Benefits of Diversity

We weren't attracting people of colour or women, and we started to think we needed employees who reflected the customer base we wanted to attract.

—*Jim Ziemer, chief executive at Harley-Davidson Inc.*[19]

The benefits of workplace diversity are many. It offers a stimulus for personal, social, and organizational growth. It provides different ideas and challenges our beliefs. It forces us to consider other points of view. And it gives us greater understanding of other people. Managing diversity aims to turn differences in employees, traditionally regarded as barriers to communication, into positive forces for efficiency and competitiveness. This is done by encouraging employees to celebrate their differences and learn to appreciate those of their fellow workers, as the feature about diversity at Proctor and Gamble demonstrates. Encouraging groups to break up and form constituent groups paves the way for employee buy-in because within the groups three essential components are in place: mutual expectations, mutual influence, and trust.[20] Viewing differences as important resources for learning can also reduce conflict, because "group members can negotiate expectations, norms, and assumptions about work in service of their goals, and conflicts that arise are settled by a process of joint inquiry."[21]

Effective workplace diversity programs enable employees to perform to their potential by removing the barriers that stifle individual expression. "Group members working with this perspective, reported feeling that their 'whole person' was known, valued, and respected by others and that they could express 'more of who they were' at work, including those things that differentiated them from others."[22] The result is a collective identity in the workforce that "includes not only race, gender, creed, and ethnicity but also age, background, education, function, and personality differences. The objective is not to assimilate minorities and women into a dominant white male culture but to create a dominant heterogeneous culture."[23] When employees are empowered to be themselves and let their individuality come out, an organization's leaders have the opportunity to define a set of values and sense of purpose that transcends the interests of any one group.

Many employers have realized the importance of a diverse work force for reaching the changing demographics of their customers. As the star forward of the Toronto Raptor's basketball team says, in response to his team signing Italian and Spanish players, "We have a lot of good basketball players on this team . . . they just so happen to be from other parts of the world. And I think that will give us a better fan base and more people rooting us on."[24] Police forces also have taken big steps in increasing diversity in their ranks to be better able to reflect the differences of various cultures and languages. The Ontario Provincial Police has attempted to reverse the dangers of racial profiling through cultural diversity programs. As Jay Hope, chief superintendent and the highest ranking Black police officer in the country says, "we call our policy illegal profiling. No police officer shall stop, detain, search, or question anyone based upon their race."[25]

Not to be left behind, diversity practices have also increased effectiveness in organized crime. Criminal Intelligence Service Canada (CISC) reported in 2005 that organized crime groups are now more reflective of Canada's multicultural makeup. Crime groups are recruiting members with certain areas of cultural expertise, since they are doing business with each other more frequently. This eliminates cultural barriers, since usually their members are from the same ethnic background, such as Asian, Italian, or Russian groups. Like corporations, they are forming cultural links that facilitate their business activity and enable them to be more productive. Said one police official, "The dynamics of organized crime are changing. We're beginning to see strategic partnerships within organized crime that you would not have seen a number of years ago. They're actually helping one another."[26]

At the accounting firm Ernst & Young LLP Canada, with 3100 employees, females comprise 55 percent of its work force and 47 percent of its managers, while visible minorities represent 17 percent, with 13 percent in managerial positions. The percentages in the big centres of Vancouver, Calgary, Toronto, and Montreal are approaching 50 percent. In contrast to the United States, where the focus is more on Black and Latino populations, Ernst & Young takes a more comprehensive cultural approach to be in harmony with Canada's mosaic of cultures. Allan Mark, partner and diversity coordinator, states:

> Our strategy has two themes to it, which is that we become successful in attracting, retaining, and promoting the best people among visible minorities, and create an environment where all our people feel they belong and can build their careers. It's also business-case driven and it's also the right thing to do. It's not about quotas and it's not about preferential treatment. It's about recruiting, retaining, and promoting the best people.[27]

The fact that the company does a lot of employee recruiting at colleges and universities reflects the diversity in Canada's post-secondary institutions.

Proctor and Gamble Canada Celebrates Workplace Diversity to Increase Cultural Competency and Sell More Soap[28]

To celebrate diversity in its work force, the 800 employees at the Toronto headquarters of Proctor and Gamble Canada set up booths that served jerk pork, samosas, henna tatoos, Romanian meatballs, and, playfully, Fruit To Go from the gay and lesbian employee booth. The celebration not only demonstrated the variety of cultures at P & G Canada, but also highlighted one of the company's core strategies: to create an environment that respects and accepts people's differences. Company President Tim Penner said, "have fun, learn a lot, enjoy your day and…increase your cultural competency."

The aim is twofold: to enrich everyone by letting them feel more comfortable about participating fully in corporate life, and to give employees a better understanding of their customers. P & G has cultural networks, such as the Asian Professional Network and the French Canadian Network, that serve as resource groups for coworkers seeking advice on targeting a specific market sector. This strategy expands the company's reach into the changing cultural makeup of Canada and around the world. The atmosphere of acceptance helped gay employees make the decision to "come out" and form the Gay, Bisexual, Lesbian, and Transgendered employees group. Said one member, "After I came out, I became incredibly more productive." Apart from the marketing aspect, there are benefits to having diverse employees involved in decision making. Said another employee, an engineer from India, "There is no point in having a team when everyone has the same ideas."

According the Jeffrey Gandz of the Ivey Business School, the benefits of diversity fall into the following areas:[29]

- **Satisfying customer needs.** The population statistics quoted above show that visible minorities make up huge sections of the market. Understanding the needs of different cultural groups and serving them in their own language makes a stronger connection with customers. The Mouvement des caisses Desjardins, a network of credit unions in Quebec, offers service and brochures in nine languages. The variety of talents in a diverse work force also helps in the design of products and in the strategies used to bring them to markets.

- **Strengthening relationships with suppliers.** With globalization, a company's network of suppliers expands to all continents, so effective relationships with suppliers are becoming more complex.

- **Empowering employees.** Managing diversity by removing barriers associated with gender, culture, age, or sexual orientation can increase personal freedom and job satisfaction for employees. A Society of Management Accountants study shows a strong relationship between diversity programs and lower absenteeism and job turnover, as well as higher commitment to the organization.[30] In addition, since white males are a rapidly shrinking segment of the Canadian work force—representing 30 percent of the labour force in 2001—the need has never been greater for organizations to realize the potential contributions of females and visible minorities.

- **Engaging in globalization.** As well as corporate expansion and relocation, global economics involves the two-way flow of workers and investments. Canada, traditionally, has relied on foreign investments for economic growth. Diversity practices are attractive factors for countries looking for locations to invest money. In this regard, Canada is successful, having the highest level of foreign investment of any of the G-7 countries. For Canadian companies seeking to become global enterprises, diversity practices are

PepsiCo Scores with Diversity Programs

PepsiCo Inc. has made great strides in both areas of cultural diversity. In terms of promoting equal opportunity, "at the end of 2004, visible minorities held 17% of management jobs at midlevel and above, up from 11% in 2000, and women held 29% of those management jobs, up from 24% in 2000."[31] In terms of better tuning in to customer needs, in 2004 about 1 percentage point of the company's 8 percent revenue growth came from products inspired by diversity efforts, including guacamole-flavoured Doritos and Mountain Dew Code Red. To develop its diversity program, the company requires each member of the executive group to sponsor a different employee affinity group. The white female CEO of PepsiCo North America, for instance, sponsors a women of colour group. A Black male executive sponsors a group of white males. "An employee affinity group consists of people of a particular race, gender, or sexual orientation, or people with a disability—with the idea that they share certain perspectives and needs within the company that can best be addressed through group discussion."[32]

Discussion Questions

1. Discuss the benefits of workplace diversity as a marketing strategy.

2. Is cultural diversity a form of stereotyping? Could it lead to hazards as a marketing strategy?

essential. "As business is done more and more through partnerships, joint ventures, and strategic alliances, so an ability to relate to other cultures becomes a key organizational requirement. It is simply inconceivable that organizations seeking to become global players could do so without achieving high levels of diversity in their workplaces."[33]

- **Becoming a good corporate citizen.** A commitment to diversity has a strong impact on an organization's reputation in the business community. Job seekers are attracted to good employers. Customers develop interest in companies that prioritize health and safety in their products. Companies that care about their employees and the environment are perceived as good corporate citizens.

Many studies relate workplace diversity to company performance. Usually, solid guidelines are necessary, such as having leadership that is committed to diversity, professional training, recruitment of diverse people, rewarding people who contribute to diversity, and holding people accountable for making progress in diversity areas.[34]

One area where diversity practices have increased equal opportunity is in name discrimination. A recent study mailed 5000 resumes in response to job ads in both the *Boston Globe* and *Chicago Tribune*.[35] Résumés were sent out for each posting using both "Black-sounding" names and "white-sounding" names. "White" names included Kristen, Greg, Neil, Emily, Brett, and Jill. "Black" names included Kareem, Rasheed, Tamika, Ebony, Aisha, and Tyrone. The results showed that "white-sounding" names are 50 percent more likely to get a response to their résumé than are those with "Black-sounding" names. The study points out the impact of cultural differences on our perceptions of job qualifications and how deeply rooted, almost unconscious, these decision-making processes are. By making a commitment to diversity, a company more closely monitors why recruiting and hiring programs are not meeting their goals and brings these thinking processes out into the open.

Diversity programs have their critics, though. In many smaller businesses with outdated human resources policies, intolerance to people's differences continues to exist. Even in the world's largest corporation by revenue in 2005, ExxonMobil, a nondiscrimination policy covering sexual orientation was cancelled in the merger of the two oil giants and its domestic partner benefits excluded gay and lesbian employees.[36]

Implementing a diversity awareness program usually has a big impact on a company's culture. The emphasis on communication, relationships, empathy, respect, and learning point to a management style that is flexible, understanding, open, and trustworthy. The key to diversity awareness is that employees must want to accomplish it—it is very difficult to force people to buy into it.

Ethics and Social Responsibility

An area of growing concern in today's organizations is the issue of ethics. The news is filled with accounts of business people involved in dishonest activities. In Canada we have former Hollinger executives Conrad Black and David Radler, John Felderhof of Bre-X, the world's largest gold mining swindle, and numerous insider stock market trading investigations. For example, Betty Ho, wife of K.Y. Ho, chairman of ATI Technologies, an international communication technology company headquartered in Markham, Ontario, was investigated in 2005 by the Ontario Securities Commission for selling four million shares that her husband gave her shortly before the stock failed to meet its earnings forecast. Incidentally, the ATI Code of Ethics on the company's website begins with "At ATI, we are committed to conducting our business with the highest level of integrity, honesty and professionalism. Maintaining high standards are also critical for maintaining investor confidence and shareholder value as a publicly traded and world-leading high-tech company."[37]

In the U.S., there are many more incidents. DaimlerChrysler has been investigated by the Justice Department for allegations that it paid bribes in a least a dozen countries and that senior executives were aware of it. In fact, before the passing of the Anti Bribery Convention in 1997 by the Organisation for Economic Co-operation and Development, several European countries, including Germany, openly allowed tax deductions for bribery overseas.[38] This spurred an anti-bribery law in the U.S. in 2002, the Sarbanes-Oxley corporate accountability law. Other investigations are more well known: Kenneth Lay and Jeffrey Skilling at Enron, Edmonton-born Bernard Ebbers of WorldCom, and William Kozlowski of Tyco International Ltd. Unethical practices are contagious in corporate life because they create a trickle-down effect. As in many situations in the workplace, when it comes to moral guidelines, employees follow the lead of their bosses. And the lies that bosses tell to employees eventually develop into cultural values, and employees adopt the old saying, "That's the way we do things around here."

What Are Ethics and Social Responsibility?

Ethics are moral principles that people use to determine what is right or wrong. In the workplace, companies that have strong ethical values and put a high value on doing the "right thing" demonstrate qualities such as fairness to all people, impartial judgment, integrity, transparency, accountability, and truthfulness. The standard treatment of ethics is generally founded on the three pillars of value, virtue, and duty. If actions produce value, they are deemed to be good. If people act according to the rules, they display good ethics. If people have virtue, they exhibit the characteristics of a morally good human being. We are adding a fourth pillar to our discussion: the principle of care, which focuses on the consequences of our actions on our relationships. Let's look at some of the principles on which common ethical perspectives are based.[39]

- **Utilitarianism**—the view that actions are ethical when they produce the greatest benefits for the greatest number of people. Organizations often change it to the lowest cost for the greatest number of people. The decision process becomes a matter of evaluating costs and benefits. One problem with the utilitarian view is that the results of actions can justify the methods used to achieve them. Placing a premium on a winning outcome can lead to the types of financial wrongdoings described above.

- **Categorical imperative**—the view that actions should be judged as universal laws. Using this view as an ethical guide, a person must ask him- or herself if the action would be right if everybody else in the world did the same. In contrast to utilitarianism, all actions are treated as ends in themselves, instead of as means to an end.
- **Libertarianism**—the view that freedom from human constraint is good, and that constraints imposed by others are evil. Supporters of a free market economy believe in a libertarian view.
- **Capitalist justice**—the view that benefits should be distributed according to the value of the contribution an individual makes to a group. Many salary systems in organizations are based on an evaluation of individual merit.
- **Distributive justice**—the view that the benefits of society should be distributed fairly and impartially among all members. People with similar qualifications should receive similar pay. This is the basic argument behind the belief in equal pay for equal work that has been presented by women in the work force.
- **Morality of care**—the view that places special value on relationships and the social consequences of our actions. In contrast to distributive justice, a caring basis for ethics is partial to those with whom we have special relationships because our own identity and sense of value derives from them. Thus, a person's or an organization's worth is increased by supporting their relationships. This view is particularly relevant in discussions of today's ethical approaches to corporate social responsibility that focus on nurturing relationships with stakeholders as a strategy for improving business. It is important to note that the caring approach emerged out of research in ethics conducted by women. Whereas the traditional male approach emphasized individuality, self-interest, and impartiality, the female approach, as proposed by researchers such as Carol Gilligan, stresses social responsibility, empathy, and compassion, and points out substantial differences in ethical reasoning methods.[40] This approach to ethics has also been called piety,

  > a disposition to acknowledge our weak and dependent state and to face the surrounding world with due reverence and humility. It is the attitude that many people—environmentalists, conservationists, and animal-welfare activists included—are attempting to recapture in a world where the results of human presumption are so depressingly apparent.[41]

Discussions of ethics in business are also influenced by the context in which ethical issues take place. According to Marc Saner and Cornelius von Baeyer, ethical issues in organizations usually fall into two categories: workplace ethics and policy ethics.[42] Workplace ethics operate at the micro level of an organization and deal with ongoing issues, such as corruption, fraud, influence peddling, and confidentiality. Policy ethics take the macro approach and deal with the issues of the day: privacy, risk factors, human rights, research methods, working conditions, equal opportunity, eating meat, wearing fur coats, or the environment. The fields of ethics and social responsibility discussed in this section generally divide along these lines. Workplace ethics provide operational guidelines to manage the everyday activities of employees, while policy ethics cover the larger area of corporate social responsibility in which organizations takes positions on issues that go beyond the sole pursuit of making money. The same general principles of ethics, however, apply to both types.

Why People Behave Badly

Ethical standards in today's workplace have been watered down for many reasons. Usually, huge amounts of money are involved, which creates great pressure to perform. When millions are at stake, ethical lines can turn into a grey zone and rationalizations can replace accurate reasoning. Consider the examples of professional athletes, already receiving inconceivably large paycheques, tying to boost their averages with performance-enhancing drugs. Large executive salaries may exert the same pressures in boardrooms. The documentary *Enron: The Smartest Guys in the Room* depicts an organization so obsessed in its final days to achieve ever higher numbers that its managers lied appallingly to provoke an energy crisis in California and then made millions from it. The Enron collapse sent its accounting firm Arthur Anderson for a crash—28 000 employees lost their jobs after the 2002 scandal.[43] In a related story, when the Enron fallout started in August of 2005, the Canadian Imperial Bank of Commerce was forced to pay over $3 billion as a settlement in a class-action suit. Though CIBC's stock price was hammered, the bank did not pursue CEO John Hunkin, who stepped down the same week with a $52-million compensation package.[44] Why did the Arthur Anderson accounting firm continue to accept glaring irregularities in Enron's accounting practices? Upper management at both companies pressured the accounting team to accept the numbers because of the revenues they were generating.[45]

When the chief financial officer of WorldCom realized the company would have to readjust its revenue upward by $130 million to meet analyst's expectations, he told CEO Bernie Ebbers, "This isn't right . . . we're making this adjustment because this is the only way we can get the numbers up to the expectations of the marketplace." Ebbers replied, "We have to hit our numbers," and orchestrated a massive accounting fraud.[46] In all, the accounting adjustments raised WorldCom's income for the quarter by $1 billion.

White-collar crime is on the rise. The RCMP's Integrated Market Enforcement Teams operate at full capacity, carrying on regular investigations. The program is funded by the government to make the country's capital markets safer for investors. In 2005, two of the big cases were Nortel Networks Corp. and Scotiabank's Royal Group Technologies Ltd. "I don't think that anyone will deny the fact that white collar crime is a growth industry," stated RCMP Chief Superintendent Peter German.[47] Yet corporate cops in Canada have limited resources. In the 1997 Bre-X gold swindle, shareholders lost $9 billion and billions more were erased from junior mining companies, but no one in Canada was charged or investigated because the case would have been too expensive to deal with.[48]

Bansal and Kandola explain that unethical practices occur because of the bystander effect. Employees "may be aware that the individuals they are observing are acting irresponsibly, yet they may do nothing to intervene because they assume that keeping silent is the norm."[49] If senior management is in the loop, more credibility is given to the wrongdoings and the longer they continue because the actions appear acceptable to the organization. Several other factors uncover some key elements of ethical practices:

- **Unethical actions are ambiguous.** Employees ignore unethical behaviour if it is not clearly spelled out that it is wrong. It must also be clear who will be responsible for addressing the issue. The more responsibility is passed from person to person, the greater the uncertainty about how serious the wrongdoing is. If ambiguity continues, employees will keep engaging in the bad behaviour.
- **Blame is shared, rewards are individual.** All employees are responsible for bad behaviour, so everyone will share the blame for irresponsible actions. However, only a certain few reap the benefits of the unethical actions, often in the form of big paycheques. As a result, employees have little incentive to expose the crime.[50]

- **Fear of retaliation.** Even though companies have begun encouraging their employees to report concerns about ethical lapses, fear of retaliation is still a big issue, and less than 10 percent of companies have a culture of dissent where employees can openly speak their minds.[51]

Ethics and Leadership

Since everything seems to start with the leader, it might be worth looking at types of leadership styles that best promote ethical values. Earlier we discussed two types of ethics: workplace ethics and policy ethics. These can be related to leadership styles, in particular transactional leadership and transformational leadership. Transactional leadership manages the routine activities of the workplace, such as setting goals, allocating resources, and directing employees to accomplish tasks and achieve organizational goals. To gain employee cooperation, rewards and formal authority are used. A transformational leader, on the other hand, is involved in developing an organizational vision and an overall strategy that not only helps to achieve objectives but engages an employee's attitudes, values, and sense of self. Both types of leaders gain respect and credibility based on their moral standing. A leader whose integrity is in doubt will have a difficult time influencing followers.[52]

The control strategies used by transactional leaders serve their self-interest, focusing mainly on physical and social needs. In contrast, the empowering strategies used by transformational leaders facilitate employees' higher-order needs for growth, autonomy, and self-development. With transformational leadership self-interest becomes collective interest.[53] As Kanungo states,

> In deciding whether the leader is ethical, the expectation is that the leader will direct and guide organizational members towards goals and objectives which will benefit the organization, its members, other stakeholders, and the society at large. It is only in the context of such benefits that leadership acts in the areas of planning, controlling, and coordinating are justified and assume moral meaning and significance.[54]

With transformational leadership, employees are able to see their own values reflected in their leader's vision and strategy.

Quality in the workplace can be linked to ethics built on customer satisfaction and employee well-being. Well-trained employees working in a positive environment have a natural inclination to do their best. Peter Drucker writes of Thomas Watson, founder of IBM, "He believed in a worker who saw his own interests as identical to those of the company. He wanted, above all, a worker who used his own mind and experience to improve his job, the product, the process and the company."[55] The management philosophy of Jonathan Demming, based on effective training, empowerment, a delegating style of leadership, the elimination of fear, and sense of job ownership, can be an effective foundation for an ethical and profitable workplace. Skilled and well-trained employees can better satisfy their customers. "Empowerment is an ethical issue because it establishes the authority of employees in the performance of their effort. It therefore affects the quality of human decisions."[56] Fear creates a workplace with negative motivators, which are expressed in the form of threats, abuse, and disempowerment. To thrive, an ethical atmosphere needs openness and trust.

Making Effective Ethics Policies

Companies today are obliged to have ethics codes. Most stock exchanges require publicly displayed codes of conduct and ethics as a requirement for being listed. In the U.K. it has been a best practice since 1992. What's the difference between effective

The Difference between Hyperbole and Lies[57]

According to Peggy Cunningham, ethics professor at Queen's University, there is a tendency to amplify accomplishments in résumés today. Up to 90 percent of people have some type of hyperbole or exaggeration in their résumé. But when the limits are pushed and exaggerations turn into lies, integrity and jobs can both be lost. Terrence Popowich was fired in 1988 from his post as vice president and chief economist of the Toronto Stock Exchange for lying about have a Master's degree from the London School of Economics. Worse still, Ottawa's John Davy served time in jail in 2002 when he lied about his qualifications to get the job of chief executive at New Zealand's Maori Television Service. In 2006 Radio Shack CEO David Edmondson admitted that he had lied about his academic record on his résumé. If a company's code of ethics is to mean anything to employees, shareholders, and customers, lying cannot be tolerated. Says Cunnigham, "The CEO is also the chief ethics officer. People aren't just looking at what he says, but also at what he does." Some things never change, though. At Radio Shack, after considering the issue, the investigation board supported Edmondson.

and ineffective ethics codes? Mark Shwartz of York University surveyed managers at four large Canadian companies. Some employees rejected rules they considered unfair. One was that inventions made by employees, even at home, were considered company property. Concrete examples were helpful for understanding rules. Codes that were written in the negative, such as "Employees shall not...", were clearer and easier to follow than those written in a positive style. Expressions such as "Business will be conducted with the highest standards of integrity" sound good, but what do they actually mean? Although all four companies' codes required staff to report violations, respondents said their decision to do so depended on various factors, such as the nature of the offence, the person who broke the rule, and fear of retribution. Some employees stated they would have difficulty reporting their supervisors. Overall, the study showed the importance of support from senior managers if ethics codes are to be taken seriously.[58]

Corporate Social Responsibility

...resources belong to society. They are derived from the air, sea, rivers, and earth, which are commonly owned and protected. One of the things I admire about Japanese culture is its recognition of the obligation business owes to society. For example, Toyota defines quality in terms of benefits to society. Genichi Tagucho defines deviation from the nominal as a "loss to society."

—William Stimson, "A Demming Inspired Management Code of Ethics"[59]

Businesses are increasingly engaging in social responsibility programs as a way of applying ethical standards of behaviour to themselves to become good corporate citizens. According to Gordon Nixon, CEO of RBC Financial Group, named Canada's Most Respected Corporation in 2005 for its fourth year running, "RBC's continued high rankings in these categories, year after year, reinforces that a company's reputation is not built on a single quarter's results, or by a single initiative, but by its sustained approach to the fundamentals of good business and ethical behaviour."[60] And for the 11th consecutive year, RBC was named the top corporation in the category of Corporate Social Responsibility. The rankings were developed by Ipsos Reid for KPMG. The survey asked 250 of Canada's leading CEOs to name the companies they most respected. Corporations were graded on investment value, financial performance, innovation, human resources management, corporate social responsibility, quality, corporate governance, and customer service.

Corporate social responsibility (CSR) refers to a company's concern and response to issues that accomplish social and environmental benefits and go beyond the narrow economic, technical, and legal requirements of making profit.[61] It has also been defined as "a commitment to improve community well-being through discretionary business practices and contributions of corporate resources."[62] The term "triple bottom-line thinking" has been applied to corporate social responsibility. It suggests that an organization's success hinges on three factors: economic profitability, environmental sustainability, and social performance.[63] Social responsibility initiatives allow a company to become proactive on social and environmental issues, instead of merely being reactive to them. In this way, companies become agents of social change. Companies are being pressured by internal and external stakeholders, such as customers, employees, politicians, and social groups, because of rapidly changing expectations about the social responsibilities of business. The forces of globalization have brought human rights and environmental issues to the surface. Nike has been criticized for poor working conditions and low wages in its overseas operations, though in response the company shocked activists in 2005 by complying with disclosure requirements, listing its more than 7000 suppliers, and agreeing to fair trade policies. The fast-food industry has been in the spotlight also in regards to obesity problems in society, especially with children.

Instead of simply giving money to help needy organizations, as was the practice in the days of corporate philanthropy, corporate social responsibility initiatives develop inroads with stakeholders to engage them in the company's operations. By collaborating with interests groups, companies develop socially responsible business models. What companies have realized is that they share many interests with their stakeholders. Frank Dottori, CEO of Tembec, a forest products company, has two critical stakeholders: environmental groups and local community groups. According to Dottori, "Once we sat down with the environment groups and asked them what they wanted, to our surprise, three of the five concerns they had were identical to our own concerns."[64] Tembec engages community members through committees made up of employees and local residents that provide feedback on business operations, which gives the company a chance to respond before confrontations arise. Energy giant Encana of Calgary uses similar employee–community groups to monitor the social and environmental impact of their projects. For instance, they speeded up approval of an 80-kilometre pipeline through B.C. by launching discussions with government, Aboriginal groups, and other interested parties. Both of these companies found that engagement was the most efficient way to create a socially responsive business.[65]

As a business movement, social responsibility has its supporters and detractors. Critics say it is too ambitious, that fulfilling social responsibilities will undermine economic performance. They claim that people's lifestyles have improved tremendously as a result of corporate profits through such things as retirement and investment funds and advances in technology. Supporters, on the other hand, complain that programs are not ambitious enough. There should be more transparency in the exercise of power, and power relationships between companies and the people and communities they operate in should reflect a greater spirit of cooperation if real social change is going to happen. In general, companies have accepted the idea that if bad ethical actions can harm a company's reputation and economic performance, good ethical actions can improve them.

The challenge for companies is to develop programs that directly relate to and benefit their business. Let's look at some examples. In 2006, Tim Horton's reinforced its reputation as a quintessentially Canadian institution in the food business by setting up shop at the Canadian army base in Kandahar, Afghanistan. But in other areas, such as using fair-trade coffee and disclosure, it scores an E, according to the 2006 *Report on Business* Corporate Social Responsibility Ranking. In contrast, Starbucks, with a B score, provides extensive social responsibility reporting, right down to CO_2 emissions and generous charity donations (1.7 percent of pre-tax profits). Cause-related marketing is a common CSR activity. MacDonald's donates money for all Big Macs sold on World Children's Day. Yoplait yogurt promises 10 cents to breast cancer foundations for each yogurt lid returned. A recent television ad had Reba McEntire announcing that Whirlpool will be donating a fridge and stove to every home built by Habitat for Humanity, a community program for affordable housing.[66] Shell Oil Company uses community volunteering programs to encourage its employees to volunteer their time to support community organizations, in some cases on company time. If literacy is your company's cause, there's much more that can be done than donating money. Getting employees involved often inspires community members to participate. This process is known as leveraging—getting the message out about the good works that you do in your community so that value comes back to the company. CSR programs such as these give a company an image, a connection to a cause to which customers can relate. In this way, they add value to the company brand. Dove soap's Campaign for Real Beauty established the Dove Self-Esteem Fund aimed at educating young girls about a broader definition of beauty and increasing self-confidence. Programs are run in participation with organizations such as Girl Scouts.

Social Responsibility and Leadership

Perhaps nowhere are ethical standards and CSR more important than at the top levels in Canada's big corporations, since they hold the most power of any leaders in the country. The trend toward better corporate citizenship is not a passing fad. Investors, social groups, and the corporate scandals of recent years have convinced many board members of the necessity for reform in corporate board practices. The result has been a significant improvement in corporate board practices over the past few years. According to the Rotman School of Management, companies scoring a perfect 100 tripled between 2002 and 2004.[67]

Canada's most influential directors represent the corporate elite, who are driving reform in board practices, or corporate governance. This small group of 16 directors has disproportionate influence in Canadian boardrooms. They represent 1 percent of all directors, yet sit on the boards of 31 percent of the companies on the Toronto Stock Exchange (TSX) and are in charge of 50 percent, or $437 billion, of market capitalization. Each one sits on at least five boards, such as those of major banks and insurance companies; media companies such as Canwest Global, Rogers, Shaw, and Quebecor; resource companies such as Noranda and Falconbridge; and technology companies such as Nortel, Bombardier, TELUS, and BCE. The influence of the elite 16 is that they represent a large number of companies and they are interconnected. Practices spread through shared directorships like a virus. Their closeness allows for easy flow of information along the corporate networks. The elite 16 have demonstrated a strong commitment to excellent corporate governance practices, and most of the companies in the elite network perform better than those on the TSX composite index. Generally, it is the companies that have a major shareholder, as opposed to companies whose shares are widely held, that are resistant to good governance practices. So widely held companies are at the forefront of change.[68]

Ethics Bill Aims to Clean Up Ottawa[69]

One of the first moves of Prime Minister Harper's government was to change the way business is done in Ottawa. In 2006, the Conservative minority introduced a 200-page Bill that would give Canada one of the toughest accountability systems in the Western world. Highlights of the ethics package include:

- Measures to reduce the power of big money in politics. Political donations will be banned from companies, unions, and associations. The cap on individual donations will be lowered from $5000 to $1000. Lobbyists will have stricter limits.
- A stronger conflict of interest and ethics commissioner to ensure objective analysis of government finances. A judicial background is required.
- A process to ensure government appointments are based on merit, in addition to greater transparency for awarding government contracts.
- A $1000 reward for whistle-blowers. A new director of prosecutions would go after bureaucrats who defrauded the system.

The Bill is a response to the sponsorship scandal in Quebec that began during the administration of former Prime Minister Jean Chretien and carried on into Prime Minister Paul Martin's government. Judge Gomery's report of the affair blamed the Liberals for secretly rewarding their friends and financing the party's campaigns in Quebec.

The Bill is not popular with everyone, however. Ethics watchdog Democracy Watch criticized the report for its numerous loopholes. Business representatives, on the other hand, complained of the added layers of bureaucracy they will face when dealing with the federal government. Business leaders will be required to make monthly reports on who they talked to in government, when, and why. Civil servants will also have to keep records of every conversation with business people and lobbyists. According to Garth Whyte, executive vice president of the Canadian Federation of Independent Business, "They're really going to add to the paper burden, and I don't see the need for that."[70]

Implementing Ethics Management—Five Questions

Although many companies have embraced the necessity of good ethics and social responsibility, others still view them as drains on corporate profits or as witch-hunts that assume everyone is guilty until proven innocent. Managers may react defensively when confronted with ethics policies. A *Globe and Mail* poll in June 2005 that asked "When picking an employer, how important is their corporate social responsibility?" showed that one-third of respondents either didn't care or ranked it low on their list.[71] How can a company emphasize ethical practices without creating an atmosphere of suspicion or meddling too much into the daily affairs of a business? Start by asking the five following questions, designed by the W. Maurice Young Centre for Applied Ethics at the University of British Columbia:[72]

1. **What is our company's strategy to manage ethics?** An ethics strategy should be integrated into the overall strategy of an organization. It should be described in concrete language, not in broad philosophical terms. The moral implications of business strategies should be fully analyzed.

2. **Who is responsible for ethics in our company?** Without a specific person designated as an ethics officer, the responsibility for ethics management will bounce between departments. Smaller companies delegate ethics management to the human resources department.

3. **Are people in our firm equipped to recognize and resolve moral dilemmas?** Ethical issues can be obvious, but often they develop in increments, unnoticeably. Employees should be given guidance for responding to ethical dilemmas. The issue is further complicated with the high degree of cultural diversity in today's workplaces. Clear and open agreement on a code of ethics helps to create a common understanding of acceptable ethical practices.

4. **Are people in our organization provided with a safe opportunity to discuss ethical issues of concern?** Research shows that employees are often afraid to point out violations of ethical behaviour. Effective reporting mechanisms will encourage employees to reveal wrongdoings before too much damage is done. Clear policies should be in place to protect "whistle-blowers." Some companies have an Ombudsman who is outside of hierarchical influence or a hotline for anonymous reporting.

5. **Do we reward or punish ethical integrity and moral courage if it has a negative impact on the bottom line?** The emphasis on short-term gains that provide instant rewards and recognition is a cultural value that quickly spreads throughout an organization. If managers preach integrity but practise cutting corners, the message employees get is that declarations of ethical values are simply window-dressing. The test comes up when ethical principles face off against business objectives. The traditional approach in business has been that ethics are important—as long as we can afford them. Rewarding ethical integrity increases the value of ethical behaviour in a company's culture, thus encouraging employees to discuss it more openly.

Work–Life Balance

In the land that helped mould the image of the corporate warrior during its boom years in the 1980s and 1990s, the Japanese word for it is *karoshi*. It means death by overwork. The typical Japanese "salaryman" in those years embodied a culture built on hard work and long hours, where workers apologized for not being the last in the office. Vacations were sacrificed for the good of the company. Executive cocktail hours ran well into the evening. The "salaryman" was a shadowy figure to his family, if they were lucky enough to catch a glimpse of him before 7 a.m. or after 10 p.m. Today, the trend has almost reversed. The younger generation are known as "parasite singles," office workers who lavishly enjoy their expendable income. Birth rates have dropped as the "salaryman's" female counterpart, the "office lady," is choosing vacations, designer goods, and dining out over getting married and having children. Male employees in some organizations are being forced to take paternity leave at full pay after their wives give birth, a policy that has been in effect for years without ever being used.[73]

Though the changes have not been as dramatic here, Canadians in increasing numbers over the past decade have reported suffering from work–life conflict. A landmark study by Duxbury and Higgins in 2001 indicates that it's getting more difficult for people to have a meaningful life outside of work.[74] Profound changes in the structure of work, in the economy, and in family life came together in the 1990s to make it harder than ever to balance personal and working lives, leaving a lot of workers with higher-than-normal levels of stress. One indicator of work–life conflict is the growing number of roles people play. We are employees, bosses, subordinates, coworkers, spouses, parents, children, siblings, friends, and community members, among other things. As the workplace gets older, more ethnically diverse, with more working women, single parents, and dual-income families, juggling our many roles becomes more complex. *Work–life conflict* "occurs when the cumulative demands of work and non-work roles are incompatible in some respect so that participation in one role is made more difficult by participation in the other."[75]

To resolve this issue, the concept of work–life balance was developed. *Work-life balance* "refers to the desire on the part of both employees and employers to achieve a balance between workplace obligations and personal responsibilities."[76] As Neault states, the elements in balance represent an interrelationship of life roles, typically including social, physical, intellectual, emotional, spiritual, and professional aspects.[77] Periods in life when things are going smoothly and people are feeling enjoyment have been called "flow" experiences.[78] Flow occurs when a person's skills and resources are equal to the level of challenge. Matching skills and resources to the demands of work and personal life creates a feeling of balance and engagement in life and in the workplace. Conversely, striving to do too much creates a feeling of stress, imbalance, burnout, and apathy, according to Csikszentmihalyi.[79] The relationship between work–life balance and effective engagement in life and work is central from an organizational communication standpoint. Creating workplaces that foster enthusiasm, satisfaction, and social and emotional involvement may contribute to greater work–life balance. Let's look at some ways that organizations have attempted to develop work–life balance programs.

Mark Hollingworth has developed Life-Maps to resolve the dilemma of work–life balance.[80] Life-Maps help people establish their strategic objectives along different axes that represent key dimensions of personal growth, such as relationships, learning, and financial management. For instance, in defining happiness objectives, Stephen R. Covey's 4Ls are applied. They represent Live (get enough money to cover your needs, and don't forget about other things), Love (define the type of social environments you want to be in), Learn (how can you develop intellectually and professionally), and Legacy (what do you want to leave for others). The 4Ls represent the basic elements of a satisfying existence.

Life-Maps extend over a three- to five-year period. They are based on techniques that bring to the surface the important parts of our lives that often get buried under other responsibilities, creating dissatisfaction and stress. Through reflection and self-analysis we become aware of our internal motivations. After determining a more clear and accurate self-perception, we can engage with others more effectively. With Life-Maps, people are able more actively to discover and pursue their unique path in life. Communication is obviously a central activity in the process of engaging in your life's interests and aligning them with the priorities of work. The goal is not to put personal interests first. It is to pay attention to all the interests that are important to you as a person. Studies have shown that it is not necessary to sacrifice family time to get ahead in your career. In fact, two studies by the Centre for Creative Leadership found that executives who make more time for family and out-of-work activities are rated higher in work performance by bosses than those pulling all-nighters at the office. Not only does family time recharge people emotionally, but the skills developed outside of work are transferable to the workplace.[81]

Many organizations have instituted work–life balance programs. Memorial University has a work–life balance company policy that promotes healthy and active living, child-care services for staff and students, and provides campus recreation and fitness facilities. Husky Injection Moulding Systems of Bolton, Ontario, has demonstrated a holistic commitment to employees since 1953 when the worldwide company of 2900 employees first started, from beautifully landscaped gardens to indoor plants, natural lighting, and fresh air. The company's values-driven culture believes that a healthy, balanced lifestyle and a positive environment have clear benefits for productivity and the bottom line. Husky estimates it saved $8 million in reduced absenteeism from its investment in employee well-being. As a result, the company made the list of the *Report on Business* Top 35 Companies to Work For two years in a row. Husky also sees work–life balance from a corporate perspective. As a corporate citizen, the company diverted

Chapter 13 / Contemporary Issues

95 percent of its waste through innovative recycling of materials, saving both the environment and hundreds of thousands of dollars in disposal costs. Companies can integrate business and environmental concerns into their business strategy in ways that are similar to the personal strategic plan used in making Life-Maps.

Workplaces can be toxic environments, though, even when they provide the physical ingredients of a healthy workplace, such as fitness and child-care facilities. Negative social and psychological conditions at work can harm employees' health by upsetting work–life balance, as can overwork and mistreatment of employees. Bill Wilkerson, president of the Global Business and Economic Roundtable on Addiction and Mental Health states:

> Ambiguity, inconsistency, uncertainty, insecurity, arbitrariness, bad decision making, self-centeredness, rewarding the wrong things in the office, the fostering of office politics and rewarding political behaviours—that's the earmark of weak leadership. And if you're a lousy leader, you're making people sick.[82]

Joan Burton, in a report on creating healthy workplaces published by the Industrial Accident Prevention Association, adds that supportive managers show respect for employees through positive feedback, effective communication, and good listening skills. Introducing fitness facilities or flexible work schedules can be simply superficial changes that contribute little to work–life balance if workplaces don't address the deeper issues of employee involvement, empowerment, and an integrated top-down and bottom-up approach to leadership. In workshops conducted by Burton, when people are asked what would make their workplace healthier, their answer is not more fitness rooms. They want their opinions to be considered and their contributions to be valued. Employees can cope with demanding challenges as long as they perceive a sense of fairness, are appreciated, and rewarded appropriately. In terms of the "flow" experiences discussed above, supportiveness from managers provides an additional resource for employees with which to counterbalance the extra challenges they may be facing in demanding tasks. Staff will go the extra mile when effective recognition programs are used.

Public policy can also play a role in creating healthy workplaces by establishing standards to prevent overwork, burnout, and presenteeism. Organizations can encourage managers to enforce simple things such as making sure people take their vacation entitlements, prohibiting excessive overtime, and limiting the use of part-time or casual staff to promote social and psychological health in the workplace. But employment standards have been traditionally weak in this area.

This chapter examined a few particularly relevant issues in organizational communication—knowledge management, diversity, ethics and social responsibility, and work–life balance. All influence a company's performance and rely on effective communication activity in different ways.

Knowledge management helps an organization continue learning, an essential requirement for high-performing companies. Learning must remain continuous because when it breaks down, as it will from time to time, knowledge gets lost. Effective knowledge management is a process that must engage employees and create an atmosphere of trust so that exchange of ideas can take place.

The issue of workplace diversity reveals a trend that has been involving greater numbers of females and cultural minorities in the workplace. Diversity, however, represents other types of differences as well, such as age, education, and sexual orientation. Two main benefits are driving the changes in diversity. Workplaces with diversity programs are more productive because they have a bigger pool of recruits to choose from. And a diverse workforce gives companies advantages in reaching a broader range of customers.

Ethics has become a very newsworthy topic in recent years, and so the pressure on organizations to respond has increased.

Ethical practices include establishing policies for ethical behaviour, appointing ethics officers, and developing leadership styles that demonstrate ethical management principles. The empowering influence that transformational leaders have on employees has been found to contribute to stronger ethical practices.

Companies in the past have exhibited corporate social responsibility activities by making financial donations. This was hard to justify to shareholders whose primary interest was profit. Today's social responsibility programs connect goodwill activities with image-building outcomes. In the long run, a corporation's reputation can be a positive influence on its bottom line.

The issue of work–life balance has become increasingly important as the number of people reporting conflict between their personal and professional lives grows.

Work–life balance involves matching the resources a person has with the challenges he or she faces both at work and at home. Various techniques have been developed to promote healthy workplaces. In the end, supportive managers and employee empowerment are at the root of the socially and psychologically healthy workplace.

Case Study

Saving Money or Saving the Environment?[83]

As the owner of a contracting company, you hire a subcontractor to take care of your waste-haulage operations. The subcontractor charges lower fees than normal, which makes your rates attractive to clients. One day you discover by way of an anonymous letter that the subcontractor you hired undercuts the competition by dumping waste into streams and swamps at night. The letter includes documents that prove the allegations.

Discussion Questions

1. Do you ignore it or cancel the contract? Apply the principles of common ethical perspectives to see how the issue can be explained.

2. Below are submissions from readers. Can you relate them to the principles that explain them best?

Reader Submissions

1. Dismiss the subcontractor immediately and report the company to the authorities. Turning a blind eye can be disastrous for your company's reputation.

2. Confirm the information before making a decision. If it is accurate, cancel the contract and contact authorities.

3. Terminating the contract is not only morally and environmentally correct, it is also smart business, since illegal dumping can lead to heavy fines and possible the closing of your company.

4. Ignore the entire issue because hiring a more expensive subcontractor will cause you to lose clients and force you to lay off staff.

5. It is not right to cancel this contract without further proof because people will lose jobs and you could be liable for a lawsuit from the subcontractor.

6. Tell the subcontractor you know about the illegal disposal methods, and give the subcontractor the chance the fix the situation before word gets out, so that jobs can be saved.

Glossary

Knowledge management, p. 258
Data, p. 260
Information, p. 260
Knowledge, p. 260
Explicit knowledge, p. 260
Tacit knowledge, p. 260
Chief Knowledge Officer, p. 261

Equal opportunity, p. 262
Managing workplace diversity, p. 262
Ethics, p. 266
Corporate social responsibility, p. 271
Work–life conflict, p. 274
Work–life balance, p. 275

Notes

1. Louise Ear, *Knowledge Management Practice in Canada*, Catalogue No. 88F0006XIE2003007 (Ottawa: Statistics Canada, Science, Information and Electronic Division, 2001).

2. Julian Birkenshaw, "Making Sense of Knowledge Management," *Ivey Business Journal* (March/April 2001): 31–36.

3. Eugene Kowch, "The Knowledge Network: A Fundamentally New (Relational) Approach to Knowledge Management & the Study of Complex Co-Dependent Organizations," *Journal of Knowledge Management Practice* 6 (June 2005).

4. David Lei and Charles R. Greer, "The Empathetic Organization," *Organizational Dynamics* 32, no. 2 (May 2003): 142–64.

5. Mark Wolfe, "Mapping the Field: Knowledge Management," *Canadian Journal of Communication* 28, no. 1 (2003): 85.

6. Dave Ulrich, "Intellectual Capital=Competence X Commitment," *Sloan Management Review* (Winter 1998): 15.

7. Etienne Wegner, "Knowledge Management as a Doughnut: Shaping your Knowledge Strategy though Communities of Practice," *Ivey Business Journal* (Jan./Feb. 2004): 1–8.

8. Fareed Hussain, Caro Lucas, and M. Asif Ali, "Managing Knowledge Effectively," *Journal of Knowledge Management Practice* (May 2004), http://www.tlainc.com/articl66.htm (accessed July 29, 2006).

9. Varun Grover and Thomas H. Davenport, "General Perspectives on Knowledge Management: Fostering a Research Agenda," *Journal of Management Information Systems* 18, no. 1 (Summer 2001): 5–21.

10. Henry Mintzberg in Stephen Bernhut, "In Conversation: Henry Mintzberg," *Ivey Business Journal* (Sept./Oct. 2000): 3.

11. L. Gupta, S. Iyer, and J.E. Aronson, "Knowledge Management: Practices and Challenges," *Industrial Management and Data Systems* 100, no. 1–2: 17–21.

12. Nick Bontis, "The Rising Star of the Chief Knowledge Officer," *Ivey Business Journal* (March/April 2002): 20.

13. Ibid.

14. Peyman Akhavan, Mostafa Jafari, and Mohammad Fathian, "Exploring Failure Factors of Implementing Knowledge Management Systems in Organizations," *Journal of Knowledge Management Practices* (May 2005), http://www.tlainc.com/articl85.htm (accessed February 18, 2006).

15. R. Roosevelt Thomas, *Beyond Race and Gender* (New York: Amacom, 1991).

16. Statistics Canada, *Canadian Social Trends* (Autumn 2003), Catalogue No. 11-008, based on 2001 census, www12.statcan.ca/english/census01/products/analytic/companion/etoimm/contents.cfm (accessed January 28, 2006).

17. Canadian Citizenship and Immigration, *The Monitor*, in Allan Allchin, *Preparing for Workplace Diversity*, (Toronto: Human Resources Professionals Association of Ontario, February 2005), http://www.hrpao.org/HRPAO/KnowledgeCentre/newscluster3/Preparing+for+Workplace+Diversity.htm (accessed March 2, 2006).

18. Howard Ross, quoted in Richard Koonce, "Redefining Diversity: It's Not Just the Right Thing to Do. It Also Makes Good Business Sense," *Training & Development Journal* 55 (December 2001): 31.

19. Jim Ziemer, chief executive at Harley-Davidson Inc. detailing a business strategy based on diversity that would compete with Japanese rivals. Today, females and visible minorities account for almost 20 percent of sales. In Carol Hymowitz, "Diversity in a Global Economy—Ways Some Firms get It Right," *Wall Street Journal*, November 14, 2005, http://www.careerjournal.com/services/print/?url=http%3A//www.careerjournal.com.myc (accessed February 14, 2006).

20. David A. Thomas, "Diversity as Strategy," *Harvard Business Review* 82, no. 9 (Sept 2004): 98.

21. Robin J. Ely and David A. Thomas, "Cultural Diversity at Work: The Effects of Diversity Perspectives on Work Group Processes and Outcomes," *Administrative Science Quarterly* 46, no. 2 (Sept. 2001): 229–73.

22. Jeffrey T. Polzer, Laurie P. Milton, and William B. Swann, Jr., "Capitalizing on Diversity: Interpersonal Congruence in Small Groups," *Administrative Science Quarterly* 47, no. 2 (June 2002): 296–324.

23. R. Roosevelt Thomas, Jr., "From Affirmative Action to Affirming Diversity," *Harvard Business Review* 90, no. 2 (March/April 1990): 107–117.

24. Jeremy Sander, "Raptors' Mosaic Attracts Interest From Abroad," *National Post*, November 1, 2006.

25. "Top Officers Ensure Diversity for OPP," *Workplace Diversity Update* 11, no. 7 (Toronto: Crownhill Publishing, July 2003): 1.

26. Jacquie De Almeida, "Organized Crime Gets Smarter," *Hamilton Spectator*, August 20, 2005, A5.

27. "Ernst & Young LLP," *Workplace Diversity Update* 12, no. 4 (Toronto: Crownhill Publishing, April 2004): 1.

28. Virginia Galt, "P & G leverages its cultural diversity," *The Globe and Mail*, April 7, 2005, B1.

29. Jeffrey Gandz, "A Business Case for Diversity," *Ivey School of Business* (Fall 2001).

30. Hymowitz, "Diversity in a Global Economy."

31. Ibid.

32. Gandz, "A Business Case."

33. Ibid.

34. J.N. Matton and C.M Hernandez, "A New Study Identifies the 'Makes and Breaks' of Diversity Initiatives," *Journal of Organizational Excellence* 23, no. 4 (2004): 47–58; Nancy Lockwood, "Workplace Diversity: Leveraging the Power of Difference for Competitive Advantage," *HR Magazine* (June 2005), http://www.shrm.org/research/quarterly/captureIDs.asp?type=2005/0605RQuart.asp (accessed October 24, 2005).

35. Jennifer Hicks, "Your name could turn off employers who discriminate," *Wall Street Journal*, from IMDiversity.

36. Ross in Koonce, "Redefining Diversity."

37. David Praddon, "Wife of ATI founder defends sale," *The Toronto Star*, June 4, 2005, D3.

38. John R. Wilke and Stephen Power, "U.S escalates Daimler bribe probe," *The Globe and Mail*, August 5, 2005, B1.

39. Manuel Velasquez, *Business Ethics: Concepts and Cases*, 5th ed. (Upper Saddle River, NJ: Prentice-Hall, 2002).

40. Carol Gilligan, *In a Different Voice: Psychological Theory and Women's Development* (Cambridge: Harvard University Press, 1983).

41. Roger Scruton, "A Carnivore's Credo," *Harper's*, May 2006, 21.

42. Marc Saner and Cornelius von Baeyer, *Workplace and Policy Ethics: A Call to End the Solitudes*, Policy Brief No. 24, Institute on Governance, October 2005, http://www.workplaceethics.ca/article.html (accessed March 8, 2006).

43. Simon Beck, "U.S. corporate governance is yesterday's news," *The Globe and Mail*, June 4, 2005, B2.

44. Sinclair Stewart, "Hunkin's millions may be beyond reach," *The Globe and Mail*, August 5, 2005, B1.

45. Pratima Bansal and Sonia Kandola, "Corporate Social Responsibility: Why Good People Behave Badly in Organizations," *Ivey Business Journal* (March/April 2003).

46. Paul Thomasch, "Ebbers told finance chief: 'We have to hit our numbers,'" *The Toronto Star*, February 9, 2005, C3.

47. Steven Chase, "White-collar crime a growth industry, committee hears," *The Globe and Mail*, May 19, 2005 B4.

48. Diane Francis, "White Collar Crooks: U.S. hits them hard," *National Post*, March 22, 2005, FP2.

49. Bansal and Kandola, "Corporate Social Responsibility."

50. Ibid.

51. Vicky Smith, "Employees need to push for ethics," *London Free Press*, January 19, 2005, Careers, B4.

52. Rabindra N. Kanungo, "Ethical Values of Transactional and Transformational Leaders," *Canadian Journal of Administrative Sciences* (Halifax) 18, no. 4 (Dec. 2001): 257.

53. B.M. Bass and P. Steidlmeier, "Ethics, Character, and Authentic Transformational Leadership Behaviour," *Leadership Quarterly* 10 (1999): 181–217.

54. Kanungo, "Ethical Values," 257.

55. Peter F. Drucker, *The Frontiers of Management* (New York: Truman Talley, 1986).

56. William Stimson, "A Demming Inspired Management Code of Ethics," *Quality Progress* (February 2005): 67–75.

57. Mark Schwartz, "A Code of Ethics for a Corporate Code of Ethics," *Journal of Business Ethics* (Springer, Netherlands) 41, no. 1–2 (Nov. 2002): 27–43.

58. Sharda Prashad, "He's not always what he seems," *The Toronto Star*, February 17, 2006, F1.

59. William Stimson, "A Demming Inspired Management Code of Ethics," 1.

60. RBC Financial Group, news release, Toronto, February 1, 2006, http://www.rbc.com/community/letter/jan_feb1994.html (accessed March 3, 2006).

61. Ruth V. Aguilera, Deborah E. Rupp, Cynthia A. Williams, and Jyoti Ganapathi, "Putting the S Back in Social Responsibility: A Multi-level Theory of Social Change in Organizations," *Academy of Management Review* 19, no. 4 (August 2005): 1–60.

62. Philip Kotler and Nancy Lee, *Corporate Social Responsibility* (Hoboken, NJ: John Wiley & Sons, 2006).

63. Aguilera et al., "Putting the S Back."

64. Robert Colman, "Corporate Social Responsibility—Where Do We Really Stand?" *CMA Management Journal* (November 2004), http://www.managementmag.com/index.cfm/ci_id/2168/la_id/1 (accessed March 27, 2006).

65. Ibid.

66. Deborah Hashey, "Generous to a Fault," *Atlantic Business Magazine*, August 31, 2005.

67. Tim Rowley and Matt Fulbrook, "Canada's Corporate Elite," Rotman School of Management, University of Toronto, December 2004, http://www.rotman.utoronto.ca/ccbe/publications.htm (accessed February 7, 2006).

68. Ibid.

69. Sean Gordon, "Massive Ethics bill aims to clean up Ottawa," *The Toronto Star*, April 12, 2006, A1.

70. Sandra Cordon, "Business Fears More Bureaucracy, Less Confidentiality with New Act," *Canadian Business*, April 11, 2006.

71. "The Weekly Web Poll," *The Globe and Mail*, June 3, 2005, C1.

72. W. Maurice Young Centre for Applied Ethics at the University of British Columbia, http://www.ethics.ubc.ca/ (accessed March 3, 2006).

73. "The Corporate Warrior Beats a Retreat," *The Globe and Mail*, March 31, 2005, J2.

74. Linda Duxbury and Chris Higgins, *Work-Life Balance in Canada: Making the Case for Change* (Ottawa: Social Development Canada, 2001).

75. Ibid.

76. Ibid.

77. Roberta Neault, "That Elusive Work-Life Balance" (paper presented at the National Consultation on Career Development, Coquitlam, B.C., 2005), http://www.natcon.org/natcon/nav_e.cfm?s=main&p=natcon2005 (accessed March 18, 2006).

78. M. Csikszentmihalyi, *Finding Flow, The Psychology of Engagement with Everyday Life* (New York: Harper Collins, 1997).

79. Ibid.

80. Mark Hollingworth, "Resolving the Dilemma of Work-Life Balance: Developing Life-Maps," *Ivey Business Journal* (Nov./Dec. 2005).

81. Kevin Voigt, "Tales from the Trenches: Balancing Work and Family," *The Wall Street Journal Online*, http://www.careerjournal.com/myc/workfamily/20041005.voigt.html (accessed April 2, 2006).

82. Janis Foord Kirk, "Unfair rule destroys productivity," *The Toronto Star*, March 12, 2005, D11.

83. Workplace Ethics 101, *The Globe and Mail*, June 1, 2005, C6.

Chapter Fourteen

Corporate Communication

Corporate communication is "an instrument of management by means of which all consciously used forms of internal and external communication are harmonized as effectively and efficiently as possible, so as to create a favourable basis for relationships with groups upon which the company is dependent."

—*C.B.M. Van Riel*, Principles of Corporate Communication[1]

Learning Objectives

- Examine the concepts and practices of corporate communication
- Identify the functions of corporate communication
- Explore the functions and practices of internal corporate communication
- Analyze the process of strategic alignment and corporate communication
- Examine external corporate communication
- Discuss methods for writing press releases

Introduction—Corporate Communication

Corporate communication is clearly a functional area of communication in organizations. It falls in the tradition of two major perspectives of communication: the rhetorical, which focuses on producing persuasive and strategic messages; and the transmissional, which focuses on communication channels, noise, message fidelity, and audience effects. Its purpose is to facilitate organizational activity by sending and receiving information that helps to achieve organizational goals. Effective corporate communication integrates a company's plan for success by communicating it clearly to internal and external audiences. In this way, all organizational activity is aligned around a common strategy.

Though limited in its beginnings to media relations, the area of corporate communication has grown tremendously in recent years. A scan through the newspaper help wanted ads will uncover various communication positions dealing with internal and external activities. Specific responsibilities involve such things as communication strategies, research and surveys, organizational image and identity, relationships with stakeholders, speech writing, internal communication vehicles such as newsletters or e-systems, employee relations, government relations, crisis communication strategies, and social responsibility. In addition, strategic planning has begun increasingly to rely on communication to give people a view of the whole organization in terms of short- and long-term goals.

Background—Public Relations

Before television, training in public relations was done in journalism and communication schools. Since the profession at the time dealt primarily with the print media, executives thought journalists were best equipped to handle it because they could write quickly and coherently. Communication schools considered this too narrow of a view and argued that mass communication would cover the area better. To add to the fray, business communication schools argued for the rights to corporate communication, claiming it was a functional area of an organization, like marketing or finance, and should be included in its business administration programs. Today, the field of public relations has expanded greatly to include many of the same functions as corporate communication. To deal with the negative connotation of the term "PR," many companies dropped the name altogether and just called it "communications."

Before the job became multi-functional, it was usually handled by someone with a different job description, such as marketing or administration. Though it allowed a company to interact with the media, often its purpose was to block the media from the inner workings of the organization and to shield top managers from outside interruption. As the profession grew, it moved away from its journalistic roots and communication schools began providing the graduates. They were experts in handling special situations, such as product launches or bad publicity, but not in the daily operations required for a smooth flow of communication. In the 1970s, the roots of today's corporate communications took hold, as management-trained professionals who could talk the manager's language created a complex and distinctive functional area, often staffed by several people.

Functions of Corporate Communication

Today's corporate communications professionals are responsible for numerous activities. Paul Argenti, author of *Corporate Communication*, has outlined the following functions for the field:[2]

Customer Communication

A man is killing time at an airport during a stopover when he spots an attractive flight attendant. He says "Hi," but she doesn't respond.

Thinking she might not speak English, he decides to rhyme off a list of airline slogans to find out which company she works for.

He tries the slogan for Swiss International. No response. He tries Air France. No response, again.

Then the woman turns to him and says, "Get lost."

"Ah," he says, "Air Canada."

—A sanitized version of a joke making the e-mail rounds in June 2004[3]

1. *Image and identity.* Image refers to the way the organization is perceived in its environment. To bolster image, corporate communications researches the needs and attitudes of its various stakeholder groups, then communicates messages to enhance the firm's image. Identity refers to the visual images of a company, such as logos, stationary, uniforms, buildings, signs, brochures, and advertising.

   But bad image management is only surface damage. Brands are killed through workplace practices and values, such as poor customer service, unreliable products, breaking promises to customers, and unmotivated employees—deeper organizational issues. The Air Canada flight attendant's attitude in the example above, though a joke, illustrates the kinds of effects employees can have on the public image of a company. Tim Horton's is well known, for example, for consistency—you always know what you're going to get. According to marketing executive Bill Moir, "the key is what the customer thinks once they try the product."[4] After Tim Horton's, the best-managed brands are WestJet, Canadian Tire, Loblaws, Cirque de Soleil, *Hockey Night in Canada*, Shoppers Drug Mart, and the CBC.

2. *Corporate advertising and advocacy.* Corporate advertising tries to sell the company, not its products or services. For example, beer and liquor producers promote drinking responsibly, as a way of creating goodwill for the companies. Advocacy ads promote a position on an issue. The slogan for Ikea says "Low Price, But Not at Any Price," expressing the company's attitude toward using cheap, Third World labour. To show social concern for humane working conditions in Third World countries, Ikea sends inspectors overseas unannounced several times a year to check on living conditions, numbers of toilets, and so on.[5] The goal, again, is to win favour with media, social and political activists, and, ultimately, customers.

3. *Media relations.* As a spokesperson for an organization, the corporate communication director attempts to shape the company's image through established media channels, such as newspapers, magazines, television, and radio. These messages are often aimed at employees as much as external audiences, though as an employee communication strategy it is very impersonal. Typical formats of communication are news releases and interviews with reporters. To prepare for interviews and ensure favourable exposure, staff will research writers and producers to evaluate their receptiveness to news stories.

   To get noticed in the parade of news releases that cross an editor's desk, many of companies resort to publicity stunts. For instance, to announce its challenge of industry giant Microsoft, the small software company Intralinux went to San Francisco where Microsoft was launching its latest operating system. A Bill Gates look-alike was matched against a Penguin, the mascot of Intralinux, in a boxing ring whose four corners were held up by Penguinettes. The Penguin pinned Gates, while a plane towing a banner that said Intralinux flew overhead. Including actors and costumes, the whole event cost about $4000. But you couldn't afford to buy the publicity it generated for the company on the evening news.

4. *Community relations.* Organizations are realizing they need to address the growing concerns in communities about the role of the organization. The focus is on giving financial help to people in need, from minor league sports, to underprivileged groups, to symphony orchestras. Financial contributions are used to stimulate positive feedback from community groups that fits into corporate communication strategies.

5. *Social responsibility and corporate philanthropy.* These two terms operate together. A corporation expresses its social responsibility, in other words its connection to the local or global community it is located in, through acts of corporate philanthropy, or by giving money to charitable causes. Michael Sabia, Bell Canada president says, "Bell believes in being connected with communities. As a corporate citizen, one of our fundamental roles is to build stronger communities ... because dynamic communities are at the heart of creativity, innovation and growth."[6] In addition to creating positive relationships with the community, social responsibility gets attention from employees. Having an active social responsibility strategy helps companies attract desirable employees and invigorates corporate culture. Canada's tech sector normally gets high marks for its corporate social responsibility, in contrast to the tobacco and oil and gas industries, for instance, which score lower.

   For some organizations, the paybacks of corporate giving are debatable. To deal with their "moneybags" image problem, big banks make considerable contributions to charitable causes. For example, in response to the 2005 Indian Ocean tsunami relief effort, TD Canada Trust gave $250 000 and matched employee donations dollar for dollar to the Red Cross for another $250 000. CIBC gave $100 000 to the Red Cross and another $100 00 to UNICEF. In all, the donations of the big five banks to various causes in fiscal 2004 ranged from $25 million to $48 million each.[7] Because stakeholders, such as owners and investors, disagree about what level of corporate generosity is enough, this information is often not publicized. To find the announcement of disaster relief aid from TD bank, you had to click a few pages into the website. According to David Nitkin, an authority on corporate giving, "The feeling is that if a bank gets perceived as a social responsibility leader, then it's not going to sell well on Bay Street."[8] What about tax incentives? Donations generally qualify as tax deductions. To help generate tsunami relief, Ottawa extended the donation deadline for the previous year's claims to January 11 from the normal December 31.

   There are two views on the issue of social responsibility. One proposes that a company should focus on profit and growth, and, when it is successful enough, then it can afford to spend money on acts of social responsibility. The other view states that social responsibility leads to success by creating numerous intangible benefits for an organization, such as greater employee commitment, a good reputation, and, ultimately, the bottom-line payoff: patronage from customers. It's a matter of perspective. For some, especially business managers, the issue is about money only. For others, including employees and the overall community, it's about a collection of related issues.

6. *Employee relations.* Internal communication is directed at employees. It begins upon hiring, with employee orientation and training programs. These not only provide information about policies and job-related skills, they also introduce employees to the values of the organization's culture. Other practical messages follow, such as explanations of pay, benefits, and safety procedures, and descriptions of products, services, and work processes. Perhaps the most important type of employee communication is in everyday relations between managers and workers. A comprehensive employee communications training program launched in 2001 at Transport Canada's Ottawa head office included skills for improving morale, active listening,

giving and receiving constructive feedback, conducting effective meetings, and using influence skills properly. Employee communication efforts aim to gain compliance for company policies, to build a positive attitude, and to gain acceptance of company values and goals. Some common channels for reaching large audiences used for employee communication are newsletters and e-mail message systems.

7. *Government relations.* Large companies in heavily regulated industries, such as utilities, tobacco, liquor, communications, and insurance, carry on regular discussions with government representatives. In some circumstances, companies lobby government groups to influence legislation that might affect them. Large users of electricity, for example, such as manufacturing plants, may pressure government groups to control rate increases, so that production costs can be kept low.

8. *Crisis communication.* To effectively address the complex issues that corporations face today, crisis management must be mandated from the top of the organization and be driven by all key business units. The role of corporate communications in crisis management is to prepare a response to potential crises and coordinate communication activity should a crisis occur. During a crisis, managing a large number of stakeholders and their diverse and often conflicting interests in a well-timed fashion becomes critically important. Planning activities include risk assessment, assigning teams to each crisis, and prepping managers for action. Executing a crisis plan involves creating a centralized crisis management centre, gathering information, and conducting presentations and interviews—all under a very tight timeframe, since delayed responses suggest confusion and lack of leadership. The purpose of crisis communication is to restore order and confidence in the company as quickly as possible. For corporate communication to operate like a special tactics unit, crisis management must be integrated into the organization's overall management system.[9]

Internal and External Corporate Communication

In terms of communication, the difference between internal and external corporate communication is in the setting and purpose of messages and the relationship between speakers and audiences. The objective is to analyze the audience or multiple audiences and adapt messages to address their specific agendas.

Internal Corporate Communication

Internal corporate communication takes place on site in the organization. Settings can be formal or informal, public or private. The direction is usually top-down, which has traditionally given employee communication a strong management bias. Training in the area today emphasizes receiver-oriented skills that focus more on the needs of subordinates. With face-to-face communication, such as interviews, meetings, or training sessions, the source is evident. Generally, though, the identity of the source is not specified. Company announcements come from the administration, not a particular person. The organization is the source, whether it's a newsletter or a website, so messages have an anonymous quality. The communication issue behind having a corporate author hinges on who is represented in that collective voice. Do employees see themselves in it? Are labour unions a part of it? Conflicting goals of individuals and groups in the organization can make people feel excluded from the message. The credibility of the source also becomes an issue if employees don't trust the organization.

The purpose of internal communication is functional: to persuade employees to become committed to the organization's goals. From simple training exercises that show the right ways of doing things, to cultural campaigns that attempt to shape workplace attitudes, employee communication relies on persuasive strategies. For example, a company might try to improve safety or reduce waste by teaching employees new ways of working or by encouraging them to buy into the value of these goals. Internal communication can make employees feel like insiders by inviting them to participate in improvement efforts and explaining clearly the rationale behind them. The effective use of employee communication involves persuading employees to participate in the organizing process.

Channels of communication carry the messages and may combine persuasive elements with other objectives. Company picnics include a social element; retirement dinners promote tradition and loyalty. The following are commonly used communication channels in organizations:

- **Print channels**—letters and memos, newsletters, bulletin boards, instruction manuals, annual reports, work rules and policies
- **Interpersonal channels**—interviews, appraisals, training, conferences
- **Group meetings**—department meetings, committees, quality circles, team meetings, speeches
- **Electronic channels**—e-mail, intranet systems, telephone and voice mail, video conferences, advertising

As with all functional messages, the types of effects each message produces is essential for determining whether persuasive strategies have hit their target. It's easier to observe the effects of messages with clear objectives, such as announcing new work processes or responding to crisis situations. Other effects are difficult to quantify, especially cultural ones. Workplaces that want to create trust and commitment in employees, for instance, by implementing communication programs, may see improvements in their bottom line, such as decreased turnover, higher productivity, and fewer mistakes and accidents. But were these improvements the result of the message? Measuring intangibles such as employee values is often done with employee surveys. Today's e-mail systems have made this type of research relatively quick and inexpensive. For example, Mercer Human Resource Consulting, a global company in human resources with offices in most Canadian cities, has developed the Mercer Culture Survey, a tool that identifies the gaps between what an organization is and what it wants to be. In this way strategic internal communication serves the purpose of aligning the workplace's culture and attitudes with its business goals. As Mercer's website states, "a company whose culture is misaligned with its business strategy can still be profitable, but its suboptimal alignment prevents it from realizing its full potential."[10] Today's organizations have designed communication strategies that fit in with their business objectives. Let's examine the role of internal communication in strategic business alignment.

Strategic Alignment Using Internal Communication

Internal corporate communication and strategic planning compliment each other in powerful ways. *Strategic planning* involves looking at the long-term goals of an organization. Communication allows those goals to be communicated to the whole organization, as well as to customers and the social and business community. The benefit of communicating an organization's strategy is that it integrates an organization so that all aspects of operations reflect that strategy. By communicating your plan for success, everyone is focused on the same goal.

The 7-S Model of Strategic Alignment

If your company's competitive strategy is to provide excellent customer service, the organizational systems and activities must support that strategy. One common experience today is that many companies promise excellent customer service only to make you

Communication Campaign Helps Gap Employees Embrace Cultural Change

The goal was to align all 150 000 of the global clothing giant's employees around a shared way of thinking called Gap's Purpose, Values, and Behaviours. This cultural transformation would better position the company for growth and make it a great place to work. Starting in 2004, the internal communication team segmented employees and devised a strategy that would start with 2000 senior managers and work like a cascade effect, eventually reaching all employees.

The managers were given plenty of time to absorb the changes, so they would feel empowered to implement the same cultural shift within their own teams. The leaders held scripted and inspiring presentations to introduce the program. Interactive workshops highlighting exercises and role plays were designed by the communication team for employees in distribution centres and field stores worldwide. The team also established a feedback channel for employees on the company Internet. Physical reminders such as posters, coffee cups, and standing displays were created to saturate every aspect of the organization with the new value system. All employee recruiting, compensation and benefits materials, existing programs, and new initiatives are put through the internal communication team's "values filter" to ensure that they directly mirror Gap's new cultural guidelines. The campaign compliments these changes with new policies on social responsibility concerning areas such as improving working conditions in developing countries where the store gets its garments.

What's the payoff in terms of strategic alignment? As one manager stated, " This … was extraordinary, clarifying for me where we'll be taking the company over the next five years, and how."[11]

Discussion Questions

1. What are some challenges in implementing a communication initiative of this size?

2. How did the Gap meet those challenges?

3. Cultural change is unpredictable. Can you think of any obstacles that might come up in the implementation of this plan as it hits the operational levels?

---

wait for long periods in voice-mail systems or waste your time with information you weren't looking for. *Strategic alignment* requires a company to look at how its strategy relates to its internal practices. Through communication, employees begin to see themselves as part of the system. The 7-S model of strategic alignment describes the activities of an organization that must be harmonized so they work holistically with each other instead of at cross-purposes:[12]

1. **Strategy**—provides a common purpose for all employees and differentiates a company form its competitors
2. **Shared Values**—goals that connect the efforts of all members; what the organization stands for
3. **Structure**—focuses reporting relationships on strategy, not authority
4. **Systems**—aligns the parts of the system, such as financial, human resources, marketing, and the general distribution of information throughout the company, with overall strategy
5. **Staff**—hiring practices reflect the competitive strategy
6. **Skills**—employees' skills promote company strategy
7. **Style**—lines up cultural and operational practices with strategy

Put simply, corporate communication is a support function that should add value to a company by helping it maximize employee resources, generate shareholder profit, and deliver quality products and services to customers.

Strategic Alignment, Structure, and Change

On a more philosophical level, the concept of strategy points out the tension between structure and change. Strategy is a fixed structure designed to respond to organizational change, but change doesn't happen only once—it's continuous. So, by the time a strategy is devised and implemented, it is dated because conditions have changed. The drawback of most fixed plans is that they are not capable of incorporating changes and adapting to them. A suitable analogy is traffic reports. By the time they are reported by drivers and announced on the radio or on customized highway signs, traffic conditions have changed. In addition, the report can quickly change the traffic dynamic as drivers respond to road congestion by taking other routes. The question becomes: do you act on conditions that may not be relevant anymore by taking a different route, or hope that things have cleared up and keep going? The 7-S model, to be effective as a change-embracing strategy, needs to be able to line up the resources of a workplace so they are working together while building in the capacity for learning and for flexibility.

Organizations have wrestled with strategy formulation since the notion of strategic management became popular. Jeanne Leidtka states, "The dilemma is that unaligned these factors work at cross purposes; aligned they drive out potentially needed change."[13] Strategic alignment based on a comprehensive internal communication system allows the constant caretaking required to respond to changes. The Gap program is a system that corrects the disruptions caused by change and sets the strategy back on course—a process known in management books as strategic planning. Strategic thinking, on the other hand, is more complex. It empowers people on the front lines of change, those involving operations and customer contact, to engage in new learning and to bring information about change into the organization's system, to remain "ever open to emerging opportunities."[14] Strategic thinking becomes "an integrated perspective of the enterprise."[15]

Much strategic alignment involves cultural change efforts. The strategic alignment program used at Gap describes a campaign that highlights cultural change. The Gap's approach is an example of a persuasive rhetorical strategy, built on persistent and comprehensive message reinforcement techniques designed to ensure conformity to strict standards. The result is a consistent framework of values, an obvious benefit for an organization with stores in many countries and mainly young and inexperienced employees involved with in-store customer contact. The company's corporate messages celebrate a successful cultural transformation. Indeed, it may be a triumph for Gap. In terms of cultural change, though, the program is highly directive and downward-driven—essentially a compliance-gaining strategy aimed at the low-skilled and low-paid bulk of the work force on the retail floor. For organizations with a higher skilled workforce, a two-way communication style might be necessary to ensure that cultural change is adopted on a deeper level. It would be simplistic to think that all internal corporate communication achieves cultural change. A definite measure of strategic alignment at the Gap, though, seems to have occurred in terms of the manager's happiness at being made aware of the company's long-term goals. The Gap campaign also builds in the need for continual realignment of strategy, because changes in the workplace coming from inside and outside the organization can cause cultural drift.

Strategic alignment efforts force organizations to see themselves as communication systems.[16] As in systems theory (see Chapter), each part of the system affects every other part. For employees to engage in a corporate strategy completely, messages must be consistent: commitment is lost when an organization says one thing but does another. To create consistent values, goals must be clearly defined. The banking industry, for instance, aggressively promotes customer service. To back up this claim, they offer more and more automatic banking services, with the ultimate goal of reducing costs. They define customer service as hours of availability and ease of access to personal automatic banking. Customers standing in long lineups inside bank branches may define it a different way and may, in fact, see it as a reduction in service. If bank tellers receive negative feedback from customers it may create a mixed message for them about how consistently customer service values are defined among all the organization's stakeholders.

Large-scale strategic alignment based on Total Quality Management systems, where employees engage in two-way participation in goal setting and problem solving, can be a very complex process. Because of the importance of employee buy-in, the communication strategy would combine persuasive and interactive strategies. This would represent a slightly different strategy than the mainly persuasive one employed in the Gap case. As employees achieve greater integration into the workplace, rapid change is difficult to accomplish without complete acceptance of change from employees.

Internal communication in workplaces has developed far beyond simply promoting organizational goals. Today, it is integrated with business objectives in a process called strategic alignment. In the same way, external communication has evolved from public relations campaigns to strategic communication programs that incorporate long-term business objectives. Let's now look at how external communication uses strategic thinking.

External Communication

External corporate communication involves interaction with stakeholders, such as the media, customers, the business community, the public, government, and shareholders. External communication takes the form of advertising and marketing, lobbying, issue management, social responsibility, and crisis management. Since audiences for corporate communication may have conflicting interests, messages are customized to address specific concerns. But care must be taken to keep a company's messages from contradicting each other. Persuasive strategies are designed to prioritize particular concerns depending on the audience. As with internal communication, it should be integrated with the company's overall strategic objectives. "Media relations programs are most often undertaken as part of a larger campaign to achieve a specific objective."[17]

Every organization projects an image. Think of the Toronto Blue Jays, the RCMP, Research in Motion, the Hudson Bay Company, SunLife. When you think of an organization, images, both positive and negative, spring to mind. One of the purposes of corporate communication is to create a favourable attitude toward the organization that will help achieve some objective. Image advertising strengthens name recognition and knowledge of what the organization does. With the many mergers today, names become composites to include their expanding functions. Northern Telecom becomes Nortel, Royal Bank becomes RBC to reflect its expanded service offerings, Pepsi Cola becomes PepsiCo, to remind people that the company sells tacos and chicken as well as pop. Web pages of organizations are designed to project an image that will appeal to its visitors. Colleges and universities show students and professors enjoying learning, in an atmosphere that is traditional yet diverse.

Government relations is important for maintaining input into policies that may affect the company. For example, manufacturing companies that use large amounts of electricity will closely monitor utility rates and use their leverage to influence possible increases. Lobby groups representing food marketing boards such as beef in the West, chickens in Ontario, or potatoes in P.E.I., use their influence to represent the interests of their members to government regulatory bodies. A primary responsibility of government relations, or public affairs, is to monitor news reports related to government activities that could have an impact on the organization. Though called public affairs, most of this communication takes place behind closed doors.

Issues management, in contrast, takes place in the public forum. Its purpose is to shape public attitudes and responses to an issue, again, in order to create a positive image for the company. Public support gives a company an edge when it comes to dealing with government regulations. Industrial companies often promote their concern for keeping a clean environment to counterbalance negative images about pollution. Countless organizations exist to conduct issues advocacy. A few examples will illustrate the point: anti-abortion and pro-choice groups, Canadian Endangered Species Coalition, Woman's Action Fund, Fathers Are Capable Too (FACT), Canadian Civil Liberties Association, Amnesty International, National Council of Bishops, Mothers Against Drunk Driving (MADD), Canadian Labour Congress, Canadian Medical Association, and Canadian Bicycle Association. Advocacy groups are abundant because they are popular and effective. When people organize, their voice gains power, which becomes a potent vehicle for change when directed at the halls of politics or corporate boardrooms. Pension fund groups have been known to get involved in issues debates. In 2005, the Ontario Teachers Pension Fund "threw a grenade into the cozy world of corporate Canada," according to Jim Stanford, economist with the Canadian Auto Workers Union. The pension group pushed for more economic equality when it suggested that aerospace giant Bombardier Inc. of Montreal should abolish its dividend payouts to shareholders before asking for financial handouts from the government.[18]

External communication has a totally different set of channels than internal communication. External channels are limited in choice to advertising in the media, sending speakers to address special interest groups (which can be covered by the press to increase exposure), news releases, and general employee contact with the business and social community. A trend in the 1990s saw companies turning to video news releases about their products or services. So, stations would fill broadcast time with canned programming pretending to be news. Turning product announcements into news stories gives a company media coverage no promotional budget could afford. In fact, companies are realizing the benefits of shifting dollars from traditional advertising into public relations. For example, AutoRef, based in Waterloo, Ontario, which produces a computerized refereeing system for tennis, hired a Toronto PR firm to sell its novel technology. The PR firm targeted the United States Tennis Association (USTA) just before the national open event. As it turns out, one of the worst examples of officiating in tennis history took place in the 2005 Open. Eager to make up for the controversy, the USTA passed out AutoRef press kits to reporters hungry for a story, who in turn wrote about the product. About $3 million in "earned media" resulted from what started as a modest $56 000 publicity budget.[19] Without the benefit of luck, though, which is usually the case, good public relations takes hard work. Maintaining close relationships with media people and having a knack for networking are essential skills.

An underutilized public relations tool is the op-ed opinion article, located with the editorial pieces in major newspapers. The article uses a company president's byline, but, of course, is usually written by communication staff. It's designed for impact and persuasion—the opinion is stated up front, and the rest of the article makes the case with facts. The key is that the subject must be timely, since that's the driving force of newspapers. Once the subject is determined, persuasive writing skills finish the job—use reasoned arguments, be personal and conversational, educate our reader, show some passion, use direct language and active verbs, express an opinion that clearly takes a side. Done right, it can win converts to the company's position, gain high-quality publicity, and reach the elite audience of opinion makers who regularly read the op-ed pages.

Corporate websites are useful channels as sources of information for journalists seeking information. But most websites do not provide adequate information for effective media coverage. What kind of information are journalists looking for? A website should include an online newsroom that shows the following three essential items:[20]

1. **Press releases**—include up-to-the-minute current and archived releases with an easy search option
2. **Twenty-four-hour contact information**—include a specific contact person by name, title, and phone number
3. **Corporate information**—include a company profile, statistics, executive biographies, and basic facts and figures, such as number of employees, annual sales, any information that can help a journalist put your company in context

From the other end of the spectrum, corporate communicators can cultivate their own backyards by building up media lists of reporters and their areas of expertise. Doing your homework can help to cut through the blizzard of news releases normally passing over a journalist's desk. A good strategy for pitching stories to the media involves developing an accurate list of reporters and their "beats." This way, your pitch goes directly to your target. The other options are contacting general features reporters or using a blanket coverage strategy where you pitch everyone in sight and hope for the best.

The Press Release

Probably the most common external corporate communication tool, the press release can be very effective if done well. Let's look at the elements of a typical press release, first, and then examine techniques for writing an effective one.

A sample press release contains the following parts:

—————————— FOR IMMEDIATE RELEASE

Halifax Ice Cream Company
375 Turnkey Road, Halifax, Nova Scotia B2E 4T9
Contact: John Chestik, 219–377–4547

HALIFAX ICE CREAM MAKER A BIG HIT WITH THE COOL CROWD

—— Halifax, Nova Scotia, April 21, 2006—Halifax Ice Cream Company. A local ice cream maker based in Halifax has been selected by cooltreats.ca as one of this year's winners of the 10 coolest new products in the country. The Halifax company appeals to ice cream gourmets with its wholesome ingredients and unique flavours, such as island berry, ocean mist, and harbour mud. Though not available outside the Maritimes, distribution of the product is sure to expand across the country this year after receiving the coveted award.

"This award will put us on the map as a premier ice cream maker in Eastern Canada and will help us tremendously to get established nationally," says John Chestik, president of Halifax Ice Cream Company.

For more information about they Halifax Ice Cream Company and where you can buy our award winning products, visit our website at www.halifaxicecream.ca or phone 1–800–442–6733.

Contact information—provide the name of the person to contact for more information, including complete address and phone number:

Announce the story with a concise title that captures attention.

Say why this information is newsworthy. Explain what the criteria is for winning the best new product award and the qualities your company showed to succeed in the competition, such as product design, packaging, flavours, ingredients, character. You might mention other winners from the top 10 list to demonstrate the elevated status your company has achieved with the award.

Include a quote by a company representative to add credibility

Conclude with further contact information.

Message Strategies for Internal and External Communication

So far we've identified our audiences and developed the format. Now let's look at style. To turn the press release into a message that will get results, corporate communicators use the storytelling approach. The message is framed around common storytelling elements such as a hero, an obstacle, a journey, and a result, all connected together with a plot or theme. Below are a few techniques that will dramatize a corporate communication message, whether it's a press release or internal communication aimed at employees, and turn it into a strong story:

- **Identification.** Organizations associate themselves with social and cultural goals to create common ground between themselves and their message audiences. In the 1970s, when Japanese cars were starting to take over market share of our domestic auto industry, the cry to save jobs, and to sell more cars, became "buy Canadian." To pick up on the healthy food momentum, companies such as Kraft, General Mills, and Kellogg's are changing the ways they advertise to children. In addressing the issue of child obesity, Kraft agreed to stop directing ads for its sugary foods such as Oreos and Chips Ahoy cookies to children under 12, replacing them with sugar-free products. Kellogg's, makers of Pop Tarts, Frosted Flakes, and Fruit Loops, also began promoting healthy eating to children by accurately describing the nutritional value of their products in age-appropriate language. So, an advertising strategy turned a negative event into a bonus by creating a new common ground with customers—the trend toward healthier eating. Part of the shift can be attributed to the influence of Concerned Children's Advertisers, a group that campaigns for responsible advertising to children.[21]
- **Framing.** A framing strategy involves constructing a point of view about an event to influence how people will understand it. It gives shape to an issue and steers the discussion about it in directions that are desirable for the company. During the last decade, the push toward privatization by governments and media promoted private industry as a more efficient manager of business than governments.
- **Storytelling.** Stories that highlight a hero overcoming obstacles are a powerful method of creating meaning for a corporate cause. The larger community identifies with the hero's values, especially when the obstacle is well understood and formidable.

Corporate Communication in Times of Crisis

The word "crisis" comes from the Greek word *krisis,* meaning decision. In times of crisis, we're pressed into decision-making activities that involve gathering information, defining situations, designing responses, taking action, and communicating problems and solutions to a wide range of stakeholders. A crisis is a test of how companies handle themselves and prioritize issues under pressure.

The business world has had its share of crises recently, from mad cow disease in the West, to potato bugs in P.E.I., to SARS in Ontario, to insider trading in the economic world. Not only has the frequency of crises increased today, but it is a growing phenomenon. According to Ian Mitroff, author of *Why Some Companies Emerge Stronger and Better From a Crisis,* "every organization is virtually guaranteed to experience at least one major crisis in its history."[22] Today's more complex business world has resulted in many different types of crises. There are natural catastrophes, such as the ice storm of 1998 that destroyed power lines for thousands of people in Quebec and Eastern Ontario, and the great power blackout in August 2003 in the northeastern part of the U.S. and central Canada. We also have planned catastrophes, such as product tampering, protest actions by political or environmental groups, and restructuring efforts by organizations themselves that shut down workplaces or move them overseas, upending entire communities. The catchy phrase that emerged from the SARS crisis expresses it well: "the new normal."

Organizations have responded by hiring experts in risk management. "In Canada, the demand for CROs [Chief Risk Officers] started to rise after the deregulation of electricity markets in 2002, when utilities and energy companies needed to manage the risk of price fluctuations as they moved from a fixed-price regime to market-based pricing."[23] By 2007, 75 percent of large organizations in North America, from finance, to health care, to energy, will have a CRO on staff. And since the position is in the executive suite, it will involve participation in setting the overall strategy of the organization, instead of simply responding to risk after the fact. John Fraser, CRO of Ontario's Hydro One, faced a drastic staff reduction when 1400 long-serving employees took early retirement in 2000. The challenge was to keep operations going smoothly and avoiding panic from managers over losing so many people. After careful assessment, he hired 125 new people and relied on consultants to reduce the risk to an acceptable level.

Risk and crisis messages especially need to be carefully developed with multiple audiences in mind because the general public interprets risks differently than managers or technical people. Technicians express risks in real, statistical terms. For instance, it may be a scientific fact that pollution from a mining plant poses less risk to health than that of car exhaust. But the general public sees dangers or disasters personally. The sight of smokestacks belching clouds of pollution is a more arresting image than cars driving by releasing invisible fumes. We are shocked by deaths in airplane crashes, even though many more people die in auto accidents. The effect of incremental dangers, which happen in small numbers over long periods of time, such as smoking or unhealthy diets, are less threatening than one-time catastrophes, such as violent crimes. Things that happen all the time are not perceived as risks, even though their cumulative effect adds up to a tragedy. So the perceptions of crisis held by the general public may not be accurate scientifically, but they are real nonetheless. The challenge for corporate communicators is to explain risks in ways that are meaningful to a variety of audiences.

There are various ways to approach a crisis. The first is to train yourself to be ready when a crisis happens. Companies can prepare for crises by developing learning processes that give managers the mental capabilities and confidence to handle them. In a crisis workshop conducted by Ian Mitroff, a giant wheel labelled with various types of crises is spun, and where it lands executives are expected to discuss everything that could possibly occur in such an event. He invites managers to exploit their inside knowledge of the company to conjure up ways to destroy it. Managers develop skills in emotional intelligence to be better able to respond to the various interests of people affected by a crisis. A flexible organizational structure enables a company to respond quickly to a crisis. Companies with rigid structures get slowed down by multiple levels of authority and procedures. The objective of crisis preparation is to be able to respond quickly and decisively to resolve a crisis before the damage escalates. According to Christine Pearson, all organizational crises give off early warning signals: "The challenge for leaders is to ... create the means that will allow them to quickly see the first signals of a crisis and their source ... [and] to separate valid warning signals from otherwise harmless 'noise.'"[24]

Keeping internal and external stakeholders informed when a crisis happens is the number one priority. Uncertainty and fear can rattle confidence and commitment to the organization. Employees who feel uninformed will have a hard time maintaining trust in and loyalty to their employer. External audiences who are left in the dark will perceive the company as unprepared and incapable. It's natural in a crisis to experience an information shortage. But engaging in dialogue to achieve a shared understanding of potential dangers and measures being taken to secure the situation are essential. A professional and realistic estimate of the level of risk must be established. Once that is done, actions can be taken to begin correcting the situation.

Internal and external communications are rapidly developing areas of organizational communication. Internal communication aims to inform employees of organizational policies and activities. Common channels of internal communication are printed and electronic memos, newsletters, e-mails, and meetings. Internal communication programs also involve employees in the development of cultural values that will improve performance. The concept of strategic alignment integrates communication programs with business objectives to more fully engage all employees in achieving organizational goals.

External communication attempts to manage information about an organization so that its public image and reputation remain favourable. Common channels of external communication are the media, advertising, presentations, and press releases. Organizations maintain communication with a large collection of audiences, such as investors and shareholders, the government, local community groups, the business community, and social groups. Strategic alignment is also important for external communication. Integrating communication programs into an organization's business strategy can enhance its effectiveness. Crisis communication is a growing area of interest for both internal and external communication. Careful preparation and training are essential requirements for managing information in a time of crisis.

Communicating Benefits Information to Employees at 3M Canada

> They're satisfied because they feel like they're involved—it's human nature.
> —Bob Jolley, Manager, Employee Benefits, 3M Canada[25]

"We tell our employees, 'this is your program—not mine or the company's ... and we all have to work together on this thing,'" says Bob Jolley, manager of employee benefits at 3M Canada. To get the message out, he hits the road, starting in Vancouver and going east to Halifax to explain what the company is doing with benefits. The philosophy at 3M Canada is that spending the time and money to talk about things such as dental coverage and insurance programs pays off big in the long run. He tells the story of how things used to be years ago when all they did to communicate benefits was to give employees a "highlight" brochure. Feedback from employees revealed that they didn't understand their benefits and felt they weren't getting value from them. Today, instead of writing memos, Jolley meets face to face with all employees to explain things clearly. But the payoff of greater employee satisfaction with their benefits is only the beginning. Employees are also highly satisfied with the company's overall "proactive approach to providing information and seeking feedback." Sharing benefits information has made it easier for the company to implement other changes.

What is there to know about benefits? Many employees don't realize the value of benefits, according to John Jackson of KPMG Consulting LP. Benefits packages often add up to 30 percent of an employee's salary. The fact that most benefits are not taxed makes employees appreciate their value even more. Informing employees about benefits can end up saving a company money, according to Mary-Lou Emmett of Pro Act Consulting in Hamilton, because it helps them appreciate the effects of inflation and rising costs of services, as well as helping them accept new products, such as generic drug substitutes. Savings for benefit expenses could translate to better packages down the road.

As always with employee communication programs, there is no one-size-fits-all method. Not all companies can afford the interpersonal approach, and scheduling conflicts can make it difficult. Casino Niagara, for instance, a 24/7 operation, set up electronic kiosks where employees can get specific information about their benefits. NCR Waterloo issues regular newsletters and enhances them with "lunch-and-learn" programs where groups can discuss specific issues. To stimulate employee interest in a generally unexciting subject, NCR holds contests, such as skill-testing questions about RRSPs, and awards cash prizes.

The key to communicating benefits effectively is to make the process interactive and frequent. Websites are informative, but are essentially booklets in electronic form. Benefit committee meetings set up as a two-way flow of information keep employees informed and involved. Benefit information that at times can be technical should be laid out clearly and simply with a view of the bigger picture. Companies can also make comparisons to other companies to give employees a clearer appreciation of what they're getting.

Discussion Questions

1. What are the barriers to effective communication of company benefits?

2. Discuss techniques for communicating employee benefits effectively.

3. What general communication principles are operating when managers communicate benefits to employees?

4. Discuss the long-term organizational effects of effective benefit communication.

Classroom Activity

External Communication

Search through newspapers or magazines for examples of corporate advertising. These advertisements will be promoting a certain image to the reader about the company instead of selling a specific product or service. Often they are full-page advertisements. Analyze the strategy that the ad uses to communicate its message. What benefits could there be for the company to project such an image? Is there a specific audience to whom the message is directed? How effective do you think the advertisement is?

Communication on the Website

Visit some company websites. Analyze the details of the website. What does the design of the website say about the company? What type of image are they trying to project to visitors? Compare the different images portrayed by public agencies, such as schools or hospitals, and private corporations, such as a bank or manufacturing company. Are their audiences different? What effect does a different audience have on the message?

Glossary

Image and identity, p. 283
Corporate advertising and advocacy, p. 283
Media relations, p. 283
Community relations, p. 284
Social responsibility and corporate philanthropy, p. 284
Employee relations, p. 284

Government relations, p. 285
Crisis communication, p. 286
Strategic planning, p. 286
Strategic alignment, p. 287
Issues management, p. 290

1. C.B.M. Van Riel, *Principles of Corporate Communication* (London: Prentice-Hall, 1992).

2. Paul Argenti, "Corporate Communication as a discipline: Toward a Definition," *Management Communication Quarterly* 10, no. 1 (August 1996): 73.

3. Tara Perkins, "Image Nosedive—Air Canada tops list of worst-managed brands," *Hamilton Spectator*, June 8, 2004, A14.

4. Ibid.

5. Bill McGibben, "Letter from China," *Harper's*, December 2005, 42–52; Ikea slogan, 45.

6. Randal Anthony Mang, "High Tech's Other Leading Edge," *The Globe and Mail*, January 22, 2005, CSR1.

7. Rob Carrick, "Most Banks Bashful about Their Philanthropy," *The Globe and Mail*, January 7, 2005, B10.

8. Ibid.

9. Caroline Sapriel, "Effective Crisis Management: Tools and Best Practice for the new Millennium," *Journal of Communication Management* (London) 7, no. 4 (2003): 348.

10. Mercer Human Resources Consulting, *About Mercer, Is Your Organization Culturally Aligned?*, http://www.mercerhr.com (accessed January 20, 2006).

11. Jill Nash, vice president of Corporate Communication at Gap Inc., "A Comprehensive Campaign Helps Gap Employees Embrace Cultural Change," *Communication World* (July-August 2004), http://www.findarticles.com/p/articles/mi_m4422/is_6_22/ai_n15787015 (accessed April 17, 2006).

12. Ethan M. Rasiel and Paul N. Friga, "McKinsey 7-S Model of Strategic Alignment," in *The McKinsey Mind: Understanding and Implementing the Problem Solving Tools and Management Techniques of the World's Top Strategic Consulting Firm* (New York: McGraw-Hill, 2002).

13. J. Leidtka, "Linking Strategic Thinking with Strategic Planning," *Strategy and Leadership* (October 1998): 120.

14. Ibid.

15. Henry Mintzburg, *The Rise and Fall of Strategic Planning* (New York: The Free Press, 1994).

16. Eric M. Eisenberg and H.L. Goodhall, Jr., *Organizational Communication: Balancing Creativity and Constraint* (Boston: Bedford/St. Martin's, 2004).

17. Susan Sommers, *Building Media Relationships* (Toronto: Irwin Publishing Ltd. Toronto, 2002), 16.

18. Jim Stanford, "Bombardier's Dividends: the case for tied aid," *The Globe and Mail*, March 28, 2005, op-ed page, A17.

19. Keith McArthur, "How Auto-Ref scored a PR ace," *The Globe and Mail*, March 22, 2005, B3.

20. Jacob Neilson and Don Middleburg, "Create a Killer Online Newsroom," *Vocus* (November 23, 2004), http://www.vocus.com (accessed March 16, 2006).

21. Mitch Moxley, "Kraft move said part of 'healthy' food trend," *National Post*, January 14, 2005, FP5.

22. Ian Mitroff, author of *Why Some Companies Emerge Stronger and Better from a Crisis*, Amacom, in Harvey Schachter, "A Recipe for Crisis Management," *The Globe and Mail*, June 22, 2005, C2.

23. Haris Anwar, "Chief Risk Officer: A valuable addition to the C-suite," *The Globe and Mail*, June 20, 2005, B13.

24. Christine Pearson, "A Blue Print for Crisis Management," *Ivey Business Journal* (January/February 2002): 72.

25. Marjo Johne, "Communicating Employee Benefits to Employees," *HR Professional* (January 2000): 21–25.

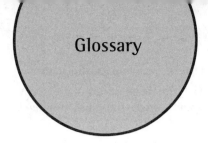

Glossary

A

accommodating approach: Used by people who want to be liked and who will give in to the other side instead of engaging in conflict.

adaptive learning: Maintains a balance of inputs and outputs.

affection: The need to be liked, respected, and important to others.

assertive style: A conflict style that handles conflicts skillfully by stating thoughts and feelings directly, yet respectfully.

autocracy: A dictatorship in which power is held by an individual or small group.

avoidance approach: Conflict is uncomfortable. Avoiders may flee when conflict arises.

B

bear hugging: A common reason people stay with an organization is that they have good relationships with the people in it. Identify what's important to people in your organization and find ways to satisfy those needs.

boundary spanners: The channels that messages from the environment travel through on their way into a system. Group members who interact with people from outside the network are boundary spanners.

bridges: Members who connect two groups by being a member of both are bridges.

bureaucracy: Power is exercised through written rules based on rational or legal authority.

C

centralization: Decision making is the right of management and is not distributed throughout the organization.

chain of command: The formal structure of an organization representing the levels of hierarchy.

Chief Knowledge Officer: The job of involving all practitioners directly in the process of collecting, storing, and sharing an organization's knowledge.

chronemics: Communication through time, such as how long we spend with different people, the amount of time we give to an activity, how long we make people wait.

closed system: A system that fails to recognize inputs from it environment and therefore deteriorates.

cognitive labelling theory of emotions: Combines emotional and mental activity in the experience of feelings. The emotion we experience is a result of how we label our perceptions.

collaboration and negotiation: Complex organizations are more ambiguous and require constant negotiation.

collaborative approach: A win–win strategy that attempts to satisfy the needs of both parties in the conflict by working together by examining issues completely and supporting each other's needs.

communication climate: A metaphor for describing people's feelings and social relationships in a workplace, as in chilly, warm, stormy

communication context: Represents a huge source of information for communicators, including the details of time and place, the relationships involved, social and cultural rules, status of participants, our level of comfort.

communicative organization: An organization where talk is action. Employees are engaged in goal-setting discussions, task directions, and job appraisals. In communicative organizations, values and goals are not only talked about by managers, they are acted on.

community relations: Messages that address the growing concerns in communities about the role of the organization.

competitive approach: Shows a high concern for satisfying personal needs without considering the needs of others.

compromising approach: Though showing a balance between personal concern and concern for others, this is a lose–lose approach where each side gives something up to reach agreement.

connection: The workplace is built on bridges that connect people, cultures, genders, and differences of opinion.

Communication connects us with our environment by creating awareness of it.

content meaning: The literal meaning of words; "what" is said.

contingency theory: Proposes that the methods organizations decide to use to achieve their goals are contingent, or dependent, on various factors in the environment.

continuous learning: Making sense of situations and learning from them requires an open mind and the ability to ask questions.

control: The closer your relationship with someone, the more influence you have over each other.

cooperative power: Power is shared equally by all members.

corporate advertising and advocacy: Corporate advertising tries to sell the company, not its products or services.

corporate social responsibility: Refers to a company's concern and response to issues that accomplish social and environmental benefits and go beyond the narrow economic, technical, and legal requirements of making profit.

crisis communication: Addresses the complex issues that corporations face, in particular, unexpected ones.

critical approach: focuses on the use of communication to express and maintain power in structures and positions of authority, communication channels, and message flow.

critical theory: Seeks to liberate workers from oppression by exposing imbalances of power.

cultural diversity: The rapid increase of females and minorities into the workplace.

culture of maybe: Describes organizations that are highly analytical. It emphasizes the gathering of all relevant facts before a decision can be made.

culture of no: Represents barriers to teamwork deriving from power and status. This organization's purpose is to control dissenting voices by stifling dialogue and alternative thinking, often to satisfy the goals of particular members or divisions of the organization.

culture of yes: A characteristic of business culture where people don't tell the truth during meetings. They say yes, but mean no. Instead of objecting to an idea in a meeting, people become quiet, then begin voicing objections informally after they leave the room to undercut the consensus that appeared to have emerged.

D

data: A collection of facts, measurements, and statistics.

debilitative emotions: Negative emotions that prevent us from feeling good about ourselves and functioning effectively.

decentralized structure: Also known as a flat structure that is more efficient than hierarchical structures because of fewer layers of authority.

decoding: Involves interpreting the receiver's messages and assigning meanings to them.

democracy: Power is held by elected officers.

dialogic: Communication is described as dialogic because through social interaction, mutual understanding is created and the self is expressed and developed.

differentiation: The degree to which a system is different from its environment, achieved through negative entropy; an organization performing a high degree of specialized, non-routine tasks with high interaction with a complex environment would have a high degree of differentiation.

directly aggressive style: A conflict style where a person attacks conflict head on, leaving the other person feeling hurt or humiliated.

dispersed leadership: Leadership is a role, not a function. Employees must be called on to exercise leadership in their areas of influence.

distributed structures: Workplaces where the employee is not physically present in the workplace, as in virtual offices.

division of work: Similar work is arranged in groups or departments.

E

employee engagement: Effective communication activities make a job meaningful to employees.

employee relations: Internal communication is directed at employees.

enactment: When people experience, interpret, and give meaning to their environments through subjective perceptions.

encoding: This stage involves formulating your idea into symbols that are shared by the receiver.

entropy: The process by which a system's energy runs down and the system ceases to exist; represents the degree to which the system is the same as its environment.

equal opportunity: Hiring, promotions, and other equality and human rights issues involving employees are followed by employees as a form of legal compliance.

equifinality: The idea that the same goals can be achieved in a number of ways.

equilibrium: A balance between entropy and differentiation.

equivocality reduction: Using communication to reduce the ambiguity in the environment.

esprit de corps: A strong organization possesses a unity of purpose and encourages initiative to establish a positive work climate.

ethics: Moral principles that people use to determine what is right or wrong.

explicit knowledge: Knowledge that can be easily expressed, as in procedures, directions, and so forth.

extensions: Technology is an extension of people because it increases our capabilities. A term coined by Canadian communication scholar Marshall McLuhan.

F

facilitative emotions: Positive emotions that make us function effectively and feel good about ourselves.

fairness and equity: Workers should support the reward systems of the organization to enable them to subordinate their interests for the good of the group and to develop commitment to their work.

feedback: A response that enables the sender to know how well the message was understood.

formal communication network: The communication network based on the formal chain of command and lines of hierarchy.

functional approach: Focuses on the operational aspects of structures and positions of authority, communication channels, message flow.

functional perspective: Associated with messages intended to create cultural values and attitudes in workers that will make the organization run better.

fundamental attribution error: Assigning an incorrect cause to someone's behaviour, often by putting too much weight on personality traits, or internal causes, and not enough on situational factors, or external causes.

G

gatekeepers: Gatekeepers are the link that controls which messages enter a network.

generative learning: Learning that enhances our capacity to create.

global village: The traditional concept of village as a small community of people connected by regular communication activity now extends to a global scale with the help of technology such as television, cell phones, and, especially, the Internet. A term made famous by Marshall McLuhan.

government relations: Attempts to maintain input into government policies that may affect the company.

grapevine: Another name for an informal network of people involved in communication in a workplace.

H

haptics: Communication through touch.

Hawthorne Studies: A series of workplace studies that discovered the motivational effects of giving human attention to workers.

hegemony: The process of a dominant group leading another group into accepting that subordination is normal.

heuristics: Routines that our mind uses to cope with complex situations.

hierarchy of needs: A theory by Abraham Maslow that explains human behaviour. We do the things we do to satisfy our needs.

horizontal communication: Fayol recognized the importance of horizontal communication between coworkers, which would by necessity bypass the chain of command.

I

ideology: A set of values that forms the basis of a worldview.

image and identity: Image refers to the way the organization is perceived in its environment. Identity refers to the visual images of a company, such as logos, stationary, uniforms, buildings, signs, brochures, and advertising.

impression management: The behaviours we use to create a desired social image.

inclusion: Communicating with people provides a sense of belonging. If we communicate effectively, we will form relationships, and our social need of inclusion will be met.

indirect style: A conflict style that attempts to communicate an unsatisfactory situation without being blunt and hurting someone's feelings.

individualism vs. collectivism: In cultures of individualism, the primary responsibility is to oneself, whereas in cultures of collectivism, it is with the group or society as a whole.

informal communication network: Communication networks established through personal, social interaction. It can take many forms as employees move around, are hired and retired, and develop new relationships. Also known as the grapevine.

information: Organized or processed data that is timely.

input: Information or materials that come into a system from the environment; can also represent a form of feedback on a system's outputs.

integration: An organization performing a high degree of repetitive, routine tasks with little interaction with a stable environment.

interpersonal communication: The process of sharing our ideas, feelings, and personal characteristics with others.

interpersonal relationship: An association in which people satisfy each other's social needs.

interpretive approach: Focuses on the meaning or symbolic significance of organizational structures and positions of authority, communication channels, and message flow.

interpretive perspective: Associated with understanding the ways in which employees make sense of organizational life in both work-related and personal ways.

intrapersonal communication: The process of thinking, or communicating with ourselves.

isolates: Isolates are characterized as being less interested in group interaction than other group members.

issues management: Attempts to shape public attitudes and responses to an issue in order to create a positive image for the company.

J

Johari Window: An instrument used for modelling degrees of self-disclosure in relationships.

K

kinesics: Communication through facial expressions, gestures, other movements.

knowledge: Information that is contextual, relevant, and actionable.

knowledge management: A process that helps organizations identify, select, organize, disseminate, and transfer important information and expertise that are a part of the organizational memory.

L

learning organization: An organization that is continually expanding its capacity to create its future.

liaisons: These members, generally gregarious and social, make connections between groups by carrying messages back and forth. They regard their integrative role as important.

loose coupling: Decentralized and differentiated structure; units of a system are fairly independent of each other, enabling each to adapt individually to the situation.

loose–tight properties: Pairs of apparent contradictions based on the individual–organizational relationship: core cultural values are centralized and collectively held, while decision making is decentralized and entrepreneurship and individual achievement are encouraged.

M

managing workplace diversity: A comprehensive managerial process that improves productivity and job satisfaction by allowing people to bring out their individual differences so that greater acceptance of each other can be achieved.

mechanistic organization: A hierarchical management structure effective in a stable, predictable environment.

media relations: Corporate communication attempts to shape the company's image through established media channels, such as newspapers, magazines, television, and radio. These messages are often aimed at employees.

message: The message is a physical representation of a sender's idea, a stimulus for a receiver.

message distortion—noise: Messages can be distorted or lose information along any stage of the communication process because of noise, which can be internal or external.

N

needs theory: A theory explaining how people satisfy their basic needs of affection, inclusion, and control through interpersonal communication

negative entropy: Constant inputs from the environment that allow a system to adapt and energize itself. In this way, differentiation with the environment is maintained.

non-assertive style: A conflict style used by a person who is unable or unwilling to engage in conflict.

norms: A group's rules for behaviour.

O

objectics: Communication through objects, such as uniforms, furnishings, status symbols.

oculesics: Communication through eye contact.

open system: A system that uses inputs from its environment to renew itself.

opinion leaders: Opinion leaders have more knowledge or are connected to more sources of information than other group members. They attain their status either through holding a formal status in the group or through expertise.

organic organization: A flexible management structure effective in a rapidly changing, unpredictable environment.

organizational culture: A system of meanings developed by a group through social interaction used for dealing with uncertainties in the environment and for creating new, ongoing systems of meaning.

output: The product or service exported back into the environment.

outsourcing: A method for using contract or casual workers to do the work that used to be done by regular staff.

P

paralinguistics: Communication through voice pitch and tone, rate of speech, and other vocal qualities.

particularism: An expedient but arbitrary and abusive form of managing workers that bases decisions on personal factors such as differences in culture, family ties, gender, or attitude.

passive aggressive style: A conflict style that is a subtle form of aggression in which the attack is concealed behind false cooperation.

pay: Monetary rewards should be seen as fair and motivating so that workplace stability is established.

perception check: A method for avoiding misunderstandings between people that uses requests for clarification.

personal authority: In contrast to position authority, personal authority is based on intelligence, experience, and character.

personal identity: The feedback we receive in interpersonal communication gives us information about ourselves that over time becomes our self-concept.

power distance: The degree to which people in a society accept differences in levels of power.

presenteeism: A work style where employees show up for work in body but not in mind

proxemics: Communication through space, such as how close we stand to different people during communication.

Pygmalian effect: Receiving positive attention can change our behaviour, which will in turn change our self-concept. How we see ourselves is greatly influenced by how others see us.

R

rational decision making: A logical, analytical approach to decision making focusing on defining the problem, identifying alternatives, applying decision criteria, making and implementing the decision.

receiver: Listens carefully for both verbal and nonverbal messages to understand the message accurately.

re-engineering: Top-down organizational change driven by senior management that aims to achieve fast change on a large scale, often producing layoffs and a big boost in shareholder value.

relational meaning: "How" the message is said. It expresses the type of relationship that the communicators have.

requisite variety: An organization's degree of complexity must match that of its environment.

restructuring: Bottom-up organizational change that focuses on the process of the work itself. A bottom-up, people-driven process, which integrates functions in a team-based structure that relies heavily on communication and interaction.

retention: Useful and effective collective meanings are preserved for future use.

retrospective sense making: The idea that sense follows action, in that people decide what an event means after it is completed.

rites and rituals: Behaviours and activities that display an organization's culture and values.

S

satisficing: Instead of selecting the best solution out of all possible options, pick a solution that will work well enough to accomplish the task.

scalar chain: Messages move vertically and horizontally through the organization

schadenfreude: The delicious sense of pleasure we feel in someone's else's bad fortune.

selection: A collective process whereby people determine which is the best meaning of a situation.

self-concept: A fairly stable set of perceptions one holds of oneself.

self-serving bias: Enhancing outcomes related to our own behaviour.

sender: The sender initiates the message.

short-term vs. long-term orientation: Western cultures in general are interested in quick, short-term pay-offs. Asian cultures, in contrast, are more patient and willing to put off instant gratification in return for long-term rewards.

social penetration theory: Describes how close relationships are formed, as people's private selves are disclosed through interpersonal communication to reveal their core personality or inner self.

social responsibility and corporate philanthropy: A corporation expresses its social responsibility, in other words its connection to the local or global community it is located in, through acts of corporate philanthropy, often by donating money, time, or resources.

Stimulus response: A behavioural approach to human communication with no interpretation stage.

Stimulus interpretation response: A meaning-centred approach to understanding human behaviour.

strange attractor: The force that makes the system constantly return to a state of order so that a new system can emerge.

strategic alignment: Requires that a company to look at how its strategy relates to its internal practices. Through communication, employees begin to see themselves as part of the system.

strategic planning: Involves looking at the long-term goals of an organization. Communication allows those goals to be communicated to the whole organization, as well as to customers and the social and business community.

system: A system is a set of relationships among interdependent parts.

systematic soldiering: A style of work described in scientific management based on workers' beliefs that increasing their output would cause layoffs. They therefore controlled output as a way of achieving group job security.

T

tacit knowledge: Knowledge represented by deep thinking structures embedded in the brain that cannot be expressed easily.

team-based organization: A company that structures itself to use teams to accomplish tasks.

teamwork: The social and emotional skills individuals need to collaborate effectively in order to accomplish tasks.

technocracy: Power is held by a body of experts.

Theory Z: A theory that combines the collective work style of Japanese companies with the individually oriented North American style.

throughput: The process by which a system transforms its inputs.

tight coupling: Centralized and integrated structure; units of a system are rigidly controlled and coordinated, since they are highly interdependent with the operation of others.

Total Quality Management (TQM): A method of changing the way quality is achieved in the workplace. Instead of tacking it onto the end of the production process, it is built into every stage of the operation.

transactional leadership: The exchange of rewards and punishments between leaders and followers.

transformational approach: Creates opportunities for leadership for all organizational members.

transformational leadership: Has the capability to literally transform situations or people by empowering and inspiring workers to achieve higher levels of satisfaction and motivation. As workers exercise greater self-direction, they are transformed into leaders.

U

uncertainty avoidance: Cultures that are comfortable living with uncertainty have low uncertainty avoidance. Workplaces high in uncertainty avoidance value stability and are fearful of risk.

unity of command: A clear line of authority according to the chain of command, which should not be bypassed.

unity of command: Employees have only one boss.

universalism: Promoted equal treatment of workers according to work-related skills and abilities instead of personal factors.

W

whistle-blowing: Refers to an employee exposing illegal or unethical practices in the workplace.

work–life balance: The desire on the part of both employees and employers to achieve a balance between workplace obligations and personal responsibilities.

work–life conflict: When the cumulative demands of work and non-work roles are incompatible in some respect, so that participation in one role is made more difficult by participation in the other

workplace diversity: The increasing diversity in today's workplaces brings with it new attitudes, lifestyles, values, and motivations. Diversity emerges from numerous differences, such as gender, culture, and age. Workplace diversity strategies aim to celebrate people's differences in order to promote greater acceptance of differences and more workplace cooperation.

Index

A

Accommodating approach, 233, 234
Accountability, 216–217, 218
Adaptive learning, 111
Administrative theory, 66–68
Aesenta Health, 91
Affection, 171
Agenda, 206
Aggressor, 202
Air Canada, 69
Algoma Steel, 210
Amazon, 139
Anchoring trap, 226
Apple Computers, 214
Applecore Interactive, 89
Arbitration, 236
Argenti, Paul, 282
Argyris, Chris, 111
Aristotle, 29
Arthur Anderson, 268
Artifacts, 124
As You Like It (Shakespeare), 169
Assertive style, 232
ATI Technologies, 266
Attention-grabbing techniques, 184
Attribution theory, 185–186
Authority, 68–70
Autocracy, 136
Autocratic manager, 241
Automobile insurance, 113
Autopoiesis, 108–109
AutoRef, 290
Avoidance approach, 233, 234

B

B.C. Bio, 132
Babe, Robert, 27
Baby boomers, 7
Banks, Jordan, 120
Bargaining, 236
Baring's Bank, 9
Barnard, Chester, 80
Baseball team, 215, 216
B.C. Bio, 132
BCE, 142
Bear hugging, 13

Beddoe, Clive, 104, 123
Behavioural approach, 78
Bell, Don, 131
Bell, Peter, 225
Bell-shaped agenda structure, 206, 207
Benefits package, 295
Benevolent authoritative system, 85
Bennett Jones LLP, 133
Bennis, Warren, 248
Berg, Dreyer, 28
Bernoe, Karen, 132
Bhutan, 91
Bias of Communication, The (Innis), 27
Birkenshaw, Julien, 258
Blabbermouth, 177
Black, Conrad, 61, 83, 145, 266
Black, Susan, 10
Blake, Robert, 86, 244
Blake, William, 151
Blaming others for your feelings, 190
Blanchard, Kenneth, 245
Blocker, 202
Blumer, Herbert, 173
Blundell, William, 4
Body shop garages, 113
Bonaparte, Napoleon, 62
Bontagnali, Gottardo, 164
Bontis, Nick, 261
Bordin, Cindy, 82
Bottom-up organizational change, 11
Boundary spanners, 103, 161
Bourden, Deborah, 89
Bowling for Columbine, 186
Branson, Richard, 249
Bre-X Mining, 9, 268
Bridges, 161
Brinded, Malcolm, 71
Brison, Scott, 70
Brown, Robert, 68
Bull-in-a-China-Shop, 176
Bulldozer, 178
Bureaucracy, 136
Bureaucratic theory, 68–70
Burton, Joan, 276
Business ethics, 9. *See also* Ethics and social
    responsibility
Byers, Peggy, 243

C

CAE, 68
Canada Post, 163
Canadian National Railway (CN), 69
Canadian Tire, 130
"Can't Buy Me Love" (Beatles), 77
Capitalist justice, 267
Car insurance, 99, 113
Casino Niagara, 295
Catastrophic comments, 190
Categorical imperative, 267
Caterpillar, 164
Cause-related marketing, 272
Centralization, 67
Chain of command, 62
Chambers, John, 210
Channel, 30
Channels of communication, 286
Chaos, 107
Charismatic authority, 68
Chauvinist Pig, 139
Chief knowledge officer (CKO), 261
Chief risk officer (CRO), 293
Chronemics, 22
CIBC, 259, 268, 284
City of Saskatoon, 239
CKO, 261
Classical management approach, 61–76
    administrative theory, 66–68
    bureaucratic theory, 68–70
    context as communication, 72
    decision making, 228
    messages/message flow, 72
    purposes of communication, 71
    scientific management, 63–66
Clemmer, Jim, 213
Climate metaphor, 87
Close Friend, 176, 177
Closed system, 100
Clown, 202
Coaching, 247
Coercive power, 240
Cognitive labelling, 187–188, 189
Collaboration, 164–165, 236–237
Collaboration and negotiation, 13
Collaborative approach, 233, 234
Collectivism, 126, 174
Communication
    corporate. *See* Corporate communication
    defined, 20
    downward, 43, 155–156
    horizontal, 67
    interpersonal. *See* Interpersonal communication
    organizational, 49–51, 54
    theoretical approaches, 42–46
    upward, 43, 156
Communication activity, 120
Communication climate, 44, 87–89, 127
Communication networks, 151–168
    communication roles, 160–161
    downward communication, 155–156
    electronic network, 162
    employee engagement, 162–164
    formal network, 154
    high-performance workplaces, 160
    importance of collaboration, 164–165
    informal network, 157–160
    upward communication, 156
Communication process, 21–25
    context, 24–25
    decoding, 24
    encoding, 23
    feedback, 24
    message, 23–24
    message distortion, 24
    receiver, 24
    sender, 22–23
Communication theory
    interactional perspective, 33–35
    mechanistic perspective, 29–31
    origins, 25–29
    psychological perspective, 31–33
    rhetorical tradition, 29
    transactional perspective, 35–36
Communicative relationship, 179
Community relations, 284
Company branding, 153
Competitive approach, 233, 234
Competitive conflict, 231
Compromiser, 202
Compromising approach, 233, 234
Conceptual filters, 31–32
Confirming evidence trap, 227
Conflict/conflict management, 229–238
    causes of conflict, 230–231
    collaboration, 236–237
    communication styles, 231–232
    conflict resolution, 232–237
    formal management techniques, 236
    nature of conflict, 229–230
    new frontiers, 237–238
    Pondy's five stages, 230–231
    quantum skills, 237–238
Conflict grid, 233
Connection, 13
Conrad, Charles, 50, 230
Consultive system, 86
Container view, 47
Content meaning, 170

Four systems of management (Likert), 84–86
Framing, 292
Fraser, John, 293
Fridge rage, 232
Frost, Joyce, 229
Fry, Hedy, 7
Functional approach, 43–44
Fundamental attribution error, 185

G

Gamer generation, 8
Gandhi, Mahatma, 248
Gandz, Jeffrey, 264
Gap, Inc., 5, 287
Gatekeeper, 161
Gatekeeper and Expediter, 202
Geertz, Clifford, 118
Gender
   female ascendancy, 7, 71
   female-male strategies, 139
   feminism, 142–143
General Dynamics Canada, 210
General Mills, 292
General Motors, 5, 142, 198
General systems theory, 35
Generation X, 7
Generation Y, 7–8
Generational change, 7–8
Generative learning, 111
George, Rick, 127
German, Peter, 268
Gidden, Anthony, 50
Gilligan, Carol, 267
Glaser, Judith, 232
Global village, 3–4
Globalization, 142
Globalization and Well-Being (Helliwell), 90
Goffman, Erving, 34
Golden Banana Award, 123
Goldhaber, Gerald, 47, 49
Goleman, Daniel, 186
Good Friend, 139
Government relations, 285, 289
Grapevine, 157–160
Great Mother, 139
Greene, George, 92
Group. *See* Groups and teams
Group cohesiveness, 199
Group communication roles, 201
Group emotional intelligence, 204
Group norms, 200–201
Groups and teams, 197–220
   accountability, 216–217, 218
   cohesiveness, 199
   conflict/diversity, 200
   contingency approach, 217

culture of teamwork, 213–214
Drucker's three kinds of teams, 214–215
effective teamwork, 211–212
groupthink, 199–200
meetings. *See* Meetings
norms, 200–201
roles, 201–202
team communication skills, 212–213
teamwork, 208–210
teamwork trend, 198
Groupthink, 199–200
Guan xi, 11
Gutenberg Galaxy, The (McLuhan), 26

H

Halo effect, 185
Hamlet (Shakespeare), 187
Happiness, 90–91
Haptics, 22
Harmonizer, 201
Harris, Mike, 90
Hartmann, Wilma, 89
Hatch, Mary Jo, 120
Hawthorne studies, 78–79
Hegemony, 140
Helliwell, John, 90, 91
Help Seeker, 202
Helplessness, 190
Hempton, Gordon, 212
Henderson, Thomas "Hollywood," 246
Heroes, 122
Hersey, Paul, 245
Heuristics, 226
Hewlett Packard Canada, 209
Heyer, Paul, 27
Hierarchy of needs, 80, 81
Higgins, Chris, 8
High-context and low-context cultures, 174
Hill and Knowlton Public Relations, 209
Ho, Betty, 266
Hoffer, Eric, 97, 109–110
Hollinger, 9
Hollingworth, Mark, 275
Holt, Derek, 138
Hope, Jay, 263
Horizontal communication, 67
Hughes, Jonathan, 236
Human body, 99
Human communication process, 21–22. *See also*
   Communication process
Human Organization, The (Likert), 84
Human relations/human resources approaches, 77–94
   Barnard, 80
   communication climate, 87–89
   context of communication, 90

Nature of Managerial Work, The (Mintzberg), 35, 67
NCR Waterloo, 295
Negative entropy, 103
Negative feelings, 189–191
Negotiation, 236
Neher, William, 54
Nemawashi, 12
Networks. *See* Communication networks
New Flyer Industries, 209
New Patterns of Management (Likert), 84
New science, 106–108
Newman, Lisa, 7
Nexen Inc., 82
Nike, 5, 271
Nitkin, David, 284
Nixon, Gordon, 270
Noise, 24, 30
Non-assertive style, 231
Norms, 200–201
Nortel Networks, 268, 289
North Atlantic Refining Company, 209

O

Objectics, 22
Objects, artifacts, space, and time, 124
Observer, 202
Oculesics, 22
Oil companies, 102
Ontario Hydro, 129, 130
Op-ed opinion article, 290
Open system, 99
Opinion leaders, 161
Opinion seeker, 201
Organic organization, 106
Organization
  defined, 46
  dialogue, as, 53–54
  interactive, 47
  metaphors, 48–49
  operational design, 47
  strategy, 46
  structural design, 47
Organizational communication, 49–51, 54
Organizational communication studies, 51–53
Organizational context, 53
Organizational culture, 44, 117–134
  changing internal communication, 129
  characteristics, 119–121
  communication climate, 127
  cultural properties, 121–122
  decision making, 228
  defined, 118–119
  elements of, 121–124
  functional perspective, 126
  interpretive perspective, 126

messages/message flow, 127
most admired cultures, 130
national cultures, 1251–26
purpose of communication, 126–127
TQM, 129–130
weak cultures, 131
Orienter, 201
Origins of communication theory, 25–29
Ouchi, William, 119, 121
Outlaw, Frank, 191
Output, 103
Outsourcing, 5
Ovechkin, Alexander, 146
Ovellet, André, 163
Overgeneralizing, 190

P

Paccar of Canada Limited, 114
Pan-Ocean Energy Corp., 102
Paralinguistics, 22
Participative management, 86
Particularism, 69
Passive aggressive style, 231–232
Pathways Communications, 4
Pay, 67
Pearson, Christine, 293
Penner, Tim, 264
PepsiCo, 265, 289
Perceived conflict, 230
Perception, 183–187
Perception check, 186
Perceptual sets, 184, 185
Personal authority, 67
Personal harassment, 239
Personal identification, 121
Personal identity, 171
Personal trait theories, 243–244
Personality, 182
Personalized power, 248
Perspective taking, 204
Persuasive communication, 29
Petroleum industry, 102
Piety, 267
Playboy, 139
Player, 145–146
Pocklington, Peter, 122
Political economy, 28
Politician, 177
Popowich, Terrence, 270
Potash, 125
Power, 136–137, 139–140, 240–241, 248
Power distance, 125
Praise, 82
Pratt, Courtney, 74
Presenteeism, 65

Press release, 291
Principles of organizational communication, 54
Principles of Scientific Management (Taylor), 63
Private Agenda Promoter, 202
Procedural Technician, 201
Proctor and Gamble Canada, 264
Progressive Conservative Party, 139
Proxemics, 22
Psychological communication model, 31–33
Public relations, 290
Public speaking, 191–192
Puddler's Tale, The, 63
Purolator Courier, 164
Putnam, Linda, 52
Pygmalion effect, 181

Q

Quantum acting, 238
Quantum being, 238
Quantum feeling, 238
Quantum knowing, 238
Quantum seeing, 237–238
Quantum thinking, 238
Quantum trusting, 238
Quantum world view, 107
Queen Elizabeth I, 139
Quinton, Mike, 198

R

Radler, David, 83, 266
Ratcliffe, John S., 221
Rational authority, 69
Rational decision making, 222
RBC, 130, 289
RBC Financial Group, 270–271
Re-engineering, 11
Receiver, 24
Recognition Seeker, 202
Redding, Charles, 44, 88
Referent power, 241
Reflected appraisal, 181
Relational meaning, 170
Repetition, 184
Requisite variety, 103
Respectful workplace policy, 239
Restakis, John, 91
Restructuring, 11–12
Retention, 109
Reverse *nemawashi*, 12
Reward power, 241
Rhetorical communication model, 29
Rifkin, Jeremy, 3
Rise of the Creative Class, The (Florida), 6
Risk management, 293
Rites and rituals, 123

Roberto, Michael, 214
Roethlisberger, F. J., 78
Rogers Communications, 8, 140
Role taking, 34
Roman, Eugene, 124
Rona Home Renovations, 100
Rothmans, 130
Royal Bank of Canada, 130, 289
Royal Group Technologies, 268
Rubin, Brent, 20

S

Sabia, Michael, 284
Sand Francisco 49ers, 245–246
Sarner, Mark, 247, 267
Sasktel Communication, 209
Satisficing, 223
Saving and losing face, 178
Scalar chain, 67
Schadenfreude, 66
Schein, Edgar, 118
Scientific management, 63–66
Scotiabank, 133
Sculley, John, 248
Seagram Inc., 142
Seeing first model of decision making, 224, 225
Selection, 109
Self-awareness, 187
Self-concept, 181–183
Self-defeated thinking, 190–191
Self-direction, 187
Self-disclosure models, 174–178
Self-fulfilling prophecy, 183
Self-organizing systems, 106–108
Self-presentation, 178
Self-regulation, 108, 187
Self-serving bias, 186
Self-talk, 192
Sender, 22–23
Sensemaking in Organizations (Weick), 103
7-S model of strategic alignment, 286–287
Shared ideas, 119–120
Shaw, George Bernard, 224
Shell Canada, 71, 143
Shell Oil Company, 272
Shelton, Charlotte, 237
Sherman, Frank A., 73
Shockley-Zalabak, Pamela, 45
Short-term *vs.* long-term orientation, 126
Shwartz, Mark, 270
Simon, Herbert, 223
Sinclair, Amanda, 217
Single loop learning, 111
Sinofert, 125